AF844007

Economic Development and Environmental Control

Balancing Business and Community in an Age of NIMBYs and LULUs

JOHN O'LOONEY

Q

QUORUM BOOKS
Westport, Connecticut • London

Library of Congress Cataloging-in-Publication Data

O'Looney, John.
Economic development and environmental control : balancing business and community in an age of NIMBYs and LULUs / John O'Looney.
p. cm.
Includes bibliographical references and index.
ISBN 0-89930-940-2 (alk. paper)
1. Land use—United States—Planning. 2. Land use—Environmental aspects—United States. 3. NIMBY syndrome—United States.
I. Title.
HD205.O46 1995
333.73'13'0973—dc20 94-45283

British Library Cataloguing in Publication Data is available.

Copyright © 1995 by John O'Looney

All rights reserved. No portion of this book may be reproduced, by any process or technique, without the express written consent of the publisher.

Library of Congress Catalog Card Number: 94-45283
ISBN: 0-89930-940-2

First published in 1995

Quorum Books, 88 Post Road West, Westport, CT 06881
An imprint of Greenwood Publishing Group, Inc.

Printed in the United States of America

The paper used in this book complies with the Permanent Paper Standard issued by the National Information Standards Organization (Z39.48-1984).

10 9 8 7 6 5 4 3 2 1

Contents

Introduction

Governing is often described as the process of deciding "who gets what, when, and how."[1] This book specifically examines how we currently go about governing when people want to use land in ways that are undesirable to their neighbors and to the larger community. Because the current governance of locally unwanted land use (LULU) issues is far from satisfactory, I attempt to suggest how such governance might be improved. The stimulus for writing this book came from observing the difficulties experienced by local government officials in the siting of unwanted community-based human service facilities. The expenditure of time, energy, and resources on such issues seemed to me to be somewhat inordinate or at least unexpected prior to my further investigation of NIMBY and LULU issues. While my initial observations of local government decision-making suggested to me that the decision-making process was neither efficient nor fair, only upon further investigation and research did I realize that in making zoning decisions related to the siting of unwanted facilities, local government officials were wading into one of the most complex areas of public governance. Moreover, my research led me to realize that the problems I observed in one local community had become so pervasive as to represent a national problem. The dimensions of this problems, I also realized, went far beyond the issue of siting social service facilities in residential neighborhoods. The "not in my backyard" (NIMBY) sentiment is a generic one applying to environmental LULUs like landfills or waste treatment facilities as well as to social ones. Moreover, while the NIMBY syndrome's ability to put a lock on development is strongest with respect to the most undesirable forms of land use, the potential for NIMBY sentiments to lead to a more generalized gridlock on development as well as to environmental injustice and racial, income, and class segregation is part of the logic of the syndrome. At the same time, however, the core of NIMBY sentiment, the belief that one's backyard exists as a sort of haven from the creative but nevertheless destructive forces of capitalism, has a long tradition in American life and is an innately attractive idea. As the pace, power, and scale of the forces of development have increased in modern times, so too have the attractiveness and power of NIMBY-like sentiments and the political ideas that attach to these.

Because my challenge in writing this book is to reconcile these two sides of the NIMBY syndrome, I found myself wrestling with some of the major themes in American political thought and everyday human concern: the balance of individual liberty, democracy, and collective responsibility; the proper role and boundaries of government; the size and scale of institutions and their power over our common "built environment"; and the dangers for democracy of our being geographically segregated by race and income. All of us have our own opinions about these larger questions, and one of the ways that we form our opinions is through experiences with the governance mechanisms that touch our own lives. For most Americans, who are not criminals, owners of businesses, or policy "wonks," a major part of their direct experience with government is related to their ownership of landed property. Gaining and maintaining legal title, reviewing and paying property tax assessments, and lobbying for zoning protection or zoning change are very basic but formative activities that define a relationship between an individual and the larger public. While land ownership is far from synonymous with citizenship, it is typically associated with higher-than-average levels of political participation, especially at the local level, where most land-use decisions are made.

In addition to the relationship between land ownership and citizenship, land ownership is also tied into the broader mythology of the American dream. To the degree that land ownership symbolizes the achievement of the great American virtue of self-reliance, the governance of land use runs up against a powerful frontier mythology. In this mythology there is unlimited space for individual autonomy and achievement: If and when there is not enough room in town for two or more persons to realize their dreams, there is always a way out, a new frontier. This mythology would lead one to believe that there is no need to compromise or to establish any common governance over land, because in the frontier myth it is an unlimited and cheap resource. It is enough to let individuals acquire the resource and in that context create a natural, "informal order" of property rights and understandings. While the frontier generally did work to reduce land-use conflicts among owners, we forget that whenever frontier land uses, such as grazing sheep versus grazing cattle, did come into conflict, violence was often the result.

Although the geographical reality on which the frontier myth was based has long since faded, the hope that this reality generated—that there can be, in the phrase of one law professor, "order without law"—lives on. The American desire for a home on the range, or at least a home in a sprawling suburb, partakes of this hope and of the dream of self-reliance and independence that it suggests. However, in the modern era, order without law is increasingly difficult. People live more closely together in cities, and there is no easy escape valve from land-use conflicts in the form of a frontier. Moreover, the forces unleashed by industrialization gave rise to a whole new set of potential land-use conflicts. While in frontier America, land used for production (i.e., the "range") could easily be one with land used for consumption (i.e., the home), the factories and heavy industry of the industrial age could not easily be situated near residences. These developments suggested that other means than "order without law" would need to be found to realize the American dream of a secure and pleasant home environment.

Despite the fact that it has been decades since the American frontier has closed, our governance of land use issues has not developed in ways that adequately meet the challenges of a more finite world. The history of planning and land-use zoning is perhaps best characterized as a qualified failure. For many critics, zoning is a poorly realized attempt to deal with the new reality of "spillover" and conflictual land uses. Simply put, they charge that it is unfair, irrational, inefficient, and inflexible. These and other charges against the current governance of land use will be a major theme of this book. Yet in another sense, the enactment of zoning legislation represents a milestone in the evolution of property rights, creating a new species of collective rights in land uses. Most contemporary zoning practices, however, realize these rights only imperfectly in ways that sit comfortably with long-standing American values and hopes. The means of realizing the American dream, of necessity, will involve the development of more refined governance structures—ones that do not assume unlimited land and space for the realization of our desires or trust too much in either markets or established politics to secure these rights. Instead, development of innovative ways to establish secure human habitats will demand new types of controls over the built environment and a new system of land tenure. Such environmental controls, moreover, will need to be put into place without also undermining liberty, human dignity, and justice for all.

The need to develop a new system of land tenure is based a set of assumptions that differ substantially from the assumptions underlying frontier mythology. Some of these new assumptions are:

- that we will for the most part live and work in relatively close quarters to each other and to the machines and waste products we create
- that we can imagine and establish new governance structures that are neither laissez-faire markets nor state-commanded orderings of the environment
- that we can assume our responsibilities to those in need of community care.

The challenge of offering new ways to govern land-use conflicts extends beyond having to overcome frontier mythology, commonplace ideas of property ownership, and the limitations of traditional policy tools. The challenge also includes confronting cherished myths about the American political process:

- that decision-making is bottom-up
- that the process is open equally to all citizens

- that public bureaucrats have our common interests at heart and can oversee in a neutral manner the competition among citizens for governmental action
- that experts can provide answers
- that citizens, whether they be producers or consumers have equal access to needed information and a truly free "marketplace of ideas"
- that the long-term result of legislative compromise and log-rolling is a consensus that serves the larger public interest.

The challenge of offering new ways to govern land-use conflicts extends further still—into the world of legal history and theory, the peculiarities of American federalism, the abstract forums of political ideology, and the varied perspectives of academic disciplines.

More concretely, however, the challenge involves a number of different stories:

- stories of the neighbor whose principal asset, her residence, is devalued because of the introduction of a landfill next door, but also of the recycling entrepreneur who cannot find any place to site a recycling center
- stories of the discriminatory treatment of persons of color in the cleanup of hazardous waste sites or the placement of group homes and social service facilities, but also of industries that cannot be operated or jobs produced because no community is willing to take risks, and of persons in need of community care who are warehoused in areas outside of any real community
- stories of the farmer who wants to continue to farm near a growing suburb, but also of the farmer who depends on the increasing value of his farm as developable land to guarantee a retirement income in his old age
- stories of the fear of being the last white or the first black in a neighborhood, of being the "sucker" who waits until the neighborhood has deteriorated to sell out at a devalued price, or the "traitor" who is first to sell out and abandon the idea of community for the "fast buck"
- stories of citizens whose government "takes" and of citizens whose government "gives," sometimes with plausible reasons, sometimes without
- stories of people who work hard to create a pleasant environment, only to have it destroyed by someone else who has worked hard to create jobs for the community
- stories of communities that accept the idea that an unwanted land use or LULU is necessary to sustain their quality of life, but not the idea that they should host the LULU
- stories of slow but systematic injustice in the allocation of rights to producers versus consumers, and stories where it is unclear that the injustice in question is anything more than accepted and necessary practice or economic reality in late 20th-century capitalism.

Finding the common threads that link these diverse stories is important if policymakers are ever to be able to establish a land-use environment where there is more justice and less tragedy than is currently evident in these stories. Finally, the challenge of offering new ways to govern land-use conflict must wrestle with a slowly developing, but insidious story of people caught in ever-larger bureaucracies and systems and of the bias toward bigness in the scale of our built and social environments and in the scope of our markets and governments.

Taken together, these stories may seem too myriad and too confusing to have any consistent moral; they are not particularly apt for discovering intentional rights and wrongs, so much as they form a touchstone for understanding the need for systemic change. The purpose of this change would be to foster greater social responsibility for the victims of discrimination and environmental toxins, but also to promote neighborhood viability, human dignity and equity, and, ultimately, liberty and democracy. One highly useful frame for understanding the stories that are associated with locally unwanted land uses and "not in my backyard" sentiments can be found in the idea of a particular tension that has been expressed variously as: the tension between the "expansion" and "exclusionary" needs of capitalism; between the "heresy" or growth values of developers and "heritage" and "habitat" values of neighbors and long-term residents; or between risk-seeking producers and risk-avoiding consumers. This very basic tension may ultimately be unresolvable, but devising satisfactory land-use policy will depend on our developing a greater understanding of it. In the process of studying the nature of our beliefs about land-use rights and values, we may also gain insight into how these beliefs play out in the political landscape. In discovering that land-use control issues are not easily isolated from the larger issues of "what is the nature of the good society" and that the collision of views regarding what is appropriate use of land in particular circumstances reflects larger beliefs about human nature, we will likely come to understand the need to address land-use control problems through systemic policy tools rather than issue-specific ones.

A second valuable frame for understanding stories about land-use conflict is that of public versus private realms. Within the private realm, market mechanisms for determining who gets LULUs, when, and how present one alternative for policy development. Within the public sector, there exists a number of policy tools which can be broken down into three species of sorts: (1) public choice based on market-mimicking mechanisms, where citizens essentially "vote with their feet"; (2) publicly sanctioned choice by experts based on regulations laying out supposedly objective, scientific, and rational criteria as well as standards for data collection and judgement; and (3) various forms of democratic choice (such as "civic republicanism" or mediated decision-making) that engage citizens and their representatives in consensus building and dialogue. Each of these policy development tools has certain strengths and weakness, the net sum of which can only be compared and judged in relation to the specific policy issue environment in question and to the overall social, political, and economic environment in which the policy will be introduced. An underlying theme of this book, stated more explicitly in Chapter 4, is that the existing governance structures (such as public sector legislatures, judiciaries, and executives at the state, national, and even local levels) are not adequate to contain the growth in the past century in private sector power. Much of the task of addressing the imbalance between private sector power to capture the public will and public sector walls for constraining this power within the bounds of legitimate public purposes is beyond the scope of this book. However, some proposals for reforming land-use governance—especially those that call for the creation of neighborhood or ward-sized districts or governments—fit neatly with the idea of increasing the ability of the public sector to limit the potentially corrupting influences of powerful private interests, without at the same time increasing the threat of big government posing an even greater threat to liberty and democracy.

The idea of a neighborhood government—one standing between the individual and the state, equipped with the flexible authority respecting approval of within-jurisdiction land uses, but limited by policies and incentives designed to promote a more equal distribution of unwanted land uses among neighborhoods—can, I argue, have specific advantages for land-use governance and the larger value of democratic choice. I also argue, however, that the pragmatic advantages of understanding and ordering the world (and property rights in particular) in terms of personhood, community, and the state, rather than in the more dichotomous terms of the individual versus the state, are not to be achieved without risk. Reordering the institutions that have traditionally maintained private/public boundaries should perhaps only be considered when evidence exists that these boundaries have already been breached and are in need of repair. Such evidence, I propose to show, is plentiful.

Finally, to understand the implications of stories related to unwanted land uses, the reader may want to keep in mind the notion that what takes place on a neighborhood or community level is also likely to take place on a national or global level. Evidence suggesting that affluent neighborhoods have escaped bearing their fair share of the LULUs may indicate that affluent regions of the country and affluent countries are also not sharing the costs of the LULUs from which they directly or indirectly benefit. While entire nations and regions of the world are likely taking advantage of the lack of adequate global governance with respect to land uses, this problem, for the most part, is beyond the scope of this book. Rather, the focus of this book is on the need, at a first cut, for innovative change in contemporary American legal doctrines of property, nuisance, and zoning, and change in the institutional structures of local government and community-level policy-making. My chosen method for discovering innovative change, however, is to move from a concrete description of environmentally and socially distinctive land uses and aspects of the built environments in the 20th century to an abstract exploration of political ideology, and from there, to proceed by way of an examination of contemporary politics and policy tools toward some concrete proposals for changes in policy and governance structures.

More specifically, the book begins with an attempt to place land-use governance issues within an historical context and traces the development of two streams or social movements that have profound effects on land-use reform—the movement for social justice and the environmental movement. The purpose of the first part of this book is to suggest that land-use issues are at the core of very complex systems of politics and policy, concepts of rights, common and positive law, social and cultural trends, and industrial and other technological capabilities. Understanding the feedback loops and system effects of these factors in land-use issues will form an important basis for attempting to craft new policy and a new regulatory framework for land use.

Conflicts about locally unwanted land uses often occasion deep political reverberations because of the major role that land and property ownership have played in American thought and because of the strong association between land ownership and core values of liberty, democracy, and responsibility.[2] The second part of this book explores the connection between concepts of property and streams of political ideologies.

In the third part of this book, I examine how the evolution of politics in the United States has affected the governance of land-use disputes. The central argument of this section is that the political mechanisms for governance so artfully designed in and for the 18th century have in the interim been captured and corrupted. Political decision-making about land use, whether at the local, state, or national level, has been negatively affected by our inability to maintain viable "classic liberal" institutions in the face of forces let loose by modernization and industrial development.

The fourth part of this book lays out four value criteria or core values that appear to be involved in most land-use disputes—efficiency, environmental quality, community viability, and equity. It is argued that part of our inability to deal with many land-use issues is that professional planners and academic researchers in the area tend to look at land-use conflicts through the lens of single value criteria. I argue, however, that one area of policy studies—the examination of what are called common pool resources—could provide a means of viewing these conflicts from a perspective that partakes of more than one point of view or core value. Moreover, I suggest that the idea of common pool resources, on which there is an increasingly useful body of literature, can provide a powerful heuristic for policy development with regard to LULUs. The logical link in using this heuristic is to view the siting of a LULU as an act of appropriation of a particular sort of common pool resource or property. In a typical common pool resource situation, an appropriator, say a farmer, will take, for example, an excessive amount of water from a common water basin, devastating what would otherwise be a replenishable resource. In a LULU situation, the person siting a LULU facility can be seen as appropriating a different, more intangible type of common pool resource or property. The property in question might best be described as the human dignity provided by one's home environment. More abstractly, however, the property that is appropriated when a LULU undermines residential amenities and community viability is what the founders called "public happiness." Public happiness is particularly undermined when neighborhood residents experience the feeling of not having any control over the environment in which they are living. The ad hoc placement of a LULU, particularly in cases where a neighborhood or community has already been the site of numerous LULUs, represents a diminution of human dignity and public happiness. This view of human dignity and public happiness as a sort of civic common pool resource that must be protected and replenished, I argue, can help us think more concretely about the governance of LULUs. The chief implication of this view is that the value of a LULU that is a necessary part of continued economic growth must be considered in light of the potential for this LULU to diminish human dignity in the process of its development.

The fifth part of this book presents a model for understanding how core values, ideologies, and politics can come together in various categorical ways and for explaining how potential solutions to certain types of land-use disputes might differ, depending on the problem category in which a specific dispute falls. In essence, I argue that whether one sees a locally unwanted land use (LULU) dispute as a problem that is structural or not and inherently win-lose or not will suggest different policy approaches or policy tools for resolving or mitigating the dispute. More particularly, this part of the book examines the strengths and weaknesses of two types of decision-making mechanisms or tools: market-mimicking mechanisms and political ones. Within the set of political mechanisms, two branches—an adversarial and a unitary (or integrative)—are identified and assessed in light of their relative ability to optimalize the core values involved in land-use planning.

The sixth part of this book explores the nature of policy innovation in the area of land-use control and property. I suggest that many policy innovations occur as a result of a cross-fertilization of distinct political ideologies or from distinct notions of how to separate or combine the public and private realms of activity. The resulting hybrid can represent either a "friendly" or "noxious" innovation, depending on what features from one ideology are mixed with the other. In particular, two approaches to land-use reform—a social republican one and social democratic one—are identified as innovative alternatives to the standard, mainstream options of laissez-faire or state-regulatory land use. I explore some of the historical record of these two alternative approaches and identify the potential benefits and limitations of these approaches with regard to contemporary land-use problems.

Next, I build on the discussion of the governance of common pool resources to suggest that further innovations in land-use control policy can be imagined. These innovations, for lack of a better term, are called framework policies because one stream of options involves "framing" a market for development rights, while the other stream of options involves "re-framing" political institutions so as to better channel and mitigate the effects of private power. Overall, I argue that in order to create market-like incentives for states and communities to act in ways that promote environmental justice, social responsibility, and community-based care, it will be necessary to establish a framework for LULU development rights that allows for limited exchanges of these rights, promotes a degree of flexibility and neighborhood control in the course of neighborhood development, while at the same time ensuring that no one community or neighborhood is forced to bear more than its fair share of unwanted developments. However, this framing of a market in development rights, properly understood, also involves some reframing of our political institutions—toward more neighborhood-level governance—to support the new socially framed market rights.

In the seventh and eighth parts of this book, I present and evaluate some contemporary policy innovations for land-use control and the siting of unwanted facilities such as toxic waste landfills. I compare and contrast these innovations to a sample framework policy that is designed to address land-use issues of both types—those involving environmental issues and those related to social justice concerns. Finally, I assess this sample framework policy in light of such concerns as legal and political viability, equity, the need for protection of open spaces, and the problem of racial segregation.

This book is designed to be of use to a number of different types of readers, including planners, policymakers, land-use and environmental lawyers, local government officials, and political theorists. However, even though the book was written so that the latter parts build on the former, not every part of the book will likely be of interest to every reader. For those who are simply interested in a statement of the problem and potential policy responses, Chapters 1, 7, and 8 would likely be of most interest. For those who have an interest in policy development, and especially how land-use policy development might be grounded in or inspired by political philosophy and theory, a reading of the entire book would be in order. Students of politics might want to be sure to read Chapter 3. For legal theorists, it is not easy to provide a guide to short-cut reading because legal issues are addressed in most the chapters. However, persons who might be reading this book only for how it addresses legal concerns would want to attend to major parts of Chapters 1 and 2; the part of Chapter 3 that addresses plan jurisprudence, SLAPP suits, and the death of property; the parts of Chapter 5 that examine judicial approaches and zoning and comprehensive planning; and the part of Chapter 8 that focuses on general, practical, legal, and ethical objections to framework policies.

NOTES

1. Lasswell, Harold. (1958). *Politics: Who Gets What, When and How*. New York: Meridian Books.

2. de Neufville, Judith I. (1981). *The Land Use Policy Debate in the United States*. New York: Plenum Press.

CHAPTER 1

The Evolution of LULU Problems

LAND-USE CONTROL, COMMUNITY, AND THE PRESSURE FOR GROWTH

Land-Use Control in the Early Republic

In constitutional republics such as the United States, the acts of governing are often organized around separate institutions—executive, legislative, and judicial—with distinctive powers. For the first century of the United States republic, the governing of land use demanded little attention from any of these institutions. Of course, elected representatives and public officials were heavily involved in the exploration, surveying, appropriation, sales, distribution, and settlement of new lands. However, beyond setting aside some public land for public uses or for the support of public institutions or public infrastructure, the newly formed federal government generally refrained from involvement in land-use controls that might affect citizens' decisions about how to use the land they owned. In fact, the passage of the U.S. Constitution resulted in a net transfer of power from colonial cities that practiced some degree of planning to the newly formed states that were more inclined to promote the new industry of land speculation and practices in line with the maximization of economic return on land investments than with planning efforts.[1]

If any branch of government was involved in land-use control, it was the local judiciary. Even here, however, government involvement was minimal because the judiciary ordinarily was limited to land-use disputes between owners of adjacent property. Settlement of these disputes was decided by recourse to the common law of property.

Much of this common law grew out of accumulated experience in settling disputes related to agriculture or hunting among land-owning gentry. Over time, the law evolved certain rules or precedents, such as the rule of first possession, that, having provided plausible solutions in the past, were now applied to new disputes. Some scholars have suggested that the common law has been able to provide a fairly efficient resolution of these disputes because the law evolved in situations where the disputes involve somewhat simple and relatively clear-cut issues generally involving just a few parties. In these cases, it is suggested that as long as the courts are able to be definite (rather than ambiguous) in the way they distribute property rights, efficiency, or the tendency for the property in question to be employed to its maximum feasible use, would be served. However, as long as a property right was left vaguely defined, the property in question would be open to dispute, and while ownership remained in doubt, the investments of labor and capital needed to extract value from the property would not be made.

While many of the common-law features of landed property evolved in an intuitive manner (such as the right to possess the agricultural fruit of the land) and have not changed much over time, other features, such as rights related to potential spillover effects, have had a much more uncertain history and are still in question today. This uncertainty is important because the essence of NIMBY and LULU issues is the perception on the part of some citizens that a property owner's use of her land has some negative and possibly illegitimate spillover effects onto others. While the existence of disputes over spillover effects is probably as old as property itself, the limited scale and scope of the potential spillovers during most of the period that the common law was evolving meant that efficiency could probably be achieved by assigning to all property the same set of clear-cut rights. When a dispute over spillovers occurs, say, when water runs off onto adjoining property because of your irrigation project, a property rule (such as related to nuisance) could be invoked by the neighbors affected by your action. Because the rule clearly gives the property right in question (such as the right not to be invaded by any physical mass whose entrance onto property is caused by another) to your neighbor, your choice is twofold: You may either give up your irrigation project or you may pay your neighbor for the inconvenience of the water run-off. Economic theory would suggest that as long as your irrigation project is of greater economic magnitude than the costs of the run-off experienced by your neighbor, you should be able to come to some agreement with your neighbor, compensating him for his loss. Economic efficiency is served in this case because the full cost of your irrigation project has been internalized or made part of your decision-making. In setting up clear-cut property rules, the common-law would seem to promote such efficiency.[2] Early common-law precedents related to nuisance, liability, possession, use, and trespass, for example, tended to favor the sharp distinctions and property boundaries that would allow for the landowner's absolute control over his or her own property and that would allow trespass of the rights by others for only the most exceptional reasons. Richard Epstein, a stern defender of property rights, for example, has noted that while trespassing would generally be prohibited, an exception might be allowed in cases, say, where a public right-of-way is blocked in a heavy snow storm such that the only way to safety would be to trespass on private property.[3]

One consequence of America's inheritance of a body of common law that featured fairly definitive property rights was that for the first century of our republic, the judiciary had little trouble applying common-law principles, and citizens had relatively little trouble complying with the social and economic consequences of the strict property rights arrangements. In addition, the existence of the frontier, coupled with cheap land policies and backed by the Jeffersonian and classical liberal ideal of a propertied citizenry, tended to fit neatly with the English common-law ideal of a man's home being his castle and refuge.

During the most recent century, however, and especially during the last few decades, governing land-use issues has demanded an ever increasing amount of attention by public officials at all levels and in all branches of government. The sources of this increase in governing are numerous. The end of the frontier and cheap land, for example, eliminated the safety valve of being able to move on whenever the land was exhausted or whenever a neighbor's behavior seemed a nuisance. More important, however, the rise of large-scale industry with its black smoke, noise, and concentrated but often transient work-force provided a never-ending source of bother for persons seeking residential havens in an industrialized world.

The effects of these trends, toward more concentrated groupings of populations and larger-scale industry, undermined to some degree the efficiency of the common law as a basis for settling disputes revolving around unwanted land uses. That is, as the magnitude of the undesirable land-use impacts increased with industrialization (for example, a noisy factory spewing smoke and foul water, and harboring transient workers is substantially more undesirable to a neighbor than most nuisances of an agricultural nature), the number of persons potentially affected by these impacts also increased. Instead of one or two adjoining property owners complaining about the nuisance of water run-off, now adjoining and nearby owners and tenant residents may have a complaint against the factory owner. With urbanization, the existence of concentrated populations further increases the number of aggrieved parties. As the scope and scale of the land use impact widens, the efficiency of common-law dispute settlement declines. The costs (which economists call transaction costs) of negotiating agreements between and among the affected parties increases geometrically as the number of parties involved increases. With the frontier closing and the pressures of industrialization and urbanization growing, the age of "easy" and efficient common- law property settlements of LULU disputes came to a close as well.

The perception of a need for planning that grew out of health problems associated with urbanization further directed this movement away from common-law understandings of property. Urban tenement housing for the laborers in the new factories provided a focus for this movement. Combining high density with poor sanitation and inadequate means of socializing youth, such housing provided another source of discomfort for citizens and spawned the Sanitary Reform movement and an urgent call for a city planning profession.[4] This movement, occurring early in the Victorian age, was concerned most directly with making cities safe for development by providing for adequate water and sewer systems and building ventilation rather than with land-use planning or common-law property rights per se. Nevertheless, it set the stage for further erosion of the common-law view of strict property rights. Similarly, the more late Victorian "City Beautiful" movement attempted to make cities more livable by providing for municipal facilities and recreation, but also failed to address land-use planning in the private sector.[5]

In fact, at the same time as these movements occurred, the courts increasingly recognized that the benefits of industrialization were not likely to be captured without some sacrifice. Specifically, the strict common-law protection of property owners against nuisances such as soot, odor, noise, congestion, and trespass would have to be balanced against the benefits of dramatic material progress for the entire community. While this judicial balancing act demonstrated the ability of the law to change with the times, it fundamentally altered centuries-old understandings of property and ignited a litigation explosion in property rights issues that continues to the present day.

Only since the first decades of this century did local and state governmental bodies act to mitigate the effects of material progress by directly ordering property rights so as to: (1) exclude some facilities and uses (Euclidian zoning); (2) control development to ensure that it pays for itself (fiscal zoning); (3) ensure that public infrastructure is available to support new development (growth management policies); (4) provide for environmental amenities (environmental zoning and land management). Taken as a whole, these measures go far beyond the minimal state intervention in the disposition of private property envisioned by most of those living during the founding of the republic.

SOCIAL MOVEMENTS PUSHING TOWARD GREATER LAND-USE CONTROL

Although land-use governance issues arising from urbanization, suburbanization, and industrialization have been evident for at least fifty years or more, these issues have recently become more salient. A number of trends, movements, and developments have brought land-use issues to our national, state, and local policy agenda.

1. The environmental movement and associated sciences that emerged in the 1960s and 1970s have heightened citizen awareness of specific health and safety dangers and personal and social costs that once were invisible. In

addition to industrial waste and pollution, the application of herbicides and pesticides has been identified as a potentially dangerous land use.

2. More citizens are aware that about two million acres of irreplaceable cropland are being lost each year to urban and suburban development. As the Department of Agriculture has noted, "The days of complacency about America's cropland supply are over."[6]

3. Similar to the loss of cropland is the loss of other vital natural resources such as water-purifying wetlands, oil and minerals, greenspace and wilderness areas, and viable soil.

4. Municipalities have attempted to control growth in ways that bring public development costs (such as for roads, schools, parks) in line with expected revenue increases from various types of development and to restrict developments that do not pay for themselves.[7]

5. The generation of huge quantities of industrial and consumer waste, as well as accumulated but untreated hazardous waste, has led to a landfill and hazardous waste disposal crisis that involves governments at the local, state, and federal levels in controversies over rights, jurisdictions, and enforcement issues. The siting of waste disposal facilities is currently the source of some of the strongest passions in the political landscape.[8]

6. A historic preservation movement has emerged that seeks to substantially expand the traditional boundaries of nuisance law into the area of aesthetics.[9]

7. Private islands of commerce (such as super malls) and residence (walled towns and neighborhoods) now eliminate public space and tightly control travel and activity.[10]

8. An economic development movement engages public-private partnerships in directing growth toward specific geographical areas.[11]

9. Deinstitutionalization and mainstreaming movements in social and correctional services call for providing community-based residential treatment and rehabilitation to persons who, in earlier periods, would have resided in hospitals, prisons, and asylums.[12]

10. Many now realize that land-use policies and movements such as rent control, gentrification, and commercial "edge city" development have done

little to better the housing and employment crisis among low-income citizens and may have even worsened this crisis.[13]

11. It is also becoming clear that some of the failure of school and housing desegregation policies to create multicultural communities can be laid at the feet of exclusionary zoning policies that segregate persons by income and class, and thereby also by race. This occurs even though intentional exclusion by race is unconstitutional.[14]

In this book, I explore how these trends and movements are challenging and changing our traditional capacities for governance in the area of land use. The challenge presented by these developments is described in terms of two recently coined acronyms that succinctly identify the issues central to discussions on land-use governance. NIMBY stands for "not in my back yard." This term captures the sense of personal invasion felt by citizens who are faced with nearby land-use developments that they find undesirable. The term NIMBY aptly describes the emotional response of citizens who are faced with being chosen to bear the full spillover costs of developments that the public or community as a whole find desirable. The citizens who cry "not in my backyard" are not necessarily saying "not at all"; rather, they are saying, "Put this development someplace else."[15] While the term NIMBY is used to describe land-use issues that are experienced at the level of individual citizens and landowners, the term LULU, or locally unwanted land use, defines a broader area of the land-use field. LULUs refer to those land uses that are generally needed by the more encompassing political or social unit, but that have specific and substantial negative spillover effects in the community where the facility or development is sited.

Although the terms LULU and NIMBY may in many instances be used interchangeably, this is not always the case. Whereas the location of a school next to one's residence may be termed a NIMBY, the school would not generally be described as a LULU. However, construction of a prison facility or hazardous waste dump would likely be described both as a NIMBY and a LULU.

PRESSURES FOR GROWTH AND THE END OF PROGRESS

Since the beginning of the first agricultural revolution in seventeenth- and eighteenth-century England, the pressures for growth have encountered numerous legal, economic, and cultural barriers. Early on, the common-law restrictions related to primogeniture and entail, customary and use rights in common lands, and dower rights placed substantial restrictions on landowners wishing to use their land to produce surplus for emerging urban markets. It is significant that many of these early common-law restrictions on property use and exchange did not survive the formation of new states in the New World. Even in the Old World, these restrictions were gradually removed by the enactment of positive laws such as the Enclosure Acts. Rather than accepting Old World common law in its entirety, the founders of U.S. jurisprudence were more significantly influenced by the work of a highly respected English jurist, William Blackstone, whose commentaries on the common law were widely circulated and accepted among lawyers in Britain and its colonies. Blackstone's notion of property as "sole and despotic dominion which one man exercises over the external things of the world"[16] reflected the values and justifications of early capitalists.[17] Capitalism at this stage in development was most in need of devices to unfetter land and labor from their feudal and customary ties to family, manor, and community. Yet, however useful this strict conception of property (that is, as a right to solely possess, use, and alienate land and other things without interference from either the community or other property owners)[18] was to eighteenth-century capitalists, Blackstone's idea of property became less useful as capitalism evolved.

Some of the first indications of a movement away from strict private property rights were evidenced in nuisance law. Under the traditional Blackstonian concept of property and nuisance principles, a judge would be mandated to grant an injunction against any party that was found to be interfering with a landowner's enjoyment of his or her property.[19] In the nineteenth century, however, judges began instead to use a balancing test that weighed the benefits of an industrial entrepreneur's activities against the purported nuisance that these activities represented for nearby landowners.[20] Instead of following a strict property right principle, judges in the middle of the nineteenth century began to use a principle based on tort law that required a finding of fault and unreasonableness before granting an injunction. Hence, even if an industrialist's activities might result in a neighbor's land being unfit for cultivation or in an actual health hazard to a neighbor, courts were reluctant to enjoin activities that provided for "public convenience" or the "wants of the community."[21] Some legal scholars have suggested that entrepreneurs could depend on the courts for favorable treatment because during this period of history, industrialization was seen either as an inevitable force or as something that rebounded to the good of the total community.[22]

The movement away from a pure Blackstonian or strict view of property was paralleled and reinforced by an evolution in the forms of property in advanced capitalist societies. Stocks in limited liability corporations, bonds, pensions, and new forms of trusts were instituted as new forms of property that involved only partial control over the property in question. That is, rather than controlling the entire "bundle" of property rights functions (for example, those related to holding, using, excluding, assigning, leasing, selling) that were typically tied together in strict understandings of property, these new forms of property provided for some separation or unbundling of the various "sticks" of the full set of property rights.[23]

These new forms of "unbundled" property facilitated economic growth but undermined traditional conceptions of property as control. As Adolf Berle and

Gardiner Means (1932) outlined in their influential book on *The Modern Corporation and Private Property*, the separation of ownership from control fundamentally transformed property rights and legitimized New Deal policies that attempted to encourage the useful aspects or rights of property while discouraging those that were socially undesirable.

Much of the evolution in property law during the nineteenth and early twentieth centuries occurred as a result of the pressure for economic growth and in conjunction with real and dramatic progress in material well-being and overall standards of living in the industrialized world. Whatever transformations in property law that were needed to support and facilitate such progress appeared to nearly all citizens and jurists of the time to be justified in light of the benefits that could be achieved through reformation of property rights.

Although it would be incorrect to suggest that material progress is at a standstill or that there are limits to economic growth,[24] there is a strong case to be made for the argument that the era of dramatic progress in achieving substantially higher levels of human material comfort may be over. As Owen Paepke explains, significant improvements in such goods and services as transportation, climate control, food production and delivery, and energy use may be limited by the laws of physics or our own inability to gain much extra utility out of the improvements that are physically achievable, but not yet achieved. Whereas in the last 100 years, long-distance travel time has been cut by magnitudes of over 1,000, within the laws of physics as they are currently known, the best we might expect in the near future would be transportation improvements that would cut only a small proportion of current travel time. Similarly, future improvements in climate control and access to affordable food would represent only marginal or imperceptible improvements in the quality of life when compared with the improvements experienced by those living through the last 100 years.[25]

Because the increments of material progress we currently experience are not (and are not likely be in the future) as dramatic as those experienced during the last century, our sense of pleasure in the change from discomfort to comfort is also not likely to be as great.[26] More important, evidence suggests that our working notions of property claims are based somewhat on a balancing of traditional property rights against the overall potential gains from material progress that would occur if property rights were adjusted.[27] That is, rather than being stagnant, the rules "defining property claims must reflect human nature and values, institutions, and technology—all of which change. Societies must be able to adapt to these changes and, pragmatically speaking, be able to overcome the ceremonial value that often attaches to particular, time-bound property ideals (e.g., those of an attachment to or a reaction against 'private property')."[28] Hence, we might expect that an end to substantial material gain from progress would have significant effects on the way we balance "ideal" conceptions of property rights against the rewards that might be achievable if we were to adjust property rights toward more utilitarian ends. That is, just as adjustments in property rights resulted from the courts' balancing the tremendous benefits of industrialization against traditional rights to exclude nuisances, so too are we likely to see other adjustments in property rights occur as a result of the decline in the rate of increase in material benefits that can be derived from further "progress." The evidence reviewed in the following chapters suggests that such a realignment of land-use property rights is taking place in discussions and rulings in the halls of justice, in decisions of citizens to incorporate,[29] in the policies of legislators and city councils, and in the executions of these policies in cities and towns.[30] These discussions and policies, however, are not all leading in the same direction; rather, ideas about property and land-use policies are being driven by motivations as diverse as academic fashion, the desire for unearned "rents" from property or the control of property, political philosophy, custom, as well as the desire to solve social problems.

Since the beginning of the end of progress in the United States, these discussions and policies have been driven by three social movements. Two of these movements—those for environmental security and social justice and civil rights—developed in contradiction to established property rights and distributions. The third movement, if it can be called that, is simply the continuation of the desires and beliefs that began with the Industrial Revolution—the desire for and belief in the possibility of material progress. Belief in such possibilities for growth tends to affect the public's consideration of other social goods such as environmental quality or social justice. When reality can no longer support such beliefs, a change in public will regarding the other social movements will likely take place.

For the sake of convenience, the beginning of the end in material progress for the United States can be marked at somewhere in the 1960s. It was during this decade that for the first time in history, the majority of citizens of the United States (or of any country) could be considered materially rich by an objective measure of comfort that took as its standard the level of comfort experienced by aristocrats during the pre-industrial period. Nearly all citizens in the United States gained substantial access to automobiles, air and other transport, telephones, electricity, running water, heating and cooling, and a variety of household appliances that in the aggregate eased life's burdens.[31]

A decline in the rate of increase in material progress should not be confused with a decline in economic growth. In fact, the 1950s, 1960s, and early 1970s experienced very high rates of economic growth even as the rapid growth in levels of material progress and personal comfort approached certain limits. Much of this economic growth had its roots in efforts to extend existing capacities for material comfort to the entire (and rapidly expanding) population.

The violence and social discord that characterized the 1960s and early 1970s were based in part on the successful expansion of material comforts to a large portion of the population. As Abraham Maslow has argued, it is only after the need for security and material comfort are met that other needs can be identified and realized. Because the system of property rights constructed to facilitate capitalist entrepreneurs was so successful, the emergence of other needs in the political realm might be predicted.[32] In this sense, the movements for social justice and environmental security emerged out of and, in some senses, in contradiction to the century-old and highly successful movement for material progress. Although both movements questioned "the system," the perceived problems that generated the rejection of established legal and economic relationships differed considerably. For the social justice movement, the primary problem had its roots in the existence of second-class citizens who had been denied their share of the fruits, both political and material, that other citizens now appeared to customarily enjoy, but that were once the prerogative only of an elite class. To alleviate the problem of social injustice, advocates demanded the extension of political and economic rights in ways that would allow a sharing of the fruits of material progress. For social justice advocates, the idea and path of material progress was not essentially questioned, only the distribution. For the environmental movement, on the other hand, the existing "careless" direction and course of material progress and economic growth were themselves identified as the problem. Despite these differences, environmentalist and social justice advocates shared a common desire to reform concepts of property rights and patterns of land use that developed from these rights.

While these two movements have had the most significant influence in directing the course of land-use reform, the issue itself would likely have earned a place on the public policy agenda if it did not also resonate among a larger cohort of citizens who consider themselves to be neither environmental nor social justice advocates. To understand how an issue as seemingly "cool" as land use could generate as much controversy and heat as has been the case during the last few decades, one needs to examine the forces at work behind the daily news of residents protesting development and landfills, farmers battling and courting developers, politicians caught taking developers' bribes, and hopelessness in a land with more square feet of housing per capita than any nation on earth.

LAND USE PLANNING CAPABILITIES AND EFFECTS

Frank Popper, a prominent scholar of land-use politics, has identified a number of the forces undermining the abilities of states and communities to serve as good stewards of the land.[33] To begin with, Popper points out, land-use planning capabilities have never been particularly strong in the United States. Although individual cities have conducted some land-use planning since colonial times,[34] these efforts were minimal and few in number. Even those colonial cities that were blessed with a founder's plan often did not extend the plan as development reached beyond the original geographical limits of the colonial town. The Commerce Department's publication in the 1920s of model acts for enabling states to establish zoning—or, more accurately, to provide local authorities with the power to set up planning commissions, pass zoning ordinances, and provide for zoning boards—rapidly resulted in nearly all states adopting versions of these acts. To some extent, Popper argues, these acts were responsible for improvements in living conditions. Residential areas were protected from such nuisances as heavy commercial traffic, factory noise, and fumes, and the provision of spacious private yards tended to promote a sense of one's home as a protected haven of privacy, unobstructed movement, and outdoor life. Yet as the critics of this "Euclidian" zoning (named after the landmark case of *Village of Euclid v. Ambler Realty Co.*[35] that established the constitutionality of zoning ordinances, but also apt in the sense that this type of zoning was based on geographic boundaries) were later to point out, these amenities came at a cost. In addition to effectively excluding low-income residents, this type of zoning often resulted in social isolation, excessive energy use, and erratic and destructive patterns of urban commercial growth and decline.[36]

The social isolation that characterizes life in the suburbs has been dramatized so much as to become a cliche, but this isolation, especially when combined with high rates of residential mobility, nevertheless is likely to have substantial social costs, including increased health and mental health risks, higher levels of family violence and hopelessness, decreased school performance, lowered chances for escaping unemployment, and increased rates of juvenile delinquency.[37]

The energy inefficiencies of this type of development are due to two factors: (1) detached single-family residences are more expensive to heat than equivalent space in multiunit structures; and (2) the urban sprawl demands greater use of automobiles and other energy-consuming means of transportation.

The more hidden costs of Euclidian zoning and associated sprawl may be the most significant ones. Jane Jacobs has chronicled these in her classic work, *The Death and Life of Great American Cities*.[38] Jacobs objects to the segregation of areas by use because the lack of multiple uses in an area results in dead zones that are boring, activity-less, and ripe for crime. In suburbia, Jacobs notes, there are few or no adult males around during the day and no stores, parks, cafes, or restaurants accessible by foot. Similarly, in single-use business districts, there is excessive use of office space during a few hours, but no use during off-hours, and, as is the case in the suburbs, there are few or no "public characters" to keep the sidewalks and parks safe and interesting. Jacobs characterizes single-use zoning as a type of madness or monomania that prevents cities from providing for healthy, multiple uses of land and urban space.

If classic Euclidian zoning by itself were the only cause of these social and economic costs, its critics might have been comforted by the fact that this type of zoning has in many areas and respects been ineffective. Popper, for example, provides a number of arguments to demonstrate that despite the existence of state enabling legislation and even the passage of specific zoning ordinances, zoning has probably been honored more in the breach than in fulfillment of land-use planning principles. He notes that much of the country, particularly rural areas that became subject to development in the 1960s and 1970s, never instituted zoning ordinances or practices in the first place. As late as 1971, for example, the Council of State Governments reported that only 30 percent of Kentucky's cities and 20 percent of its counties had zoning. While many communities have adopted some zoning since this time, a considerable amount of development has occurred and continues to occur without even the slightest relationship to zoning-based planning.[39]

Second, Popper argues that even communities that have adopted a strong planning stance in terms of enabling ordinances are often constricted by a lack of staff to enforce the ordinances and the existence of arbitrary planning boundaries and multiple, overlapping jurisdictions and special districts. Arbitrary boundaries can mean that communities will have no control over developments that lie immediately outside their own boundaries even though these developments might have severe impacts on them. Even within a single community, the existence of school districts, housing, hospital, recreation, utility, and port authorities, water and sewer commissions—some of which have their own powers of eminent domain and the right to ignore local zoning ordinance—can go a long way toward voiding whatever plans have been established. The extreme case might be seen in Los Angeles, where, as Popper notes, over 342 special districts exist.[40]

Third, Popper suggests that communities are constrained in their planning strategies by the practices of neighboring communities. If one county takes a strong growth-management stance, it may nevertheless be the victim of the pollution and traffic produced by growth in a neighboring county. Moreover, in limiting growth in this case, the community will forgo the added tax revenue provided by within-county growth that would have helped remediate some of the negative effects of growth.

Finally, Popper concludes:

> "A determined developer could almost always get around the intent of a plan by obtaining a variance, especially if he was willing to bribe or make campaign contributions to a few underpaid local government officials. In most communities, developers had no need to engage in such improper behavior. Development interests—builders, realtors, and their political and financial allies—were heavily represented in local government and ran planning commissions and zoning boards."[41]

Houston as a Counter Example

If the elimination of classic Euclidian zoning were all that was needed to prevent the harms of social isolation, energy inefficiency, and lifeless urban and suburban environments, then, according to Popper's analysis, the critics of this type of zoning should have little to be concerned about because zoning of this type does not appear to have been particularly effective. The case of Houston in this regard is telling. Houston is often cited as the only large American city that lacks a zoning ordinance. If zoning has a substantial effect on land use, it should be apparent in a comparison between Houston and similar cities that differ chiefly with respect to the latter cities' having a set of zoning and other planning ordinances.

Most observers have had difficulty discovering significant differences in land-use patterns between Houston and zoned cities. The distribution and location of industrial firms and retail sites in Houston differ little from patterns found in zoned cities. In both cases, firms tend to locate close to transportation arteries and nodes, and retailers are found to cluster together so as to capture some of the spillover effect of people attempting to shop for a number of different items at one time or to comparison shop. Houston does appear to have more strip development than is the case in zoned cities, and low-income housing is more plentiful, but there are few instances of commercial developments invading quiet neighborhoods, as might be expected. In essence, the differences between zoned and unzoned cities appear to be marginal and not always favoring the zoned cities. For example, whereas apartment complexes in zoned cities tend to provide a narrow range of densities, those in Houston tend to provide a much broader range of densities, more accurately reflecting existing differences in wealth and desires for housing amenities. That is, in Houston the poor tend to be housed in more high-density apartments and the wealthy in more low-density apartments than is the case in zoned cities.[42]

The Houston case suggests that zoning may have some effects at the margin of land-use issues but that ordinary forces of economic and demographic growth and migration, business economies of scale and scope, and political opportunism are often sufficient to overwhelm or undermine the intended effects of zoning policies. These forces have been particularly strong during the post-World War II decades.

PLANNING IN THE AGE OF THE AUTO

If there were no other factors in evidence, the recent importance of NIMBY and LULU issues could be explained by the simple pressures for growth that increased population places on an environment that no longer can use the frontier as a release valve for social pressures caused by demographic growth. The post-World War II baby boom by itself would likely have been enough to place substantial pressure on cities and towns to allow developers to put into place the infrastructure needed to support the bulge of children who would be attending schools and using recreation facilities, and later, the young adults who would join the nation's work force and who would need their own low- and moderate-income housing. While the increase in population was indeed dramatic, it was by no means unprecedented. Similar explosions of population had occurred at other times without having as dramatic an effect on the salience of the land-use issue in American politics.

Instead of being a simple case of population expansion, the prominence of land use issues during the last few decades has its origins in a confluence of forces that model post-World War II growth like no other. Perhaps the most significant of these forces was the dramatic rise in automobile ownership. Because of the Great Depression and World War II, car ownership had been constrained, but once the pent-up demand that fueled a postwar economic boon was released, Americans bought cars in unprecedented numbers. Because cars are useless without an adequate road system and space for parking, the explosion in car ownership was accompanied by a similar rate of increase in road building and capacity expansion. Moreover, the pace of this expansion was heavily determined by federal subsidies for road building that ranged from 70 percent of cost for regular roads to 90 percent of the costs to construct the interstate highway system.[43] The development of roadways specifically for individual car use intensifies this impact. It has been estimated, for example, that trips by private car to work take from six to forty-five times as much road space as would be the case if the same trip were taken by bus.[44]

As more space is devoted to automobiles, the density of urban development is lowered, making mass transit less economically viable or practical from a personal point of view. Cities with more miles of road per capita tend to be characterized by greater sprawl and higher energy consumption,[45] higher costs per mass transit trip,[46] longer average time spent traveling,[47] and more per capita spending on roads.[48] Although the exact costs of urban and suburban sprawl are difficult to calculate and often still a matter of debate,[49] Edmund Fowler argues that most evaluations of the costs and benefits of the automobile fail to take into consideration the opportunity costs of having very valuable downtown real estate used as space for parking. Fowler estimates that in North American cities, a single car takes up to three to four thousand dollars' worth of parking space, and he concludes that when one adds this cost to other estimated costs (for example, an estimated 6.7 percent loss of property values due to expressway noise) and incalculable costs (such as jobs displaced by highway construction), "there is no way one could justify, financially, making room for more cars in any downtown core."[50] Fowler's point should not be taken to mean that owners of parking lots do not appropriately price parking spaces and that these spaces are not generating a market rate of income—in some areas these spaces go for several hundred dollars a month. Rather, Fowler's analysis is suggesting that there is a certain absurdity in spending so much on daily auto storage, and that in a better planned urban environment, the transportation expense would be more reasonable. Building roadways and parking areas in turn necessitates an even greater dependence on the automobile. Cities such as Los Angeles that devote nearly two-thirds of their downtown land to parking and roadways end up pushing any new development and housing further from downtown, intensifying the need for people to own cars to get from place to place in the highly sprawled landscape.[51]

Because of the high level of federal subsidization of highway development and the fact that the interstate system tended to substantially direct growth toward its nodes and away from existing highways, localities usually had little choice in the crucial decisions that would affect their future prospects. Groups that might have some influence in these decisions, local developers and public works authorities, did not usually question and generally favored even the largest of projects.[52] Those who were most likely to feel negative impacts of such development were generally unorganized and powerless.[53]

The Problem of Scale

The opportunities for growth and "creative destruction" occasioned by the construction of a nationwide transportation system were not lost on businesses. Alfred Chandler has chronicled the steady expansion of scale and scope in American business operations.[54] The interstate highway system and improved shipping and communications meant that companies could expand their geographical reach while reducing their administrative costs per sales unit. This process began with the expansion of the railroad system in the 1880s but accelerated sharply during the post-World War II era as trucks and autos became the pervasive mode of transportation. The rise of regional and then national supermarkets, retailers, producers, insurers, distributors, and other business operators during this period had two major effects on land use: First, the scale of these operations grew ever larger, far beyond what architects and planner describe as "human scale." An empirical indicator of this growth in scale can be found in calculations of the amount of space per worker in industrial plants. Survey data indicate that the amount of space per worker in suburban industrial plants has probably grown at somewhere on the order of three to four times since the early 1920s.[55] Office space per worker has also increased in the postwar period. The City of Toronto Planning Department, for example, has documented an increase of four square meters per downtown office worker between 1960 and 1988.[56]

Because of the increase in the geographical scope of markets, the average size of industrial plants, retail stores, and corporate headquarters expanded proportionally. Wal-Mart's new superstores dwarf the average general purpose store, and the new mega-malls—like the recently built, 78-acre, 4.2 million square foot Mall of America presenting a 2200 percent increase in scale over the average-sized shopping center—are merely the latest round in what seems to be the ever-increasing scale of facilities development.[57] Business analysts who have studied the success of Wal-Mart explain, however, that the success of Wal-Mart is not based so much on the size or scale of the individual stores. Rather, it is the result of the use of new communications networking that allows for all the stores to act as one very large store in directing supplies of goods from low-demand areas to high-demand areas.[58] Consequently, it would be wrong to conclude that the forces of global competition are necessitating an increase in size of facilities on individual pieces of land. Instead, as markets have become more global, many businesses have simply assumed, in a traditional fashion, that they need to centralize operations in one place, ignoring the potential for communication technologies to allow for a design of production and other facilities to a more human scale. If more work and office facilities were to remain within human scale dimensions, fewer such facilities would be considered as LULUs by those living nearby.

Even in areas such as electrical power generation, where there are limits on the economies of scale and scope (because energy is lost when it is transmitted over long distances), a bias toward bigness has been evident during the post-World War II era. The typical energy-producing plant, especially a nuclear one, now costs several billion dollars to bring on line and often requires several square miles of land and huge amounts of water to operate. However, recent rounds of federal deregulation of power production that essentially require electric utilities to buy power at market rates from any producer may change the drive toward large-scale production facilities. This deregulation of energy production has set in place incentives for increased efficiency and local cogeneration. According to some observers, one outcome of this process may be the production of substantial amounts of power from small-scale, low-impact operations. If this were to occur, it would reduce or eliminate the need to construct one type of high-impact LULU—the large-scale power plant.[59]

Second, large-scale production, distribution, and retailing have generally occurred at the expense of "mom-and-pop," smaller-scale operations. These smaller businesses are believed to provide a "sense of place" for many community residents. More important, however, such places also are thought to provide an arena for the exercise of neighborhood-level democracy and informal social control and responsibility.[60] The negative impact of retail malls and shopping centers on the viability of aging downtowns has become a cliche in planning circles and has resulted in millions of dollars being spent in attempts to revitalize mainstreet America, while preserving historic values.[61] In general, these efforts have not been particularly effective. They have been thwarted primarily by the forces, including public subsidies for infrastructure development, that support large-scale developments. But "main street" redevelopment efforts have also, in some cases, been undermined by their advocates' failure to understanding the limits of their plans. That is, it may be futile to make over a rural-based, town center when the overall prospects for economic growth in rural areas are dim.[62] The effects of large-scale environments on democratic values and social responsibility are larger topics that will be addressed in more detail in a later chapter. Intuitively, however, one can understand that participatory democracy demands repeated engagements with the same people. Complex interests and values are less likely to be aggregated, compromises formed, or policy consensus built if many of the same people do not meet on a regular basis in informal settings. Large-scale facilities undermine this possibility. Similarly, the development of a sense of social responsibility and cooperative norms may demand a more localized setting and one in which people have a sense of developing long-term informal relationships.[63] In such settings, people learn about each others' reputations and can adjust their behavior and expectations accordingly without having to resort to legal sanctions to establish a workable level of social responsibility.[64]

SINGLE USE AND THE PROBLEMS OF SPRAWL AND HOMOGENOUS DEVELOPMENT

The effects of large-scale, automobile-dominated development are intensified by zoning ordinances and conventional development practices that emphasize single-use land planning. Single-use land planning occurs when land in a particular area is used for a single purpose only, such as for retail space, housing, industry, or general business. While development around the automobile tends to deconcentrate urban development, single-use land planning makes the automobile that much more necessary. In communities characterized by single-use development, to complete daily tasks such as getting to work, shopping, picking up children from school, obtaining insurance or banking services, or seeing a doctor or other professional, it is often necessary to make numerous trips to separate parts of the city by car. In contrast, multiuse land development, where several types of spaces can exist within a single area, has been shown to reduce dependence on the automobile and lower time and energy costs for residents in these multiple-use areas. Also, segregating housing from other uses will often require individual households to purchase goods and services, such as washing machines, day care services, tools, and workshops, that once could be provided in a more communal fashion.[65]

In addition to the private costs of deconcentrated, single-use, auto-dominated development, this type of growth involves substantial public costs as well. Urban scholars Peter Newman and Jeffrey Kenworthy, estimate, for example, that the city of Melbourne would save on the order of $40,000 (Australian) if a developer placed a new house within the existing urban district rather than at the fringe of the city. These savings would occur because development on the fringe involves building new roads, schools, sewers, and utility lines as well as providing new facilities for police, fire, and child care.[66] Other researchers, in a similar manner, estimate that providing government services to a subdivision that does not border on any previously built-up area will cost about 28 percent more than would be the case if the development were near or within an already developed area.[67] Furthermore, Edmund Fowler documents that newer, more sprawled cities are spending a larger percentage of their budgets on sewage and sanitation.[68]

The pattern of post-World War II land-use development is based not just on the expansion of new, large-scale, segregated-use developments, but also on the replacement of existing housing and business building stock. For example, one study found that in 1985, over half of the U.S. housing stock had been built since 1960 and that a fair proportion of this new stock (over a third) had been built to replace older housing. Fowler argues that much of the replacement of older housing was unnecessary and economically inefficient. It was only because of tax incentives and policies that allowed and supported large-scale land speculation that development could prosper. A major effect of this development was to replace low- to- moderate-income housing with higher-rent developments.[69]

Furthermore, during the post-World War II era, housing developments became more large-scale and commodity-like, rather than singular expressions of individuality. In earlier periods, a single area might include dwellings of various sizes and richness, the style of which was a result of individuals doing much of the designing and contracting themselves. These residences would be added onto and subdivided as families went through various stages of household expansion and contraction and economic gain and loss. In the post-World War II era, however, housing was often developed en masse by subdivision developers who built in a single style for persons of a single economic and family-size category. As the family grew in number or wealth, it became easier for such families to simply move to another subdivision to meet their needs for living space or status-based consumption. This process increased both neighborhood transience and the tendency for families of a single socioeconomic class to be clustered together. Increased transience reduced the value of a key intangible feature of neighborhoods—the permanence of neighbor and neighborhoods—and tended to increase the primacy of residents' concerns for the economic values of their property. As Fowler has argued, maintaining homogenous housing was a major factor in maintaining the commodity or exchange value of property while at the same time undermining the capabilities of communities to organize around political and workplace issues.[70] In recent times, this tendency toward protected, homogenous residential developments has taken on an even more definitive shape—enclosed neighborhoods built and operated by corporations in conjunction with neighborhood associations. "Each neighborhood," David Guterman writes about these master-planned communities, "inhabits a planned socio-economic niche—$99,000, $113,000, $260,000 homes. They are labyrinthine, confusing in their sameness. . . . It is possible to drive through miles of them without seeing a single human being." [71]

As post-World War II housing dynamics and patterns developed, NIMBY and LULU problems began to be more prevalent. Nearly any intrusion of something "different" into a homogenous and highly segregated neighborhood or subdivision could be considered suspect. Moreover, as large-scale development and wholesale "redevelopment" began to be the norm, the suspicion that new developments could threaten the viability of neighborhoods was confirmed. The legitimate fear that large-scale developments would ruin neighborhood life was unfortunately extended beyond its initial scope such that any development that did not exactly fit into the plan for homogeneous subdivisions was to be viewed as a threat. As a consequence of rejecting all non-planned development, the opportunity for interesting land-use diversity and for the social and environmental benefits of small-scale, multiuse development was also rejected. The logic of taking a strong NIMBY stance is powerful. Without some assurance that the rate of growth and the scale of development will be contained and that there will be some limits on the extent to which land in a neighborhood will be transformed into non-residential uses, neighborhood residents might have very good reasons for fighting any and all development. They understand that if they do not keep the "developer's nose" from entering the neighborhood "tent," then development, like the camel in the old Arabic saying, will soon take over the entire tent. That is, under current land-use governance, there is no guarantee that tomorrow's developments will not be of the type and scale that would undermine, rather than support, the character and quality of the neighborhood. Home owners and residents in the immediate path of development rightfully fear that they will be the ones to bear the costs of intrusive and noxious developments. Even though limited development could provide substantial benefits to private individuals, to the neighborhood as neighborhood, and to the public at large, in an age of NIMBY attitudes, residents may decide to take a zero-tolerance stance to all development. At the same time, however, these residents will likely continue to behave in a manner that supports further development of the intrusive, large-scale type. This paradoxical behavior needs some explanation.

THE POLITICS OF LAND-USE REFORM AND THE FREE RIDER PROBLEM

Attempts to protect the intangible values of human habitat, those found in traditional neighborhoods, downtowns, historic areas, and places that maintain a human scale and a link to the natural environment, run up against what political scientists call the free rider problem. As individual consumers, each of us would like to maintain these intangible values and habitats, but we also want to get the best deal on our purchases of goods and services. If large-scale producers, retailers, and service providers have a price advantage, as Alfred Chandler suggests, we will be tempted to stroll through areas that are charming in character, but purchase goods and services from low-cost, large-scale providers. Our hope is, however, that others will not follow our lead, but will instead make their purchases from the traditional, mom-and-pop producers and retailers. Unfortunately, the logic of self-interest suggests this will not be the case. Without being able to easily communicate what our preferences would be overall, individuals will take the view that others will support the higher-priced, but human-scale shops and workshops, and that their individual "defection" to low-cost providers who are working out of LULU facilities will not have any substantial effect on the survival of human-scale businesses. However, when most individuals take this "free-rider" approach, the fate of smaller-scale business is sealed. Because of free-rider problems, mom-and-pop operations are likely to be doomed even where all the consumers in an area would be willing collectively to pay the premium needed to keep these operations going. Without collective action, however, few, and certainly not enough, individuals are willing to be the ones to pay the entire premium themselves.

The forces toward ever-larger-scale operations also combine with the "logic of collective action" to exacerbate the situation. Those who have studied this logic suggest that while it may be relatively easy to coordinate a small group of people so as to overcome free-rider problems and capture the benefits of collective action, the coordination of larger groups of people involves some inherent difficulties.[72] Besides the proportional expansion of typical organizational costs, coordinating large groups is less likely to occur because an individual's share of the overall benefit is likely to be less than in cases where benefits are spread among fewer people. As a consequence, the costs of providing leadership for collective action in large groups usually outweigh the benefits that will accrue to individuals who initiate the action. Hence, no one starts a movement to address free-rider problems. Because large-scale development necessarily increases the size of the group of neighbors affected by the development process while at the same time increasing the stakes of the small group of developers (and the owners of the specific neighborhood properties they seek), the logic of collective action works against those resisting development. That is, as developments increase in scale, the more difficult it will be for citizens to organize similarly large-scale collective action to resist the developments. Fortunately for those resisting large-scale developments, the size of the proposed facility's effect on a community can bring visibility to their cause and, in doing so, may sometimes counter the negative effects of the logic of collective action.

Frank Popper's description of the politics of land-use reforms in the United States tends to confirm that a free-rider problem exists in this policy area. Popper suggests that those who want to reform traditional laissez-faire land-use policies have to do more than convince a majority of citizens to favor such reform. In an ideal democracy this achievement would be enough to place reform on the policy agenda, but in real political situations, it is often the coherency and concentration of political will that govern policy development. In this respect, Popper believes that the opponents of land-use reform have the upper hand. He suggests that the sentiments in favor of land-use reform are likely "to be relatively lightly held and weakly expressed; that is diffused. But opposition to land-use reform is strongly felt and cogently articulated; that is concentrated."[73] The political landscape that Popper describes is shaped by the fact that opponents of reform have more to lose individually than proponents have to gain individually. This situation is evident in the relative turnout of persons at public hearings. Opponents of overall land-use reform generally turn out in larger numbers than do supporters and tend to present more expert testimony and speak with a more coherent voice than do proponents.[74] Moreover, the plea of these opponents of reform often appears to be more immediate, personal, and heartfelt than that of the proponents of reform. This is the case because the costs of land-use regulations are often immediately felt and borne by a small, but politically powerful group of people, while the benefits tend to be long-term in nature and diffused among residents in general. Additionally, the costs, as Popper notes, tend to be concrete (for example, a specific number of jobs lost), while the benefits tend to be abstract (the preservation of an historic environment or a reduction in future transportation costs).[75]

This process was recently witnessed in a public hearing about a proposed sign and billboard ordinance in Athens, Georgia. The hearing was packed with persons from the outdoor advertising industry who felt that their jobs were on the line if the new ordinance was passed. Citizens in favor of the new ordinance numbered less than a handful and were generally associated with the nearby university. Although those favoring the ordinance displayed a certain command of the general issue, the opponents had commissioned a poll that specifically addressed the question of support for further regulations of signage. Additionally, because of the social differences between the two groups, the group favoring more regulation could easily be characterized as coming from the "ivory tower" and being anti-business.

GENERAL VERSUS SPECIFIC LAND-USE CONTROLS

It is important to distinguish between more general, standard-setting land-use politics and policymaking from the politics that surround specific decision-making that affects individual neighborhoods and plots of land. Examples of the general type would be state and local land-management policies, the plans that specific zoning and signage ordinances are based on, wildlife habitat or endangered species protection laws, and so forth. The specific type is exemplified in the politics involving specific pieces of land and can be seen in fights over re-zoning or zoning variances.[76] In the former instance, the free-rider problem and the difficulties involved in large-scale collective action will provide an advantage to those who wish to develop land. Even where the public overwhelmingly desires to enact a strong land-use law, the legislative process will tend to favor the opponents of reform. Popper's analysis of a number of state land-use laws suggests that only in California, where the voters enacted legislation directly through a ballot initiative, did a strong measure of land-use reform emerge from the political process. In states where the legislature originated and finalized land-use reform laws, the degree of actual land-use management tended to be minimal. According to Popper, weak laws were the result of the strong and well-organized efforts of anti-reform groups. These groups of developers, businesses, road contractors, realtors, bankers, trade unionists, and insurers have large and established lobbying organizations, collectively provide the largest share of campaign funds for elected officials, have access to the information channels, and possess a knowledge of how to exploit popular attitudes with respect to private property rights and free enterprise values. Opponents of reform, moreover, have been known to outspend proponents by margins of better than fifty to one.[77]

Because of the strong popular sentiment for environmental and growth management land-use reforms in the late 1960s and early 1970s, it was politically wise for governors and legislators to take some action that could be characterized as pro-reform during this period. However, as Popper's analysis of the resulting legislation demonstrates, the regulations enacted often contained numerous and serious loopholes and constraints. Specifically, Popper notes:

1. Exemptions of developments of particular types. For example, in Florida state land-use law exempted agricultural, highway, utilities, and hotel construction.

2. Thresholds that limit intervention to only the largest projects. Such thresholds, Popper reports, often led to developers building a project in a number of phases, each of which was below the threshold. The effect of this loophole was to worsen urban sprawl in many cases.

3. Numerous restrictions on the powers of the body charged with regulating the land use. In some states, for example, the commission or agency in charge of implementing the land-use law cannot question developers' estimates of impacts, regulate land owned by the state itself, make binding decisions, or review the nature of potential impacts (such as a state's need for additional power generation) that are not directly specified in the enabling legislation.

4. Provision for substantial representation of development and pro-growth interests in regulatory bodies.

5. Gaps between state and local jurisdiction through which regulated interests can slip. For example, Popper describes a situation in which state regulatory agencies only review local actions every five years, providing plenty of time for development-hungry localities to avoid regulation.

6. Insufficient staffing and financing of regulatory agencies.

7. Inadequate provisions for citizen participation. For example, in Pennsylvania, strip-mining proposals demand public notice and hearings only if the proposed site abuts an existing home. Even when notice is required, it is published in a relatively obscure journal. Moreover, Popper suggests that in Pennsylvania, citizen challenges to the regulatory agency's decisions demand a high level of proof and involve complex legal processes.[78]

Popper's description of general land-use law tending to follow the dominant interests of powerful political actors in the legislative process has its parallel in local zoning change and variance decisions with respect to specific pieces of land. However, at the small scale or neighborhood level, the political dynamics are not always in developers' favor. While traditional and state- and regional-level land-use laws have had little effect on most development, there are some instances where developers' plans run up against existing zoning restrictions and organized, neighborhood-level resistance. In these instances, the political dynamics—related to "free riders," the logic of collective action, and the distribution of costs and benefits across the population—cease to support development interests exclusively. A threat of a specific LULU-type intrusion into a neighborhood takes the issue of land-use regulation out of the realm of abstraction. Negative development impacts that from a community- or state-wide perspective appear as distant and diffuse suddenly become concrete for the persons in neighborhoods that will be directly affected by development. At this neighborhood level, because the development costs to a small group of residents are significant and tangible, the logic of collective action suggests that this small group should be able to organize to resist this development. Hence, in contrast to the dearth of citizen participation in public hearing on the regulatory framework of land-use law, one can read every day in the newspapers of citizens participating in protests of specific land uses that affect their neighborhood and the immediate environment.[79]

Even at the neighborhood level, however, land-use decisions tend to follow interest-group politics. Only in certain areas, for example, do the political dynamics work in favor of more strict land-use regulation. These areas tend to be town-sized, with strong economies, and dominated by upper- and upper-middle-class residents, who are often new to the area, have high levels of education, and do not depend on land use or development for their livelihood. The stereotype of a strict regulation proponent would be a well-off couple recently retired to a thriving resort area who only wanted to stop development after being able to build their dream house in an undisturbed location that nevertheless provided easy access to shopping and services.

In other areas, however, the political dynamic tends to dictate against land-use controls and NIMBY-like controversies. These areas are generally more economically depressed and dependent on land development and high rates of growth to provide hope for economic regeneration. Rural areas with high unemployment rates and strong individualist and private property ethics tend to be very pro-growth, as do high-growth urban areas where ownership is dominated by business interests—even though the residents might be from a lower socioeconomic group.

The political dynamics surrounding land-use issues can help explain in part why the siting of LULUs tends to occur in neighborhoods and areas that are economically and politically less powerful than in other neighborhoods: There is less of an interest-based resistance to such development in these neighborhoods. However, even when the interest might be strong, resistance in these areas tends to be more difficult. These neighborhoods generally do not have an excess of persons with the time and talent to organize, they usually do not have easy access to technical and legal assistance, and they often do not contain as high a proportion of residents who are also homeowners.[80] As a result, the siting of industrial waste disposal sites, large-scale commercial and industrial facilities, social service and correctional institutions, and other high-impact LULUs has been easier to carry out in these areas.[81]

Because of these varying dynamics, local government officials have not as a group taken a consistent stance on land-use issues. Instead, some call strongly for "neighborhood protection" while others promise jobs and economic opportunity. In many communities that do not fit the profile associated with advocates or opponents of strict land-use control, local politicians have generated statements that call for a balancing of interests, with only those who closely monitor these officials knowing exactly how they might weigh these interests in particular cases.

A VICIOUS CIRCLE OF LULU DEVELOPMENT

A central premise of this book is that the siting of particular facilities and the overall "built environment" can have substantial long-term effects on the quality of life for individuals and can shape in very acute ways the dynamics of neighborhood growth and decline. Simply put, the location of high-impact LULUs in areas that are not prone to resistance can potentially accelerate a cycle of decline in the value of a neighborhood as a place for human habitation. A vicious circle occurs: As high-impact LULUs are concentrated in particular areas, these areas become stigmatized as "waste disposal" sites and thereby become less desirable for other types of development, especially residential development. This process further reduces or limits residential and many business land values in the area, often depressing the local economy and making the area more desperate for economic growth. Such land-value reduction places pressure on local landowners to try to sell their property for whatever purposes while they still can. It also induces these owners to petition for a rezoning that would allow them to sell their property for a more high-impact use. Those who cannot rezone or sell will often attempt to move out of the neighborhood anyway, with the property being rented out to persons who have even fewer economic and political resources with which to resist further intrusions. And the circle begins again.

This negative spiral dynamic that appears to accompany the heavy concentration of LULUs within a single neighborhood, community, or region parallels the "fight or flight" syndrome identified by biologists. In this syndrome, an animal faced with a potential threat will choose to fight or flee the area depending on the signals provided by the situation. Animals will only rarely stake out some middle ground between these two alternative behaviors. Rather, the signals that give impetus to a fleeing movement will initiate chemical reactions that reinforce this movement. As a result, animals will tend to continue fleeing until they have escaped from the danger area. Although human behavior does not have the same instinctual base as animal behavior, it has long been recognized that some policies tend to set up feedback loops and cycles while others tend to set up feedback systems that lead to ever more undesirable outcomes.[82] Niels Prak and Hugo Priemus have described such a process at work in the decline of neighborhoods. The process is based on three intermeshing "spirals of decline": technical, financial, and social. A backlog on housing maintenance leads to a lower quality of stock, a rise in operating costs, and lower rent revenue, which in turn lead to less spending and, hence, to greater backlog in maintenance. Lower quality encourages residential mobility, which leads to a decreasing social control, higher vacancy rates, and vandalism, which once more decreases the quality of the housing stock. The higher mobility lowers rent revenue, which in turn leads to a lowering of admission standards and an influx of lower-income tenants, which again encourages mobility, and so forth.[83]

More System Effects

Just as the politics of land use is played out in terms of feedback loops and "chaotic" system effects, so too are other aspects of the land-use picture created in part by such effects. The impact of specific behaviors and events in an interactive system can be intensified and exaggerated by other behaviors and events occurring at the same time.[84] As the immediate consequences of large-scale development, for example, ripple through a community and interact with larger national trends in systematic ways, the initial impact of the development can be dwarfed by the systemic impacts. For example, large-scale operations demand that labor of a particular type move wherever the operation is sited. When a large-scale business locates in a new area, the resulting in-migration can be dramatic and set off an economic boom in that area. The intensity of the boom, however, can overwhelm existing community infrastructure and service capabilities. Frank Popper, for example, describes how the construction of regional airports and large-scale utilities can stimulate "destructive" levels of growth. He cites the town of Rock Springs, Wyoming, to illustrate his point. As a result of an energy industry boom, the town became the site for the construction of a very large power plant and a number of other installations for supplying the needs of this plant. During the mid-1970s, the population was growing at over 20 percent per year and increased from 12,000 in 1970 to 60,000 in the early 1980s. Popper writes:

> Already, Rock Springs had an overloaded sewage system, high prices, large new bonded indebtedness, traffic congestion, deteriorating schools and roads, a water shortage, and a high crime rate with particularly unpleasant drug, prostitution, and racketeer problems. No housing was available. The affluent construction workers were sleeping in tents, campers, and trailers in a climate where winter brought subzero temperatures for weeks at a time. Rock Springs had virtually no recreational facilities. The town's mental health caseloads had increased tenfold, and its per capita suicide rate was the third highest in the country, behind only San Francisco and Las Vegas. . . . Much of Rock Springs had become as dangerous, ugly, and unpleasant as any urban ghetto. Rock

Springs and Sweetwater County were developing public services sufficient for the new residents, but by the time the facilities were ready, most of the construction workers would be gone, and the permanent residents would have to absorb the costs of what would then be excess facilities."[85]

MIGRATION AND THE TRANSITORY COMMUNITY

In addition to overwhelming community capacities to absorb growth without undue negative consequences for their quality of life, large-scale enterprises create and exacerbate inter-regional and urban-rural migration patterns and social transience. The post-World War II era of large-scale development has also seen extraordinarily high levels of migration in the United States. Although Americans have always been more mobile than peoples of most other nations, the rate of migration in the postwar period has been unprecedented. This migration has occurred in a number of directions. During the 1950s and 1960s, millions of African Americans left Southern farming communities for job opportunities in the industrial north.[86] In a parallel movement, millions of farmers across the nation gave up their rural life for better prospects in the cities; city residents meanwhile were moving in large numbers (35 million between 1950 and 1970) to the suburbs; and later, as the "rusting" industrial plants in the Northeast and Northwest were retired, workers pulled up roots and moved to the Sunbelt, where the lack of mass transit systems made the automobile a necessity rather than a luxury. Finally, retirees and those who could afford it bought land, built second homes and moved in part or in whole to areas—on the sea coast, in the mountains, on rivers—that afforded the charms and amenities associated with earlier time and a more human scale of development.[87] The result of this large-scale migration is a nation of citizens who move on average once every six years.[88] While traditional economists suggest that this mobility can have positive economic effects and improve employment rates, there may be hidden costs to such transience. In addition to the abandonment in areas affected by out-migration of perfectly usable community infrastructure, high levels of transience have been associated with a variety of social ills from poor school performance to increases in family violence, divorce, and crime.[89] Although the state of current research suggests that we may be unable to know the exact nature of the trade-off between the costs and benefits of increased residential mobility, there is a good economic argument to be made that public policies (such as tax deductions for job-related moves, facilitation of long-distance commutes, and so on) and the tendency for negative mobility effects to lag behind actual residential moves have probably skewed citizen choices toward greater mobility than they would otherwise desire.[90]

From a policy and political development perspective, increased transience also has the effect of further undermining collective action efforts that might mitigate free-rider problems and put some social limits on large-scale development. Residential mobility combines with large-scale development to form a synergistic barrier against the kind of politics that might address the problems associated with out-of-control growth and boom and bust cycles.[91]

The forces of rapid development also interact with the market for property to exacerbate growth-related problems. This process takes different forms in different settings. William Whyte describes how rapid in-migration into a formerly rural area leads to a proportional increase in property values and property taxes. Land-rich but otherwise poor property owners are forced because of skyrocketing taxes to sell large tracts of land to developers who can make a profit by creating a new suburb or siting an industrial plant, regional landfill, or shopping center.[92]

In the case of large-scale industrial or commercial uses, the impact on the remaining residents is substantial. While tax rates quadruple, the value of the land in terms of providing the amenities of pristine beauty, exceptional quiet, freedom from traffic, and clean-smelling air plummets. Such a rapid decrease in the quality-of-life values relative to the costs of owning property fuels the development dynamic. Where residents once might have banded together to resist a LULU, once the process has begun or reached a certain point, the dynamic takes the opposite direction: Resident landowners begin to run over each other in their rush to develop their own land or sell to someone who will.

When the pressure is for development of residential areas and housing, the dynamic is a little different. If the new residents of this suburb are wealthy and have few children and build large homes, the increases in the tax base caused by the development will, in the long run, likely pay for the roads, sewers, schools, human services, sidewalks, and utility infrastructure that must be put in place to serve the new residents. If, as is more often the case, these new residents are of low to moderate income, have a growing family, and build only modest houses, the increased tax base will not pay for the increase in services that will be needed. A study conducted by Lawrence Livingston and John Blayney dramatizes this point.[93] This study concluded that even $80,000 houses (at 1971 prices) built on the outskirts of Palo Alto would not pay for themselves and that the city would be better off buying up available land and letting it lie fallow and off the tax rolls than to allow residential development of the land. While the Palo Alto study perhaps presents an extreme case, the effects of this type of development have led municipalities and counties across the nation to attempt to assess impact fees or practice forms of what has been called "fiscal zoning" (that is, exclusion or control of development that does not provide a net fiscal return).

Because new infrastructure and services for new residents often have to be built or provided in large-scale units, even developments that may eventually pay for themselves in the long run can have severe short-term impacts and result in large increases in the taxes that old residents of the community must pay.

RAPID DEVELOPMENT AND THE WASTING OF COMMUNITY

In more urban settings, the interaction of rapid development and associated increases in the market value of property has a number of effects that stem primarily from the tendency of the more livable and desirable areas of a city to attract a disproportionate share of large-scale, big-money development. Jane Jacobs documented this tendency in her classic work on *The Death and Life of Great American Cities*. According to Jacobs, the most lively, safe, and desirable parts of city tend to have mixed uses that allow for plentiful street life throughout the day and evening. However, because these mixed-use areas have these desirable traits, the demand for property in these areas increases, resulting in a proportional increase in property values and rents. The desirable nature of the area attracts large-scale businesses that can afford to pay higher rents, while slowly or rapidly eliminating those usually small-scale businesses that can no longer afford the higher costs. Eventually, according to Jacobs, only large insurance companies, banks, and corporate headquarters can afford the desirable location. Others who cannot afford the increased property taxes will be forced to flee.[94] However, this trend toward single-use development undermines the very factor—multiple use—that made the area lively and desirable in the first place. To maintain urban life, Jacobs argues, area development must be balanced and kept to a relatively small scale; high-rent, upscale properties should be mixed with lower-rent properties that will allow for start-up businesses, specialty retailers, residential uses, and artist workshops.

When this balance is not maintained, Jacobs suggests, urban life will eventually deteriorate, and rampant growth in some areas will be matched by total neglect and stagnation in other areas. In these latter areas, property values will decline precipitously and seemingly in defiance of the laws of urban economics. This uneven and unexpected pattern of growth can be seen in the values of a range of properties extending from a city center to its outskirts. Urban economic theory suggests that property values would show a fairly steady and even decline as one moves away from the city center.[95] In actuality, in many cities the pattern of property values does not exhibit this trend; instead of a steady decline in values, in areas just outside of the city center, property is sharply discounted from the expected value. Some of this unexpected lowering of property values can be attributed to racial prejudice and segregation, but some is also likely due to the systemic effects of unchecked and uneven growth that Jacobs describes. Eventually, the disequilibrium caused by the existence of "dead zones" in areas that should have high property values due to their location becomes too great. The exceedingly low costs of "dead zone" property tempt investors, small-business entrepreneurs, and potential home-buyers to take a chance on redeveloping an area. When these new urban pioneers are successful, the process that Jacobs describes begins all over again.

A recent example of this dynamic can be seen in the process of "gentrification." In the early 1980s, a number of urban pioneers brought new economic life, needed investment, and racial, class, and economic balance to blighted areas of the inner city. Taking a chance on bottomed-out property values, they renovated, rebuilt, and restored individual residences, and made it viable for existing landlords to invest in properties that had once been abandoned. These initial investments were risky, but once a crucial mass had been reached, the dynamic of growth began to take over, and a seemingly healthy process led to the eviction of thousands of low-income residents who could not stop what had once been a good thing. Too much of this good thing resulted in a displacement of residents from their home community, an exacerbation of hopelessness, and increased commuting costs for those who had to get out of the way of gentrification.[96] It also led to a renewal of racial, class, and cultural segregation, as those who were in the position of being displaced began to resent the "yuppies" who were new to the community. What had once been a movement toward community was transformed into another NIMBY issue—though one not usually associated with the term—for this time the poor were crying, "not in my backyard."

LAND-USE PLANNING AND THE IDEAL OF AN INTEGRATED COMMUNITY

Because of this path of development, the environmental and social justice movements contain elements that have worked to undermine the bias toward established understandings of property rights—rights that are commonly understood to be supportive of material progress. Whereas the environmental movement has put land-use issues at the top of its list of priority policy change goals, the social justice movement has been less vocal and less coherent in its critique of land-use policy. For many in the vanguard of social justice issues, land use problems are seen as peripheral. The abstract nature of an issue like land-use management also makes it a hard one to sell to an active civil rights community, especially if few people in this community are themselves landowners. Charles Little, for example, quotes one civil rights activist as saying, "Open space does not draw a great deal of attention down at the pool hall."[97] Also, land-use control is sometimes not a salient issue in social justice circles because such controls sometimes involve a reduction in immediate job opportunities. Land-use regulation will likely remain a low priority issue among the broad base of social justice advocates as long as unemployment is high and good jobs remain elusive. In some circumstances, moreover, social justice advocates will take the side of developers and oppose environmentally driven land-use restrictions. The obverse is also true: That is, middle-class opponents of locally unwanted low-income housing projects have sometimes invoked existing environmental impact requirements to block the construction of such housing in their area.[98]

Nevertheless, the movement for social justice, community, and civil rights, like the environmental movement, has explicitly questioned distributions of property and property rights in land. This questioning is based on the argument that these distributions and rights have led to large numbers of persons being left out of the benefits of material progress and segregated into ghettos of the propertyless, the underclass, and the "socially undesirable." In terms of land-use issues, this movement has promoted legal and policy changes in exclusionary zoning laws, tenant-landlord law, adverse possession,[99] land covenant law, and in policies related to housing segregation of racial and ethnic minorities, rent control, urban development grants, and the institutionalization of the handicapped, delinquent, mentally retarded, insane, and others in need of community care.

The vision of the social justice movement has been one of a free, just, and integrated community in which the fruits of progress and property rights are shared and secured. The land-use and other policy changes that have been achieved by this movement, however, have often been incremental in nature and in some cases have led to outcomes of the "one step forward, one step back" variety in relation to the overall vision. A number of cases illustrate the problems encountered and the partial victories achieved by social justice advocates when they grudgingly accept incremental changes. The following sections briefly describe three of these instances: the desegregation of housing and schools, the deinstitutionalization of care and correctional institutions, and the enactment of rent control.

Desegregating Housing and Schools

Ostensibly, the social justice movement has had considerable success in changing laws that kept people of one racial group from purchasing and residing on property that had been set aside for another group. Martin Luther King's successful challenge of the Chicago ordinances that promoted housing segregation was, as Nicholas Lemann tells us, a key victory and essential boost to a flagging civil rights movement during the early 1960s. This victory came in the wake of a series of defeats of King's efforts to promote economic justice and job opportunities for African Americans in the Chicago area. King's more successful attempt to change housing ordinances that limited the land ownership and residency options of African Americans was based on the high visibility of the injustice caused by these ordinances and by the lack of laws prohibiting discrimination in the housing market. Racial segregation in housing could be seen every day by any resident who traveled the length or breadth of the city. The high visibility of this phenomenon was especially evident when compared with less visible de facto prejudice and injustice evident in diminished employment and economic opportunities. Further, constitutional legal precedents set during the early part of the century had already outlawed the most egregious ordinances in support of racial segregation. In one key 1917 case concerning the constitutionality of racial zoning, Louisville's president of the National Association for the

Advancement of Colored People, a Mr. Warley, negotiated a real estate contract that made his purchase of land owned by a Mr. Buchanan, a white, contingent on his (Warley's) ability to reside at the property he proposed to buy. Under Louisville's ordinance barring persons of color from occupying a residence upon a block where the greater number of houses were already occupied by whites, the real estate contract could not be executed. The Supreme Court justices struck down the Louisville ordinance as an improper use of the police power and as being in direct violation of the Fourteenth Amendment. The police power of local government to promote public health, safety, and welfare, though broadly constituted, the court reasoned, could not be used to interfere with the right to acquire and enjoy property, or to take away property rights without due process of law and the equal protection of the laws. One commentator has noted that "in this way, racial zoning was found unconstitutional, in a case not concerned with discrimination against blacks, but rather with preventing a white man from disposing of his property to whom he pleased."[100]

As *Buchanan v. Warley* indicated early on, government action to enforce racial segregation directly through zoning ordinances that would deny a traditional property right, such as that of disposing of one's property as one sees fit, were too blatant and visibly unjust to be successful. A property right that includes an absolute discretion to dispose of one's property as one sees fit could, as *Buchanan v. Warley* evidenced, prevent discrimination from occurring when it is against the will of the parties involved. However, this same right could also institutionalize racial segregation in cases where it is the desire of one or both racial groups to do so. In fact, this property right became the customary legal basis for "voluntary" segregation during the years between 1917 and 1967. In 1967, in *Reitman v. Mulkey*, the U.S. Supreme Court found that a clause of California's constitution that forbade counties and municipalities from restricting the absolute discretion of property owners to dispose of their property was unconstitutional because, in the words of Justice White, it "was intended to authorize, and does authorize, racial discrimination in the housing market" [101]

While the U.S. Constitution was fairly clear with respect to outlawing state action that authorized discrimination, the question of whether individuals could use restrictive deed covenants to maintain racially defined land-use patterns was not as easily answered. While such covenants were barred in 1948 by the Supreme Court decision in *Shelley v. Kraemer*, for practical purposes, it took the combined action of the 1968 passage of the Fair Housing Act and the Supreme Court's decision in *Jones v. Alfred H. Mayer Co.* to effectively end any state authorization of or direct acquiescence in racial discrimination as it concerned the purchase, financing, or rental of property.

Nicholas Lemann states that the success of the civil rights movement in eliminating legally supported housing discrimination had a substantial effect on African American communities in central cities across America. Middle-class and professional blacks used their new-found rights to purchase suburban properties and associated amenities in areas where they once would have been effectively thwarted in their attempts to do so. This exodus of middle-class African Americans from inner city areas was not without cost, Lemann suggests, because it left these areas without the human and social capital that is so important to successful communities. This transformation of inner city racial islands from areas that were relatively safe and economically and culturally viable to economically and socially blighted ghettos has been described and illustrated in both the scholarly and popular literatures and media.[102] After the pillars of these inner city communities left for their place in the suburbs, these neighborhoods were left with a population of "underclass" persons and only a "shadow economy." Children in these neighborhoods are often born illegitimate, and raised in families characterized by high rates of abuse and neglect, and by dependence on state welfare programs. With the exodus of the business and professional classes, these neighborhoods also came to lack essential and high quality services, fair-priced goods, and productive role models for children.

Individual African Americans who were able to leave the racially defined islands created by segregation obviously benefited from the increased freedom that fair housing and desegregation policies brought about. Unfortunately, for those without the resources to exit the inner city, the result of desegregation policies was not as auspicious, and was in many cases unfavorable. In addition to leaving inner city communities without sufficient purchasing power, human capital, and leadership, the exodus of middle-class African Americans from these communities likely had a catalytic or accelerative effect on the twin paths of urban development that have become known as "edge cities" and "gentrification."

Theoretically, these two developments would seem to be contradictory. Gentrification is based on the re-entry of generally young, white, urban professionals into run-down and low-cost inner city areas and properties that offer opportunities for renovation and negligible commuting costs to downtown offices. Edge city development is driven by businesses and corporations moving their facilities to suburban nodes of a larger metropolitan area. This move is made possible by the creation of transportation infrastructure and communication systems that have reduced the cost advantages of downtown business locations.[103] Additionally, as corporations downsize and their workforces become more professionalized, the demand for labor more nearly matches the supply of middle- and upper-middle-class residents of the suburbs. While supply of clerical and other lower-skill labor is still a problem in edge city locations, the total private costs of these locations, which include the costs of crime and other quality-of-life amenities, appear to be as low or lower in edge cities than in the downtown business district.

The emergence of edge cities, theoretically at least, should be neutral with respect to the effect on economic opportunities for minorities. That is, all things being equal, middle-class African-Americans and other minorities who have the resources to move out of the central city areas should be able to benefit in ways equal to whites from edge city development. However, recent research suggests that this may not be the case. Urban geographers studying the emergence of edge cities have concluded that these "cities on the side of cities" do not just occur at random. Rather, they tend to develop on the opposite side of the central city's suburban area to which African-American and other minorities have traditionally migrated. The ability of edge cities to be exclusive is often based on a combination of factors such as traditional land-holding patterns, subdivision planning approval processes that encourage high-income developments, the lack of housing authorities, and the unavailability of mass transit. With these features in place, it is not always necessary for edge cities to enact explicitly exclusionary zoning ordinances.[104]

While edge cities and gentrification appear to be two different paths of urban development—one intensifying development in the inner city and the other doing so at selective edges of a metropolitan area—these developments are alike in having a common effect on racial minorities. Edge cities have tended to reduce the access of middle-class blacks to employment opportunities by increasing the commuting distance from suburbs that have high levels of minority residents to predominantly white edge cities. Gentrification has a similar effect on low-income residents of inner cities. While edge cities were being developed around high-tech or automated industries, central business districts continued to develop as centers for service-oriented businesses in finance, insurance, and the like and as corporate headquarters for industrial empires. The new jobs being created in these districts tended to be very high-tech or professional positions, on the one hand, or secondary labor market positions such as those filled by clerks, busboys, fast food attendants, janitors, and so on, on the other hand. Such positions, as many observers have noted, offer almost no upward mobility. However, Harold McDougall argues that central city areas still offer more employment opportunities than do suburban areas for low-skilled or non-professional workers.[105] Consequently, as gentrification pushes low-income residents farther away from the city center, it increases the distance and the cost of the commute to the remaining available jobs.

De Facto Racial Islands and the Law

From a social justice perspective, the effectiveness of efforts to rid the nation of laws and law-supported practices on which de facto racial segregation was thought to exist was limited, unfortunately. Some of this limited effectiveness can simply be traced to continued racial prejudice and some to the tendency for racial and cultural groups of all types to want to live and work with others who resemble themselves and with whom they can feel comfortable and understood. A major explanation for continued racial residential segregation can be found in the behavior of racial groups rather than in individual prejudice or legal barriers to integration. This theme will be picked up again in the last part of this book.[106]

Nevertheless, for some advocates of social justice, the very law and policy-based efforts to eliminate racial segregation have ironically become dual-edged swords in their battle. McDougall, for example, has complained that:

> HUD, despite these changing demographics, has maintained a policy of desegregating inner-city neighborhoods along racial and class lines, which policy often prohibits funding of low-income housing renovation and new construction in them. The belief is that the poor should be dispersed among the suburbs. Yet, jobs for the less affluent are disappearing in the suburbs, and integration there has usually been more trouble than it is worth."[107]

Whereas land-use law once directly supported the ability of white citizens' to restrict a land use by minority citizens, elimination of these legal supports alone was not sufficient to establish real incentives for the creation of integrated communities. Instead, as the critics of zoning laws have suggested, as long as the courts hold that standard zoning practice is a legitimate use of government's policing powers, these practices will continue to be exclusionary in nature. One critic has decried: "Zoning is a class act! It separates classes of land and classes of population. . . . Behind the beneficial classification of land use lies a hidden agenda: the classification of people." [108]

In 1971, the Supreme Court in *James v. Valtierra* and *Shaffer v. Valtierra* decided that zoning laws that had the effect of discriminating by income or wealth did not necessarily violate the Fourteenth Amendment's guarantee of equal protection and due process. Justice Black argued for the majority that "a lawmaking procedure that 'disadvantages' a particular group does not always deny equal protection." In constitutional terms, the court decided in these cases, as it had already done in some school district cases, that wealth is not a "suspect class" that would demand the special protection afforded in the Constitution to classifications of race, religion, and national origin.

Justice Marshall dissented from the majority opinion, arguing that "singling out the poor to bear a burden not placed on any other class of citizens tramples the values that the Fourteenth Amendment was designed to protect."[109]

Inclusionary Zoning

With versions of exclusionary zoning[110] receiving a general blessing from the U.S. Supreme Court and most state constitutional courts, advocates for social justice have concluded that some other social policies are needed to counter the negative effects of exclusionary zoning. One proposed remedy has been inclusionary zoning policy. Under inclusionary zoning policies, cities require as part of the permitting process that developers include housing or other facilities designed for low- and moderate-income residents. The vision behind inclusionary zoning policies is explicitly based on ideas of social justice: Inclusionary policies define a community "where all members are made part of the whole."[111] Specifically, inclusionary zoning is designed to address the needs of those who have traditionally been denied access to affordable housing, whether as a result of exclusionary zoning, urban redevelopment, the expansion of the central business district, gentrification, or the conversion of single-room-occupancy housing. Inclusionary zoning can be seen as a mechanism that parallels environmental protection approaches that demand environmental remediation of any development efforts. In fact, the early enactment of San Francisco's inclusionary zoning ordinance was explicitly based on legislation requiring environmental impact statements related to proposed development. In the case of inclusionary zoning, the environmental impact to be studied and remediated is the impact on human habitat rather than non-human habitat; in other respects, the purpose and mechanism of inclusionary zoning are essentially the same.

The typical inclusionary zoning ordinance, such as one put in place in San Francisco, requires that commercial developers engaged in replacing or renovating existing housing stock provide for (or subsidize indirectly) a measure of low to moderate-income housing. The amount of housing that has to be provided depends on a formula that takes into account the relationship between square footage of office space used per employee and the housing needs of such employees. The formula used in San Francisco also takes into consideration: (1) the fact that only 40 percent of all office employees in the city reside in the city and that on average 1.8 working adults occupy each residential unit in the city; (2) whether the developer uses governmental assistance in providing for housing; and (3) whether the housing being developed is for moderate- or for low-income residents.[112]

As with exclusionary zoning, the constitutionality of inclusionary zoning has not gone unquestioned. As a policy, inclusionary zoning has many of the attributes and problems associated with affirmative action. Both sets of policies can be thought of as a remedy for problems that are caused by color-blind policies that nevertheless result in discriminatory effect. That is, although the typical exclusionary zoning ordinance is color-blind, the actual effects of this zoning are not. Inclusionary zoning, like affirmative action policies, attempts to remedy this situation by providing those who have been excluded from reasonable access to affordable housing at least some guaranteed access. However, like affirmative action, inclusionary zoning presents similar constitutional problems. These problems arise because the remedy for exclusionary zoning is for practical purposes designed on explicitly discriminatory categories of race and income. As such, even though these categories are being used to redress discriminatory effects, they nevertheless invite substantial scrutiny.

Only one state supreme court, the New Jersey Supreme Court in the Mount Laurel II decision, has mandated inclusionary zoning as a remedy in a suit charging that existing exclusionary zoning harmed low-income citizens wishing to move to Mount Laurel. Some state courts have followed some of the reasoning in Mount Laurel, with California's Supreme Court, for example, requiring that zoning laws be judged on their effects on the welfare of a region as a whole, not just on residents of a particular town.[113] Other states have generally failed to follow the lead of the New Jersey court, and in some states (such as Virginia) the state supreme court has struck down inclusionary zoning ordinances.[114] Nevertheless, local governments in some other states have successfully enacted inclusionary zoning ordinances.

The federal courts have generally avoided exclusionary zoning cases that might call for an inclusionary zoning remedy. The combined effect of the Euclid decision and the *Warth v. Selden* (1975), and *Village of Arlington Heights v. Metropolitan Housing Corporation* (1977) decisions has been to limit the rights of potential residents of a municipality (or outsiders) to challenge exclusionary zoning. Unless outsiders can prove that they were specifically and personally harmed by the ordinance or that the ordinance was passed out of an intent to discriminate, the federal courts are unlikely to interfere in local exclusionary zoning laws. The problem for outsiders wishing to sue to change local ordinances is the difficulty in proving standing, or the right to sue. While standing requirements are intended to ensure that plaintiffs are bringing action to vindicate their own interests and will thus participate vigorously in the litigation, the value of such requirements has been questioned in a number of areas affecting the right of citizens to protect environmental qualities in which they do not have a direct personal interest. As a consequence of such difficulties, the legal significance of inclusionary zoning remedies has not received much attention from the federal courts.

However, debate on inclusionary zoning has not been lacking. Robert Ellickson, for example, has argued that inclusionary zoning could easily have a number of negative side effects that in some cases hurt those the ordinance was designed to assists. This is the case, Ellickson argues, because inclusionary zoning constitutes a tax on new construction. Such a tax, he suggests, will reduce the overall amount of construction and thereby on balance aggravate the housing and job prospects of the income groups the program was designed to assist. Ellickson also finds the in-kind requirement (that is, that builders supply some low-income housing as part of new construction projects) to be extremely poor public policy because non-transportable subsidies of this type are highly inefficient. They force, for example, families to occupy a particular housing unit to receive a subsidy, even though another unit would meet the family's need more effectively.[115] Ellickson notes that estimates of the value of such in-kind benefits indicate that they are less than half as efficient as more transportable housing allowances.[116]

Ellickson's most damning arguments against inclusionary zoning concern its tendency to have negative effects on equity and other democratic values. Ellickson questions, for example, why "owners of land ripe for development or redevelopment bear the brunt of the tax, while owners of recently built buildings are free of the inclusionary taxes until they choose to redevelop."[117] In a similar vein, Ellickson argues that the number of inclusionary subsidized units is far lower than the number of persons eligible for these units, and that in many cases it is middle-income rather than low-income persons who receive these units. He asks, "Why should a government transfer large amounts of wealth to a few fortuitously selected middle-income households?"[118] Finally, Ellickson objects to the particular mechanism—housing trust funds—by which inclusionary zoning is effected. Selection of this mechanism is based in part on the courts' tendency to be hostile to general purpose development taxes and to require a strong "nexus" or connection between the revenue raised from taxes or fees on new developments and the impacts (or infrastructure costs) that these developments occasion. In legal terms, the linkage of development and impacts is called the "exaction standard." Requiring that the linkage be at least proportional—that the benefits of the policy equal or exceed the harm—is known as the harm-benefit theory.[119]

Proponents of inclusionary zoning believe that Ellickson and other critics may be throwing out a perfectly useful tool even though its potential defects might be correctable or of little real consequence. Ronald Silverman, for example, suggests that the question of "who really pays" for inclusionary zoning is much more complex than Ellickson implies. Depending on the various elasticities of demand and looked at from the point of view of a general equilibrium analysis, the answer to this question can vary considerably from place to place, but in most cases will involve a broader group than Ellickson implies; that is, one that includes landowners, developers, suppliers of capital and labor, and potential purchasers of the new construction.[120] Law Professor Alan Mallach argues that even if some landowners end up bearing some costs in the form of a reduction in land values, this is not necessarily unfair or unreasonable because public policy commonly and legitimately affects land values in the normal course of doing business.[121] Daniel Mandelker and Bruce Gelber also concur in this view and suggest that the U.S. Supreme Court would likely uphold inclusionary zoning if it were to be challenged. Mandelker argues that the Supreme Court is unlikely to discover that any of the problems posed by inclusionary zoning are of a serious constitutional nature. Specifically, Mandelker finds that inclusionary zoning meets the constitutional tests for substantive due process, takings, and equal protection. Due process standards are met because states and municipalities have broad powers to serve the health, safety, and general welfare of a community. The argument that inclusionary zoning is an unwarranted type of socioeconomic engineering that violates due process does not hold, Mandelker suggests, because constitutionally approved exclusionary zoning essentially works in a similar manner. As long as a reasonable argument can be made that inclusionary zoning promotes community welfare (such as by providing for low-income housing), it will likely meet due process tests. Mandelker also notes that the Supreme Court is unlikely to apply the exaction doctrine of subdivision law to inclusionary zoning cases. The exaction doctrine (which prohibits forcing private individuals to pay for public goods) does not apply because most inclusionary zoning does not shift the costs of facilities that are normally assumed by the public sector onto the private sector. That is, except for public housing, the costs of low-income housing are normally borne by the private sector. "Inclusionary zoning," Mendelker writes, "merely requires a modification in the economic mix of housing provided by the developer."[122] Finally, Mendelker argues that the courts have not found any equal protection problems in instances where inclusionary zoning set-asides apply only to developments above a minimum size.[123] While opponents of inclusionary zoning do not dispute Mandelker's overall analysis, they do note that some state courts are likely to apply the exaction doctrine or other state constitutional provisions that might limit inclusionary zoning policies.[124] Also, they argue that despite the seeming constitutionality of inclusionary zoning, its desirability as public policy has not been established. John Costonis, for example, suggests that even those who favor provision of low-income housing might want to shun inclusionary programs that promise more than they deliver and that foist the costs of this subsidized housing onto the developer and prospective buyers. Costonis suggests that the spirit if not the letter of the "takings clause" of the Constitution (which requires just compensation whenever government takes property for public purposes) is violated by inclusionary zoning, which requires that "an individual or discrete group be unfairly singled out to provide a benefit."[125] Costonis suggests that inclusionary zoning tends to transform developers into public utilities (for the provision of housing) without providing them with the conventional rights of such utilities (such as a fair rate of return).

The call for inclusionary zoning, generally espoused by persons who share the vision of a socially just and integrated community, represents an effort to address the problems created by the combined and agglomerative effects of exclusionary zoning, historical racial and class discrimination, and the built environment as it currently exists. Inclusionary zoners may be attempting to do what seems right and plausible at the moment to address the problem of homelessness and the lack of affordable housing. However, these actions to solve an immediate problem may ignore the potential for long-range perverse effects, as well as alternative policy options. As will be argued later in this book, inclusionary zoning (in some, but not all, instances) is an example of a detailed and problem-specific regulation that could easily have numerous unintended systemic effects. At the least, inclusionary zoning in central city areas could continue to have the long-term effect of maintaining segregated districts. A more indirect and systemic effect of inclusionary zoning might be for businesses to decide to locate elsewhere. Even advocates of inclusionary zoning admit that inclusionary zoning can work only when there is substantial demand for development. This tendency may explain in part why inclusionary zoning has been more effectively practiced in high-demand areas such as San Francisco. However, one of the most important potential effects of inclusionary zoning is an invisible one inherent in the basic nature of such zoning policies: In Costonis's words, they "require the government to dance with the developers."[126] That is, regulations of this type provide opportunities for developers to attempt to influence their application, negotiate exemptions, avoid application thresholds, and cheat on the quality of in-kind contributions. Government officials, for their part, may be tempted or influenced by developers' bribes and campaign contributions to apply or interpret the law in a selective manner or to negotiate unequal deals with different developers. At the core of the "dancing with developers" issue is a question of the proper roles of the public and private sectors and the nature of the regulations that define and guide these roles.

School Desegregation

School districting represents a second way in which governance of land and boundaries has a strong potential for promoting or undermining social justice. Metaphorically speaking, exclusionary zoning has a direct parallel in the way school districts are drawn. Exclusionary zoning tends to gerrymander specific areas for specific uses. The exclusion of other uses has the unstated but commonly recognized effect of excluding residents or business persons of a particular type, income, or socioeconomic status. The drawing of school districts, if conducted in a particular fashion, tends to result in districts and individual school catchment areas that include persons of a particular socioeconomic class or racial group while excluding others who are from a lower strata or a different racial group. In addition to the effect of segregating children by class and race, exclusionary school districts have resulted in unequal financing of education. Because a large proportion of school funds have traditionally come from property taxes, school districts that chiefly contain properties of lesser value cannot afford to finance education to the same degree as districts containing property of higher value.

As with exclusionary zoning, the U.S. Supreme Court has upheld the constitutionality of school districts that were not specifically established to foster racial segregation. The Supreme Court has been willing to intervene significantly *within* a given school district to void government action that resulted in segregation, but the court has refused to intervene in the actual determination of the districts themselves. Yet it is this latter issue—the drawing of the school districts—rather than the allocation of particular students to specific schools within a district that primarily accounts for the level of racial segregation in U.S. schools. The key case in setting the bounds of judicial action on school desegregation is *Bradley v. School Board of the City of Richmond*, Virginia. The reasoning of the Court of Appeals in this crucial case was twofold: First, the power to structure internal governments is reserved to the states; and second, this power cannot be abridged unless it can be established that the racial composition of the schools in a state's cities and counties is the result of "invidious state action."[127] In the court's majority opinion it was recognized that some of the inter-district racial segregation may have been caused by such government action as the location of public housing, but the court concluded that "the root causes of the concentration of blacks in the inner cities of America are simply not known."[128] The U.S. Supreme Court did not overturn this decision and was similarly reluctant to intervene in 1974 when its *Millikan v. Bradley* decision let Detroit's school districts stand intact.[129]

When one considers the combined effects of exclusionary zoning and patterns of urban migration, inter-district school segregation is hardly surprising. As R. J. Johnston states, "although the Court would not allow new school districts to be created to avoid integration, it was not prepared to recognize that one of the raisons d'etre for residence in suburban districts, and the white flight to those districts in recent years, has always been educational provision and the nature of the school environment."[130] The close link between residential zoning that excludes by income and segregation due to separate suburban schools has been recognized by a number of scholars.[131] However, because the federal courts have not recognized this linkage as amenable to a constitutional law remedy, some observers have concluded that we have reached a limit in the support that judicial action can provide to the movement for further integration.[132]

Rent Control

As the constitutionally based means of challenging land-use policies have been exhausted, other means have been attempted. One consequence of high rates of growth and intensive development is the displacement or exploitation of renters that occurs as landlords attempt to establish the highest possible use of their land. Often, this highest possible use will involve a conversion of rental property to lower-density condominiums or a rezoning of properties for office or business use. From the point of view of renters, this conversion of property is an unwanted land use even it if only takes place nearby, because the dynamics of urban development will dictate that there is no limit to the growth process and that "they will be next in line for conversion." The landlord's goal is to capture these higher-valued uses, either through actual conversion or rezoning or through a rise in rents for the existing facilities.

In some jurisdictions, rent control has been established to mitigate the effects of substantial development on renting residents. Theoretically, rent control should ensure that a supply of rental housing is available to low- or fixed-income residents. As numerous reports of New York's and other rent-control housing markets make clear, the real rent-controlled housing markets bear only minimal resemblance to what was intended by those who draft rent-control ordinances. Those who gain from these ordinances tend to be those who are fortunate enough to have found a rent-controlled apartment, rather than those who are in particular need of such an apartment. Because the price differential between controlled and non-controlled units can be on an order of a few magnitudes, the effect of the ordinance in many instances has been to have some landlords subsidize persons who may in fact be wealthier than the landlords themselves.

The most important drawback to rent control, however, is the tendency for these controls to reduce the investment in rental market housing. If one conceives of rental property as only one of numerous possible investments that the owners of these properties can make, then as rent control reduces the value of rental property,[133] owners will move their investment to alternatives such as stocks or bonds. If this is not feasible, they will work even more diligently to convert rental housing into condominiums or cooperatives that can be sold to higher-income buyers. Hence, rent-control measures that were designed to improve the lot of the poor in situations of high growth and urban transformation can actually exacerbate the situation. The increased rate of rapid conversion toward condominiums in turn pushes up general land values and property taxes and results in more high-value development and less diverse neighborhoods, which begins the process of growth and decline all over again.

Rent control, Robin Malloy's analysis suggests, may have other effects that reinforce the patterns of development—of large-scale development, over-building of transportation systems, and the spatial mismatch of low-income persons and jobs—described in an earlier section of this book. As rent control reduces the supply of rental housing, persons who otherwise would have lived within a central city are forced to move elsewhere and commute to their work in the city. This puts more pressure on transportation planners to increase the scale of highways and other facilities, with an attendant increase in traffic and pollution and loss in quality of life. The split citizenship and loyalties of those who work in one area while living in another, moreover, make it harder to organize politically to solve development-related problems or to enact effective public policies.

Rent control, like inclusionary zoning, places the burden of solving a social problem on a single group of citizens who are not themselves responsible for the entire problem, but who appear in the immediate proximity to the problem. Like inclusionary zoning, rent control does not violate the letter of the Constitution, but it may violate its spirit.

COMMUNITY CARE OF "UNWANTED" CITIZENS

The social justice movement has also been concerned with a fourth type of land-use issue—the siting of care facilities for citizens who as a group are generally unwanted by society or who have been viewed as not fitting in with the mainstream of American life. These groups include the mentally ill or incompetent, the incorrigible, the socially maladjusted, children in need of care and supervision, the economically dependent and homeless, the chronically ill, youthful and not-so-youthful delinquents, the developmentally disabled, and recovering alcoholics and other drug addicts. Traditionally, many of these persons were provided for in large institutional settings: asylums, prisons, detention centers, residential schools, orphanages, hospitals, sanitariums, and industrial workshops.

The deinstitutionalization movement began in the 1960s and grew out of numerous critiques of the institutional treatment. Criticism of institutional approaches to treatment and rehabilitation cut across a number of disciplines. Critics from social work and other therapeutic disciplines argued that institutions often had a iatrogenic effect: Because these institutions represent an exception to normal ways of living, they tend to cause as much mental illness, deviancy, and maladjustment as they cure. This effect could be traced to institutional routines, structures, prohibitions, and supports that had no counterparts in the communities to which institutional residents were one day to return. Moreover, by concentrating persons who did not fit into mainstream society, institutions often reinforced the behavior or condition that they were designed to ameliorate; at the very least, such institutions could not provide role models for living a normal life. Institutional therapy, furthermore, could have long-term effects due to the labeling of residents—by others and by themselves. Such labeling, it was argued, could lead to a self-fulfilling prophecy. Finally, institutional settings were likely to create long-term dependency, these critics contended.

Critics from sociology, politics, and law saw institutional treatment as excessively restrictive, and they implied that treatment in such involuntary settings was an abridgement of constitutional rights and an improper extension of state power.[134] Criticism from these social disciplines helped initiate the deinstitutionalization (or normalization) movement, which was designed to transfer chronically mentally ill, disabled, delinquent, and orphaned persons from long-term, medically oriented residential settings to community-based care. This community care was generally to take place in the least restrictive settings,[135] a legal mandate that was ordinarily translated to mean involvement in group home care.[136] Group homes are thought to promote normalization through a familial-like setting and through opportunities to work alongside "normal" persons and to attend regular public schools.[137] Reviews of the deinstitutionalization movement suggest, however, that it was less the criticism from social disciplines than it was the economic opportunities inherent in deinstitutionalization policy that fueled the movement. Richard Warner's study of this movement identifies the potential for states' cost savings as the driving force behind deinstitutionalization.[138] Closing expensive state-run institutions was made possible by the introduction of federal-level disability programs. The theory behind deinstitutionalization was that expensive institutions could be closed as more effective community-based housing and treatments were made available. Ideally, this would be a win-win situation: State-level political and program executives could reduce state expenditures and institutional residents could get better treatment. In actuality, most critics of deinstitutionalization would suggest this did not occur. Instead, after more than three decades of deinstitutionalization and, for example, an 80 percent cut in the number of patients in mental hospitals since 1955, many of those who were to benefit from community-based care still receive little or no treatment in the community.[139] Most important for this study, many of these deinstitutionalized persons are either re-institutionalized—but without adequate services—in boarding and nursing homes, jailed, or made homeless. The major barrier to effective community care has obviously been the lack of state and local commitment of resources to care for these persons. However, the NIMBY syndrome and the tendency of zoning ordinances when combined with land markets to steer community-based care homes toward the less affluent areas of a community have also played a role. Studies of the siting and siting opportunities for community care housing suggest that community-based homes are most likely to be found in physically and socially deteriorated neighborhoods that are not appropriate for persons who have mental, emotional, or behavioral impairments. For example, Elizabeth Markson and Mary Ann Diroberts found that both the elderly in need of care and the mentally ill in community-based residences tended to reside in settings where low expectations are the norm and where there are few resources for rehabilitation.[140] Nancy Scott and Robert Scott's study of the availability of community care settings for deinstitutionalized persons suggests that the great majority of available units are likely to be in deteriorated neighborhoods.[141] When availability is combined with the state's interest in keeping costs low, the result is a disproportion of community care facilities being placed in low-income neighborhoods. The American Bar Association has specifically identified the tendency of zoning laws that restrict group homes to special areas as a major factor in the creation of "group home ghettos." Such ghettos, one observer noted, "are a unique and degrading form of institutionalization that impedes the habilitation process." [142] This ghettoization process will tend to have a negative effect on property values and will likely reinforce the decline or flight syndrome described above. As community care facilities are placed in the areas where political and economic power are weakest, more resident-owners will flee the area, making more properties available for rent, reinforcing the tendency to locate community care facilities and other LULUs in the area, and starting the flight syndrome over again.

Even if the state were to put adequate resources into community-based care facilities, without addressing the land-use problems associated with deinstitutionalization, achievement of one of the key goals of deinstitutionalization—to have formerly institutionalized citizens living normal lives in normal neighborhoods—would be thwarted. Instead of living in an abnormal and dysfunctional institutional setting, these individuals would simply reside in an abnormal and dysfunctional neighborhood.

Specific measures to overcome zoning barriers to siting community care facilities in normal residential settings have been only partially effective. Some advocates for excluded citizens have been effective in using judicial theories of superior sovereign immunity (that is, actions by the state take precedent over those of a local government) to overcome local restrictions. This tactic, however, can be ineffective if the group home is not being operated directly by the state.[143] A more effective tactic has been explicit state policy regulating the zoning of such homes. However, Patrick Bergin reports that unless legislative intent is unequivocally expressed, courts have generally been reluctant to invalidate local zoning laws that place reasonable conditions on group homes. The equal protection clause of the Constitution has been used somewhat successfully to thwart local exclusionary zoning of group homes. However, the key Supreme Court decision in this regard, found in *City of Cleburn v. Cleburn Living Center, Inc.*, did not recognize any standard of review that was more than the minimal level of scrutiny that would be applied to any citizen. Hence, even though the Court decided in favor of the retarded citizens whose home had been excluded from a residential area, the failure to recognize a higher standard of scrutiny suggests that in many instances the courts will not question local zoning that tends to exclude special need citizens, but that does not do so directly.

Passage of the Fair Housing Act Amendments in 1988 substantially reduced the ability of individual property owners or local governments to restrict the housing options of physically or mentally handicapped citizens or of citizens with different familial status. Interpretations of this Act suggest that it would also apply to persons in need of drug and alcohol rehabilitation, but may not apply to halfway houses for delinquents or paroled adults. The Fair Housing Amendments provide for legal remedy to discrimination that is based not just on intent but also on discriminatory effect. However, local zoning measures that simply limit the number of persons in particular zones do not alone establish discriminatory effect.[144] Hence, local governments can still use lot size, residence caps, and similarly broad zoning mechanisms as long as there is no obvious discriminatory effect. The very establishment of these zoning mechanisms, however, can preclude efforts to test the exclusionary nature of the ordinance itself. That is, most providers of community care facilities, whether public or private, will normally attempt to establish such facilities in a low-cost manner. Hence, because most exclusionary zoning mechanisms raise the price of land and buildings in exclusionary neighborhoods and zones, few providers of community care are likely to desire to build or purchase facilities in these high-cost areas. As a result, even though there is a discriminatory effect, it is one that operates through voluntary market-based choices.

Additionally, key features of the Fair Housing Act Amendments have not been fully clarified in national-level court decisions. For example, there is still some questions as to whether the amendments would make unlawful ordinances or state law that would require a certain degree of dispersion of community care facilities. A City of St. Paul ordinance that precluded the placement of licensed residential facilities for retarded or mentally ill persons within 1,320 feet of existing facilities was not found to be discriminatory.[145] The dispersion question is important because without the ability to prevent group home ghettos, one of the prime purposes of normalization is undermined. Furthermore, as will be explored in more detail later in this book, dispersion of LULUs is likely to be important with respect to achieving the goals of community responsibility and stable and sustained mixed-use development.

Similarly, court interpretations of the Fair Housing Act Amendments have not fully clarified the degree to which local governments can use the definition of family to exclude unwanted individuals or groups. Traditional zoning law, for example, has allowed cities to draft ordinances that would exclude or restrict student rentals in single-family zones. However, ordinances designed to limit the number of unrelated persons in a single-family zone that have been challenged by those desiring to operate community care facilities have been variously upheld and struck down, depending on particular district court interpretations of the Fair Housing Act.

Overall, while the Fair Housing Act Amendments have provided social justice advocates some leverage for overcoming exclusionary effects of private or public land-use acts, these amendments have not provided a comprehensive framework for dealing with LULU issues or for establishing guidelines for community responsibility for deinstitutionalization.

Social Justice Reforms and Centralized Regulation

Like the original Fair Housing Act and federal court cases defining the area of federal government interest in land uses that have discriminatory effects, the Fair Housing Act Amendments represent another in a long line of efforts to reform land-use policy through more centralized regulation. This movement toward centralized regulation has generally been an unquestioned feature of progressive land-use reform. For example, in 1973 the Rockefeller Brothers Fund Task Force on Land Use and Urban Growth declared in a report on *The Use of Land* that "where a regulatory decision significantly affects people in more than one locality or state, regional, or even federal action is necessary."[146]

Even though it is generally acknowledged that local governments may have more intimate knowledge of the land and related conditions, the tendency for specialized local interests to unduly influence local government policymaking is seen as simply too great to allow, especially when this influence is used to favor powerful interests at the expense of the powerless. The Douglas Commission that was formed in 1968 to study urban problems suggested that strong measures by state and national governments were necessary to deal with the restrictive zoning policies that represented a "conspiracy against low-income housing" and that separated "low-income persons from job opportunities."[147] As part of a reform package, the commission recommended that municipalities with fewer than 25,000 people or less than four square miles in area be denied land-use control rights. Some of the inadequacy of governing LULU problems that have social justice features can be attributed to the lack of implementation of this and other recommendations for more regional control of land uses. However, a review of the effectiveness of the centralized regulation that has been implemented (such as the Fair Housing Act) suggests that this approach to reform has not been as successful as social justice reformers would have desired.[148]

THE ENVIRONMENTAL MOVEMENT AND ENVIRONMENTAL JUSTICE

The second social force undermining growth-based property and land-use rights is the environmental movement. Although this movement has many branches, it intersects land use and property rights issues in a very direct manner as well as in numerous indirect ways. For example, addressing the preservation of open space, sensitive coastal zones, wetlands, wilderness areas, and endangered flora and fauna will often require direct public sector intervention and the reinterpretation of traditional private property-use rights. However, protection from the harms of air, water, noise, and solid waste pollution can often be understood as an extension of common law protections against nuisances or the harmful spillover effects of one neighbor's use of his property. Although some of these environmental land-use problems, such as the elimination of wetlands and endangered species, might be handled as specific cases of negative land-use spillovers and might thereby logically fall under an expanded use of nuisance law doctrine, the expansion of nuisance doctrines involved could result in putting government even more into the position of "taking" from some while "giving" to others. Even if such action is, strictly speaking, constitutional, it can wound our sense of equity in ways similar to those redistributions evident in the more social justice area of land-use issues.[149]

Perhaps because of its more direct relationship with land-use issues, the environmental movement has engendered the most successful and comprehensive efforts to reform land-use policy. To create a sense of need for policy change in the social justice area of land-use reform, one has to generate an understanding of complex social dynamics, the indirect effects of growth-management policies, and the role of racial and class prejudices that exacerbate existing tendencies in zoning policy. However, unmanaged growth alone can easily be seen as a direct threat to environmental values. Strictly speaking, it seems plausible for social justice reforms to take place in collaboration with high levels of growth-induced destruction of the environment. That is, regulation that ensures equity with respect to both the benefits and costs of land development—no matter what level of environmental impact occurs—would seem to be sufficient to meet social justice criteria. On the other hand, environmental land-use reform, its advocates suggest, is more likely to demand comprehensive land-use planning along a number of dimensions. The analysis presented in this chapter, however, suggests otherwise. At least to a moderate degree, the genesis of both types of problems is essentially the same: large-scale, sprawled, single-use, segregated, and unrestricted development. Such development, it can be argued, leads to communities not accepting the responsibility for either the social or environmental damage that their land-use policies support. These characteristics of the existing system of land use and the consequences for social responsibility occur under both a laissez-faire, non-zoning condition and under current standard zoning conditions. Zoning, as some observers have noted, may only add a layer of political validation to the market's power to determine the general pattern of land use in any given geography.[150]

These features of contemporary land use tend to work together in synergistic ways. For example, single-use and segregation of land uses allow for even larger-scale development than would be unacceptable under a more mixed-use plan. In turn, large-scale development creates more demand for segregation of unwanted uses or for uses (such as low-income housing) that threaten the more intangible value of social status. Similarly, as uses are segregated, it becomes more feasible for affluent citizens to select areas that are free of LULUs, while leaving the less affluent areas subject to ever more dense and dangerous concentrations of these unwanted developments, both social and environmental. The lower quality of life in areas where LULUs are concentrated in turn results in greater efforts of citizens to segregate themselves from the more "troubled" neighborhoods, while making such neighborhoods the low-cost choice for the siting of unwanted community care facilities. Because of these synergistic effects, single reforms (such as fair housing legislation, suspect class categories, and so on) directed toward achieving social justice, which might appear to be directly addressing the problem, often are without substantial effect.[151] However, because environmental and social justice land-use problems can be seen as having, to some extent, a common origin, it may be feasible to craft policies that will, to some degree, address both problems simultaneously. This task will be addressed in the last part of this book.

Scale and Environmental Impacts

The scale of industrial and commercial development leads to environmental degradation because the impact of any single development can destroy the potential for maintaining any kind of ecological balance in the area affected. Large-scale industrial developments that produce air- or water-borne pollutants will tend to concentrate toxins in areas adjacent to the plant, intensifying the destructive effects of these substances. Both the land and air have a certain potential for renewal and self-cleaning. This potential is overwhelmed by concentration of noxious elements.

Even though small-scale, mixed-use developments may involve as much total transformation of a natural landscape, the effect of this transformation can often be minimized or directed at the least sensitive elements in the total ecological system. For example, in a type of zoning known as cluster zoning, owners and developers are provided incentives for developing in areas that are least likely to be significantly disrupted by development, and further incentives are provided for keeping intact geographically contiguous areas that can be preserved for wildlife or used for low-intensity farming. As Randall Arendt suggests, the rationale for cluster zoning is to protect aquifers, riverfront land, fields and pastures, wildlife habitat, and scenic features that are in some respects irreplaceable.[152]

The potential for keeping negative environmental impacts at a low level is undermined, however, when the scale of development increases. For example, as the average size of an industrial site's land-use footprint has grown by a magnitude of four since the early 1920s, the impact of the siting of these behemoths has probably grown by an even larger magnitude. This is the case because large-scale development often cuts across the traditional migratory and other paths that animals within a single ecosystem need if they (and the ecosystem as a whole) are to survive. Large-scale development, moreover, often precludes the kind of protection afforded by cluster development; large-scale facilities often demand radical transformation of the landscape. Extensive grading, watercourse re-direction, artificial drainage infrastructure, and large amounts of paved parking are often needed to build and use a large-scale facility. Parking provides just one illustration of the large-scale effects: Whereas small-scale facilities can often locate parking in areas that allow for natural drainage, to supply the same level of per capita parking for large-scale facilities, natural drainage effects are not adequate, and extensive paving has to be put into place. This paving increases the concentration of run-offs during rains and the potential for a concentrated pollutant to have a noxious effect on the environment.[153]

Landfills as a Typical Environmental LULU

The increase in the effects of large-scale facilities on the environment translates into increasing numbers of LULUs and protests by adjacent residents. Perhaps the most significant recent increase in these types of LULUs is associated with the development of landfills and other waste disposal processes. Landfill-related LULUs are generated due to a number of interrelated factors. First, the scale of landfills has increased due to certain recognized economies of scale and the general population increases evident in most jurisdictions that operate landfills. More important, the scale of these operations is likely to increase, due to a perception that new landfill regulations will make all but the largest dumping operations economically impossible. Specifically, federal regulations, collectively known as Subtitle D, require landfill operators to install expensive liners and drainage systems and to engage in more regular testing for noxious elements that might leak out of the areas that have been lined. Because of the expense of these systems and their management requirements, most localities, especially those with few resources, realize that they will likely need to work with other communities on a regional basis, building large-scale facilities, in order to meet the EPA's Subtitle D requirements.[154]

In addition to arguing that Subtitle D "protections" are insufficient to prevent landfill run-off and the poisoning of underground aquifers, many environmentalists dispute the assumption that protection from contamination can only occur and be economically viable if large-scale landfills are built.[155] These advocates would prefer that the scale of such landfills be reduced so that the localities generating the waste have an interest in long-term monitoring of the disposal site. They reason that because these sites will never be completely safe, strong incentives and procedures are needed to ensure continual and long-term oversight of their pollution potential. Subtitle D regulations, they argue, will simply give people a false sense of security.

A second reason for landfills' having become a more substantial LULU issue is the generally heightened awareness of and sensitivity to the dangers of unseen pollutants. Where landfill impacts related to noise and odors may have once extended only to immediately adjacent properties, these impacts in terms of a measurable decrease in property values have been detected at distances as far as a few miles.[156] Disposal of more hazardous materials is likely to affect property values at even greater distances.

A third reason for the increased tendency of landfills to be seen as serious LULUs is the awareness that in many areas where landfills and other waste disposal sites are located, the wastes being processed are often not local in nature. The saga of the barges of waste from New York City that were rejected by city after city dramatized the increased willingness of communities to reject waste materials that they did not themselves create. Finally, the willingness to accept waste that was not locally created is increasingly being tested, due to the sprawl of most urban, waste-creating areas. As cities have grown in geographical reach, there is little nearby or local land that affords appropriate landfill sites. Hence, cities must resort more and more to persuading other outlying or rural areas to accept massive amounts of waste that they did not create and for which they are often not willing to accept responsibility. In one study, economists estimated that it would be necessary to pay a nearby community $227 per household to compensate these residents for the external costs of the landfill.[157]

When waste disposal involves more hazardous substances, the issue of equitable burden sharing or communities taking responsibility for their own waste products becomes more acute. Jean Peretz has described the frustration of states whose commercial hazardous waste treatment and disposal capacities are being aggressively used by other nearby states. States with excess capacity, Peretz says, believe that other states that are currently using this capacity have not aggressively pursued siting of waste facilities and sometimes are impeding the establishment of such facilities through enactment of restrictive provisions.[158]

Deconcentrated or Sprawled Development

When the effect of large-scale development is combined with deconcentrated or sprawled development, the potential impact on the human and natural environment is magnified. In addition to the tendency of large-scale facilities to concentrate toxins and overtax the cleansing capability of air, ground, and water resources, an additional effect of large-scale development is the tendency to cover over the "design of nature."[159] That is, a large-scale facility will often have to bulldoze the existing landscape to meet the large-scale needs. When one adds sprawled development to this process, the damage is even greater, because instead of having all the large-scale facilities concentrated in one, say, urban setting, which would at least leave numerous acres undeveloped, sprawled development extends the damage across these acres. However, such sprawl does little to mitigate the intensity effects of large-scale development. Rather, sprawl tends to require the addition of more large-scale highways to connect the large-scale institutions and facilities, thus increasing the environmental damage overall without leaving areas free from development. Concentrated but small-scale development can potentially allow for some sensitivity to the features of the natural environment within a concentrated urban area, while saving acres of existing, natural areas. Sylvia Lewis has chronicled the success of Boulder, Colorado's, efforts to save the open spaces and natural habitats that surround the town. "The town that said no to sprawl," Lewis reports, has been able to save scenic views and create numerous protected areas that maintain natural environments while allowing for plentiful opportunities for recreation. Using a special local sales tax as funding, the city of Boulder purchased over 17,000 acres. Management of these acres includes leasing for ranching and farming, prairie and wetland preservation, and wildlife preserves.[160]

Partly because Boulder is a highly desirable area, the growth-management policies implicit in the land purchase have not negatively affected the local economy or local government's budgets. A spokesperson for the Boulder Area Board of Realtors has suggested that the creation of open space has been good for business, helping to keep the area highly desirable and to maintain low vacancy rates.[161] Additionally, Lewis reports that the cost of this purchase per acre per year to the taxpayers has been approximately $75, inclusive of management fees; alternatively, the per acre per year cost of providing services to these areas would have been on the order of $3,200.[162]

Perhaps the classic case of the environmental movement's success in reducing urban sprawl can be found in Portland, Oregon. Based on Oregon's land-use program, development in the Portland area is contained inside a regional urban growth boundary. The creation of this boundary was the result of a political compromise between two traditional land-use enemies: developers and environmentalists. Such a compromise was possible because the allowed density of development inside the boundary was raised, pleasing developers, while at the same time development outside the boundary was restricted, thus protecting open undeveloped space and pleasing environmentalists. The Portland compromise, however, is vulnerable in a number of respects. It is being undermined by piecemeal rural/agricultural developments that are more in the character of subdivision developments than the "farm dwellings" specified in the guidelines. It is also being criticized because it is sometimes easier to develop outside the boundaries than inside, because of the lack of administrative flexibility and fairness, and because it results in the displacement of those who cannot afford new housing when redevelopment projects occur. Also, the NIMBY syndrome is finding greater support from urban and suburban residents faced with higher-density development than they desire.[163]

Sprawled development not only gobbles up prime agricultural land and irreplaceable natural resources, but is also an indirect source of motor vehicle-related air pollution. To the extent that deconcentrated development leads to greater use of trucks, buses, and automobiles, it also worsens air pollution. Worldwatch Institute reports that in OECD member countries, motor vehicle sources of pollution account for 75 percent of carbon monoxide emissions, 48 percent of nitrogen oxides, 40 percent of hydrocarbons, 12 percent of particulates, 3 percent of sulfur dioxides, and 17 percent of all carbon dioxide released from fossil fuel.[164] The adverse health and natural resource effects of smog and acid rain are well established, and the potential for negative impacts from a greenhouse effect has gained greater credence in recent years.

Urban geographers Peter Newman and Jeffrey Kenworthy have discovered a strong relationship between urban density and gasoline consumption.[165] Extrapolating from their study, it is possible to estimate that air pollution in U.S. cities could be cut by more than half if densities in these cities were increased to the level of comparable European cities. Nevertheless, it must be conceded that even as regionwide pollution levels are lowered by increasing density levels, there exists some danger that atmospheric concentrations of auto-related pollutants might continue to remain at high levels in many areas. This danger exists because even though the number of automobile trips is decreased by reducing sprawl, the remaining trips may be more highly concentrated.[166] However, increases in urban density can make both mass transit and electric vehicles more cost effective.

Furthermore, concentrated but small-scale developments can maintain viable aspects of a natural environment. This is particularly the case in urban areas that promote neighborhood gardening programs and that contain and link neighborhood parks and greenways.[167]

To argue that environmental concerns can be eliminated by policies that are designed to encourage small-scale, concentrated, mixed-use development would be foolish. In fact, environmental policy at the federal level has traditionally ignored the broader and more systems-based understanding of the land-use origins of environmental problems in favor of an effort to define and proscribe particular environmental crimes. For example, the Environmental Protection Agency, acting under legislative authorization, has generally taken a command-and-control approach to the major sources of air and water pollution, giving less attention to the non-source-specific and "cross media" aspects of pollution control. Meanwhile, our increased exposure to chemical pollutants and toxins has suggested to many observers that "our society is now saturated with human-made, mostly chemical, toxic threats to human health and the natural environment."[168] The environmental threats tend to permeate the entire system of production and consumption, going to the core of our desire for high levels of consumptions.

Moreover, the United States leads the world in the production of hazardous waste, with an estimated 250 million metric tons per year.[169] The EPA has identified 22,000 hazardous waste sites nationally, and even though nearly half of all Americans are living in counties that contain waste sites that are on the EPA's National Priority List for cleanup, it is generally recognized that despite the existence of laws mandating a cleanup, the process has been much slower than expected.[170] One could conclude, in fact, that post hoc policies of environmental control have been a substantial failure when compared with expectations. Part of this failure may be due to the lack of real enforcement,[171] but another part is perhaps due to the strategy itself.

An argument can be made that if we are to progress beyond post hoc policies of environmental control and policing[172] and toward more preventive policies that attempt to reduce the initial production of toxic emissions and other harmful wastes, land-use controls and decentralized decision-making that provides for community participation will likely play a major role.[173] It is true that some environmental problems such as air or water pollution, or the scarcity of natural resources can potentially be addressed through such preventive actions as source-reduction, re-engineering, and the use of more effective pollution-control technologies or more efficient production technologies. However, for other problems, such as elimination of genetic resources or entire species and the destruction of sensitive wetlands or other ecologically necessary features of the environment, the only preventive "technology" available is the wise management of the land itself. Moreover, as will be outlined in a new governance proposal for land-use control in the last part of this book, effective governance mechanisms for land-use controls can go some way toward providing incentives for industries and businesses to reduce pollutants, waste generation, and other nuisances.[174]

Environmental LULUs and Centralized Control

In comparison with federal and state efforts to address local land-use issues related to social justice concerns, efforts of a similar nature to address environmental impacts have been much more extensive. Specific federal acts have been passed to control air and water pollution, the disposal of high- and low-level nuclear waste, and the management of hazardous waste and of more traditional solid waste. Additionally, many of these federal acts have state parallels and enforcement bodies.[175]

In addition, a number of states have passed growth-management and land-use control legislation designed to limit unwanted environmental impacts. Despite more extensive legislation of environmental land use, one cannot conclude that centralized regulation has been any more effective in this area than it was with respect to the regulation of land uses for purposes of achieving social justice. The relative ineffectiveness of state growth-management legislation has already been described. Chapter 3 of this book will examine in more detail why more centralized control of land uses for environmental purposes may not have been as effective as originally believed possible.

It should be acknowledged that progressive local and regional agencies responsible for environmental quality have begun to move away from command-and-control approaches to land-use regulation and have begun to embrace more system-oriented policies. Such policies that focus on watershed protection, river basin management, and source reduction hold substantial promise. Unfortunately, these policies have yet to become the norm.

A Merging of the Movements: Environmental Justice

Although the environmental and social justice movements have generally had different and sometimes opposing land-use reform agenda, recently these movements have coalesced around a particular issue set: the seemingly inequitable siting of toxic waste dumps and the greater prevalence of temporarily obsolete, abandoned derelict sites (TOADS) in poor and minority communities. A short citation of recent research into TOAD sites can illustrate the confluence of social justice and environmental land use issues. Researchers at Rutgers University recently[176] studied the prevalence of TOADS in twenty-one mid-sized cities in New Jersey. They discovered that deserted commercial, industrial, and housing properties and unbuilt sites are likely to become toxic waste dumps, makeshift housing for the homeless, and crack houses and that these sites were more likely to exist in communities with many poor and minority residents and a weak economic base. The findings of these researchers are not unexpected, but they help focus our attention on a key feature of individual land-use decisions: Such decisions tend to have consequences for the environment, the community at large, and the habitat of particular individuals who live in these blighted areas.

The TOADS research is one of the latest in a series of studies that have examined what is being called the issue of "environmental justice." Broadly speaking, the idea of environmental justice is invoked when facilities-siting decisions result in those communities that have benefited little or not at all from the production or consumption of products that result in unwanted waste having to host a toxic production, waste treatment, or other LULU facility. Hence, Southern communities containing landfills that are primarily used to store waste created in the process of producing goods for consumers from other parts of the country might call for environmental justice. More particularly, however, the movement for environmental justice has been focused on the question of whether and to what extent officials in industry and government responsible for siting decisions have chosen to locate LULUs in poorer communities and neighborhoods or in communities that are populated by minorities. Because these neighborhoods often tend to be politically unorganized and without the resources needed for effective opposition, they are perhaps considered to be the path of least resistance for siting officials concerned with the potential for rejection of their proposed land use. Representatives of such neighborhoods have charged siting officials with using a PIBBY—"Put it in blacks' backyard"—strategy for identifying sites for the placement of unwanted facilities.[177] While neighborhood representatives have invoked the idea of environmental justice, and specifically the Equal Protection Clause of the U.S. Constitution, to challenge the siting of LULU facilities, a recent review of such cases suggests that courts will generally follow the reasoning used in housing segregation cases and reject equal protection arguments unless the plaintiff can prove specific intent to discriminate.[178] Although several cases making equal protection claims about the siting of LULU facilities have yet to be decided, those that have been decided have tended to reject the claims of poor and minority neighborhoods that specific sitings of LULUs occurred because of developers' or siting officials' discriminatory intent.[179] Some legal experts are suggesting use of other legal strategies as a means of addressing environmental justice issues, including use of lawsuits based on the Federal Water Pollution Control Act and Title VI of the Civil Rights Act as well as the Medicaid Act, which can be specifically used to challenge the disproportionate impact of pollution on a minority community.[180]

Because direct legal challenges to perceived environmental injustice have not to date been particularly successful, affected neighborhoods and their champions have resorted to other strategies, including vocal and physical political protests, civil disobedience, use of general land-control laws and environmental statutes, and advocacy for more effective legislation and governmental policy. The role of each of these strategies in developing effective governance of LULUs will be examined in further detail in later chapters. It should be noted, however, that in 1993 alone, three bills were introduced into Congress that would substantially change the context in which some LULU siting decisions are made. For example, a bill called the Environmental Justice Act, introduced by Congressman John Lewis (D-Ga.), would prohibit further siting of toxic chemical facilities in up to 100 environmental high-impact areas if it is shown that proposed facilities would exacerbate the significant adverse health impacts already evident in the areas in question. Other proposed legislation would amend the Solid Waste Disposal Act to require consideration of "community information statements" that outline the demographic characteristics of the areas near the proposed site and their existing LULU burdens prior to issuing a permit for a hazardous waste facility. Similarly, but more forcefully, sponsors of the Environmental Equal Rights Act of 1993 would prohibit approval of hazardous or solid waste facilities in "environmentally disadvantaged" areas, defined as poor and minority areas that already have facilities of this type.[181]

While at the time of this writing these bills had yet to be enacted, the Clinton administration, recently issued an executive order calling on federal agencies and recipients of federal grants to begin to consider environmental justice in their decision-making. An estimation of the specific effects of this order or of the more extensive legislative proposals is unfortunately impossible, not just because the policies have yet to be fully implemented, but primarily because our knowledge of the full extent of environmental injustice is still at a preliminary stage. Existing studies do make a good case that waste storage, treatment, and disposal sites, facilities discharging noxious chemicals, and social service facilities such as homeless shelters and group homes tend to be located disproportionately in poor and minority neighborhoods. However, these studies have only been able to establish that the current distribution of LULU facilities is one that does not favor low-income and minority residents. They have not been able to demonstrate either an initial intention to discriminate or proof that this distribution pattern would have existed even if people did not continually move in and out of various neighborhoods for reasons unrelated to the siting of specific LULUs (such as in order to acquire cheaper housing or better schools). Furthermore, as with many areas of research, the findings of environmental justice studies are open to methodological dispute. Vicki Been, a professor of law at New York University School of Law, for example, has noted that there does not appear to be any consensus as to the best way to define the areas of LULU impact for the purposes of accurately identifying the presence of environmental injustice. Some studies use census tracts, others use zip code areas or distance circles, and still others use entire municipalities. The variations in land mass, for example, within any group of census tracts, municipalities, or zip code areas can substantially affect findings.[182]

Despite some methodological problems, the evidence for a pattern of disproportionate distribution of LULUs is substantial—sufficient in the minds of many observers to warrant legislative and other action.[183] These studies, for example, have found that:

* While African Americans in 1980 constituted about 12 percent of the U.S. population and 20 percent to 30 percent of the population in the Southeast, residents living near three of the four Southeastern U.S. host communities for hazardous waste disposal sites studied by the General Accounting Office were predominantly African American.[184]
* Nationally, in 1987 persons of color were nearly twice as likely to reside in a zip code area containing commercial hazardous waste facilities as were whites.[185]
* The average household income and home values of areas containing hazardous waste facilities are lower than those in surrounding counties.[186]
* Hazardous waste sites in New Jersey and hazardous waste incinerating sites in Texas and Louisiana were more likely to be found in minority communities than would be the case if such facilities were spread evenly among the various population groups.[187]
* New York City zip code areas that contain predominantly minority populations (such as Harlem) tend to host a much higher number of homeless shelters and programs than do areas in the city with more whites.[188]
* Minority neighborhoods in Oakland, California, house 50 percent of the population but 75 percent of the social services facilities.[189]

Most recently, the *National Law Journal* published a series of reports on environmental justice. The journal's research on 1,177 Superfund sites confirmed the findings of earlier studies that hazardous sites are more likely to be located in minority areas. What these reports added to the growing aggregate of data suggesting injustice in the siting of waste facilities and other LULUs was an indictment of the federal government's efforts to address pollution-caused ills in minority communities. In particular, the journal reporters found that government officials, while often tardy in taking action to clean up polluted sites, were especially delinquent and weak-willed in exerting efforts to identify and clean up such sites in minority areas. Fines for violations of the Resource Conservation and Recovery Act, for example, were 506 percent greater in white areas than they were in minority areas. It took 20 percent longer to get a hazardous waste site in a minority area declared a Superfund site.[190] While the environmental justice movement has the potential for pulling together the disparate strands of land-use reform, much of the legislative and policy proposals that are currently being put forth by participants in this movement are narrow in scope (for example, addressing only hazardous waste or only residential facilities of a certain size) and unlikely to resolve the full range of concerns and values—including, in addition to equity and environmental values, those regarding efficiency and community viability—that land-use governance structures and policies should address. Attempting to offer alternative policy proposals is an ambitious task and one that, I believe, involves forays into political theory, politics, sociology, and law prior to offering any specific policy alternative. The reader may find these forays worthwhile for a few reasons. First, they can provide a ground of understanding how particular land-use policies might fit within the larger context and problem of governance in our age—that is, an age when government's very legitimacy is widely questioned. Second, development of new land-use policies is fundamentally different from most policymaking processes in that new land-use policies are likely to touch our common everyday assumptions about the proper relationships between citizens and their governments and the more complexly woven, 200-year-old fabric of legal rights and federal institutions. Finally, in taking forays into the theoretical environment surrounding land-use policy, the reader may discover, as I have, that this environment offers a rich source of inspiration about innovative policy design. That is, the policy alternatives that I offer in the next-to-the-last chapter of this book grew out of an understanding of how it is possible to draw ideas and tools from different ideological traditions so as to forge new policy "hybrids" that do not fit neatly into any of the traditional ideological boxes. Instead, in the tradition of American pragmatism, these policies represent, not the result of purebred policymaking, but rather a conscious policymaking of a mongrel sort—one that is not particularly pretty, but essentially healthy.

NOTES

1. Hagman, Donald G., and Juergensmeyer, Julian. (1986). *Urban Planning and Land Development Control Law*, 2nd edn. St. Paul, Minn.: West Publishing Co.

2. Coase, R. H. (1960). "The Problem of Social Cost." *Journal of Law and Economics* 3:1.

3. Epstein, Richard. (1991). "Property and Necessity." *Harvard Journal of Law and Public Policy* 13:1:6.

4. Hagman and Juergensmeyer, *Urban Planning*, pp. 14-16.

5. Ibid., pp. 16-17.

6. DeGrove, John M. (1991). *Balanced Growth: A Planning Guide for Local Government*. Washington, D. C.: International City Management Association.

7. Lowry, Ira S., and Ferguson, Bruce W. (1992). *Development Regulation and Housing Affordability*. Washington, D. C.: Urban Land Institute.

8. See, for example, Anderson, John E. (1987). "The Toxic Danger." *American Demographics* 9:45; Liner, Blaine. (1992). "Beyond the Turf Battles." *National Civic Review* 81:1:5-8. See also other articles in *National Civic Review* symposium on "The Civic Environmentalist" in the same issue.

9. Costonis, John. (1989). *Icons and Aliens*. Urbana and Chicago: University of Illinois Press.

10. Guterson, David. (1992). "No Place Like Home." *Harper's* (November), pp. 55-62; Guterson, David. (1993). "Enclosed, Encyclopedic, Endured." *Harper's* (August), pp. 49-56.

11. Grossman, Howard J. (1987). "Regional and Public-Private Partnerships: Forging the Future." *Economic Development Quarterly* 1:1:52-59.

12. See Florida Department of Health and Rehabilitative Services. (July 1, 1983). *Guidelines for Zoning and Special Community Housing*. Pamphlet 10-1.

13. Malloy, Robin Paul. (1991). *Planning for Serfdom*. Philadelphia: University of Pennsylvania Press.

14. Merriman, Dwight, Brower, David, and Tegeler, Philip. (1985). *Inclusionary Zoning Moves Downtown*. Chicago: American Planning Association; Garreau, Joel. (1988). *Edge Cities*. New York: Doubleday; Johnston, R. J. (1984). *Residential Segregation, the State, and Constitutional Conflict in American Urban Areas*. London: Academic Press.

15. Dear, Michael. (1992). "Understanding and Overcoming the NIMBY Syndrome." *American Planning Association Journal* 58:3:288-300.

16. Blackstone, William. (1979; originally 1766). *Commentaries on the Laws of England*. Volume 2 (Chicago: facsimile reprint) p. 2. As cited in Levy, Michael B. (1983). "Illiberal Liberalism: The New Property as Strategy." *The Review of Politics* 45:476-94.

17. Levy, Michael B. (1983). "Illiberal Liberalism: The New Property as Strategy." *The Review of Politics* 45:476-94.

18. Epstein, Richard. (1991). "Property and Necessity." *Harvard Journal of Law and Public Policy* 13:1:2-9.

19. Smith, George P., and Fernandez, Griffin W. (1993). "The Price of Beauty: An Economic Approach to Aesthetic Nuisance." *Harvard Environmental Law Review* 15:53-83.

20. Kurtz, Paul. (1976). "Nineteenth Century Anti-Entrepreneurial Injunctions—Avoiding the Chancellor." *William and Mary Law Review* 17:621.

21. *Barnes v. Calhoun, N.C.* (2 Ired. Eq.) 199 (1842); *Bradsher v. Lea, 38 N.C.* (3 Ired. Eq.) 301 (1844).

22. Kurtz, "Anti-Entrepreneurial Injunctions," pp. 621-640.

23. Gray, Thomas. (1980). "The Disintegration of Property." In *NOMOS*: Property, Vol. 22, edited by J. Roland Pennock and John W. Chapman. New York: New York University Press, pp. 69-85.

24. The Club of Rome's predictions of an end to economic growth have proved to be overly pessimistic.

25. Paepke, Owen. (1993). *The Evolution of Progress: The End of Economic Growth and the Beginning of Human Transformation.* New York: Random House.

26. Scitovsky, Tibor. (1992). *The Joyless Economy: The Psychology of Human Satisfaction.* New York: Oxford University Press.

27. Pollock, Frederick. (1883). *The Land Laws.* London: Macmillan and Co.

28. Reynolds, Larry R. (1985). "Institutionally Determined Property Claims." *Journal of Economic Issues* 19:4:481-489.

29. Couglan. (1980). "Comments on Professor Sato's Paper." In *Proceedings: Respective roles of State and Local Government in Land Policy and Taxation,* edited by G. Lefcoe, pp. 51-53, comments that "the primary reason for incorporation of the last three cities to be incorporated in Los Angeles County was to gain local control of land-use decisions" (p. 53).

30. For a discussion of how ideas of property tend to change over time so as to adjust to new circumstances, see Nelson, Robert. (1977). *Zoning and Property Rights.* Cambridge, Mass.: MIT Press.

31. Scitovsky argues in *The Joyless Economy* that Americans have been particularly prone to consuming goods and services that promote comfort, but have been less keen on using the fruits of material progress to develop our capacities for pleasures that stimulate.

32. Park, Han S. (1984). *Human Needs and Political Development: A Dissent to Utopian Solutions.* Cambridge, Mass.: Schenkman Publishing Co.

33. Popper, Frank. (1981). *The Politics of Land-Use Reform.* Madison, Wisc.: University of Wisconsin Press.

34. For example, James Oglethorpe's plan for the city of Savannah has helped preserve a sense of that more pedestrian-oriented era in the older parts of the city. The National Commission on Urban Problems' *Building the American City* presents a short history of the development of zoning and land-use planning in the United States.

35. See 272 U.S. 365, 47 S.Ct. 114, 71 L.Ed. 303 (1926).

36. See Merriman, Bower, and Tegeler's *Inclusionary Zoning Moves Downtown* and Johnston's *Residential Segregation, the State and Constitutional Conflict in American Urban Areas* for a discussion of exclusionary effects. For a discussion of the energy costs of urban sprawl, see Real Estate Research Corporation, *The Costs of Sprawl* (Washington: Government Printing Office, 1974).

37. Mulroy, Elizabeth A., and Lane, Terry S. (1992). "Housing Affordability, Stress and Single Mothers: Pathway to Hopelessness." *Journal of Sociology and Social Welfare* 19: 3 (Sept.): 51-64; Shelton, Beth Anne. (1987) "Variations in Divorce Rates by Community Size: A Test of the Social Integration Explanation." *Journal of Marriage and the Family* 49:4: 827-32. Simmons, Roberta G., Burgeson, Richard, Carlton Ford, Steven, and Blyth, Dale-A. (1987). "The Impact of Cumulative Change in Early Adolescence." *Child Development* 58:5:1220-34; Levine, Edward M. (1986). "Sociocultural Causes of Family Violence: A Theoretical Comment." *Journal of Family Violence* 1:1:3-12. Sampson, Robert J. "Neighborhood and Crime: The Structural Determinants of Personal Victimization." (1985). *Journal of Research in Crime and Delinquency*. 22:1:7-40.

38. Jacobs, Jane. (1965). *The Death and Life of Great American Cities*. New York: Random House.

39. Popper, *Politics*, pp. 8-55.

40. Ibid., pp. 8-55.

41. Ibid., p. 10.

42. Siegan, Bernard. (1972). *Land Use Without Zoning*. Lexington, Mass.: D.C. Heath; O'Sullivan, Authur. (1993). *Urban Economics*, second edition. Boston: Irwin. One reason for the relatively minor differences between Houston's land-use outcomes and those of zoned cities is the existence of state constitutional law that allows individuals to adopt restrictive covenants that limit the development prospects of future owners. Homeowners and subdivision developers have used such covenants as a sort of mutual protection pact against unwanted types of development. This process is sometimes referred to as the Coase solution, after R.H. Coase who first suggested that when parties are affected by potential negative externalities or nuisances, private negotiations among property owners would lead to an efficient solution to the externality problem. It should be noted that not all states allow for the use of restrictive covenants. In Georgia, for example, such covenants are limited to seventeen years. Historic preservation groups attempting to use these covenants, such as by buying historic properties and then reselling them with a covenant restricting inappropriate development, have often discovered that their legal footwork was for naught once the time limit on the covenant expired.

43. Urban Systems Research and Engineering. 1976. *The Growth Shapers: Land-Use Impacts of Infrastructure Investments*. Washington, D. C.: Government Printing Office.

44. Economic Council of Canada. (1971). "The Challenge of Rapid Urban Growth." in *Urban Problems: A Canadian Reader*. Edited by Ralph Krueger and R. Charles Bryfogle. New York: Rinehart and Winston.

45. Newman, Peter, and Kenworthy, Jeffrey. (1989). *Cities and Automobile Dependence*. Brookfield, Vt.: Gower Publishing.

46. Goldberg, Michael A., and Mercer, John. (1986). *The Myth of the North American City: Continentalism Challenged*. Vancouver: University of British Columbia Press.

47. Michaelson, William. (1977). *Environmental Choice, Human Behavior, and Residential Satisfaction.* New York: Oxford University Press.

48. Fowler, Edmund P. (1992). *Building Cities That Work.* Montreal: McGill-Queen's University Press.

49. For example, Dale Keyes has argued that proposals to address urban sprawl may have only moderate effects, say, on the order of a 10 percent to 20 percent savings in energy used for urban travel. See, Keyes, Dale. (1979). "Channeling Metropolitan Growth: In What Direction, Toward Which End." *Law and Contemporary Problems* 43:239-51.

50. Fowler, *Building Cities*, p. 43.

51. Gruen, Victor. (1964). *The Heart of Our Cities.* New York: Simon and Schuster.

52. Popper, *Politics*, pp. 8-55.

53. See Robert Caro's biography of Robert Moses (*The Power Broker: Robert Moses and the Fall of New York.* New York: Knopf, 1974) for a detailed narrative of how development professionals could promote and control the course of highway development, while essentially ignoring the interests of unorganized citizen groups.

54. See, Chandler, Alfred D. (1990). *Scale and Scope: The Dynamics of Industrial Capitalism.* Cambridge, Mass.: Belknap Press.

55. Hoover, Edgar M., and Vernon, Raymond. (1959). *Anatomy of a Metropolis.* New York: Doubleday; Vernon, Raymond. (1960). *Metropolis 1985.* Cambridge, Mass.: Harvard University Press.

56. City of Toronto, *Cityplan '91,* Report No. 5, February 1990.

57. Guterson, David. (1993). "Enclosed, Encyclopedic, Endured." *Harper's* 287:1719:49-61.

58. McGrath, Michael, and Hoole, Richard. (1992). "Manufacturing's New Economies of Scale." *Harvard Business Review* 70:3:94-103. Also, Stalk, George, Evans, Philip, and Shulman, Lawrence E. (1992). "Competing on Capabilities: The New Rules of Corporate Strategy." *Harvard Business Review* 70:2:57-69.

59. Easterbrook, Greg. (1993). "The Future of Electric Power." *Atlantic Monthly* 272:1:42-46.

60. Brandeis, Louis. (1934). The Curse of Bigness: Miscellaneous Papers of Louis D. Brandeis, edited by O. Frankel. New York: Viking Press.

61. See, for example, Waters, John C. (1983). *Maintaining a Sense of Place: A Citizen's Guide to Community Preservation.* Athens, Ga.: Institute of Community and Area Development.

62. Thompson, Wilbur R. (1987). "Policy-Based Analysis for Local Economic Development." *Economic Development Quarterly* 1:3:203-13; Jacobs, Jane. (1984). *Cities and the Wealth of Nations.* New York: Random House; and Jacobs, Jane. (1969). *The Economy of Cities.* New York: Random House.

63. Wilson, James Q. (1993). *The Moral Sense.* New York: The Free Press.

64. Ellickson, Robert C. (1991). *Order Without Law: How Neighbors Settle Disputes.* Cambridge, Mass.: Harvard University Press.

65. Fowler, *Building Cities*, pp. 29-98.

66. Newman and Kenworthy, *Cities and Automobile Dependence*, pp. 83-85.

67. Bahl, Roy W., and McGuire, J. Michael. (1977). "Urban Sprawl: Policies for Containment and Cost Recoupment." In *Local Service Pricing Policies and Their Effect on Urban Spatial Structure,* edited by Paul Downing. Vancouver: University of British Columbia Press.

68. Fowler, *Building Cities That Work*, pp. 29-98.

69. Ibid. pp. 29-98.

70. Ibid. pp. 29-98.

71. Guterman, David. (1992). "No Place Like Home." *Harper's* 285:1710:55-64.

72. Olson, Mancur. (1971). *The Logic of Collective Action.* Cambridge, Mass.: Harvard University Press.

73. Popper, *Politics*, p. 94.

74. Healy, Robert, and Rosenberg, John. (1979). *Land Use and the States*, 2nd. edn. Baltimore: John Hopkins University Press.

75. Popper, *Politics*, pp. 92-115.

76. Rose, Carol. (1983). "Planning and Dealing: Piecemeal Land Controls as a Problem of Local Legitimacy." *California Law Review* 71:837-912.

77. Popper, *Politics*, pp. 92-115.

78. Ibid. pp. 92-115.

79. Kmiec, Douglas. (1981). "Deregulating Land Use: An Alternative Free Enterprise Development System." *University of Pennsylvania Law Review* 130:28-130.

80. Verba, Sidney, and Nye, Norman. (1972). *Participation in America: Political Democracy and Social Equality.* New York: Harper and Row; Verba, Sidney. (1987). *Elites and the Idea of Equality.* Cambridge, Mass.: Harvard University Press; Caro, *The Power Broker.*

81. Bullard, Robert D. (1990). *Dumping in Dixie: Race, Class and Environmental Quality.* Boulder, Colo.: Westview Press.

82. Prak, Niels L., and Priemus, Hugo. (1986). "A Model for the Analysis of the Decline of Postwar Housing." *International Journal of Urban and Regional Research* 10:1:1-7.

83. Ibid., pp. 1-7.

84. Briggs, John. (1989). *Turbulent Mirror: An Illustrated Guide to Chaos Theory and the Science of Wholeness.* New York: Harper and Row.

85. Popper, *Politics*, pp. 40-41.

86. One and a half million African Americans migrated from the South during the 1950s alone. See Garreau, *Edge Cities*, p. 154.

87. Lemann, Nicholas. (1991). *The Promised Land: The Great Black Migration and How It Changed America.* New York: Knopf. See also Popper, *Politics*, pp. 30-33; and Bluestone, Barry, and Harrison, Bennett. *The Deindustrialization of America.* New York: Basic Books, 1982.

88. Based on an annual mobility rate of 17 percent per year (source: *Statistical Abstract of the United States*, U.S. Bureau of the Census, Current Population Reports, P-20, No. 456).

89. See citations in Note 31. Also, Crutchfield, Robert D., Geerken, Michael R., and Gove, Walter R. (1982). "Crime Rate and Social Integration: The Impact of Metropolitan Mobility." *Criminology* 20:3-4:467-78.

90. For example, Rossi, Peter H., and Shlay, Anne B. (1982). "Residential Mobility and Public Policy Issues: 'Why Families Move' Revisited." *Journal of Social Issues* 38:3:21-34.

91. Orbell, J. M., and Uno T. (1972). "A Theory of Neighborhood Problem Solving: Political Action vs Residential Mobility," *American Political Science Review* 66:471-89.

92. Whyte, William. (1970). *The Last Landscape.* New York: Anchor Books.

93. Livingston, Lawrence, Jr., and Blayney, John. (1971). *Foothill Environmental Design Study: Open Space v. Environment.* San Francisco: Livingston and Blayney; Frieden, Bernard. (1979). *The Environmental Protection Hustle.* Cambridge, Mass.: MIT Press.

94. California's Proposition 13, which limited increases in property taxes, was in part a response to the state's unprecedented rate of growth and success. The rapid influx of new people that came with this success placed pressure on the market for housing and land, which in turn raised property values and property taxes. The property tax revolt was led by long-term residents of the state who did not want to be forced to sell their property simply because their income was not adequate to pay the ever-increasing taxes. While accomplishing this purpose, the cap on property values, however, has other less positive effects. For one, the market in housing has been skewed. Long-term owners of property who pay relatively minimal taxes are loath to sell their property even if they could be better off in terms of the amount and type of new housing they might purchase to replace their old home. This market rigidity exists because purchasers of new housing will often have to pay many times the taxes on a new residence (with a value similar to their old one) that they would if they were to keep their old one. One result of Proposition 13, therefore, has been to exacerbate the affordable-housing crisis in the state. Although owners refused to let go of old property, some nevertheless moved to other properties, while keeping their old residence off the market. This strategy tightened the housing market further, leading to even more dramatic increases in house prices.

95. This pattern is predicted by a general equilibrium theory that hypothesizes that businesses will locate at geographical points that optimize their access to business-supporting services, transportation nodes, and sources of labor. The solution to such equilibrium equations generally suggests a central city location as optimal for most businesses, resulting in a rise in the rents in these locations and a pattern of decreasing property values as one moves away from the city center.

96. McDougall, Harold. (1985). "Regional Development: Who Gets the Short End?" In *Inclusionary Zoning Moves Downtown,* edited by Dwight Merriman, David Brower, and Philip Tegeler. Chicago: American Planning Association.

97. Little, Charles. (1976). *Shifting Ground: New Priorities for National Land Use Policy.* Washington, D.C.: Library of Congress: Congressional Research Service.

98. Tucker, William. (1977). "Environmentalism and the Leisure Class." *Harper's* (December), pp. 49-50.

99. Adverse possession is the legal doctrine that allows for strangers, but not family members, partners, or other known shareholders in land, to gain property rights by squatting for a period of time on the property. If the title holders do not take action indicating their

objection to the adverse possession, the squatter gains full title. Because the law excludes known shareholders or heirs of a partial share of property from taking adverse possession, many Southern African-Americans, who are partial heirs of property or relatives of such heirs, have been unable to gain full title to the property where they have been residing for decades. As a consequence, these squatters have been unable to protect their residences from invasions by such industries as the kaolin mining industry. Source: Conversation with Randall Johnson, University of Georgia School of Law, December, 1993.

100. Johnston, *Residential Segregation*, p. 80.

101. *Reitman v. Mulkey*, 387 US 369, 1967, p. 838.

102. For two more conservative analyses see Mead, Lawrence. (1992). *The New Politics of Poverty.* New York: Basic Books; and Murray, Charles. (1984). *Losing Ground: American Social Policy 1950-1980.* New York: Basic Books.

103. See generally, Garreau. *Edge Cities.* Leinberger, Christopher, and Lockwood, Charles. (1986). "How Business is Reshaping America." *Atlantic* 258:4:43-63.

104. Whether edge cities are part of a tendency toward racial segregation is a matter of debate. Joel Garreau, one of the discovers of the edge city concept, argues that class is the key determinant in the development of these cities. If this were the case, however, we would likely be seeing a greater tendency toward racial integration in metropolitan areas as a new black middle class emerges. However, this does not seem to be the case; (for example, see Sander, Richard. (1988). "Individual Rights and Demographic Realities: The Problem of Fair Housing." *Northwestern University Law Review* 82:3:874-939). See also Leinberger and Lockwood, "How Business is Reshaping America.

105. Harold McDougall's argument is based in part on a theory about the causes of poverty that has come to be known as the spatial mismatch theory. This theory suggests that racial segregation in urban areas increases poverty because racial minorities tend to be segregated into residential areas that are distant from the greatest number of job openings. Because of the complexity of assessing not only the level of existing job openings but the appropriateness of the openings for those residing in segregated neighborhoods, proof of the spatial mismatch theory has been difficult to establish. Early studies by John Kain (1968) suggested a spatial mismatch effect that decreased employment opportunities by an estimated 20,000 jobs in the Chicago area. David Ellwood's (1986) research did not find any evidence of the spatial mismatch effect, but Keith Ihlanfeldt and David Sjoquit's (1990) critical assessment of Ellwood's data and their own study of data from another area (Philadelphia) tended to support the existence of a mismatch effect. For example, they found that the average commute time for blacks was twenty-six minutes compared with 18.5 minutes for whites. In his review of the spatial mismatch evidence, O'Sullivan (1993) estimates that the "mismatch is responsible for about a quarter of the gap between black and white employment rates, leaving three-quarters to be explained by labor-market discrimination, differences in education, and other factors" (p. 339).

Recent research by Philip Kasinitz suggests that social networks are perhaps more important as a cause of residents in inner city neighborhoods not having access to jobs. Kasinitz found that even when industries that hire low-skill labor are located near a depressed neighborhood, residents were often not hired. Some of the tendency to not hire these residents was due to the stigma associated with the neighborhood and the company's negative experiences with a few attempts to hire from the neighborhood. However, most of the lack of local hiring was due to the existence of social networks that gave persons who were recommended by existing employees a first shot at a job opening. See McDougall, Harold. (1985). "Regional Development: Who Gets the Short End?" In *Inclusionary Zoning Moves Downtown.* Chicago: American Planning Association; O'Sullivan, Authur. (1993). *Urban Economics.* Homewood, Ill.: Irwin; Elwood, David T. (1986). "The Spatial Mismatch Hypothesis: Are There Teenage Jobs Missing in the Ghetto?" In *The Black Youth Employment Crisis,* edited by Richard B. Freeman and Harry J Holzer. Chicago: University of Chicago Press; Kain, John T. (1968). "Housing Segregation, Negro Employment, and Metropolitan Decentralization." *Quarterly Journal of Economics* 82:175-97; Ihlanfeldt, Keith R., and Sjoquit, David L. (1990). "Job Accessibility and Racial Differences in Youth Employment Rates." *American Economic Review* 8:267-76; and Kasinitz, Philip. (1993). "The Real Jobs Problem." *The Wall Street Journal,* November 26, p. 8.

106. Sander, "Individual Rights," pp. 874-939.

107. McDougall, "Regional Development," p. 64.

108. Davidoff, Paul. (1985). "Zoning as a Class Act." In Merriam, Brower, and Tegeler, *Inclusionary Zoning,* p. 1.

109. *James v. Valtierra* and *Shaffer v. Valtierra,* 402 US 137, 1971, p. 685.

110. Fiscal zoning can be thought of as a type of exclusionary zoning that occurs when cities or other local governments exclude households or other land uses because they would impose fiscal burdens on the local government. High-density housing and mobile homes, for example, have been cited as types of housing that contribute less to the public coffers than the government must expend to provide for the public infrastructure needs (such as roads, schools, libraries, and so on) of the citizens residing in these housing types. Similarly, the fiscal impacts of new commercial developments or developments on the fringe of an urban area can represent a short- or long-term negative fiscal impact on local governments.

Because of the differences in state constitutions and law, some types of fiscal zoning ordinances (such as those defining density limits or lot sizes) have generally, but not in all cases, passed constitutional muster, while others, such as the prohibition of mobile homes or the exclusion of multifamily housing districts from a municipality, have generally been ruled invalid. (For a review of the determinant of valid exclusionary zoning practices see Mann, M. S. (1976). *The Right to Housing.* New York: Praeger; Blasser, Brian, and Weinstein, Alan C. (1989). *Land Use and the Constitution.* Chicago: American Planning Association; Wolf, Haar. (1989). *Land-Use Planning: A Casebook on the Use, Misuse, and Re-Use of Urban Land.* Boston: Little, Brown and Company.)

111. Davidoff, "Zoning," p. 1.

112. Sedway, Paul. (1985). "The San Francisco Downtown Plan: Office Boon Brings Housing Boon." In Merriam, Brower, and Tegeler, *Inclusionary Zoning,* pp. 163-168.

113. *Associated Home Builders v. City of Livermore,* 18 Cal. 3rd 582, 557 P2nd 473, 135 Cal. Rptr. 41, 1976.

114. *Fairfax County v. DeGroff Enterprises,* 214 Va. 235, 198 S.E. 2nd 600, 1973.

115. See Ellickson, Robert C. (1985). "Inclusionary Housing Programs: Yet Another Misguided Urban Policy?" In *Inclusionary Zoning Moves Downtown,* edited by Dwight Merriman, David Brower, and Philip Tegeler. Chicago: American Planning Association, pp. 83-91.

116. Rydell, C., Barnett, C., Hillestad, C., Murray, M., Neels, K., and Sims, R. (1981). "The Impact of Rent Control on the Los Angeles Housing Market." Washington: Rand Corporation, N-1747-LA.

117. Ellickson, "Inclusionary Housing," p. 85.

118. Ibid., p. 87.

119. This is commonly known as the exaction doctrine of land use, which was developed as part of the regulation of subdivisions. Under this doctrine, municipalities may not require subdividers to dedicate land for public facilities unless the need for the facility is generated by the subdivision. Daniel Mandelker (1982, 1985) suggests that when this doctrine is applied to inclusionary zoning, it requires that the development that falls under inclusionary zoning actually generate a need for low- and moderate-income housing.

120. Silverman, Ronald. (1985). "Panel Comments." In *Inclusionary Zoning Moves Downtown*, edited by Merriman, Brower, and Tegeler. Chicago: American Planning Association. pp. 91-94.

121. Mallach. (1986). "The Fallacy of Laissez-Faire: Land Use Deregulation, Housing Affordability, and the Poor." *Washington University Journal of Urban and Contemporary Law* 30: 35.

122. Ibid., p. 35.

123. Mandelker, Daniel. (1985). "The Constitutionality of Inclusionary Zoning: An Overview." In *Inclusionary Zoning Moves Downtown*, edited by Merriman, Brower, and Tegeler, p. 35. Also, see Gelber, Bruce. (1985). "Panel Comments" on Mandelker's article in the same book.

124. Mandelker, "Constitutionality," specifically Netter, Edith M. (1985). "Panel Comments" on Mandelker's article in the same book.

125. Mandelker, "Constitutionality," specifically Costonis, John. (1985). "Panel Comments," p. 52 in the same book.

126. Costonis, "Panel Comments," p. 53.

127. Johnston, *Residential Segretation*, pp. 105-36.

128. *Bradley v. School Board of the City of Richmond, Virginia*, 462 F.2d p. 1066 (1972).

129. Ibid.

130. Johnston, *Residential Segregation*, p. 134.

131. Orfield, G. (1978). "If Wishes Were Houses Then Busing Could Stop." *The Urban Review* 10:108-24; Redwine, S. (1981). "Busing Across District Lines: The Ambiguous Legacy of Milliken v. Bradley." *Houston Law Review* 18:585-609.

132. Whereas the federal courts have been reluctant to find constitutional issues in de facto inter-district segregation, state courts, relying on state constitutions, have been less timid. The inequality of school financing that is part of school district gerrymandering has been successfully contested in numerous state courts and is being litigated in most others.

133. Rent control reduces values by reducing the rate of return and the ability to make rapid adjustments in cash flow so as to respond to changes in market prices of inputs such as fuel, maintenance, materials, and so on. See, Malloy, *Planning for Serfdom*, pp. 56-59.

134. Friedman, P. (1976), *The Rights of Mentally Retarded Persons*. New York: American Civil Liberties Union; ACLU monograph series.

135. Lippincott, Marcia K. (1979). "A Sanctuary for People: Strategies for Overcoming Zoning Restrictions on Community Homes for Retarded Persons," *Stanford Law Review* 31: 767-68.

136. American Bar Association. (1978). "Zoning for Community Homes Serving Developmentally Disabled Persons." Developmental Disabilities State Legislative Project of the American Bar Association on the Mentally Disabled. Reprinted in *Mental Disability Law Reporter* 2:294-95.

137. Bergin, Patrick (1987). "Exclusionary Zoning Laws: Irrationally-Based Barrier to Normalization of Mentally Retarded Citizens." *Journal of Land Use and Environmental Law* 2:3:237-68.

138. Warner, Richard. (1989). "Deinstitutionalization: How Did We Get Where We Are?" *Journal of Social Issues* 45:3:17-30.

139. Mechanic, David, and Rochefort, David A. (1990). "Deinstitutionalization: An Appraisal of Reform." *Annual Review of Sociology* 16:301-27.

140. Markson, Elizabeth W. and Diroberts, Mary Ann. (1985). "After Deinstitutionalization, What?" *Journal of Geriatric Psychiatry* 18:1:37-56.

141. Scott, Nancy J., and Scott, Robert A. (1980). "The Impact of Housing Markets on Deinstitutionalization." *Administration in Mental Health* 7:3:210-22.

142. Bergin, "Exclusionary Zoning," p. 251.

143. Gailey, J. Benjamin. (1981). "Group Homes and Single Family Zoning." *Zoning and Planning Law Reporter* 4: 97-98 (cited in Bergin).

144. *Doe v. City of Butler, Pennsylvania.* C.A.3 (Pa.) 1989, 892 F.2d 315.

145. *Family Style of St. Paul, Inc. v. City of St. Paul, Minn.*, D.Minn. 1990, 728 F.Supp. 1396.

146. Reilly, William. (1973). *The Use of Land.* New York: Crowell, p. 27.

147. National Commission on Urban Problems. (1968). *Building the American City.* Washington, D.C.: U.S. Government Printing Office, p. 243.

148. Sander, Richard. (1988). "Individual Rights and Demographic Realities: The Problem of Fair Housing." *Northwestern University Law Review* 82:3:874-939.

149. Kmiec, "Deregulating Land Use," pp. 28-130.

150. See Seigan, Bernard. (1972). *Land Use Without Zoning.* Lexington, Mass.: Lexington Books, for an argument that zoning has few major effects on how people decide to use various pieces of land.

151. Sander, Richard H. (1988). "Individual Rights and Demographic Realities: The Problem of Fair Housing." *Northwestern University Law Review* 82:3:874-939.

152. Arendt, Randall. (1989). "Open Space Zoning: A Land Use Alternative." In *Balanced Growth: A Planning Guide for Local Government,* edited by John M. DeGrove. Washington: International City Management Association.

153. Fowler, *Building Cities*, pp. 29-90.

154. Gottinger, Hans-Werner. (1991). *Economic Models and Applications of Solid Waste Management.* New York: Gordon and Breach Science; McConnell, Virginia, Cumberland, John, and Gordon, Patrice. (1988). "Regional Marginal Costs and Cost Savings from Economies of Scale in Municipal Waste Treatment: An Application to the Chesapeake Bay Region." *Growth and Change* 19:4:1-13.

155. Pallats, Leonard. (January 12, 1994). "Are Big Regional Landfills Better for Rural Georgia." *Athens Banner-Herald*, p.7.

156. Nelson, Authur, Genereux, John, and Genereux, Michell. (1992). "Price Effects of Landfills on House Values." *Land Economics* 68:4:359-65.

157. See, Roberts, Roland, Douglas, Peggy, and Park, William. (1991). "Estimating External Costs of Municipal Landfill Siting Through Contingent Valuation Analysis: A Case Study." *Southern Journal of Agricultural Economics* 23:2:155-65.

158. Peretz, Jean. (1992). "Equity Under and State Responses to the Superfund Amendments and Reauthorization Act of 1986." *Policy Sciences* 25:2:191-209.

159. Whyte, *The Last Landscape*, pp. 207-21.

160. Lewis, Sylvia. (1990). "The Town That Said No to Sprawl." *Balanced Growth*, edited by John DeGrove. Washington, D.C.: International City Managers Association.

161. Ibid., p. 26.

162. Ibid., Lewis.

163. See, Kasowski, Kevin. (1991). "Oregon: Fifteen Years of Land Use Planning." In DeGrove, *Balanced Growth: A Planning guide for Local Government.* Washington, D. C.: International City Management Association, pp. 125-30; and Nelson, Arthur. (1991). "Blazing New Planning Trails in Oregon." In DeGrove, *Balanced Growth*, pp. 130-38.

164. Renner, Michael. (1988). *Rethinking the Role of the Automobile.* Washington, D. C.: Worldwatch Institute, June.

165. Newman, Peter, and Kenworthy, Jeffrey. (1989). *Cities and Automobile Dependence.* Brookfield, Vt.: Gower Publishing.

166. Keyes, "Channeling," pp. 239-51.

167. Gratz, Roberta Brandes. 1989. *The Living City.* New York: Simon and Schuster; Hayden, Dolores. 1984. *Redesigning the American Dream: The Future of Housing, Work and Family Life.* New York: W.W. Norton.; and McRobie, George. 1981. *Small is Possible.* London: Abacus.

168. Mazmanian, Daniel A., and Morell, David L. (1991). "EPA: Coping with the New Political Economic Order." *Environmental Law* 21:4:1477-91. Also, see Tarr, Joel M. (1985). "Industrial Wastes and Public Health: Some Historical Notes." *American Journal of Public Health* 76:9:1059; Leepson, M. (1982). "Toxic Substance Control." In *Environmental Issues: Prospects and Problems.* Washington, D.C.: Editorial Research Reports.

169. Information drawn from *The Tampa Tribune*, April 22, 1990.

170. Anderson, John E. "The Toxic Danger." (1987). *American Demographics* 9:45. Also, see Greider, William. (1992). *Who Will Tell the People.* New York: Simon and Schuster.

171. Greider, *Who Will Tell*, pp. 120-89.

172. Swanson, Charles, Chamelin, Neil, and Territo, Leonard. (1992). "Agricultural, Wildlife, and Environmental Crimes." In *Criminal Investigation*. New York: McGraw-Hill.

173. Mazmanian and Morrell, "EPA," pp. 1477-91.

174. See Mazmanian and Morrell, "EPA," pp. 1477-91, for a description of how collaborative community-management plant oversight and performance contracts might provide a strategy for mitigating environmental impacts of industrial facilities.

175. See Federal Clean Air Act of 1970, 1977, 1990; Federal Clean Water Act of 1977, 1987; Federal Atomic Energy Act of 1954, 1982, 1987; Federal Low Level Radioactive Waste Policy Act of 1980; Federal Resource Conservation and Recovery Act of 1976, 1984.

176. Greenberg, Michael, Popper, Frank, West, Bernadette, and Schneider, Dona. (1992). "TOADS go to New Jersey: Implications for Land Use and Public Health in Mid-sized and Large U.S. Cities." *Urban Studies* 29:1:117-25.

177. Bullard, Robert D. (1990). *Dumping in Dixie: Race, Class and Environmental Quality;* Been, Vicki. (1993). "What's Fairness Got To Do With It? Environmental Justice and the Siting of Locally Undesirable Land Uses." *Cornell Law Review* 78:1001-87.

178. Been, "What's Fairness," p. 1004.

179. Ibid. pp. 1001-87

180. Brown, Alice L. (July, 1993). "Environmental Justice: New Civil Rights Frontier." *Trial* 29: 48.

181. Ibid. Also, see H.R. 2105, 103rd Congress, 1st Session, 1993; H.R. 495, 103rd Congress, 1st Session, 1993; and H.R. 1924, 103rd Congress, 1st Session, 1993.

182. Been, "What's Fairness," p. 1015.

183. For an additional review of the data on environmental justice see Austin, Regina, and Schill, Michael. (1991). "Black, Brown, Poor, and Poisoned: Minority Grassroots Environmentalism and the Quest for Eco-Justice." *Kansas Journal of Law and Public Policy* 1:1: 69-82.

184. U.S. General Accounting Office. (1983). *Siting of Hazardous Waste Landfills and Their Correlations with Racial and Economic Status of Surrounding Communities*. Washington, D.C.: U.S. Government Printing Office.

185. Commission for Racial Justice, United Church of Christ. (1987). *Toxic Waste and Race in the United States*, pp. 4-53. Cited in Been, "What's Fairness," pp. 1010-11.

186. Ibid., pp. 4-53.

187. Ketkar, Kusum. (1992). "Hazardous Waste Sites and Property Values in New Jersey." *Applied Economics* 24:647-53; Bullard, Robert. (1983). "Solid Waste Sites and the Black Houston Community." *Social Inquiry* 53:273.

188. Chira, Susan. (July 16, 1989). "New York's Poorest Neighborhoods Bear the Brunt of Social Programs." *The New York Times*.

189. Gabriel, Stuart A., and Wolch, Jennifer. (1984). "Spillover Effects of Human Service Facilities in a Racially Segmented Housing Market." *Journal of Urban Economics* 16:339-45.

190. Lavelle, Marianne, and Coyle, Marcia. (September 21, 1992). "Unequal Protection: The Racial Divide in Environmental Law." *National Law Journal*, p. S2.

CHAPTER 2

Property Law, Ideology, and the Dilemma of Habitation

THE IDEA OF PROPERTY AND LAND-USE PLANNING IN THE UNITED STATES

The idea of property and the particular distribution and sphere of property rights has been the stuff of ideological debate since ancient times. Because property plays a major role in marking the boundaries between what is private and what is public, property rights issues become more salient during periods of doubt about the public's or government's ability to solve social problems. Much of the current debate about regulation and privatization is based on such doubts. Advocates in this debate often base their arguments explicitly or implicitly on a coherent set of values, outlooks, and preferred policy tools that, taken together, form more or less coherent ideologies. This chapter first briefly explores the particular legal context in which ideological arguments arise in the United States, then sets out the concepts central to four of the ideologies that are most actively at play in land-use disputes. Finally, these ideologies are examined in light of Karl Polanyi's ideas about habitation, in particular his argument that habitation should be seen as a unique form of property that is potentially destroyed when included in the scope of supposedly "self-regulating" markets.

Property Rights

In the previous chapter, a number of land-use ills of a social justice and environmental type were attributed in part to individuals' exercise of property rights without consideration of their neighbors, and more specifically without consideration of the effects on the dynamic pattern of community development.

Individual decision-making about land uses is based on particular notions of private property rights. The movements for social justice and for environmental protection have included calls to reconceptualize and clarify the rights of those who are negatively affected by others' exercise of their property rights. In a more radical sense, however, some members of these movements have called for a major transfer of property rights away from individual owners and toward collective ownership of certain property use rights. Such a transfer would appear to violate our commonsense notion of property as something that is generally unchangeable.

However, as Robert Nelson suggests, property rights are not static; rather, they tend to evolve over time, with new property rights emerging through "the spread of common practices that reflect strong immediate pressures."[1] Only after the practices have been in place in some areas do they spread and become formalized in law. Nelson suggests that zoning laws, for example, reflect a number of practices (such as Los Angeles' turn-of-the-century segregation of industrial and residential uses) that were already in place. A tension is created, however, when there is not an accepted legal basis for incorporating the emerging practices into new, legally defensible property rights. Such is the case, for example, when the courts stretch our understanding of the state's police powers for preventing harm in order to approve zoning that calls for lot sizes of at least two acres. The ostensible rationale for such a policy—that such lot sizes are necessary to prevent the spread of fire—is weak at best and is provided only because the real reasons for such zoning—to relieve pressure on the rural environment, to reduce fiscal burdens, or keep out "undesirables"—are not legally defensible.[2]

The creation of new property rights will often create a new relationship between the individual and the state. For example, zoning can be seen as the creation of a right that did not exist prior to the passage of a zoning ordinance. This right—to prohibit others from using their land in specific ways—establishes an obligation on the part of the state to enforce the prohibition.[3] Similarly, the call among some environmentalists for a transfer of property rights from human owners toward the trustees of individually endangered species or whole ecosystems would have the effect of creating a new trustee-like institution that would mediate between individual property owners and the state. For the most part, however, policy analysts have tended to support either the establishment of more clearly drawn private property rights or greater centralized state control as the means of dealing with problems such as real or potential environmental degradation. As will be explored in more detail in the latter parts of this book, these two dominant policy options—clarification of individual property rights or expansion of state power to act as a trustee of the environment—may be less viable than the formalization of new property rights and local collective responsibilities. However, before exploring the policy potential of making adjustments in traditional conceptions of property rights, it may be worthwhile to describe in more detail the origins and concepts of the current system of property rights.

Land Use and Intangible Property

While scholars and researchers of various political opinions can agree that the evolution of capitalism and material progress have had significant effects on the theories of property in use in the judicial system, there is much less agreement as to whether the evolution in law and public policy that has occurred in reaction to the pressures for progress has been a healthy one overall. Among those who see this evolution as an unhealthy one, there is even less agreement about the exact "nature of the disease" that has been created as a result. Students of property rights law and some advocates for social justice, moreover, are not even sure that landed property per se is all that important in the modern world.

The publication in 1964 of Charles Reich's article on "New Property" (the idea that recipients of government benefits and grants have a property right in these) gave clear and early expression to the desire by those in the social justice movement to fashion new concepts of property as part of a community-building strategy. The fact that Reich's "New Property" article has become the most cited article in recent legal literature indicates how important the idea of property is to the workings of a just society. Reich's article, with its emphasis on property in government largess, also points out that land is no longer the dominant form of property in contemporary society.[4] Intellectual, shareholder, entitlement, and limited liability forms of property obviously account for a greater proportion of wealth in advanced capitalist states. However, despite its relative decline in the overall scheme of property values, it is the thesis of this writer that landed property and land-use planning is still central to realizing the other more intangible forms of property. If industrial or personal uses of property are zoned or developed out of a community, the intangible forms of property will not be realizable in that community and will therefore likely be reduced in value.

The fact that our property laws have evolved in support of entrepreneurs who own marketable intangible properties has muted some of the real danger of land-use controls' having a chilling effect on liberty. At the same time, however, when support is given disproportionately to types of intangible property that have market value, other types of intangible property may be left undeveloped and unsupported in our legal and public policy systems. At various point throughout this book, I will suggest that these other pre-capitalist types of intangible property are important to the way we think about governing the tangible or landed form of property.

Examination of James Madison's 1792 essay, *Property*, provides some insight into how this Founding Father conceived of the relationship between land and other forms of property. Madison wrote:

> In its larger and juster meaning, [property] embraces every thing to which a man may attach a value and have a right; and which leaves to every one else the like advantage. In the former sense, a man's land . . . is called his property. In the latter sense, a man has property in his opinions and the

> free communication of them. . . . Government is instituted to protect property of every sort; as well that which lies in the various rights of individuals, as that which the term particularly expresses.[5] (pp. 101-102)

Laura Underkuffler's review of Madison's essay points out that Madison's broader understanding of property as including the freedoms of conscience and expression as well as physical liberty, and the ability to use one's intelligence and creative powers, "is radically different from the ordinary understanding of property today."[6] Underkuffler also quotes from others in the founding era to suggest that property had a substantially broader meaning during that period. Joseph Story, for example, saw property as existing not only "in things, . . . but in actions." Similarly, Alexander Hamilton noted that one could have a property right in an office. Underkuffler identifies the origins of this broader view of property in the writings and expressions of English Whigs such as John Locke. Locke and other Whigs tended to see property as the total moral space that an individual can fill. The beginning of this moral space is found in Locke's idea that "every man has a PROPERTY in his own person."[7] From such a beginning, property in possessions and estates is created by intermingling one's labor with the things available in nature, while leaving behind "good enough and plenty" for others to do the same.

The implications of this comprehensive idea of property are significant. The value of property in this view is to mediate between an individual's rights and the power of government as well as to establish a baseline of capacity for human dignity and citizenship. In much of the remainder of this book, I will argue that individual and traditional property rights in land may be a necessary but are likely not a sufficient, condition for realizing the more comprehensive goals of property ownership.

The Unique Legal Context of Land-Use Planning in the United States

The U.S. Constitution is somewhat unique in that it provides some of the most explicit protections of private property in the world. Although these protections are explicit, they are not unambiguous. Rather, the protection of property rights, though legally guaranteed, has to be balanced against other constitutional powers and rights such as those concerned with securing the general welfare of the populace. Consequently, land-use issues are subject to a greater degree of legal dispute in the United States than is commonly the case in nations that give more weight to governmental prerogatives than private rights. Land-use disputes in the United States are often played out in the courts, and the larger role of judicial interpretation of property rights in land-use disputes in the United States is reflected in the relatively high number of lawsuits related to land use, acquisition, and disposal issues and in the observations of social critics who, from de Tocqueville on, have noted that the judicial branch of government in the United States takes on responsibilities that in most other nations would be assumed by the legislative or executive branches. As one observer has written: "As a practical matter, the courts have had a major planning function—perhaps *the* major function—for the system of land-use regulation in the United States."[8]

The unique constitutional protections provided to private property in the United States are derived in part from a liberal view of property as something that individuals earn by mingling their labor with the resources that nature provides. According to John Locke, the premier theorist of this view of property, property is forged by individuals out of a state of nature and only becomes subject to public power upon the voluntary agreement among individuals to form a social contract.[9] In contrast to this Lockean view of the origins of property, most nations have adopted a more Hobbesian approach to property. According to Hobbes, "the introduction of Propriety is an effect of Common-wealth. . . . From whence we may collect that the Propriety which a subject hath in his lands, consisteth in a right to exclude all other subjects from the use of them; and not to exclude their Sovereign."[10] The Hobbesian approach to property rights is evident in the lack of specific constitutional guidelines as to public sector regulation, acquisition, and disposal of property. In a Hobbesian or traditional world, property is something that belongs to the sovereign and that individuals can use only at the discretion of the sovereign. This view of property is still evident even in such seeming bastions of liberalism as Canada and Britain, where Parliament can still determine fundamental law.

In a more subtle way, traces of the Hobbesian view of property are evident in the everyday practice of real estate law in the United States. For example, the vast majority of property in the United States is bought and sold as "fee simple" property. Although Americans commonly think that their purchase of landed property gives them exclusive rights to the land, the "fee simple" term is a reminder that ownership rights in property have traditionally implied that the owner has a number of obligations or fees that he or she must meet or pay to retain ownership. In some cases, ownership is linked to a number of obligations or fees, while in other cases such obligations are few in number or the simplest to fulfill. Fee simple ownership implies that ownership of land comes with the fewest possible implied duties, but duties nonetheless.

The medieval or feudal fee system of ownership was part of a larger social system that severely limited the market for land. Devices such as entail were used to ensure that large tracts of property remained intact. While such limited property rights would be highly inefficient from the perspective of a classically trained economist, the fee system was an integral part of providing for security. For example, entail would ensure that estates did not become so small or fragmented as to be unable to provide for their own, or their king's, defense. Because property is always dependent on power, the system of property rights will tend to reflect the power relationships in the larger society. In feudal societies, where most property is landed property and most goods are derived directly from land, these relationships revolved specifically around land and land-use rights and responsibilities. The medieval system of property and property rights is just the inverse of the understanding of landed property that is common today. The modern fee simple ownership arrangement implies that one can divide one's property both geographically and abstractly (that is, in terms of rights to lease or sell aspects of the property such as mineral rights) as one wishes, without having to consult the state or the community. This is the case because the state or community is not entitled to any fees over and above such customary ones as property taxes. By way of contrast, during the medieval period, property in its geographical and abstract senses was encumbered in numerous ways. Practices like entail restricted the division of property and the existence of pre-ordained fees on property rights meant that these rights were considered to be highly divisible, rather than indivisible, as conservative and libertarian legal theorists believe.[11] What is important for our purposes is that the medieval idea of property as divisible made possible a set of restraints on the ability of markets to undermine stable human habitats and communities.

The idea that property rights are not unitary but instead could be broken into various separate and alienable components has come to be known by legal theorists as the "bundle of rights" notion of property. The bundle-of-rights idea provided a great deal of flexibility to feudal societies. Property rights and obligations substituted for the absence of a developed currency system and national market. The bundle-of-rights idea did not disappear with the emergence of capitalist society; rather, it was privatized. That is, instead of divisible property rights being used to define the relationships of security, these rights became part of the overall market system. Instead of purchasing the entire bundle of rights or fee simple, it becomes possible to purchase only that part of the property that one needs, such as the rights to water or minerals that lie on the property. As the bundle-of-rights concept was privatized, it was also transformed into something essentially different. The original bundle-of-rights idea suggested not only that property rights could be divided, but that some rights are more under the control of the individual property owner than others. That is, some of these rights can be more easily possessed by the community or the state than others. Under the new bundle-of-rights theory, every property right is equally protected; these rights are indivisible from property ownership per se.

Hence, the classical idea of property as a bundle of divisible rights has generally been associated with a more Hobbesian notion of property as belonging to the sovereign, with certain bundles being doled out to citizens in return for various fees. This classic bundle concept also implies a high level of entanglement between, and a potential for confusion of, the public and private sectors. In contrast, Locke's idea of property as something that an individual wrests from nature, suggests that in the beginning at least, property is a private and indivisible thing and that the line between public and private is a relatively sharp one. These contrasting approaches to property are evident in the comparison of the allocation of mineral rights in the more Hobbesian-oriented European nations with the more

Lockean-oriented United States. In most European countries, mineral rights belong exclusively to the state, even in cases where ownership of the land's surface is private; in the United States these rights are part and parcel of the ownership of the surface property. [12]

While the contrast between the United States and European nations is relatively stark with regard to basic ideas of property, a similar, but not as dramatic contrast can be seen between the United States and Canada—two nations with fairly liberal traditions of property rights. While the majority of land in both nations is held in fee simple, where ownership of land is subject to payment of taxes and to expropriation through eminent domain in cases where a social need arises, Canadian governments have interpreted the "fee" part of fee simple much more broadly. For example, in British Columbia, the Limited Access Highways Act gives the "Minister of Highways the right to expropriate up to 5 percent of an individuals's property fronting on a provincial limited access highway without any right to compensation." A similar act in the United States would be considered unconstitutional, not because of the taking of property per se, but because of the failure to pay just compensation.[13]

The more explicit protections of private property in the United States are found in the Fifth and Fourteenth Amendments of the Constitution. The Fifth Amendment provides that governments in the United States cannot take private property without ensuring substantive due process and just compensation. Substantive due process has been interpreted to mean that government's actions to acquire property have to be related to a public purpose. For example, zoning regulations, to be constitutional, have to have some "reasonable relationship" to the promotion of health, safety, morals, or general welfare. The takings clause of the Fifth Amendment protects private property owners because it demands that governments provide "just compensation" for the property that is taken for public use. Interpretations of this "takings" clause suggest that government actions that do not invade the land, that leave a reasonable beneficial use of the property, or that are taken to prevent a harm are generally not considered takings that would require compensation. Other, more drastic physical invasions of private property or reductions in property values that go "too far," however, would demand compensation. The Fourteenth Amendment protects private property owners by requiring that laws affecting property be applied in a manner that would not discriminate for or against any individuals or groups. As was described in the section of this book that treated exclusionary zoning, the courts have generally refused to invalidate laws that did not directly and purposefully discriminate against classes of individuals who have traditionally been protected by the Constitution. Specifically, the discriminatory effect would need to be related to race, creed, or national origin in order for most U.S. courts to invoke the equal protection clause as the basis for voiding laws. Very simply put, laws, regulations, and uses of the power of eminent domain that seem to have a legitimate public purpose and/or that prevent harm are generally considered valid by the U.S. courts.

Hence, interpretation of the clauses of the Constitution that protect private property have not severely restricted governmental powers in this regard; however, the fact that constitutional protections exists and that so many issues of governmental control over property are brought to the courts makes the U.S. system of land use and regulation somewhat unique in the world.

Property and Legal Formalism

Because the courts have such a major role in the regulation and acquisition of land in the United States, theories of law and economics and related ideologies are important to the way land-use policy is enacted. For such policy to be legitimate, however, judicial decision making must be seen as a principled exercise of power that is above politics. One way in which this is supposed to occur is through the invocation of what is known as legal formalism. Legal formalism, according to Roberto Unger, has two parts. For legal rulings to be accepted, they must first embody an understanding of human association that is defensible. Second, they must be based on legal reasoning that invokes purposes, policies, and principles that are impersonal.[14] Only the coupling of neutral rules and fundamental principles would enable a judicial branch to distinguish itself from the realm of politics where self-interest is dominant, Unger argues. Additionally, legal formalism acts to protect judicial actors from the charge of being anti-democratic. Because judges are more often appointed than elected and are chosen exclusively from those with an elite education, legal formalism, in the eyes of critical scholars, is a sort of necessary fiction. If it did not exist, it would be necessary to invent it to justify the existence of a judicial branch that makes decisions in cases where social cohesion is most fragile.[15]

Legal formalism, which calls for judicial deference to the legislature, also implies that rules will be applied to disputes according to accepted principles.[16] This can provide some obvious benefits when neutrality is a primary value. But application of formalism to land-use control also has substantial drawbacks, especially if the rules in question are outdated. The formal structure of law was designed to address fairly simple disputes between two parties; it is much less capable of designing basic social policies. In fact, because the courts tend to rely on an adversarial system (that is, the litigants themselves) for the information on which decision are made, they are disadvantaged, especially when neither party to a dispute has the resources or skill to generate information. Also, because of its reliance on precedents that were formed in other times, formal legal processes can often result in policies that are "out of touch with basic economic and social needs."[17] Complaints against the use of legal processes have been made based on the relatively elite position of most members of the judiciary.

The drawbacks of legal formalism have been particularly evident in the construction of land-use controls or zoning ordinances. In essence, zoning has been built on the long-standing legal concepts of "nuisance" and public "police powers" to prevent harm to the public at large. These formal legal concepts, however, form a fairly narrow basis for the kind of exclusionary property right that has been created by municipal zoning ordinances. According to Robert Nelson, while zoning was established on the basis that it prevents nuisances or harm, it in fact has much more extensive purposes and effects: protecting the overall quality of life in neighborhoods, maintaining individual property values, and fulfilling the desire for environmental and aesthetic protection. Moreover, these positive effects are not independent of the more negative or exclusionary effects of zoning described in the first chapter. Because zoning was initially designed to help prevent costly nuisances and costly nuisance actions, but has been discovered to have many other, perhaps as important or more important effects, Nelson argues that the intellectual and legal foundations of zoning are a "legal fiction" since there is a substantial gap between the "actual substance and consequences of zoning . . . and its intellectual justifications."[18] The price of this intellectual dishonesty in the legal system is substantial, Nelson suggests:

> Significant amounts of lawyer time and client money are taken up in constructing legal arguments that have become little more than formalities. The confidence of the average citizen in the legal process is diminished by the absence of persuasive justification for zoning and of clear explanations for judicial decisions. Finally, communities are required to make significant expenditures solely to comply with the formal requirements of zoning law . . . and [waste] money in preparing comprehensive community land-use plans.[19]

Because much of our zoning has been based on the need to contrive elaborate but "fictitious" legal justifications, as a society we may be avoiding a necessary struggle with fundamental issues and values. The purpose of the rest of this chapter is to explore how the idea of property is seen from within particular ideologies or political philosophies.

Disputes Through Legal Indeterminacy

In times of social change, disputes that in less turbulent times might have remained at the level of conflicts among stakeholders or individual interests can become disputes over principles and ideologies, on the one hand, or over the nature of the "facts" of legal discourse itself. Because of the central nature of land-use issues, both types of "disputing by other means" have become evident in the legal environment of land-use questions. The drawbacks of legal formalism became so evident in some cases, especially those involving the interpretation of property rights under conditions of dynamic change, that astute observers came to believe that either the law must be viewed as a more flexible instrument or it would break under its own weight.

If the role of the courts in resolving the propriety of governmental action in land markets is predicated on legal formalism, legal and language theorists who argue that ordinary language is open to numerous interpretations are cutting at the root of legal formalism. Because of the open nature of language, disputes will naturally occur over the meaning or relevance of interpretative rules. Texts that can be read (or in critical terms, deconstructed) in numerous ways are in this regard thought to be ripe for unlimited judicial discretion. As such, objective and neutral interpretation of legal rules would be impossible and the law itself would be indeterminate. Many of the scholars associated with the critical legal studies movement make this argument.

Some legal theorists have agreed that rules may be open to varied interpretations, but that it may nevertheless be possible to limit judicial discretion by accepting a set of principles that can then be used to interpret the rules in question.[20] Critical scholars have, in turn, argued that the principles themselves would demand interpretation, opening up the process for indeterminacy again.

The seemingly indeterminate nature of the "facts" of language has affected judicial policy in the land-use area in several ways. As will be explored below, the awareness of the indeterminacy of language has been directly used to justify a particular political philosophy—communitarianism—that has major implications for land use and regulation. In the broader political environment, however, indeterminacy, or worse yet, vagueness in legal language has been magnified by the incentives that politicians have to appear to please everyone, while not offending anyone.

Although a degree of indeterminacy may exist in legal rules that are designed to be clear, a further unbinding of judicial discretion occurs when the legislative bodies do not attempt to create clear language or even deliberately construct law that is vague or overly abstract. Observers of political behavior believe that legislators operate in this manner because it is in their interests in many cases to appear to be satisfying a number of differing and competing constituent demands through passage of legislation, while in fact not fully satisfying any one set of demands. In particular, vague legislation can provide the appearance of action, while at the same time avoiding the offense of negatively affecting powerful interests. Theodore Lowi and other political scientists have described legislative bodies that enact vague laws with the expectation that agencies will develop more specific regulations. The effect of this strategy is not only to provide political cover and afford powerful special interests another chance to achieve anti-democratic purposes, but also to create a situation in which rule by law is something that can be achieved only through increasingly high levels of judicial interpretation. This interpretation in turn is often conducted through ideological lenses.

PROPERTY AND IDEOLOGY

Disputes Through Ideology

At one level, governance of land-use issues is based on codes of land-use laws and property rights. Previously, I touched on how these code of property law have changed over time, reflecting a change in underlying ideas of property, and of how property laws function to support specific goals such as economic development. The immediately preceding section briefly touched on the vagueness that is increasingly built into the law, a political reality that reinforces the view that judicial interpretation will necessarily be subjective or indeterminate. This revelation of the subjective or indeterminate nature of the "facts" of legal discourse will necessarily undermine the legitimacy of the status quo, but it does not thereby provide insight into what would be a legitimate basis for governing the acquisition, use, regulation, and disposal of property. To gain such insight, it is necessary to explore how property laws are themselves built on and in turn support more basic norms, values, and political forms. Property laws in this sense reflect the social choices that citizens make with respect to whether they give priority to freedom, equality, security, or some other value and whether their lives will be organized around individual choices, group choices, or dictated by a "sovereign" who chooses for individuals.

When such values, norms, and preferred political forms cohere in a systematic way, they form ideologies. The rest of this chapter explores alternative ideologies as they might inform our understanding of land-use issues and reform. The following draws heavily on Robin Paul Malloy's descriptions of competing approaches to law and economics. Malloy contrasts four basic choices: conservative, communitarian, libertarian, and classical liberal. The first two ideologies—conservative and communitarian—involve a conceptual framework in which liberty is understood as liberty for the state, the community, or groups of citizens. The latter two—libertarian and classical liberal—understand liberty as liberty for the individual and view this type of freedom as fundamental.[21]

Communitarian and state-centered frameworks focus on the importance of groups or state-appointed experts and planners at the expense of individual decision-makers. The difference between the two group-oriented ideologies is found in the level at which legitimacy is validated. State-oriented or conservative ideologies, for example, are legitimized at the state level, where the individual is liberated and enhanced through the enhancement of the state. Communitarian ideologies, on the other hand, find their legitimacy at the community level, and individuals are liberated and enhanced by meeting the needs and promoting the will of identified groups or classes. Whereas conservative discourse tends to be sprinkled with references to tradition, patriotism, and "the people," communitarian discourse tends to be progressive or leftist in nature, and is characterized by references to ethnic groups, classes, sexes, or races. To push the stereotype to the extreme, state-oriented, conservative ideologies could be used to justify fascism, while communitarian ideologies taken to a logical extreme could lead to the dehumanization and loss of personal identity for persons who do not share the common goals of the collective.[22]

Individual-oriented ideologies rely on individuals' subjective viewpoints and experiences as the primary frame of reference for understanding liberty and rights, and such ideologies are suspicious of conceptions of group rights and state power. Although the two streams of individually oriented ideologies—libertarian and classic liberalism—agree on the primacy of individualist views, natural rights, and autonomy, they disagree on the extent to which governing institutions should balance public and private power or promote social welfare and human dignity. The libertarian approach, constrained by a rigid view of the primacy of the private realm and the minimalist role of the state, is precluded from addressing issues of welfare, human dignity, and maldistributions of power. Classic liberalism, on the other hand, sees these issues as legitimate and demanding of attention.

CONSERVATIVE IDEOLOGIES

Contemporary conservative ideology often appears as individualist (rather than state-oriented or communitarian) because conservative theorists such as Richard Posner offer a view of property rights that supports the maintenance of a free market system. The rights of individual ownership of property, however, do not derive from either a natural rights perspective or from a view that considers the need for a balance of private and public power. Instead, property rights and other individual rights are derived from a view of society that considers the status quo as given and the "free market system as a desirable *end* in itself."[23]

Conservative positions on the bundle-of-rights idea of property might vary depending on the context of the discussion. In general, conservatives would likely agree with the idea that property is mutable as long as there is a free market for the various rights that are unbundled and if the unbundling can be justified as an action leading to greater total wealth. However, contemporary conservatives tend to accept the libertarian propositions that property is unitary, and that the possession of property is an indicator of an essential (if not the essential) civil right. Conservative beliefs in the immutable nature of property do not extend to other forms of property, such as those identified by Madison or the "new property" that Charles Reich has purported to discover in largess and entitlements of the welfare state. Hence, for conservatives the unity of property is secondary to utilitarian concerns. Like chameleons, conservatives will borrow the colors of libertarian ideology in their quest for efficient social structures.

Conservatives, as Malloy points out, have identified social arrangements that lead to wealth maximization as the most desirable and have accepted neoclassical economics as the model for such social arrangements. This blind acceptance of neoclassical economics, however, masks a number of value assumptions. As these assumptions are clarified, the statist perspective of conservative ideology becomes visible. For example, one assumption of this ideology is that the current distribution of wealth and resources is given and that persons without resources or jobs have no claim on social resources. This assumption reflects the value judgment that efficient, wealth-maximizing markets preclude certain types of inherent human rights to a share of the world's resources.

According to Malloy, conservative ideology purports to decide issues rationally and objectively, but actually supports laws and institutions that favor persons "already in possession of a disproportionate share of political and financial power."[24] The supposed objective, rational and scientific policy analysis that is made possible by use of neoclassical economic concepts is, Malloy suggests, a sham. Such analysis acts as a pseudoscientific screen for decisions that favor the interests of those who are already in power and also favor the state's interest in maximizing total wealth (of which the state receives a share) rather than individual rights and happiness. As evidence of the non-objective nature of the wealth-maximizing, neoclassical model, Malloy shows how wealth-maximizing principles can be employed to justify *or* undermine the same policy objective. For example, he notes that the voluntary nature of the exchange of money for sexual favors would, under traditional criteria for economic efficiency (such as Pareto or Kaldor-Hicks), argue for legalization of prostitution. On the other hand, he notes that conservative philosophy can easily identify other effects of prostitution (on family life or street crime) that would need to be factored into the wealth-maximizing equation. Depending on how one weighs these other effects within the equations, conservatives could accept or reject prostitution. This degree of indeterminacy would be less damning in an ideology that did not assert as one of its strengths a scientific rationality.

Additionally, the neoclassical model of economics assumes: (1) that property and resources are freely moveable, an assumption implying that the hardships of families who are being forced to uproot and relocate due to market adjustments are not substantial or significant; (2) competition, implying that adversarial relationships are generally desirable; (3) equal and full access to information, implying that the current distribution of education and access to information are acceptable; and (4) that individuals can and should act rationally and in their self-interest, implying that the aggregation of these individual choices is best for society. Each of these assumptions is open to substantial challenge.

In all, Malloy suggests that conservatives should be faulted not for using neoclassical market principals per se, but for the "almost dogmatic manner in which Posnerian conservatives employ the model as an end in itself"[25] and the tendency of conservatives to "dress up ideology in the academic legalities of neutral and objective inquiry."[26] Malloy argues that when the facts of policy issues, which in themselves are "a matter of subjective interpretation," are "submitted to an indeterminate mode of economic analysis, that itself rests upon certain assumptions," our conscious participation in moral and humanistic decision making is marginalized.[27] The marginalization process can be seen in a number of land-use siting issues. The siting of a waste treatment facility, for example, usually begins with an analysis of the economics of siting a facility in particular areas. First, factors are identified, such as land costs, leakage rates of soils and other land features at various sites, proximity to waste-creating facilities, transportation costs, acceptable risks to nearby populations, density of populations that could be affected, and so forth. Whether particular factors are identified and included in the analysis is by no means assured. If, for example, one accepts the contention that toxic waste that has been treated through high temperature incinerators is 99.99 percent transformed into harmless substances or that solidification processes immobilize inorganic waste by mixing it with cement,[28] risks assessments might not even enter into the economic analysis of the site location for these types of facilities.

Next, the "facts" related to each of these factors are translated by "experts" into economic values that are then manipulated within economic models. Often these models are computerized so that certain basic assumptions are transparent only to those who constructed the computer model. In North Carolina, for example, experts attempting to site a waste treatment facility used low population density as a prime assumption in the economic analysis of the suitability of various locations. The analysis was conducted through use of an automated geographical information system that identified a number of "suitable" sites—all rural. Because the key assumption was hidden in the model, citizens had little basis for questioning the results (that is, that none of the "acceptable" sites were found in the more urban areas, even though these were the areas where the waste to be disposed originated).[29] Without the existence of environmental activists who also had the skill to uncover the hidden assumptions in the model, the facility would have been sited in an area that was not responsible for the wastes that would be treated.

Economic modeling of the cost-benefit variety is not without its benefits. It can, for instance, help to make explicit the factors under consideration and the weights that are being given to each. In this way, it could enable disputants to understand each other's configurations of concern. However, when such modeling is used as a rationale for judicial decision-making or other less democratic policymaking, the potential for hidden assumptions, arbitrary weights, and overall abuse is large. This is particularly the case when policymakers give full weight to tangible and easily measurable values, but discount the intangible forms of property.

Although conservatives purport to respect property rights, these rights do not typically include in full measure the rights that Madison describes in his essay on property. Rather than viewing individuals as having rights in their opinions and in the communication of these opinions, as Madison suggests, conservatives tend to limit their view of property to the traditional sense of land or other tangible items. The conservative ideal of wealth maximization is limited to storable wealth. Also, Posner's wealth-maximization construct differs from those of Adam Smith and other classic liberals in that the latter would be reluctant to subsume natural rights, human dignity, and welfare rights within wealth-maximizing equations that monetize, discount, or even ignore these values.

Consider another typical land-use problem—the exclusionary nature of traditional zoning—under the conservative constructs of the law and economics school of thought established by Posner and others. Within the constructs of this conservative approach, one must undertake a determination of the costs and benefits of measures such as inclusionary zoning that are designed to remediate the exclusionary effects of traditional zoning. At the same time, the conservative approach permits one to avoid the underlying and difficult measurements of the costs of segregation by race, class, or handicap or the difficult questions that revolve around whether certain persons are able to engage in the debate on the issues, or whether these individuals would be able to participate in exchange relationships. As Malloy writes:

> The discourse of wealth maximization validates voluntary contract transactions without asking whether some people have been systematically deprived of an opportunity to acquire the wealth necessary to bargain voluntarily. In this way Posnerian approaches to law and economics deprive certain individuals of the opportunity to participate in the market. These approaches are conservative because they are grounded in and continue to promote values biased in favor of prior distributions of wealth, power, and resources.[30]

The limitations of conservative ideology can be seen in the historical maldistribution of land in the Hawaiian Islands, where the government has traditionally owned 45 percent of the land, while nine private owners possessed another 45 percent. Within a conservative ideology, addressing this maldistribution of land would be difficult if not impossible unless an indirect case could be made that the concentration of land ownership creates monopolies. Contrary to conservative ideology, the Supreme Court upheld a state law that allowed the state to take land from one private owner and give it to another, who had been previously excluded from ownership.[31] One rationale for legitimizing what may at first glance seem like a "taking" by the state government might be found in the classic liberal proviso first noted by John Locke. Locke's proviso is the counter and limit to his idea of property as something created through one's labor and the corresponding legal idea of first possession; according to Locke, one could generate property in this manner as long as there was "plenty and enough left" over for others to do the same.[32]

COMMUNITARIAN IDEOLOGY

Communitarian approaches to law and economics can be found in the thinking of a number of progressive and leftist scholars and social theorists.[33] However, communitarians make fewer claims of objectivity and rely less on expert-devised systems of analysis. Instead of accepting the autonomous individual as the basis for normative judgments, communitarians often deny that individuals can hold preferences or even have an independent identity that is not somehow mediated by life in groups or in society as a whole.[34] Moreover, for communitarians, experience in a community is intrinsically good, rather than simply an instrumental means to fulfilling pre-existing individual desires.[35] The process of group self-definition, communitarians argue, is a fundamental mode of expression and should be protected from unwarranted intrusion by the state.[36]

Communitarians also place an emphasis on neutral dialogue and equality of treatment. The distributions of education, information, and resources that are accepted as a basis for analysis by conservatives become the very issues of concern in communitarian discourse. Whereas conservative approaches to law and economics are at root justified by utilitarian ideas of economic efficiency, communitarian approaches are utilitarian only to the extent that the greatest good for the greatest number can be achieved without undermining equality.

In maximizing the "good" in a communitarian society, some communitarians argue that the state be allowed to take whatever actions are necessary as long as the results do not lead to greater differences in economic or political power. The political process in this respect would protect groups of individuals because the first principle of treating everyone equally should restrain groups from taking action against each other. That is, groups will not take action to enact harm-producing laws that would also apply to themselves.

A number of communitarians, however, would restrain state action to allow communities to "flourish as realms of empathy and concrete personality." Subordinating these communities to the will of the state, it is thought, would magnify the problem of dominance by the collective.[37]

Rather than rely on the aggregation of individually rational decisions as market theorists do, communitarians demand that *group* discourse be rational, consistent, and neutral. However, in contrast to proponents of legal formalism who might use these same criteria, communitarians are not nearly so tied to legal precedent as a guide for meeting these criteria. For communitarians, discourse is rational when decisions to distribute resources unequally are justified in persuasive dialogue; it is consistent when the justification for unequal distribution does not conflict with basic equality principles; and it is neutral in that claims for unequal resources based on superior power or access to resources are not legitimate. Under these discourse principles, for example, groups could not claim better treatment because they are superior, more knowledgeable, or retain some traditional source of authority.[38]

Malloy argues that communitarian approaches presume a basic equality of outcome, reject natural rights, and reject neoclassical market justifications for resource distributions. In the place of markets and individual rights, communitarians emphasize *neutral* political processes. In these processes "individuals can have their rights reduced," Malloy writes, "as long as there is an element of equality in the process of reduction."[39]

From a classic liberal or libertarian point of view, the communitarian approach places too much faith in political processes that may come to be dominated by special interests or by the managers of public agencies and other public decision makers. Malloy believes that just as conservatives give too much credence to market dynamics, communitarians are perhaps not skeptical enough of public sector dynamics, especially their potential for ignoring natural or individual rights. In communitarian ideologies, one's rights can become contingent on a political process. As a self-described classic liberal, Malloy sees communitarian ideologies are flawed because they would likely allow taxation and regulation at levels substantial enough to undercut the existence of a private sphere strong enough to counterbalance public power.

Communitarians tend to support the idea that property rights are in fact divisible and mutable. The shaping and distribution of the various bundles of rights, however, should be determined by social processes that are guided by a vision of social justice rather than by the utilitarian idea of wealth maximization.[40] In this view, communitarians have been able to draw upon a large body of legal realist theory and literature. Legal realists argue that property is not a thing as such, but rather a set of contingent and disaggregated human relationships that are played out in real contexts. Chief among these is the relationship between state power and citizens; the state's monopoly of physical force allows it to exclude others from property as well as include itself in property-use decisions related to the public interest. The state itself, however, can be captured by specific interests or audiences. Legal realists have noted, for example, that the prime common law indicator of property—first possession—is itself a notion that is culturally contingent. Possession rules, these scholars point out, will differ for different audiences. In classic cases, scholars have shown that there are substantial differences in the way first possession is understood among whalers vis-a-vis fox hunters, or between Europeans and Native Americans.[41]

Malloy identifies critical legal studies as the primary mode of discourse for communitarians. Critical Legal Studies (CLS) advocates, like legal realists, have been effective in showing that existing law and institutions—especially those that conservatives take as given and as a distillation of accumulated wisdom about efficient outcomes to conflict—are in fact socially chosen. Moreover, the choice of laws and institutions, CLS scholars contend, is biased in ways that reflect the dominance of particular classes. In taking legal realism to its logical conclusion, CLS scholars ask why this should be so.

Standards versus Rules

The question for Malloy and others classic liberals is whether a realist view of law requires a total rejection of legal formalism and legal rules. This question in communitarian and CLS circles is played out in discussions about the difference between formal rules and less formal standards. Communitarians believe that there is a difference and that the rules on which legal formalism is based should be replaced by standards. Rules are formalistic in that they apply equally to individuals in nearly all contexts. Standards, on the other hand, may result in different outcomes depending on the context. Under a rule-based society, parties can be held to a contract if they entered into the contract and included contract terms that are allowed by the rules of contracts. Alternatively, in a standards-based society, the legitimacy of a contract is not known until the context of the bargain has been examined. Factors such as levels of education, wealth and power, the history of the relationship, and the like would need to be examined before a contract could be declared valid.

Legal formalists and classic liberals argue that although a review of legal rules for direct bias and coercion should be part of legal processes, the extensive adoption of standards in lieu of rules could result in a reduction in individuals' rights and in the benefits of certainty. As a consequence, individuals would find it impossible to act without extensive and continuous intervention by the state or community overseers.

Standards demand that society continuously discover the meaning of the standards in new contexts. Individuals will have to be continuously re-educated to understand new interpretations of standards. For communitarians, legal standards represent a way of respecting differences among various groups or communities. Standards send out a message that questions of authority are never really closed. Rather, the dialogue that occurs in court serves to bridge communities and the larger society. Standards suggest an open-ended dialogue about the reasonable relationship among various communities or within a single community. Standards would allow judges to attempt to decide whether the community had used its police powers (such as to effectively exclude others) in ways that would lead to an undermining of the ideal of community itself. Hence, a sort of meta-standard for communitarians would be that communities' abilities to exclude others would need to be limited, because strict exclusion results in a decrease in a community's capacity to develop sympathy for others. Because the capacity for sympathy is at the root of the communitarian ideal, exclusion would need to be limited in some fashion. Paradoxically, however, exclusion is part of the nature of communities. The shared purposes of community at the very least provide a symbolic message that only some types of individuality will be realized in the internal life of particular communities.[42]

Because of this paradox of exclusion, and because communities are often built around cultural understandings that are obscure to those on the outside, only open-ended standards would allow courts to balance the claims of the universal ideal of community against the claims of specific communities. Adjudicating these claims by way of rules, communitarians argue, would involve placing all communities on a sort of Procrustean bed of rigid law, one that was insensitive to what Jurgen Habermas has called the "lifeworld" of communities, where concrete individuals understand each other with reciprocal empathy.[43]

In contrast to standards, rules, especially if they are general, can clearly frame the decisions to buy, sell, or enter agreements, but the decision and outcomes of the decisions that result from purchase, sale, or open agreements among individuals are left to individuals.

In terms of land-use policies, two types of communitarian standards can be identified. The strong community autonomy standard would generally allow communities, neighborhoods, or residential associations a great deal of leeway to restrict the use or transfer of property so as to form walled communities based on shared interests or characteristics such as age, behavior, or family status. A weaker community autonomy standard would give more credence to the paradox of exclusion, conceiving of communities with flexible boundaries built around shared purposes and characteristics, but not walls that would foreclose dialogue among groups.[44]

Libertarian Ideology

Libertarian approaches to the idea of property have been articulated by two modern scholars, Richard Epstein and Robert Nozick. These sophisticated libertarian scholars generally accept the ideas that property should be established through the rule of first possession and that the bundle of rights that form private property relationships is unitary.[45]

According to Epstein, the bundle of property rights includes three rights that form the basis of three fields of property law: the right to possession, use, and disposition. The right to possession is the right to exclude and forms the basis of trespass law. Use rights must be added to possession rights if one is to be able to do anything productive with property. The common law of nuisances, Epstein suggests, is based on use rights that enjoin others from unreasonable interferences with an owner's use of property. Finally, disposition rights are needed if individuals are to be able to realize the differences in the value of exchange on the one hand and the value of the current use on the other. For Epstein, tort law allowing application of sanctions to those who would interfere with advantageous relations among individuals has its origins in the disposition rights "stick" of a tightly bundled set of property rights.[46]

Epstein suggests that even though the common law was created to deal with disputes among private parties, the lessons of this law should apply to the relations between citizens and the state. In particular, he and other libertarians believe that the common law of property, which has successfully guided relationships among free holders of property, provides a good model for understanding what might be appropriate in the relationship between the state and citizens. Epstein admits that common law has allowed some fraying at the edges of the unity of the three property rights, but that it has on the whole respected this unity. For example, the common law of trespass allows for exceptions in cases—say, when a public road is blocked and the only way to get home is to trespass on private property—where the common and ordinary use of land and houses would require an exception. These "necessity" exemptions from the rule, Epstein argues, should be few and should "work to the advantage of all individuals who are required to relinquish some of the property rights that they possess."[47] In the same way that necessity criteria limit the exemptions to unified and strict private property rights in the relations among individuals, so too, Epstein argues, should necessity guide the creation of exemptions to these rights in the relations between citizens and the state. That is, for libertarians, when the state carves out exemptions to the strict common law concept of property as a unified bundle of rights, the justification has to demonstrate necessity and provide evidence that the exemption would benefit all citizens.

What libertarians such as Epstein object to is the state's undermining of common- law property institutions such as the right of exclusive possession on the basis of "fairly feeble, often very poorly articulated, police-power justification."[48] For libertarians, zoning provides a vivid example of the undermining of common-law property institutions. In Epstein's characterization, the law of zoning is one that goes far beyond live-and-let-live, necessity-type exemptions to property rights; instead, it reverses the field of freedom from the private owner toward the state, saying in effect that "as long as 'we the people' allow you to do anything, we can prohibit you from doing everything else with respect to the property."[49]

It should be understood that libertarians do not wish to outlaw the unbundling of property rights per se; rather, they would limit the choice of whether and how to unbundle rights to those who are the owners of these rights. That is, government cannot and should not force individual property owners to do so as a result of either positive law or judicial interpretation—without just compensation. For example, it is perfectly all right for individual property owners to separately sell the rights to possess and use property, while maintaining the right to dispose of a piece of property themselves (as is commonly done with leases) or, alternatively, to sell a right to the subsurface minerals, exclusive of other use rights, and so forth.

What libertarians object to is not the unbundling of rights by the owners of those rights, but the unbundling that occurs by government fiat. For example, Epstein would question the validity of the Supreme Court decision in *Andrus v. Allard* that upheld the state's prohibition of the sale of eagle feathers that were lawfully acquired and ruled that such prohibition did not constitute a takings.[50]

Libertarians, in contrast to conservatives and communitarians, identify individuals as the key reference point for discussions about liberty; they suggest, for instance, that personal autonomy should be protected even if such autonomy appears wasteful to the nation or larger community. Epstein, for example, argues that disposition rights in property include the right to waste or destroy one's own property. At the same time, however, libertarians such as Epstein argue that the greater danger is not an individual's waste of property under a libertarian system of rights; rather, it is the danger that under a system based on collective or communitarian ownership, property will remain unused and negativism will triumph: "Absent the unanimous agreement of all members of society about how resources are to be deployed, they could well remain unused."[51]

In terms of the environmental damage that occurs as a result of "tragedy of the commons" problems (such as where open access to property provides incentives for overuse of a resource), libertarians stand squarely on the side of those who believe that privatizing the ownership of such common-pool properties as air, water, and public lands would be the preferred solution to the "commons" problem. With a system of private property rights in place, they believe, the market would allocate use rights in accordance with efficiency principles. As overgrazing (of land), overdrawing (from water basins or fisheries), or pollution (of air) begins to occur, the increased scarcity would dictate a higher price for these properties and would correspondingly reduce demand, bringing such properties back into a state of viable, if not sustainable, use. Although self-interest might guide private owners toward protecting the value of their investment, critics could argue that the exclusive right of disposition that is implied in the common law and libertarian ideas of property would always leave the commonwealth subject to the perverse desires of individuals to waste, horde, or destroy resources.

There is no universal principle that would allow one to choose between the dangers of communitarian property and those of libertarian property. In both cases there is a potential that property will be destroyed through overuse as well as a danger that it will be hoarded and thereby not used to supply legitimate human needs. There is some empirical and theoretical evidence, explored later in this book, to suggest that both of these ideological conceptions of property may be flawed in certain respects.

Libertarians and the Minimal State

Epstein recognizes the essentially arbitrary nature of the choice among property theories, but argues for a libertarian approach with respect to most property.[52] His argument is based on the idea that unitary property in the hands of private citizens who can claim title by first possession, subsequent inheritance or assignment requires only a minimal state. In contrast, Epstein writes, "the theory of common ownership requires much more extensive public control, for someone must decide how the rights in question are to be packaged and divided amongst individuals."[53] Libertarians, like Epstein, tend to fear a system of original property rights such as communitarian ones that invite continued state intervention and the potential for ever increasing expansion of intervention rights. According to Epstein, the same justification of common ownership could be extended to arguments as to how individuals acquire ownership rights in themselves. The implication for Epstein is that individuals could never be secure in their ownership.

Epstein, in a line of thought perhaps more indicative of conservative ideology, also believes that some weight in the argument over the approaches to property rights needs to be given to the way society in the past has organized its property institutions. In the absence of clear principles as to how property rights might be reshuffled, Epstein suggests that the rules of the game should remain the same and that the burden of persuasion should rest with those who would want to displace the existing unitary property entitlement system.

Robert Nozick has fleshed out many of the libertarian ideas of private property and the minimal state. Whereas Epstein's work suggests that he believes that "state of nature" thought exercises may be of limited value in comparison with the practical, in medias res understandings to be found in common law, Nozick, following Locke, uses the state-of-nature model to discover the appropriate limits of state power. In a natural state, Nozick suggests, individuals will organize themselves primarily in ways that will afford them a measure of security. Such organization will often involve the development of a warrior class that can specialize in public defense. While this arrangement for security, Nozick argues, would naturally arise from a state of nature, numerous other functions do not. From a libertarian viewpoint, these other functions are suspect because there is potentially no limit to the expansion of state powers once one moves away from the type of mutual agreement that might be forged in a state of nature.

Libertarians and Absolute Rights

Nozick and other libertarians base their ideas of law and economics squarely on the bedrock of absolute individual rights. In contrast, conservatives, communitarians, and classical liberals would all restrict certain personal freedoms such as the freedom to destroy one's own property in oneself by suicide or to destroy one's personal freedom by voluntarily accepting slavery. Conservatives would tend to reject this freedom to destroy on the basis of the state's right to maximize wealth for the good of all; communitarians would probably reject the voluntary slavery choice on the basis that such a choice would undermine social justice and equality over the short and long terms. Classical liberals would draw on notions of natural law and basic human dignity to reject self-destructive choices. For example, in classic liberal Lockean terms, certain types of property, such as property in life and liberty, are inalienable; such inalienable property does not truly belong to individuals, but is rather possessed by God or inherent in nature.[54] Nozick and libertarians reject such limitations on personal freedom as being paternalistic. As Nozick writes, "my non-paternalistic position holds that someone may choose (or permit another) to do to himself *anything*."[55]

Libertarians in this respect accept the theory of natural rights that asserts that liberty and property are independent of and prior to the establishment of the state. As Epstein states, "trespass is not wrong because the state prohibits it, it is wrong because individuals own private property." [56] At the same time, they reject natural law that might restrict the freedom of individuals or the free play of individuals within a market.

Libertarians, Markets, and Decentralization

Libertarians support free markets, not because they tend to maximize wealth, but because they emerge from the choices of free individuals. Whereas conservatives would allow the regulation of markets to achieve the greatest aggregate wealth, libertarians would only allow market regulation or the intervention of the state into markets when it was directly related to minimalist needs. As part of this desire to constrain the state, libertarianism suggests a particular spatial structure for government. As Nozick suggests, decentralized government is more congenial to human association and is closer to the state-of-nature circumstances that act as the model for generating property rights.[57] Such communities should support associations of like-minded people finding and consuming their own preferences.

Gordon Clark, however, suggests that this libertarian "imperative of decentralization" cannot stand alone; instead, it must be balanced by an "imperative of centralization" because of the need for individuals who are victimized by the community to appeal to a higher authority.[58] Under a libertarian regime (and a classical liberal one), communities give up their powers to higher levels of government in a process that mirrors the voluntary relinquishment of individuals of rights to the community. In this conception, instead of communities being granted powers by state or federal governments, it is the state or federal governments that are granted powers by localities. This strong version of home rule has generally not been accepted by the courts. In fact, U.S. localities have been forced to labor under the assumption, explicated in the Dillion Rule (named after Justice Dillion), that they exist only at the pleasure of state governments and that they possess only those powers that have been expressly delegated to them by the state government.[59]

Libertarians would argue that the imperative to centralization, like the voluntary relinquishment of rights by individuals, should only affect those minimal sets of powers that would logically and voluntarily be given up in a state of nature. Hence, libertarians like Epstein have been particularly critical of the New Deal and post-New Deal efforts to create a welfare state. All actions, especially those by the central government, that promote social welfare by taking property from some citizens and redistributing it in the form of social benefits to other citizens are in this view illegitimate.

While conservative and communitarian ideologies tend to give priority to and expand the public sphere of life so that it potentially dominates the private sphere, the libertarian ideology does just the opposite; it shrinks the public sphere and expands the private sphere of action so that the private arena potentially dominates the public one.

Classic Liberalism

Classic liberalism accepts many of the assumptions of libertarian theory: the primacy of the individual and of human freedom, the importance of natural rights, and the need to constrain the power of the state through a system of full, but not absolute, private property rights.[60] Where classic liberalism differs from libertarianism is in its acceptance of natural law as it relates to issues of human dignity and welfare and in its belief in the need for an equilibrium between the private and public spheres of human freedom.

Classical Liberals and New Property

Where Nozick, Epstein, and other libertarians reject the Lockean notion of the inalienability of some property rights, classic liberals accept that there are essentially two types of property: the kind of property such as landed property that can be alienated, and the kind of property such as one's life or liberty that cannot be alienated even if one so desired. Additionally, classic liberals draw heavily on Adam Smith's idea that the state can rightfully intervene in markets to establish or maintain human dignity. Hence, classic liberals concern themselves not only with the rights of those with tangible property to alienate or dispose of that property as they see fit, but also with the broader, more abstract, and inalienable property rights of those who may not own any real estate. In this respect, Charles Reich's argument for a type of "new property" could fall into the classic liberal tradition. Reich believes that in the modern world, the concept of property as a secured part of a bundle of rights should no longer be applied to land-based property alone, but instead should be extended to the more dominant forms of property in the modern age—entitlements from large institutions. Entitlements such as job security and welfare, Reich thinks, should be given the same level of protection as has traditionally been given to landed property. Critics of Reich's argument believe that he may have stretched the idea of property rights too far, especially since there is a danger that property in entitlements from large institutions might forge a new feudal-like dependency under the guise of property rights.

As an alternative to the creation of new property, more mainstream classic liberals such as Michael Levy suggest that Locke's proviso about possession of property (that "enough as good be left in common for others"[61]) be revived in the modern world. Such a revival would take the form of mechanisms, such as extensive public education and training opportunities, that act to create equal opportunities to earn or create property.[62] Property that was earned in this manner would recapitulate the earning involved in the first possession of property and therefore would constitute a right that did not require dependency.[63]

In classic liberalism, individual liberty is the primary value, but as this liberty is broadly conceived as being liberty in both a public and private realm, the institutions of democracy and a free market are crucial to the realization of liberty, but still secondary to the basic value of freedom itself.[64] Private property obviously protects autonomy and liberty, but it can also be argued that in capitalist economies, it magnifies human differences and reduces the number of autonomous centers of power. As Madison warned in "Federalist No. 10," "the most common and durable source of factions has been the various and unequal distribution of property."[65] By "factions" Madison is referring to citizens who are united by a common passion that is adverse to the community.

Modern observers have added to Madison's insight by suggesting that liberty is endangered directly by the reduction in the relative liberty of the majority of people who own little or no property, and indirectly "by generating irrational attempts to restore equality."[66] Capitalist democracy undermines the social context of the balance between the public and private realms in which the values of classic liberalism are easily generated and maintained. Inequality in material standing will tend to divide the citizenry between those for whom the private sphere seems oppressive and oligarchic and those for whom this sphere represents the ultimate in positive personal freedom. The former group will tend to see the public realm as being more desirable and more democratic, while the latter will tend to see the public realm as a mere extension of private freedoms. Classical liberalism stands against both of these tendencies and maintains that the public and private realms must be kept in balance. In this regard, if the market is inadequate to provide the material prerequisites of basic human dignity, such as food, shelter, medical care, and education, government action to provide for these goods is tenable within the bounds of classic liberal philosophy. Similarly, public action to balance private sector coercion is also legitimate.

Classic Liberalism and the Moral Sense

Classic liberalism draws on the kind of knowledge we would gain by using economic concepts to enhance our analysis of social policy, but it also asks that we complement this knowledge with moral judgment. Moral discourse, in turn, helps us to interpret our experiences and our natural sense of merit and propriety, and to forge from this dialogue some general rules of social morality.[67]

Classic liberals, in contrast to libertarians or conservatives, would not object to government action to assist those who are ill-housed; however, they would apply a market analysis to determine if a proposed policy was the most efficient means of reaching a moral objective. Application of market principles would suggest to many classic liberals, for example, that housing vouchers would be preferable to rent control or public housing as a means of providing shelter to those who do not have it. Rent control and inclusionary zoning, they would assert, discourage the production of rental housing and often result in benefiting individuals who are not the targets of the housing goal.[68] Public housing would be rejected because its monopolistic characteristic—one type of housing fits all—provides less utility and satisfaction for those receiving the benefit than could be obtained through use of vouchers. Because utility is defined as an individual function and community (beyond voluntary contractual associations) has no independent value in classic liberal ideology, market-based schemes would generally be favored by classic liberals.

The policy instruments of classic liberal thought are well known to most Americans under the rubric of federalism. The mechanisms of federalism were particularly designed to deal with the paradoxes of power and control. The key paradox for classic liberals is related to the need to maintain individual (private) autonomy and the ability to join in shared (public) activity. These paradoxes, as Charles Handy notes, also include: "the need to make things big by keeping them small; to encourage autonomy but within bounds; to combine variety and shared purpose, individuality and partnership, local and global, tribal, region and nation state, or nation state and regional bloc."[69] Federalism is composed of a number of key principals, including: (1) subsidiarity or the placement of power at the lowest point; (2) interdependence or the deliberate spreading of power; (3) dual citizenship, or being a citizen of more than one level of government; (4) development of common or general standards, regulations, language, and currency (broadly speaking, currency refers to agreement about units of measurement that will be used to describe the "good" and "ills" of social organization—in terms of land-use issues, for example, it may be useful to attempt to develop some common measures of the value of a locally unwanted land use); and (5) separation of powers, which implies that management (executive powers), monitoring (interpretative powers), and governance (rule-making powers) occur in segregated units.[70]

Classic Liberalism and Legal Rules

The philosophy of classic liberalism is built on the pessimistic assumption that "men are not angels" and that power therefore needs to be fragmented into various boxes of separate and overlapping functions and separate realms of interest (that is, public versus private), all of which need to be balanced against each other.[71] This diffusion and separation of powers helps explain why classic liberals prefer legal rules to standards. Governance policy and rule making in classic liberal thought properly belong to the legislative branch of government. The rules that are created out of the dialogue among representative legislators form the heart of democratic (or more correctly, republican) values. These democratically created rules provide concrete guidance to administrators who function to carry out the will of the people and to judges who interpret within the narrowest boundaries how the rules apply to specific contexts. If judges were to apply standards to specific contexts instead of rules, classic liberals argue, they would be overstepping their authority because they would in essence be creating law. Because judges are typically not elected or at least not elected to carry out this function, replacing rules with standards would have a substantial anti-democratic effect. While classic liberal thought prefers rules to standards, it makes a distinction between general rules and specific ones. General rules, liberals believe, have advantages over standards with regard to maintenance of individual rights and spheres of power. Specific rules have no such advantage and can even represent a more dangerous form of anti-democratic governance. Specific rules and regulation are those that apply only to some individuals, some contexts, or some areas. Zoning that is site-specific, subsidies that apply only to specific projects rather than to a whole class of projects, or public-private partnerships that are not open to all comers are examples of specific rules.

In contrast, general rules are those that can be supported and easily understood by a majority of citizens and that tend to apply to citizens across the board. Special interest legislation would generally not result in general rules, and a workable set of general rules could be overwhelmed by a plethora of special interest laws that make it difficult for citizens to know the general rules. In terms of land-use issues, general rules could include, for example, generalized cluster or performance zoning, the allocation of public resources to general purpose items such as streets, sewers, parks, and education and training facilities. General rules also imply limitations on the ability to change the rules to favor particular persons or groups. For example, zoning variance procedures under a general rules society would be eliminated or severely restricted. The issue of general versus specific rules will be treated in more detail in a later part of this book.

IDEOLOGY, INSTITUTIONAL IMPROVEMENT, AND THE DESTRUCTION OF HABITAT

Ideology in Context

The four basic ideologies described in this chapter are obviously ideal types. Many citizens do not possess or follow any one coherent ideology. However, citizens' views tend to cluster around one or more of these ideologies, and justifications for public action, especially judicial ones, are usually couched, if only implicitly, in the language of one of these philosophical systems. Hence, these ideologies have practical consequences, influencing judicial decision-making and public policy.

Although classic liberalism formed the original bedrock of a peculiarly American form of governance and property ideals, the emergence of these other competing ideologies have measurable historical roots. Conservative ideology in a number of forms has flourished among those who have been the "winners" in American society. Conservative property rights emphasize the positive capabilities of unleashed capital, especially as capital is protected by a state that is interested in achieving a viable and important place in the international order. In the aftermath of world wars and cold wars, conservative theory is given greater credence as part of an overall effort to create a secure state. Similarly, the roots of communitarian ideology can be found in the reaction to severe social dislocation caused by failures of laissez-faire economic systems to protect basic features of community life. Karl Polanyi has noted, for example, that as soon as the neoclassical or laissez-faire economic market had essentially been established through a combination of legislative acts (such as England's Enclosure Acts) and reinterpretation of common law (for example, to allow for capitalists to build factories without concern for pollution or the use of child labor), English society attempted to protect itself. Parliament enacted legislation to protect public health and safety and to provide for education, housing, and improved factory conditions.[72] Although these early attempts to protect the community were conducted without reference to a coherent ideology, the continual, if more evolutionary, assault of competitive markets on communities has led to a number of more ideologically coherent reactions. A large body of sociological work, for example, has argued somewhat persuasively that twentieth-century urbanization and mobility in the United States in particular have so changed social relations that community, as a phenomenon separate from transitory and instrumental associations has disappeared.[73] In the terms of Ferdinand Tonnies' famous distinction between Gemeinschaft and Gesellschaft, social relations over time have moved from intimate, community-based solidarity to impersonal, market-mediated, social aggregations.[74] The argument in the first chapter of this book suggests that urbanization by itself need not destroy community, but that when urbanization is combined with hyper-mobility and land-use planning that fosters homogenous, single-purpose, large-scale development, such destruction is difficult to avoid. The search for community has been multipronged and has resulted in every form of utopian visioning, from a nostalgic desire to revive craft-oriented and royalist communities to various forms of socialist, Marxist, and Maoist states. Marxian critiques of the dynamics of capitalism have provided ideological weight to much of the reaction against classic liberalism. While the specter of actual Soviet-style socialism appeared to diminish the desire of many in the West to experiment with rigid communitarian models, it did induce a number of social thinkers to begin to consider with more seriousness how communitarian values and structures could be instituted without undermining important individual freedoms.

Finally, libertarian ideology originated in a reaction to the rise of the large bureaucratic state that seems to have accompanied modernism (and especially the building of national security mechanisms). Libertarian sentiment, based on the frontier mythic ideal of the self-made individual, has blossomed as a coherent ideology most prominently in the constrained soil of a highly regulated economic landscape.

Ideological Appeal

Conservative ideology is ultimately limited in its appeal because it primarily rests not on a universal ideal of human association, but rather on a more narrow nationalism. This nationalism in the contemporary form of conservative thought is of rather shallow type, being based on the ideal of wealth-maximization. This ideal, as any scholar of religion can attest, cannot speak effectively to our larger moral or social nature or to our desire for liberty. Nonetheless, conservative ideologies will remain popular to the degree that nationalism is an effective rallying cry for economic and political elites.

On the other hand, libertarian and communitarian arguments are effective and potentially have deep, if not broad, appeal precisely because they address, though in obverse ways, weaknesses in the contemporary form of the classic liberal society. The libertarian ideology appeals to our desire to escape the false and instrumental "community" of a hyper-regulated economy and the political and discretionary use of state police powers. Data showing that as much or more of governmental subsidies goes to upper-middle class and wealthy citizens as goes to the poor are fodder for the libertarian argument that everyone, even the poor, would be better off if the state simply went out of business and let private citizens organize themselves.[75] In this regard, libertarians of an "anarcho-capitalist" variety have gone so far as to propose not entirely implausible schemes for the elimination of public police powers entirely in favor of private syndicate protection.[76] As will be explored in more detail in the next chapter, libertarians' cynical view of contemporary democracy is not without some justification.

Alternatively, and pointing to many of the same phenomena and experiences, communitarian ideology strikes a responsive chord precisely because the welfare regulatory liberalism that underpins much of contemporary social policy has left so many citizens isolated from each other in lifeworlds that are only bridged through money-mediated relations. Although market mechanisms can provide valuable measures of consumer satisfaction, these same mechanisms can do little to satisfy human needs for belonging to a productive and supportive community.[77] E. F. Schumacher has noted, for instance, that markets tend to equate everything with everything else, giving them a price and making them exchangeable. "To the extent that economic thinking is based on the market," Schumacher writes, "it takes the sacredness out of life, because there can be nothing sacred in something that has a price."[78] As the philosopher Hannah Arendt would argue, contemporary social policy that puts consumption first also tends to ignore a traditionally important aspect of humanity—homo fabricus, or man as creator.[79]

Liberalism and the Ecological Understanding

Additionally, the regulatory liberal state has emphasized a liberal tradition that excludes much of the classic liberal's moral sense of the limitation of markets. In this corrupted liberalism, both man and nature are identified as commodities that can be dissected, detached, and consumed in measurable, though regulated, quantities. In this respect, the understanding of natural ecology and constraints on environmental sustainability have provided added weight to a communitarian critique of liberalism. In ecological studies, nature is viewed as a complete system with interdependent parts; the dissection and detachment of any one part has the potential, in essence, of destroying or severely damaging the whole. This more holistic view of man and nature goes beyond the typical view of planning in liberal society. Planning in market-based societies is usually only thought to be justified upon proof of market failure, especially the type of market failure that is due to negative externalities. Such externalities occur when economic transactions, such as the production and sale of a cleaning agent, result in negative side effects (such as pollution of the air and ground near the factory where the agent is produced). Because markets do not typically reflect these side effects, planning, regulation, or even public control or ownership are commonly thought to be justifiable. (Some libertarians, however, believe that such market externalities can be readily handled through the courts after refinements in the law of nuisance. Environmentalists, however, believe that this is impossible because of the problems with legally proving causation when there are a number of contributors to the nuisance, such as when there is non-point pollution.) Most developments known for their NIMBY or LULU quality are thought to pose some degree of a negative externality, at least for persons whose residence or business adjoins the development in question. The noises, congestion, pollutions, disease, odors, and other nuisances that neighbors inflict on each other are all features of negative externalities that accompany development.

Land development and other economic activity can also have positive externalities. The private provision of basic research that will benefit the entire society is an oft-cited example of a positive side effect of individual economic activity. When the public at large cannot be excluded from the positive spillover of private economic activity, and when private individuals would therefore supply less of the desired good than is feasible or socially desirable, public intervention may be justified just as it is justified in cases of negative externalities. The intervention in the case of positive externalities is justified on the basis that the economic activity in question forms a "public" good. In economic terms these are goods that have substantial positive spillover effects and that cannot be packaged so that only paying consumers will reap the benefits and nonpayers will be excluded. National defense is the stereotypical public good. [80] In addition to clearly defined public goods, public finance economists have identified a number of goods that do not meet the public good criterion of excludability, but that nevertheless are thought to generate social benefits that are not easily captured by the market. These goods are termed "merit goods," and education is often cited as a merit good in that it is the kind of good that, though it can be packaged so as to exclude others, has positive spillover effects and may not be privately consumed in quantities that would result in optimal levels of total benefit.

Classic liberals (and most conservatives) have little trouble with public planning and market intervention in cases of clearly defined public goods (that are non-excludable) or spillover effects that are diffuse in nature (that is, that cannot be easily attributed to any one or a few parties). However, following the logic of methodological individualism, classic liberals are extremely circumspect in their definition of cases that merit public intervention. First, liberals would tend to agree with libertarians that many cases of market failure of the negative externality type can be handled perfectly well through private negotiation between neighbors. That is, if property rights are well delineated, a property owner whose use of her property causes a nuisance will typically agree to pay the neighbor who is unjustly victimized by the nuisance a payment sufficiently large to avoid recourse to the courts. A residual number of hard cases will reach the court for final settlement.

If a settlement is not possible between neighbors, liberals of the public-choice school of thought would place a further hurdle before those who would call for public intervention.[81] Public-choice liberals argue that there needs to be a test to ensure that public intervention does not cost more (in terms of regulatory cost or lost efficiency) than the original market failure. The proper test, they suggest, would be for individual citizens to choose among and between a variety of public or local, state, and regional governments. By "voting with their feet," citizens would individually determine if the public intervention (or set of interventions) in question were worth the cost. The state, it is believed, should support numerous localities and public associations, such that individuals would be allowed choices. Through their freedom of travel, citizens would gravitate toward the localities that in their view represent the best value in terms of providing for public goods and controlling negative externalities.[82]

Mobility, Ideology, and Institutional Improvement

A key assumption being made by public-choice theorists is that mobility is both possible and desirable. As was argued in the first part of this book, mobility after a certain point may have system effects on the built environment and indirectly on social welfare that overwhelm whatever short-term benefits are achieved through choosing the jurisdiction that best meets one's needs. Albert O. Hirschman has succinctly articulated the dilemma of mobility in his classic work on "Exit, Voice, and Loyalty." According to Hirschman, dissatisfaction with organizations and governments can be articulated in two basic ways: through "exit" from the organization, or through giving "voice" to dissatisfaction. These two modes of organizational development and progress have different features, but are nevertheless intertwined in fundamental ways. Exit, in Hirschman's view, is an inherently unsatisfactory way to promote progress because it is generally lacking in informational content; exit communicates the fact of dissatisfaction, but not the reason. Voice, on the other hand, can communicate information-rich messages that can therefore become the basis for sensitive, strategic, and efficient change and development. Whereas exit signals the need for a change, the lack of information in the signal could lead to change in the wrong direction. Voice is less likely to lead to such perverse results.[83]

While voice has some superior qualities, it can be a weak or ineffective instrument for governmental improvement if exit is not also a credible threat.[84] At the same time, if exit is made too easy, citizens will be less inclined to use their "voice" option to effect improvements in the organizational environment. Hence, Hirschman recommends that public policy be concerned about developing some mechanisms for establishing loyalty within governmental organizations.

In terms of the ideological categories delineated in this chapter, Hirschman's explications of the dynamics of "exit, voice, and loyalty" suggest a rough correspondence of "exit" with liberal and libertarian approaches, "voice" with communitarian approaches, and "loyalty" with conservative approaches to law and economics. Overall, Hirschman's dynamic model of governance suggests that no single ideological viewpoint is sufficient to contain a full understanding of the conditions for organizational amelioration of the human condition. This line of reasoning will be picked up later in a discussion of hybrid ideologies. What Hirschman's work suggests for the current argument, however, is that the "exit" option by itself and the hyper-mobility that it implies is probably not desirable in a number of contexts.

Specifically, developing governance structures and policy that support "exit" as the primary choice for human behavior and association is suspect in several situations identified by public finance economists. First, when the citizen-consumer is unaware of the alternatives and their consequences, multiple and continuous "exit" can lead to general chaos rather than to rational choice. The argument here suggests that public-choice concepts perhaps assume a kind of knowledge on the part of citizens to understand and choose governmental jurisdictions as one would choose which fruit or clothes to buy. The more realistic view suggests that the number of factors in the choice are too great to include in any decision-making equation; rather than choice, citizens will tend to "satisfice" within the bounds of limited knowledge.[85] A potentially more efficient alternative to choosing among jurisdictions would be to reform the government of which one is a member; "exit" options that are too easy undermine this alternative. Some observers would argue that the liberal emphasis on easy "exit" may be one of the causes of a crisis of legitimacy in contemporary democracy. According to this argument, "exit" and mobility are being subsidized through personal and business deductions for job-related moves. As more people move more often, they have fewer ties to any one community and are therefore less likely to participate in democratic institutions in general and in local politics in particular. The evidence for such a decline in community-level democracy can be seen in the extremely low turnout for local government elections.

The larger, more generally communitarian, critique of the dominance of the "exit" option is that exercise of this option is based on the ownership of resources sufficient to allow exit from one community and re-entry into another. As with all market transactions, "exit" rewards those who have sufficient resources to pull up roots in one place, explore a number of alternative locations, and still have resources left over to purchase a new residence in another place. Over time, as is evident in the United States residential mosaic, the wealthy will cluster in new, amenity-rich, but homogenous enclaves, while the poor are relegated to the housing and residences that have been left behind.[86]

Exit and the Destruction of Habitation

At an even more general and more important level, near-exclusive reliance on "exit" or market mechanisms would be especially problematic if we were to discover that the destruction (creative or otherwise) wrought by markets is not simply an outcome of negative externalities, but is built into the very operations of large-scale, supposedly self-regulating, markets themselves. Karl Polanyi argues this very point. He suggests, and more recent anthropological work tends to confirm, that liberal approaches to law and economics are based on what he terms an economistic fallacy: the mistaken idea that human beings innately behave as economizing agents and would act in ways consistent with utilitarian values even if they lived in non-market-based societies. Polanyi's anthropological studies suggested to him that far from being a typical economic mechanism, markets have been the exception in economic history, and the situations where markets were the dominant mechanism were fewer still. Polanyi pointed out that the "great transformation," from non-market feudal estates to accumulative capitalism seen in modern Western society, was unprecedented in history precisely because it entailed a well-planned effort to work around and undermine existing community-based economies. "The road to the free market was opened and kept open by an enormous increase in continuous centrally organized and controlled interventionism," Polanyi wrote.[87] To Polanyi, there was substantial irony in economies being substantially planned products of state action. These market systems, as the supposed natural and best reflection of inherent human character, should have evolved naturally and universally, but instead appeared forced and planned.[88]

In his critique of market-dominated economies, Polanyi made two important points, one of which is especially relevant to our understanding of land use and property. His first point is that the introduction of markets into society was planned not simply as a way to determine the appropriate price of cloth or cheese, but also as a way to create an autonomous and self-regulating system for the entire society.

The market would allocate all resources in society and would in the course of its operation "clear itself," making efficient use of these resources. However, this pure and efficient operation of the market would occur if and only if labor and land were also included in the goods that were to be treated as commodities for sale.

For Polanyi, this acceptance of land and labor as commodities did not seem reasonable because commodities are by definition objects that are produced for sale, but land (nature) and labor (human life) are obviously not commodities. Polanyi wrote, "Labor is only another name for human activity which goes with life itself, which in turn is not produced for sale but for entirely different reasons, nor can that activity be detached from the rest of life, be stored or mobilized."[89] When labor is made into a commodity, Polanyi explained, it changes not only the life of an individual, but entire cultures, and usually in destructive ways. This destructive change occurs as the contexts for previously appropriate economic activities (such as the shared grazing of animals) are eliminated. The dislocation, job insecurity, dismal working conditions, alienation, and "natural rates of unemployment" that characterize modern capitalist economies, Polanyi would argue, are not simply market externalities but are instead inherent in the very possibility of a self-regulating market.[90]

Polanyi points out that just as human labor is not logically or legitimately viewed as a commodity, land is also something that is of a different quality than what we would normally consider a commodity. "Land," Polanyi writes, "is only another name for nature, which is not produced by man."[91] The treatment of land as a commodity, like the treatment of labor, tends to detach land from an integral whole. Nature, for Polanyi as for many ecologists today, can only be understood as a whole system of relationships—the relationship with humans being only one of an interwoven complex of interdependencies. Polanyi suggests that isolating nature and forming a market from it is "perhaps the weirdest of all undertakings of our ancestors."[92] It is weird, Polanyi suggests, because land, like human nature, can fulfill a number of vital functions beyond the narrow economic one laid out in a system of tradable property rights. Polanyi explains that land can provide some stability in a person's life, a place for habitation, a basis for physical safety and food production, a landscape for contemplation, and so forth. In classic liberal terms, Polanyi would argue that commodification of land would undermine some of the basis for human dignity. Most classical liberals, however, would argue that this dignity could be restored in one of two ways: by giving the market's victims a portion of the stream of added wealth created as a result of societywide adoption of a self-regulating market; or by providing these victims with some "new property" in the positions or benefits created by large capitalist institutions, as Charles Reich has suggested.

Polanyi's rhetoric suggests that this monetary compensation for the loss of direct rights to nature would be insufficient. He, like many an environmentalist in his wake, raises the specter of market allocations of land and nature ultimately leading to such things as the denudation of forests and severe dust bowls created by erosion of the soil. Empirical evidence on this point is mixed but generally supports Polanyi's fears. Studies of American private sector forestry and agriculture report that private sector stewardship of the land has not been entirely insensitive to the long-run economic values of land as a renewable resource (for example, a comparison of United States private forestry operations and Canadian public sector ones suggests that private owners may even be less likely to ignore the long-term economic value of the land than their public sector counterparts).[93] However, this sensitivity appears to extend only to the narrow economic qualities of land renewal designed for economically productive activity. That is, market systems may provide ample incentives for reforestation of property with a single species of tree designed to meet the needs of the forestry industry, but such systems will be much less likely to support the maintenance of land as a mixed habitat for wildlife, as a source of genetic variation, or as a stable buffer against the vulnerability of monocultures to ecological disasters. The value of these more complex relationships and long-term interdependencies is given short shrift in market-dominated societies.

Additionally, dependency theories of capitalism would suggest that as capitalism has evolved into a world economic system, the full extent of environmental degradation will be felt primarily at the periphery of the world system, rather than at its core.[94] Evidence for this effect appears to exist in the substantial differences in environmental practices in Third World (periphery) nations when compared with First World (core) nations. Periphery nations are generally known to have less effective land-use and other environmental controls than do core nations. The superior wealth of these core countries allows them to be able to purchase both consumer goods and environmental goods.

As Ernest Sternberg has pointed out, the outstanding feature of Polanyi's thought is that "this conception of noncommodifiability emerges not from a pious humanistic wish, but from a plausible, historically grounded examination of the market economy. His analysis tells us that planning, policy, and design are often not only justified, but urgently required to protect and reconstruct the integrity of human life and its environment."[95]

Critics of Polanyi have suggested that his discussion of "habitation," or the integral relationship between human life and the environment, opens his work up to charges that it is simply another instance of crude organicism, or the belief that the world is one organic whole that should never be penetrated by persons acting individually or in their economic self-interests. The dangers of this view, Sternberg recounts, are the familiar dangers of the extreme versions of conservatism and communitarianism: a romantic view of national and native traditions, the diminishment of enlightenment values of personal dignity and responsibility, and the elitism of those (professional experts or native shaman) who alone can understand and interpret the organic whole.[96]

Sternberg defends Polanyi against these charges by pointing to Polanyi's separate treatments of the characteristics of labor and land. The implication for

Sternberg and for this argument is that Polanyi recognized particular characteristics of the whole as being somewhat unique domains with their own domain-specific features. As Sternberg concludes, Polanyi's conception of planning would allow us to seek out the "meaningful, technical, ecological, and morphological interrelationships" in the separate domains of "landscapes, ecosystems, urban form, community, technology, work, and industry." [97]

As a theoretical foundation for planning, Polanyi's work suggests a need, not to reject markets outright—he explicitly outlines a number of roles for the market in society, including as a guarantor of consumer choice, an allocator of resources, and means of accounting—but rather to understand the limits of markets as instruments of human freedom. Markets, for Polanyi, are like all social institutions: a means for both liberty and constraint. As Sternberg suggests, "Planning raises moral questions not because it introduces constraint where there was none, but because it shifts the balance of constraint."[98] As classic liberals would add, however, this planning needs to be justified, especially in terms of the balance between the private and public realms.

The next chapter reviews some of the particular features of contemporary land-use politics in terms of the balance between private and public power. In this review it is argued that while the power of the private and public sectors has grown due to industrialization, the overall balance of power between these two realms has shifted during the last century toward greater private sector control over the levers of public governance. The impact of this shift in the balance of power for land-use decision-making is explored.

NOTES

1. Nelson, Robert. (1988). "A Private Property Right Theory of Zoning." *The Urban Lawyer* 11:4:725.

2. Ibid., p. 715.

3. *Vickers v. Gloucester Township*, 37 N.J. at 266, 181 A.2d at 147 (1962).

4. Reich, Charles. (1964). "The New Property." *Yale Law Journal* 73:373-87.

5. Madison, James. (1906). "Property." *The Writings of James Madison*. Edited by G. Hunt. p. 101. Cited in Underkuffler, Laura. (1990). "On Property: An Essay." *The Yale Law Journal* 100:135.

6. Underkuffler, Laura. (1990). "On Property: An Essay." *The Yale Law Journal* 100:13.

7. Locke, John. *Second Treatise of Government* § 27 in *Two Treatises of Government*. (P. Laslett rev. ed., 1988) (3rd edn. 1698) (emphasis in the original) cited in Underkuffler, Laura. (1990). "On Property: An Essay," *The Yale Law Journal* 100:136.

8. Nelson, "Private Property Right," p. 202.

9. Locke, John. *The Second Treatise of Government* (1st edn. 1690).

10. Hobbes, Thomas. (1968). *Leviathan*. Harmondsworth, England: Penguin, p. 297.

11. Whyte, William H. (1970). *The Last Landscape*. New York: Anchor Books.

12. Leman, Christopher. (1987). "The Concepts of Public and Private and Their Applicability to North American Lands." In *Land Rites and Wrongs*, edited by Elliot Feldman and Michael Goldberg. Cambridge, Mass.: Lincoln Institute of Land Policy.

13. Goldberg, Michael. (1987). "Evaluating Urban Land Use and Development." In *Land Rites and Wrongs*, edited by Elliot Feldman and Michael Goldberg. Cambridge, Mass.: Lincoln Institute of Land Policy.

14. Unger, Roberto M. (1983). "The Critical Studies Movement." *Harvard Law Review* 96: 561-675.

15. Clark, Gordon. (1988). "Adjudicating Jurisdictional Disputes in Chicago and Toronto: Legal Formalism and the Urban Structure." In *Land Rites and Wrongs*, edited by Elliot Feldman and Michael Goldberg. Cambridge, Mass.: Lincoln Institute of Land Policy.

16. Ibid., p. 229.

17. Nelson, "Private Property Right," p. 203.

18. Ibid., pp. 168-69.

19. Ibid., p. 169.

20. Tushnet, M. (1983). "Following the Rules Laid Down: A Critique of Interpretivism and Neutral Principles." *Harvard Law Review* 96:871-927.

21. Malloy, Robin Paul. (1991). *Planning for Serfdom*. Philadelphia: University of Pennsylvania Press, pp. 61-83.

22. Ibid.

23. Ibid., p. 66.

24. Ibid., p. 68.

25. Ibid., p. 66.

26. Ibid., p. 68.

27. Ibid., p. 70.

28. Ristoratore, Mario. (1988). "Siting Toxic Waste Disposal Facilities: Best and Worst Cases in North America." In *Land Use Rites and Wrongs*, edited by Elliot Feldman and Michael Goldberg. Cambridge, Mass.: Lincoln Institute of Land Policy.

29. Personal interview with Bill Shiner, economic development planner, Vinson Institute of Government, University of Georgia, Athens, Ga.

30. Malloy, *Planning for Serfdom*, p. 70.

31. *Hawaii Housing Authority v. Midkiff*, 104 S.Ct. 2321 (1984).

32. Locke, John. *The Second Treatise of Government*, edited by T. Peardon. 1952. (1st edn. London: 1690). Indianapolis, Ind.: Bobbs-Merrill.

33. Barber, Benjamin R. (1984). *Strong Democracy: Participatory Politics for a New Age*. Berkeley : University of California Press; Bowles, Samuel, and Gintis, Herbert. (1986). *Democracy and Capitalism: Property, Community, and the Contradictions of Modern Social Thought*. New York : Basic Books; and Unger, Roberto M. (1975). and *Knowledge Politics*. New York : Free Press.

34. Alexander, Gregory S. (1989). "Dilemmas of Group Autonomy: Residential Associations and Community." *Cornell Law Review* 75:1-61.

35. Unger, *Knowledge*, pp. 561-675.

36. Cornell, Drucilla L. (1985). "Toward a Modern/Postmodern Reconstruction of Ethics." *University of Pennsylvania Law Review* 133:291.

37. Alexander, "Dilemmas," p. 33.

38. Ackerman, Bruce. (1980). *Social Justice in the Liberal State*. New Haven, Conn.: Yale University Press.

39. Malloy, p. 71.

40. Garber, Judith. (1990). "Law and the Possibilities for a Just Urban Political Economy." *Journal of Urban Affairs* 12:1:1.-15.

41. Cohen, Felix. (1954). "Dialogue on Private Property." *Rutgers Law Review* IX, pp. 357-87; Rose, Carol M. (1985). "Possession as the Origin of Property." *University of Chicago Law Review* 52:73-88. Mensch, Elizabeth, and Freeman, Alan. (1991). "Introduction." *Property Law* Vol. 1. New York: New York University Press.

42. Alexander, "Dilemmas," p. 52.

43. Habermas, Jurgen. (1987). *The Theory of Communicative Action, Vol. 2. Lifeworld and System: A Critique of Functionalist Reason*. (Thomas McCarthy, trans.). Boston, Mass.: Beacon Press.

44. Alexander, "Dilemmas," pp. 59-61.

45. Epstein recognizes that rules of first possession may vary because of custom and that first possession as a universal principle cannot be justified by reference to any objective facts or non-ethical premises. See Epstein, Richard. (1979). "Possession as the Root of Title." *Georgia Law Review* 13: 1221-43.

46. Epstein, Richard. (1992). "Property and Necessity." *Harvard Journal of Law and Public Policy* 13:1: 2-9. It should be noted that only a small minority of United States jurisdictions follow "tortious interference with economic advantage" doctrine in a manner that Epstein would likely consider sufficient.

47. Ibid., Epstein, p. 7.

48. Ibid., Epstein, p. 8.

49. Ibid., Epstein, p. 8.

50. *Andrus v. Allard*, 444 United States 51 (1979).

51. Epstein, "Possession," p. 1237.

52. Epstein is willing to concede that for property that has not been possessed, such as he resources on or beneath the ocean floor, it may be feasible and even desirable to employ other, more collectivist, concepts of property. This concession, however, is based on the fact that it is possible to begin with a blank slate.

53. Ibid., Epstein, p. 1239.

54. Andrew, Edward. (1985). "Inalienable Right, Alienable Property and Freedom of Choice: Locke, Nozick and Marx on the Alienability of Labour." *Canadian Journal of Political Science* 17:3:529-50.

55. Nozick, Robert. (1974). *Anarchy, State, and Utopia.* New York: Basic Books, p. 58.

56. Epstein, Richard. (1985). *Takings: Private Property and the Power of Eminent Domain.* Cambridge, Mass.: Harvard University Press, p. 6.

57. Clark, Gordon. (1988). "Adjudicating Jurisdictional Disputes in Chicago and Toronto: Legal Formalism and Urban Structure." In *Land Use Rites and Wrongs*, edited by Elliott Feldman and Michael Goldberg. Cambridge, Mass.: Lincoln Institute of Land Policy.

58. Ibid.

59. Garber, Judith. (1990). "Law and the Possibilities for a Just Urban Political Economy." *Journal of Urban Affairs* 12:1:1-15.

60. Malloy, pp. 16-60.

61. Locke, *Second Treatise*, Book II, Chapt. 27.

62. Levy, Michael B. (1983). "Illiberal Liberalism: The New Property as Strategy." *The Review of Politics* 45:576-94.

63. Mensch and Freeman, "Introduction," pp. xi-xxiv.

64. For a discussion of markets and freedom see Friedman, Milton. (1962). *Capitalism and Freedom.*

65. Madison, James. (1986). "Federalist No. 10." *The Federalist Papers.* Reprinted in *Classic Readings in American Politics*, edited by P. Nivola and D. H. Rosenbloom. New York: St. Martin's Press, p. 30.

66. Mensch and Freeman, "Introduction," p. xv. See also Baechler, Jean. (1980). "Liberty, Property, and Equality." *NOMOS* 22, 269-88.

67. See Malloy; Smith, Adam. *Moral Sentiments*, p. 264.

68. See discussion of inclusionary zoning in the first part of this essay, especially Ellickson's critique.

69. Handy, Charles. (1992). "Balancing Corporate Power: A New Federalist Paper." *Harvard Business Review* 70:6:59-73.

70. Ibid.

71. Madison, *The Federalist Papers*, especially No. 10.

72. Polanyi, Karl. (1957). *The Great Transformation* Boston: Beacon Press. Also, Sternberg, Ernest. (1993). "Justifying Public Intervention without Market Externalities: Karl Polanyi's Theory of Planning in Capitalism." *Public Administration Review* 52:2:100-09.

73. Bender, Thomas. (1982). *Community and Social Change in America.* Baltimore: John Hopkins University Press.

74. Tonnies, Ferdinand. (1988). *Community and Society.* New Brunswick, N. J.: Transaction Book. Alexander, "Dilemmas," pp. 1-61.

75. Howe, Neil, and Longman, Phillip. (1992). "The Next New Deal." *Atlantic* 269:4:88-105.

76. Friedman, David. (1989). *The Machinery of Freedom: Guide to Radical Capitalism.* La Salle, Ill.: Open Court.

77. Thurow, Lester. *Head to Head: The Coming Economic Battle Among Japan, Europe, and America.* New York: Murrow.

78. Schumacher, E. F. (1975). *Small is Beautiful—Economics as if People Mattered.* New York: Harper and Row. pp. 45-6.

79. Arendt, Hannah. (1965). *On Revolution.* New York: Viking Press.

80. See generally Stokey, Edith, and Zeckhauser, Richard. (1978). *A Primer for Policy Analysis.* New York: W. W. Norton. Haveman, Robert. (1976). *The Economics of the Public Sector.* Santa Barbara, Calif.: Wiley. For a discussion of merit goods, see Campbell, Richard, and Hepburn, Lawrence. (1992). "Educational Choice: Is it Really a 'Panacea' for What Ails American Schools?" *Kansas Journal of Law and Public Policy* (Summer):61-73.

81. Utilitarian legal theorists (usually of a conservative libertarian bent) similarly suggest a test for more than market failure per se is needed to justify public intervention. For example, Frank Michelman has suggested that prior to implementing regulations of land uses such as those involved in land zoning or building height limitation, a number of issues need to be considered in addition to the existence of the failure of private markets for restrictive covenants, including: settlement costs, the transaction costs of making compensation when "takings" occur, the demoralization costs to landowners who expected to be able to use the land in ways allow prior to the regulation, and the anxieties of landowners and productions losses occasioned by not compensating those with such expectations. See Fischel, William. (1988). "Utilitarian Balancing and Formalism in Takings." *Columbia Law Review* 88:8:1581-99.

82. Buchanan, James, and Tullock, Gordon. (1962). *The Calculus of Consent.* Ann Arbor, Mich.: University of Michigan Press. Mueller, Dennis C. (1979). *Public Choice.* Cambridge, England: Cambridge University.

83. Hirschman, Albert O. (1970). *Exit, Voice and Loyalty.* Cambridge, Mass.: Harvard University Press.

84. Marlow, Michael L. (1992). "Intergovernmental Competition, Voice and Exit Options and the Design of Fiscal Structures." *Constitutional Political Economy* 3:1:92.

85. Simon, Herbert. (1960). *New Science of Management Decision.* New York: Harper and Row.

86. Downs, Anthony. (1973). *Opening Up the Suburbs: An Urban Strategy for America.* New Haven, Conn.: Yale University Press. McDougall, Harold. (1985) "Regional Development: Who Gets the Short End?" In *Inclusionary Zoning Moves Downtown,* edited by Dwight Merriam, David J. Bower and Philip Bower. Chicago, Ill.: American Planning Association, pp. 57-82.

87. Polanyi, *Transformation,* p. 140.

88. Sternberg, "Justifying," p 103.

89. Polanyi, *Transformation,* p. 72.

90. Sternberg, "Justifying," p. 105.

91. Polanyi, *Transformation,* p. 72.

92. Ibid., p. 178. Cited in Sternberg, "Justifying."

93. Leman, Christopher K. (1988). "A Forest of Institutions: Patterns of Choice on North American Timberlands." In *Land Use Rites and Wrongs*, edited by Elliot Feldman and Michael Goldberg. Cambridge, Mass.: Lincoln Institute of Land Policy.

94. Wallerstein, Immanuel. (1991). *Geopolitics and Geoculture: Essays on the Changing World System.* New York: Cambridge University Press.

95. Sternberg, "Justifying," p. 106.

96. Ibid., p. 107

97. Ibid., p. 107.

98. Ibid., p. 108.

CHAPTER 3

Land-Use Politics

Ideological views of property rights provide an essential background for understanding the evolution of the politics of land use in America. Although our nation was founded on classic liberal ideals and institutions, the founders could not have predicted or planned for the changes wrought by massive industrialization, urbanization, the closing of the frontier, and the abolition of slavery. Whereas in the founder world, common law was adequate to address most land-use issues and disputes, the forces of change in the nineteenth and twentieth centuries rendered this generally private ordering of land use obsolete and unsatisfactory. More important, as this chapter explores, the delicate balance of private and public sector power conceived by the founders was upset by the rapid expansion and concentration of private sector power and resources. The expansion was due most directly to unprecedented growth in technological capability and private economic wealth, while the concentration was based on the establishment and development of a new legal entity, the corporation. One often-proposed means of redressing the imbalance of private and public power has been to place greater power at the national level. It is at this level, proponents of this strategy argue, that government can match the concentrated power and expertise of large corporate entities. This chapter explores this notion, by first examining the classic liberal or Enlightenment conception of self-regulating politics. The classic notion of self-regulating politics, I attempt to show, was not designed either to create good or virtuous government, as the Progressives sought, or to handle the contemporary reality of interest group influences on governmental processes. Specifically, I argue that at the national level and especially with respect to environmental land-use issues, the classic idea of politics as a balance of interests has been transformed and corrupted in part (and ironically) by the expectation that politics be conducted in a virtuous and rational manner. When the expectation that government be not just fair, but also good is combined with classic liberal political institutions that were not designed to fulfill this expectation and with the power of private interests to "create reason and information" designed to support their notions of "the good," a corrupted form of liberal governance—interest group liberalism—is created. The dynamics of interest group liberalism, I point out, have made governance of land-use issues untenable from the point of view of classic American or liberal ideals. While a contemporary alternative to the classic liberal organization of politics—European corporatism—exists and could work to right the contemporary imbalance of public-private power, I argue that this approach to the problem has disadvantages that would make it undesirable as an alternative governance structure for controlling land use in the United States. Next, I examine how in the local politics of land-use planning, classic liberal, but specifically federalist ideas about the legitimate spheres of legislative, judicial, and administrative decision-making breakdown. Finally, I attempt to identify how the global forces of production and consumption affect our conceptions of land-use rights in the contexts of local, national, and global politics and markets.

SELF-REGULATING POLITICS AND THE IDEAL OF VIRTUE

The Enlightenment ideal of a self-regulating market in the private realm had its public sector counterpart in a conception of politics as a delicate balancing of interests and powers. As the short review of classic liberalism suggested, this balancing was accomplished through a separation and overlap of governmental powers between and among branches and levels, and an insulation of the public sphere from the private. Most Enlightenment proponents of this self-regulating system did not have any illusions as to politics ever being either a product or producer of human virtue. Rather, they thought and assumed the opposite—that men would "not be angels" and that "factions," or groups dedicated to achieving their individual or special interests, would abound.[1] They did believe, however, that a political system with these balancing features might be able to prevent a natural, and according to the ancients, a fated devolution of democracy into tyranny, even though citizens might in many cases remain creatures of self-interest.[2] The founders invoked traditional classic liberal ideas for constraining the tendency of democracy to devolve into tyranny; that is, they designed institutions so as to separate power among levels and branches of government and to check the powers of one branch or level with overlapping power in another branch or level. Because power could not be easily concentrated in this institutional system, it was believed that adversarial private sector interests could and should remain free to form various coalitions. Over time, it was thought that all the participating parties would join winning coalitions and achieve some satisfaction; in the meantime, protection of individual rights as well as the expectation of today's winners eventually being on the losing end of a majoritarian decision would hold temporary majority factions in check. The classic liberal model of politics also mimicked the market in that the participants, like market participants, did not necessarily have to be rational, or altruistic or act in the public interest for the decisions to have a legitimacy. This classic liberal mechanism, like Adam Smith's market, did not depend on the existence of virtue, and even assumed the opposite, in order to work.

The fact that the American version of self-regulating politics was designed to operate without having to remake citizens into models of virtue is often lost on contemporary Americans. This is the case because at least since the Progressive Era, Americans have been increasingly demanding that their political leaders and procedures be virtuous in nature. The explicit interest-based deal-making of the log-rolling, you-scratch-my-back, I'll-scratch-yours, variety has ceased to be the dominant mode of political discourse and has been replaced instead by a conception of politics as an arena where competing rationales battle for their rightful place on the policy agenda. Reform-minded Progressives and their heirs have been effective in exposing the dirty little secret that legislative politics is not clean. What these reformers ignored, however, was the key insight of the Founding Fathers—that the effort to clean up politics and to create virtue in the land would only lead to a different type of corruption, one that in the French and Russian revolutions led to the overwrought, zealous, and holier-than-thou reigns of terror by citizen-bureaucrats, Robespierre and Lenin. Virtue, like beauty, would seem at first to be a trait universally recognized, but in most cases virtue, like beauty, is defined in the eye of the beholder. An emphasis on virtue in politics ultimately results in the reign of some subjective or even personal view of "the right" that is disguised in the clothes of a universal rationale. Briefly put, an over emphasis on virtue in politics is often the precursor of tyranny. For the Founders, virtue might or might not arise from democratic debate, but tyranny would surely not arise from the combat of ever shifting alliances among factions. Moreover, in the classic liberal structures of governments, virtue need not be a universal quality, but like the powers of government, could be divided into separate domains of virtue. Hence, the virtues of action and obedience would be nurtured in the executive branch, judgment and fairness in the judicial branch, and imagination and craftsmanship in the legislative branch. Each of these virtues, if taken too far or if raised to the status of the universal virtue, could themselves become the basis for tyranny. If illuminated either in part or in whole, the workings of these separate virtues with and against counterpoised virtues would never result in a particularly pretty or virtuous whole. The old saw about the imprudence of watching either sausages or legislation being made is an apt metaphor for the essential unvirtuousness of democracy. Contrary to fashionable and modern views of democracy, more sunlight or public exposure of the inner workings of democracy by itself may not be the best treatment for the "corruption" of the system, especially if the power to bring light to bear on the situation is held by only a few citizens, and the effect of sunshine is to create repulsion and avoidance rather than empathy and understanding of the flaws of democracy.[3]

An argument can be made that the Progressive reform agenda, the scholarship of a number of realist schools of thought, the muckraking tradition of journalism, and the movement for openness and sunshine in government have all had a somewhat perverse and unintended effect of undermining faith in democratic politics while simultaneously magnifying the political power of those who hold the torch and offer to wield the scalpel. The exposure of corruption, deal-making, and irrationality in politics during the Progressive Era resulted in a call for a different kind of politics, one that is driven by information, expert analysis, substantive debate, and rational policymaking. To accomplish this, professionals would need to be brought into government at all points, both to forge policy that was economically efficient and to manage the implementation of this policy in a businesslike fashion.[4] Although Progressives maintained the traditional separation between the policymaking branches of government and the administrative branch, rational, unsentimental, information-driven decision-making by professionals was the dominant mode of action in both branches.[5] The "good government" movement begun by the Progressives has been carried on by a number of those who believe in the possibility of creating a virtuous politics. In the area of land-use control, "planning" and the scientific objectivity of the professional planner have represented this movement toward information-driven decision making.[6] In contrast to the politics of factions outlined by the Founders and fueled by creative exchanges of political resources, the politics of virtue is fueled by information and the goal is the creation of a policy ideal that best fits the informational inputs.

The difficulty with virtue-oriented politics is that information is not a free good, and when it is generated by paying customers, it is rarely neutral. William Greider, who has chronicled the rise of an information-based politics in environmental issues, suggests that while the early reformers wanted to bring sunshine and rationality to politics, and had noble and progressive goals, the nature of information politics generally dictates that an information elite will be advantaged by this form of politics. For Greider, the change from a back-room politics by deal-makers to a back-room governance by experts has not necessarily been an advantageous one, especially when expertise is heavily subsidized by powerful corporations and interest groups. The Progressive movement's tools of information and neutral expertise, Greider asserts, are themselves a commodity that the wealthier and more powerful interests in society have a particular advantage in producing. In addition to experience in employing professional marketing techniques, these interests, Greider notes, are provided substantial subsidies in the form of business and other tax deductions for research, education, and public policy lobbying. As a consequence, governments, especially at the federal level, are now surrounded by the sponsored intelligence of private America.[7]

With respect to local zoning and public development, the movement from political decision-making based on bargaining among interests to decision making by expert planners has been well chronicled. For example, Robert Caro has described in detail how Robert Moses, the former head of a number of public development authorities in New York, was able to successfully impose his development plans on communities that did not want them. Moses was successful because he essentially controlled the generation and flow of information and expertise on numerous public development projects. Only when Moses attempted to impose one of his development plans on a more affluent Central Park neighborhood was his control of information and expertise challenged.[8]

However, governance of local zoning issues often involves, in addition to the potential for "sponsored information," another type of problem—the generation of irrelevant information. That is, observers who have compared actual land uses to those that were planned for the land in question have noticed that much of the information generated for land-use planning quickly becomes operationally irrelevant. In essence, the comprehensive land-use plans that are generated by local governments are often ignored when it comes to the actual passage of zoning ordinances. As Robert Nelson has argued, these plans are created because of the legal requirement that professional planning undergird zoning actions. As one of the authors of the 1924 Standard State Enabling Act has stated, "Justification of a zone plan . . . comes from the fact that those who made the plan made it purposely, and more or less scientifically and organically."[9] As with other information- and expert-based policymaking, professional land-use planning has generally been used as a means of sustaining the legal fiction that zoning ordinances are based solidly on rational comprehensive planning. The planning theory of zoning, then, has provided municipalities the camouflage they needed to continue to practice whatever type of zoning they liked without judicial interference and without excessive citizen complaints or participation. After the production of a comprehensive plan, the average citizen may have a sense of achievement but is usually unaware that "comprehensive plans are more often than not disregarded."[10] Scientific planning and the application of information, in addition to being subject to corrupt influences, can act to deceive the public into believing that the greater good has been considered in decision making.

The Cost of Entrance

Another unintended effect of the open and good government movement has been an increase in the cost of entry into politics. This increased price of admission involves not only the price of lobbying an ever more open legislative process, but also influencing the supposedly uninfluenceable administration of policy by the executive branch. As "realist" scholars and journalists uncovered unvirtuous back-room deals, they also exposed another dirty secret of modern bureaucratic government: Politics and policymaking do not stop at the voting booth or even at the doors of the legislative chambers. Instead, political decisions of who gets what, when, and how are also likely to take place within the back rooms of the massive and complex bureaucracies and in the deliberations of supposedly neutral and bipartisan blue-ribbon commissions. These alternative arenas for politics are clearly a phenomenon that classic Enlightenment liberals did not anticipate. The size of the executive branch during the late eighteenth and early nineteenth century was such that there were few difficulties with legislative oversight.[11] With the rise of the administrative or bureaucratic state, all this changed.

As numerous historians have noted, large-scale public bureaucracies arose in an environment where economic and technological factors and military security interests dictated a substantial increase in the scale and scope of all enterprises, both public and private.[12] While it would be comforting to believe that the administrative and regulatory state arose as a public sector counter to the increased scale of private sector power, this was not the case. Instead, much of the regulatory apparatus of the administrative state was created at the behest of and to the advantage of large-scale corporate interests.[13] As Karl Polanyi might have noted, the community of corporate interests could not stand a true laissez-faire market system. The close-knit relationship between regulatory agencies and the groups being regulated has been observed by a number of scholars who now speak of "iron triangles" and "subgovernments" dominating public policymaking.[14] These subgovernments are composed of bureaucracies, interests groups, and a congressional committee or subcommittee that exchange contributions, information, resources, rulings, and assistance (such as with constituent complaints) and form cozy relationships of mutual dependency. Policymaking that takes place within these triangles often is at variance with the larger, more general interests of citizens who are not part of the interest group being regulated. While average citizens might have some chance of influencing their own legislator, the cost of entering into subgovernment politics is far beyond the resources of the average American.[15]

Moreover, as the logic of collective action suggests, even if average citizens could muster the time and resources to enter into subgovernment policymaking, the expected gain from engaging in each political battle within each subgovernment would often be too small to induce average citizens to do so. Simultaneously, if such citizens were to enter into subgovernment policymaking, the regulated interests would likely raise the entrance ante of spending on information, expert testimony, campaign contributions, and the like.[16]

The dynamics of subgovernment governance are seductive and particularly corruptive of classical liberal ideals. They tend to "make conflict-of-interest a principle of government rather than a criminal act" and create "structures of power with impressive capacities to resist central political control."[17] This resistance is powerful because the public is often shut out of policymaking at the most crucial and creative "problem identification" phase.[18]

Instead of the classic liberal ideal of a small number of general laws that apply to all citizens and that can be readily understood by most citizens, subgovernments tend to generate innumerable specific laws and rules that favor some interests. While each particular advantage may be only marginal in its effect on the overall public interest, the cumulative effect of numerous subgovernments can be substantial.[19] The most detrimental effect, however, is on democracy itself. When citizens discover that the government is not of, by, and for the people, but rather of, by, and for various subgroups of people, their faith in democracy is undermined, and their trust in the even-handedness of the law is destroyed.

Subgovernments and Lawlessness

Another key feature of the rule by subgovernments is a certain lawlessness. When law becomes so complex and detailed that its basic purposes, outlines, and features cannot be determined by average citizens, it begins to exist only in the realm of lawbooks, lawyers, and courts. While such an existence is not trivial and may be a feature of life in a complex, technologically sophisticated society, when taken to an extreme or raised to a public philosophy, it also tends to make the law appear arbitrary and obscure, belonging only to a special class of people.[20] Unfortunately, the dynamics of the political process make law by subgovernments, or even more narrowly by regulatory agencies or organized interest groups alone, a seductive option. The power of organized interest groups to administer to their own needs began somewhat modestly in areas such as agriculture, where the technique could appear to be justified as a means of decentralizing decision making. As Theodore Lowi explains, administration by organized groups involves "an ethical and conceptual mingling of the notion of organized private groups with the notions of 'local government' and 'self-government.' "[21]

Organized interest group governance offers an even more compelling seduction to legislators and public officials: It can help politicians avoid conflict more effectively by delegating substantial authority to regulatory bodies and their allied interest groups. Avoiding conflict allows politicians to appear more effective in their role as conflict resolvers and to avoid the wrath of constituents who might be the losers in any particular policy debate. William Greider quotes Representative Mike Synar of Oklahoma as saying,

> We [legislators] defer the tough decisions to the regulatory agencies. . . . The bureaucrats look at the legislative record and they can see the issues where we didn't want to make a decision. So they know they're in no hurry either. Why make a decision that will make the same people mad at them, if Congress did not want to make it? Then the lobbyists move in and overwhelm the agency. If a lobbyist sees he is going to lose in Congress, he'll say to us: "Let the agency decide." Then the regulatory side of his law firm will get another shot at it.[22]

The Vagueness Mechanism

The mechanism through which legislators devolve authority onto regulatory agencies is vague, malleable, or even hollow law. In essence, legislators pass the buck to executive branch agencies, but in doing so seem to offend no one. In local land-use actions, governmental boards instruct professional planners to keep comprehensive land-use plans at a very global level; these plans tend to be noncontroversial and to have few practical effects. Instead of confronting people with immediate and difficult choices, they focus on the distant future and establish little guidance on the decisions that will need to be made in the near term.[23]

If the regulatory agency or planning body uses its discretion to subsequently enact regulations that provide teeth to the enabling act, legislators can argue that they did not pass or vote for those regulations or that it was not their intention for the law to be used in that manner, and subsequently make a show of calling for oversight hearings or directly overriding the comprehensive plan. The idea of expert-driven policymaking—or specifically in land-use governance, the planning theory of community zoning—has maintained a life beyond the point that it can be reasonably defended. That is, planning theory can provide legislative justification and political cover for politicians who want to please landowning voters. It can also offer legal support to judges who might otherwise have to strike down zoning regulations as unconstitutional "takings" of property. However, the mere provision of political coverage and legal backing cannot easily sustain a process (that is, comprehensive planning) that is both costly and ultimately without political legitimacy.[24]

The typical case of vagueness in governance involves regulatory agencies generating only imprecise and often malleable regulations from the vague laws that Congress or other governing bodies pass. As agency discretion is magnified, rule by law and the classic liberal notion of general rules are further undermined. Greider has characterized the resulting effort by interest groups to bargain for special treatment, for exclusion from a regulatory program, or for delay of the implementation of a law as a sort of "grand bazaar" in which law is bought and sold in agency and interest group board rooms. This represents a profound change from the classic liberal idea of political log-rolling as a necessary evil, but one to be confined to legislative branch negotiations. Such bargaining was justified because it eventually would result in clear, precisely worded general rules. However, in the world of interest group liberalism, market-like log-rolling as a style and mode of governance has been adopted as a universal good even by those branches of government for which this style is inappropriate.[25]

The effect of this type of regulatory regime on environmental land use in the broad sense of the term has been substantial. Greider chronicles a number of these effects, including:

- the Inspector General's discovery that 80 percent of the EPA's case files on hazardous waste violations "showed no evidence that the violators had ever complied with the enforcement order."[26]

- the ineffectual governance of government-created wastes and locally unwanted land uses. The General Accounting Office estimates that federal agencies violate the clean water law at twice the rate of private industry. Even when federal facilities are operated by private corporations such as Westinghouse or General Electric, these companies have, until recently, been shielded from liability for pollution by having federal departments pay contractors' fines. As Greider concludes, "taxpayers have often been put in the position of underwriting violations of the law."[27]

- the continual delay in the enforcement of clean air laws, causing a Brookings Institute scholar to conclude that "it is possible that the entire [clean air] program has generated little reduction in air pollution."[28]

The Corporate Citizen

The lack of effective environmental law enforcement is particularly evident with respect to corporate violators. Known violators of environmental laws are often able to continue operations and to continue to receive tax deductions, limited liability protections, and other benefits afforded to law-abiding corporations. This phenomenon can be explained in part by the extension of full "citizenship" rights to corporations. Such consideration of corporations as persons has long been viewed among many legal scholars and historians as an anomaly in the law.[29] The legal basis for this extension of constitutional rights to corporations took place during the 1880s when the common law of nuisance was also being reinterpreted to favor the expansion interests of industrial capitalists.[30] It is impossible in this book to explore in depth all the problems and the social effects of this trend. However, it is possible to point to a major problem with accountability that has its origins in the "corporate citizen" doctrine. When an average citizen disobeys the law in a substantial manner, the sanctions that are applied include a revocation of many of the rights of citizenship. However, when a corporation is caught breaking laws, the sanctions are generally not so definite or predictable. Most often, corporations will offer the resignations or firings of the guilty executives and enter into consent agreements with the court to refrain from further wrongdoing. However, the corporation itself continues to possess all of its citizenship rights, including those that provide for lucrative tax deductions, credits, and liability limitations. Moreover, such law-breaking corporations are generally not restricted from winning government contracts. As Greider has documented, this slap-on-the-wrist deterrence strategy has been particularly ineffective in getting corporate "outlaws" to change their behavior. Part of the problem is traceable to a jurisprudence system that relies on individually identifiable guilt, rather than collective corporate responsibility. Corporate executives can always blame wrongdoing on individual employees, while escaping blame for corporate policies and incentive systems that induce employees to disregard the law.[31] Other cultures that have sanctioned the development of large corporate organizations as a necessary part of modernization and development have been more effective in limiting the potential for corporations to escape punishment. For example, in contrast to the American system of jurisprudence based on individual guilt, Japanese jurisprudence and corporate law and culture are based more on the maritime law principle of the "captain of the corporate ship" being responsible for all that takes place during his or her watch.

The ability of corporations to evade pollution control laws has been assisted by the federalist structure of American government. Because most of these violations are registered in a single locality or state, corporate transgressors of pollution-control law have been able to move operations or expand their market across jurisdictions to escape even the minor stings of punishment. This growing corporate lawlessness has not escaped the attention of environmentalists. In October 1993, the Western Organization of Resource Councils, for example, drafted a "Citizen's Guide to Bad Actor Laws" and has, along with other environmental groups, lobbied for passage of such "bad boy"[32] deterrents as (1) disbarment from governmental contracts of corporations that commit environmental crimes; (2) blocking of permits and licenses based on an examination of a corporation's past behavior or compliance record; and (3) complete dissolution of the corporation through revocation of the state's charter. Environmental groups have had some success in using existing "bad actor" laws and cite enabling mechanisms such as local "bad actor" ordinances in Palmer, Massachusetts, and Fort Bragg, California, sections of federal law such as 510(C) of the federal Surface Mining Control and Reclamation Act, state environmental laws such as Maryland's that allow easy permit blockage, and corporation statutes such as those in New Mexico that have fairly open-ended grounds for charter revocation.[33]

Acting to control corporate lawlessness is difficult in an environment characterized by interest group liberalism. For example, in 1989, the Justice Department drafted a set of more severe sentencing guidelines for corporate violators of federal law, but backed off from these after corporate lawyers brought political pressure through executive branch channels.[34] Additionally, the legal fiction of corporations acting in the capacity of citizens works to the advantage of those who would go to great lengths to hide or disguise their bad behavior. Tactics such as corporate name changing, ownership change, nesting ownership in a maze of holding companies, and using "contracting out" relationships to insulate the core of the company from responsibility are often used to frustrate those who would desire to rein in corporate lawlessness. Consequently, for "bad actor" laws to work, they will have to be combined with adequate disclosure requirements and sufficient resources dedicated to enforcement.[35] Unfortunately, competition among states to attract business headquarters has created pressure to reduce restrictions on corporations to a lowest common denominator.

Governance in an Interest-Group Liberalism Environment

To summarize, the existence of interest group liberalism works against the self-correcting nature of classic liberal conceptions of government for a number of reasons: (1) market principles of bargaining have been extended to domains of government (such as administration) where they are inappropriate and essentially undercut the separation of branches and powers that classic liberals believe is fundamental to effective constraint on tyranny; (2) interest group liberalism effectively undermines the classic liberal ideal of creating a broad legislative domain in which varied interests overlap, conflict, and bargain in the process of creating law. As Madison in "Federalist No. 10" suggested, factions should not be allowed to form and mature in isolation from each other, but instead should be forced into confrontation with one another; and (3) interest group liberalism creates such a plethora of specific law that it undermines the capacity of citizens or even skilled and experienced legislators to comprehend the law as an integral whole and to make adjustments according to a commonplace understanding of this whole. The complexity of this maze of specific law invites paralysis and dependence on interest group-produced information and expertise.

As Theodore Lowi points out, interest group liberalism is essentially a conservative mechanism, one that supports existing, powerful private sector interests in capturing, if not the whole ship of state, then the key, perhaps hidden, steerage mechanism of this ship and directing it to their own ends. Interest group liberalism is also similar to conservative ideology in that they both involve applying a single model for understanding, that is, a market-based model, to political governance structures where the model is inappropriate.[36]

The Lack of Criticism of Interest Group Liberalism

Communitarian critiques of interest group liberalism have been somewhat late in coming because many of the elements of interest group liberalism have been dressed up in communitarian rhetoric and practices. In many situations, for example, policymakers in the forefront of developing interest group liberalism would include legislative language explicitly recognizing group interests, including the interests of the "the poor," racial minorities, businesses, and so forth. This seeming thrust of interest group liberalism toward direct democracy and "citizen participation" has often not been recognized for what it is: an attempt to avoid the hard choices of power. As Lowi observes, many of the "citizen participation" clauses in modern legislation denote interest groups as the equals of government officials, even though representatives of these groups are rarely chosen democratically from among their membership, and the aggregate of all citizen representation is rarely balanced in terms of all the interests in society.[37]

For the most part, libertarians suggest that the problem that interest-group liberalism seems to present for democratic governance is an artificial one. They believe that if government did not extend beyond the minimalist state, the threat of interest group liberalism would be substantially diminished. Mancur Olson makes a libertarian-like argument when he contends that free-ranging interest groups will eventually nourish a bloated state. Such a state, he notes, will acts in numerous ways, including using its police and planning powers, to clog the arteries of the economic system. Over time and without a war or other interest group-destroying event, nations with ever higher political participation by interest groups will decline in terms of wealth-creating capabilities relative to other nations.[38]

EUROPEAN CORPORATISM: A DIFFERENT KIND OF INTEREST GROUP LIBERALISM?

In developing his critique of interest group liberalism, Lowi referred to "corporatism" as a potential cognate for the interest-group liberalism terminology he eventually chose to describe developments in American politics. Although Lowi thought these terms to be equivalent, many observers of European corporatist relations would differ with this assessment. Both corporatism and interest group liberalism (or pluralism) are characterized by interest groups in close interaction with (or co-optation of) the state. The difference between American pluralism and European corporatism can be grasped by visualizing two types of umpires in a political "game." In American interest group liberalism, the state acts as a sort of neutral and passive umpire, validating the "winner" of the competitive battle among interest groups. The state in this system merely defines the terms of the contest and awards the prizes to the victors. With corporatism, on the other hand, the state is seen as a very active and even participatory umpire who is provided with powers that are commensurate with those brought to the game by recognized interest groups.

European-style corporatism has not escaped criticisms similar to Lowi's critique of the anti-democratic nature of interest group liberalism.[39] Nevertheless, modern versions of corporatism do seem to stand in contrast to crude Italian fascist-style corporatism that often is identified as the original, but undeveloped, model for the more modern forms of this governance structure. Some scholars, for example, have noted that modern versions of corporatism often coexist with extended equal rights, referenda, proportional representation, ombudsman systems, and other features of well-developed democratic states.[40]

Political scientists who have studied seemingly successful versions of corporatism have suggested that corporatism requires a state system that is strong enough to maintain independence from the interests in society, yet not so strong as to develop a transcendent interest that would disallow participation of interest groups.[41] What sets corporatism apart from interest group liberalism most emphatically is the role of the state in providing for and promoting particular forms of broad-based organization of interests. That is, instead of allowing narrow interest groups to coalesce more or less freely around a particular narrowly focused government agency, bureau, or office or congressional subcommittee as is the case with American-style pluralism, corporatism requires that the state recognize and sanction only broad-based interests. In return for recognition, interest groups are required to exhibit a degree of social responsibility.

In creating a role for interest groups within what Peter Katzenstein has called a "para-public" system of institutions, interest groups are in turn expected to come to an agreement on policy and to constrain social conflict. In essence, interest groups are organized into a recognizable institutional framework, but are then bound to that framework.[42] In general, descriptions of modern European corporatism will make reference to tripartite structures involving representatives of business, labor, and government, broadly defined. Hence, European corporatist governance structures (like interest group liberalism and contrary to classic liberal principles) allow a market-like mode of bargaining and negotiation to enter into the processes of the administrative state. The crucial difference between corporatist models of administrative bargaining and those of interest group liberalism is that in the former, private participation in governance is not free-formed, left to chance, or founded on the cruel logic of collective action that dictates disproportionate power for narrow special interests. Instead, corporatist states (as Polanyi might have suggested) have taken steps to *frame and limit the market for participation in public administrative policymaking*. In this ideal conception of corporatism, Lowi's fears about interest group liberalism are partially addressed. Instead of narrow interest groups being able to find a special niche in the political landscape, they are forced to join with larger, more primary group interests and to bargain within these larger groups prior to further bargaining with other broad-based interest groups of a different sort. For example, a textile manufacturer would not be allowed to directly lobby a textile regulatory agency, as typically occurs in the United States. Under some corporatist regimes, even a textile manufacturing association would not be recognized as a legitimate negotiator with government. Instead, only the broadest based association of all manufacturers or even all businesses would be authorized to enter the public policymaking process. That is, special manufacturing interests, such as textile producers, would have to join with a broader group of manufacturing or business interests before being recognized. In Germany, for example, the government often selects the German Chamber of Commerce as the key business interest group with which to negotiate. However, in Germany, participation in the chamber is not a choice for holders of business licenses; all businesses must be members. Consequently, when the government negotiates with private interests, it does so in arenas that involve participation by broad groups of interests. Because European unions or labor councils are for the most part similarly organized in broad groups that cut across narrow crafts or specific industries, the varied interests of labor are also aggregated and reconciled before they are allowed into the policymaking arena.

From a realist perspective, both corporatism and interest group liberalism possess a valuable quality. That is, they both implicitly recognize that in the modern industrial world, the complexity of the governance tasks will typically mean that important details of policymaking will be decided in the administrative and judicial arenas. The essential complexity of private sector behaviors and technologies drives this tendency toward the need to institute ever more complex public sector regulation, while traditional elected officer holders typically lack the time and expertise to perform this function. Instead, these details of policymaking are delegated to administrative and judicial actors who are more equipped for the task. Unfortunately, while these administrators and judges are more equipped to deal with complexity than are elected officials, they nevertheless possess less political legitimacy. As such, bringing the public into these alternative governance structures represents a means of maintaining democratic values. In this respect, corporatism would seem to be superior to interest group liberalism because it is designed to bring to the table a much larger part of the whole public, and to bring in more than just the self-interested public.

From a classic liberal perspective, corporatism has several potential weaknesses. First, the general division of interests into two (or a few) broad categories of business and labor may be somewhat contrived. Although these categories of interest are indeed broad and are likely to subsume a number of variations on the themes of labor and capital, the framework for organizing these interests suggests that a minority group within each camp would have difficulty emerging even if it represented an actual majority when aggregated across groups. It could be argued that the corporatist frame for organizing groups is based on an outdated schema (such as industrial relations) that identifies economic growth and job security as the priority social goals. Within this frame, emerging issues such as the environment are likely to receive less than their due. Evidence of this potential weakness can be seen in some corporatist nations. For example, observers of corporatist governance in Germany have noted recent failures of some interest groups and para-public institutions to resolve conflict and to adequately represent the group members. This failure of representation has been especially acute with regard to individual members' concerns about the environment. As Christopher Allen, a scholar of European politics, has noted, "The Green Party . . . is a prime example of a movement that arose out of the inability of existing institutions to address, mediate, and solve contentious issues."[43]

As with interest-group liberalism, the practice of corporatism must deal with the legitimacy issue. That is, for the primary aggregations of business interest on the one hand or labor interests on the other to be considered legitimate and worthy of para-public status, they must take place within a democratic context. Some corporatist societies have made progress in ensuring that recognized interest groups are representative, but many are still experiencing problems in this respect. When corporatist institutions are not thoroughly democratic, they will likely act in ways that are similar to special interest groups with respect to the development of information and expertise for use in policy debates. That is, information will be built and financed around the interests of those with entrenched power, status, and wealth, rather than arising from the broad interests of the membership.

A Strong Independent Civil Service

Another key feature of corporatist governance is the development of a strong independent civil service that is capable of standing up to organized interests. One of the elements in the development of subgovernments is the similarity of background, training, and interests of regulatory agency managers and interest group representatives. They share subject matter content, similar reference groups, information sources, and experiences. As such, personnel in each camp are often interchangeable, leading to the infamous "revolving door" syndrome in which public sector managers see private sector interest groups as the primary source of future job prospects, and interest group lobbyists position themselves for high-level government positions. This situation is anathema to classic liberalism's strict separation of the public and private realms.

Perhaps because European corporatism is more straightforward about the fact that private sector interests are being given an explicit role in public policymaking, these states have developed strong civil service systems to counter the corrupting tendency of revolving door relationships. The French bureaucracy, which is known generally as one of the most competent, honest, and efficient in the world, counters the revolving door syndrome by assuring top level public sector managers of attractive lifetime careers in public administration. Additionally, these top-level bureaucrats are explicitly selected and trained for careers in the public sector. The Ecole Nationale d'Administration, the highly selective and demanding school that graduates future public executives, for example, trains generalist managers rather than content-specialists. Because of such training, these public sector managers adopt a more exclusively public viewpoint than their American counterparts, and are less likely to be taken in by narrowly constructed interest group arguments. Also, because the civil service career path is strictly unitary (that is, one cannot get on and off as in the United States) and is considered at least as attractive as private sector employment, these public administrators are less likely to be tempted or swayed by the prospects of future lucrative employment in the private sector.[44]

Although in European states, the strong civil service is part of an overall corporatist structure, classic liberals such as Theodore Lowi have suggested similar reforms of the American civil service system. Lowi, for example, calls for a major expansion of the Senior Executive Service. The effect of such an expansion, he suggests, would be to rotate generalist, public-oriented managers among public agencies so as to diminish the chances of their being captured by any one interest group.[45]

Classic Liberal Versus Corporatist Solutions to Corrupted Liberalism

Classic liberalism and European corporatism represent two potential roadmaps out of the inefficient and anti-democratic political landscape of interest-group liberalism. Classic liberalism would restore the walls separating public from private and limit the conversation about their proper interaction to the legislative branch. Corporatism would recognize and validate private group interests in the legislative branch of government, but would also construct para-public institutions as part of the administrative branch of government and would recognize and validate private group interests in the formation and implementation of policy within this branch. In terms of the ideologies explored in the previous chapter, corporatism can be seen as a combination of communitarian and conservative ideological elements. It is communitarian because group rights are recognized as primary, and it is conservative because the state is charged with establishing the framework for private interest influence.

However, corporatism has to construct a somewhat rigid and potentially elitist civil service system in order to maintain a balance of interests in the administrative domain of the public sector. Corporatism, in this respect, is dependent on the traditional distinctions between an aristocratic guardian class, representing the interests of the state, and a merchant class, representing private commercial interests. Modern corporatism has eliminated the family membership requirement for entrance into the guardian class; strict selection procedures and extensive training are believed to be sufficient to instill a public-oriented code of honor.

Whereas corporatism depends on a sort of caste system for separating public and private realms, classic liberalism is based on the idea that average citizens can have a role in both realms. Classic liberals believe, for example, that it should be possible and is indeed desirable for a figure like Harry Truman to be both a haberdasher and president of the Republic. Business experience is thought to be a qualification for government service rather than a disqualifying factor. These citizen-guardians, moreover, ideally provide a flexible bridge between government and the private economy, resulting in numerous cross-fertilizations and an increased understanding of the requirement of both realms.[46] From these understandings, institutional inventions in the form of efficient provision of public goods and merit good are realized. Business becomes more profitable and efficient because government learns from merchant-legislators how to create market-enhancing infrastructure and, just as important, learns about the limits of public provision of goods and services. These limits exist because government largess must be paid for through taxation of private wealth. High rates of taxation, as conservative or supply-side economists constantly remind us, have the effect of reducing incentives for people to begin new enterprises or expand old ones.[47]

Caste Versus Flexible Systems of Public-Private Boundaries

Economic historians suggest that the gains of moving out of a caste-like system for separating the public and private realms and into a more flexible system of ordering public and private roles can be considerable. In part, this is the case because there appears to be substantial economic costs involved in maintaining a strong class system in an age of rapid technical change. For example, many observers have traced the relative economic decline of Britain and the rise of the American industrial power over the past century to the different values each society places on membership in the guardian class vis-à-vis the business class. With little or no status or power differences in America between these two classes, creative merchants would enter government and creative politicians would engage in private enterprise, with concomitant gains in national product. However, in Britain, the existence of a class difference between those who were engaged in trade and those who were "above trade" may have had a substantial effect. That is, although trade and industry were the engines of Britain's early economic growth, the more successful British merchants and industrialists willingly gave up their quest for wealth and economic expansion to be able to join the society of the upper or guardian class—a class that did not get its hands dirty. Successful merchants found, Jane Jacobs writes, "ostentation, largesse, and achieving the status of patrons more satisfying than attending to productive investment. Their own industriousness suffered in favor of guardian pastimes. . . . They found hobnobbing with guardians more congenial than keeping in close touch with suppliers, customers, and competitors."[48]

While too rigidly restricting the movement of individuals between the world of private sector commercial enterprise and that of public sector duties and honors is economically inefficient and usually results in political elitism, making movement between these realms too easy is not without its own pitfalls. Unless citizens are acutely aware of and educated to the different moral systems and ethical precepts that attach to commercial versus governmental activity, the gains of creating a flexible bridge between the public and private sectors will be lost due to an increase in corruption.[49] Effective governance systems will need to have a certain degree of flexibility of interaction between the public and private sectors while at the same time controlling for the potential of private sector interests to overwhelm public interests or vice versa.

Corporatism and classic liberalism represent two models of such control, while fascism and interest group liberalism represent the corrupted versions of these models, respectively. Corporatism controls the potential for private actors to "self-deal" by limiting and structuring the channels through which individuals with private interests communicate their desires to the state. An elite corp of public sector guardians, who are kept in a separate institutional compartment, maintain these limitations, but on the whole private sector interests are given access to the administrative sector of the state. In a classic liberal system, corruption is controlled through limiting the range of private interest access to government (for example, access to the administrative sector is denied). Flexibility is achieved by having individual citizens function in both commercial and public servant roles. With organized, private interest access to the state limited to the legislative branch, corruption can be controlled because all political maneuvering and policymaking is restricted to a single arena. In this limited arena, activities are potentially transparent to all citizens (or to their representatives, at least). However, once politics is expanded to include the administrative sector of the state, classical liberals argue, the cleansing effects of "sunshine" and citizen participation are not likely to be sufficient to prevent corruption, because some interested citizens will be much more likely to work to achieve their interests than others.

Corporatism, as its early critics have noted, can be corrupted by elite guardians working in collusion with selected (usually the most powerful) interest groups to assume control over the state and the economy under the aegis of national interests or national security. Although such fascist versions of corrupted corporatism seem to have been limited in modern times by broad public acceptance of civil rights, a more typical failure of corporatism can occur when these guardian elites collude with organized interests to capture unearned rents in the short term, but fail to make the necessary long-term adjustments required by global economic competition. Some observers have suggested that European nations' failures to create sufficient jobs (especially when compared with American achievements in this area) are a sign of the failure of corporatist systems to adjust to new economic realities. Critics of European welfare states suggest that the system of social welfare payments in these nations represents a social safety valve that is necessary in a para-public economic system. Without such a safety valve, the obvious favoritism that the system gives to a corps of elite industrial workers and governmental civil servants, at the expense of growth and flexibility in the overall economy, would be unacceptable.[50]

Addressing the Public-Private Paradox: Lessons of Corporatism Versus Classic Liberalism

While corporatism is designed to frame, and thereby control, the nature of the bargaining between public and private actors in the policymaking process, there is reason to believe that the benefits of corporatism are not easily transferred from one social, cultural, and political context to another. If corporatist institutions are to operate as desired, it is likely that such institutions will need to be situated within a supportive culture and that such institutional arrangements would need to be adopted as a whole cloth, rather than piecemeal. In fact, there is some evidence to suggest that a piecemeal grafting of corporatist institutional structures onto an essentially classic liberal governance mechanism and political culture will afford new and expanded opportunities for corruption. This is the case because liberal political cultures have never answered the question of exactly what the appropriate ethical guidelines are for persons acting as part of a para-public organization. In the United States, for example, norms for what is appropriate activity for private citizens who are members of para-public organizations such as hospital or economic development authorities are still not firmly established. In my own study of a local industrial development authority, for example, I discovered that the predominantly business members of this authority were unsure about the exact nature of their obligation to act in the public interest and according to public sector ethics. They questioned whether they should be held to the rigid standards of public accountability, merit system personnel procedures, and "sunshine" provisions. They sensed that their role was to bring the virtues of private sector flexibility to this institutional innovation, but had no guidelines as to where this flexibility ended. Because of the relative newness of such para-public institutional arrangements in America, the cultural and ethical groundwork has not been fully established. As I and a number of other observers of para-public innovations have discovered, the potential for corruption is high in these institutions, not because Americans are any more innately corrupt than Europeans, but because the full cultural and political ecology of corporatism has not been introduced here. Instead, only pieces of the corporatist reform alternative have been introduced, with predictably unimpressive results.[51]

Establishing coherent, "whole-cloth" governance reforms is essential because each alternative governance scheme has its own peculiar way of handling what has been called the public-private paradox. Simply put, this paradox suggests that the public and private realms of life must be separated, but not by too much. Separation is needed because these realms represent two very different ways of living: Public sector actors are supported by taking, while private sector actors are supported by trading. Each demands a somewhat unique set of virtues—ones that if transferred to the other realm would likely become vices. Yet, while the virtues of, for example, a public sector warrior or bureaucrat would be misplaced in the commercial realm, there is nevertheless a need for these public sector actors to exchange information, ideas, and technologies with their private sector counterparts. Similarly, the private citizen will need to get close enough to the workings of government to be able to have influence, but not so close as to control the government outright.

Both corporatism and classic liberalism have established methods for dealing with the public-private paradox. Corporatism addresses this paradox by using something like a caste method. That is, it ensures broad private representation in all aspects and branches of government, but demands in return that citizens essentially choose to be either a public figure or a private one. One caste, a group of highly trained and skilled public administrators, acts as guardians of the public interest against the other caste of private actors. The private sector group is let into governance coalitions as partners on important boards and councils, but its members, in turn, are expected to behave responsibly. Under most corporatist arrangements, private sector partners would find it difficult to join the public sector corps of administrators without extensive retraining. Similar barriers are often in place to prevent the public bureaucrats from easily entering the private sector. Because few persons in either realm ever cross over to the other, a single, fairly coherent, and understandable set of moral expectations can be outlined, taught, and followed by persons within each realm. Because the separate moral responsibilities of public and private actors are so well defined, it is possible for these actors to come together in corporatist institutions with little danger that the shared experience will be morally confusing for one group or the other.

In contrast to corporatism's caste-based method for dealing with the "separate, but close" paradox, classic liberalism's "flexible method" of dealing with this paradox is more demanding of the moral understanding of average citizens. Such citizens are expected to know when, where, and how to ethically cross back and forth from what Jane Jacobs has called the guardian and commercial moral syndromes. Classic liberal institutions were designed to clearly demarcate between the times and places where one's public persona and related ethical guidelines are activated and those where private roles and morals are engaged. That is, under classic liberal regimes, institutional structures such as public-private partnerships that could potentially confuse a citizen-representative would simply not exist. Such sharp lines between the public and private realms would assist citizens in meeting the demands of the "flexible method." Additionally, classic liberal requirements for rule of law, not of men, and for general rules, rather than specific rules or context-dependent standards, reinforced the notion that private persons would be limited in their ability to craft laws that would favor their own interests or harm those of their enemies. Laws would have to apply to all persons in the same way, and special treatment of particular groups, businesses, or industries would be prohibited. (This type of restrictive classic liberal structure helps to explain why classic liberal nations have made only relatively primitive attempts to craft industrial policies.) Similarly, classic liberal institutions would limit the scope of activity of private citizen-representatives primarily to the legislative branch. In the other branches of government, however, citizen-representative participation would be limited, if not entirely outlawed, as being a form of unfair and unwarranted influence on what is meant to be neutral administration and adjudication of the will of the legislature.

However, as William Greider and other observers of interest group liberalism have demonstrated, these sharp public-private boundaries set up by the founders have been eroded during the course of the last several decades. Organized interests have penetrated sectors of the administrative state that were once reserved for public personas and have, moreover, helped create new para-public institutions such as public authorities that often lack democratic accountability or structures for delineating and enforcing a clear set of public ethics.

Although advocates for both corporatism and classic liberalism offer plausible responses to the problems posed by interest group liberalism and the public-private paradox, comprehensive application of the principles of either of these ideologies to land-use control issues is problematic. This is not to say that land-use and environmental policymaking at the national level would not benefit from either a return to strict classic liberal approaches or the adoption of corporatist institutions of governance. Either of these approaches would be superior to the current interest group liberalism arrangements. However, both theories of governance assume that the key policies being made will apply at a national or at least a regional level. Land-use issues and policies for the most part are local in nature. When compared with national politics, local decision making offers far fewer opportunities for either the organization of broad interests (as would be suggested by corporatism) or for the clash of numerous individual interests (as would be called for in classic liberal thought). The trouble that local land-use politics poses for democratic theory has not gone unnoticed by American legal scholars and political theorists. Moreover, as is explored below, the issues they have raised put in question the legitimacy of over forty years of zoning and planning.

Local- Versus National-Scale Land-Use Planning and the Idea of Legitimacy

In addition to traditional classic liberal ideas for constraining the tendency of democracy to devolve into tyranny (that is, separation of power among levels and branches of government), the Federalist founders also argued, contrary to the conventional wisdom of the time, that large republics would be particularly effective in legitimizing democratic politics.[52] James Madison pointed out that controlling "factions," or groups that would impose their will at the expense of others, would be much easier in an extended republic where the large variety of factions would ensure that no one group would continually rule over the others. Having a large number of different interests represented in a polity makes it more difficult to establish secure winning coalitions because the issues will change over time. As today's enemy is potentially tomorrow's friend, a large republic with numerous interests makes it less likely that any single faction will want to poison its relationship with other factions; it will forbear putting salt into wounded groups because it knows it may need to call on that group for assistance in the future. Because of these tendencies, political theorists have generally recognized that legislatures that contain a large number of interests tend to be more deliberative and less hasty in their consideration of issues, more likely to craft compromise legislation, and more likely to "reflect on the true public welfare."[53]

The Founders' view of the proper size of democratic republics is implicitly critical of the potential legitimacy and fairness of most local government decision making. If the interests in the locality are too few or too homogeneous, the more deliberative, careful, and public interest-minded outcomes that legitimize democratic decision making are not to be expected. As Carol Rose has pointed out, the domination by factions in localities can take a number of different forms, including: (1) corruption (because it is easier to identify and influence the few powerful people whose support is needed and who can be "bought"); (2) the formation of small well-organized groups or "cabels" that dominate the community. Madison and other eighteenth century observers were aware of this possibility long before Mancur Olson discovered the underlying organizational "logic" of small groups gaining a disproportionate share of power; and (3) the development of uncontrollable passions, or the action of popular whims or long-standing prejudices that create a mob-like majority.[54] In essence, at the local level, factions are thought to much more easily "subject others to sudden destruction or to permanent political disability."[55]

Decisions on land-use issues are thought to be particularly vulnerable to rule by faction rather than by reflective legislative deliberation and due process. As Frank Michelman and Carol Rose suggest, any single local land-use decision usually involves only a very limited number of people or interests; when this situation is combined with the fact that local governments generally are only authorized to decide on very few types of issues overall, there are often not enough interests at stake to create the kind of clashes of interests that promote deliberation or that "permit the development of coalitions and the benefit-trading and mutual forbearance they entail."[56]

In effect, many of the forces promoting lawlessness, corruption, unequal interest-group influence, and "rude and crude" politics that have been identified at the national level with respect to environmental regulation are likely to be magnified at the local level. Just as Congress would rather not decide the hard issues and confront the true costs of its decisions, local and state governments are also loath to establish clear, general-purpose land-use law that is subsequently enforced. Instead, as with their counterparts in the federal government, local and state legislators have created a number of administrative bodies for the regulation of land-use issues. A large number of land-use issues are relegated to such para-public bodies as planning and zoning boards and zoning variance commissions as well as to public authorities for schools, hospitals, utilities, ports and transportation, housing, and recreation. Membership on planning boards, zoning councils, and zoning variance commissions invariably is weighted toward those citizens who are interested in the development and market potential of land.[57] Similarly, representation on the boards of public authorities that have powers of eminent domain (such as port, housing, recreation, industrial development and hospital authorities) is also dominated by the organized interests of those who would benefit from the expansion, location, or relocation of public facilities.

Although the civil rights and environment movements have undoubtedly played a major role in publicizing the problems with the "politics" of local land-use control, early identification of these problems occurred in the 1930s and 1940s, when city planners began to notice that zoning variance procedures tended to make a mockery of the original intentions of planners, and judges began to worry about the vagueness, and therefore constitutionality, of the ordinances establishing zoning variance boards. Later, as urban scholars documented the haphazard fashion in which zoning adjustment boards granted variances, the lack of procedural safeguards by these boards, and their failure to rely on technical expertise, some courts were moved to tighten up on these boards.[58] A number of studies conducted in the 1950s and 1960s concluded that variances were generally doled out in such an easy fashion as to make a mockery of the zoning ordinances themselves. The advice of professional planners was generally ignored and the vast majority of developers got what they wanted. In some areas they began to view a variance as a right rather than a privilege.[59] Although variances were less likely to be granted in contested cases, this provided additional proof that the system was basically arbitrary and political instead of ordered by a rational plan for community development.[60]

As a result of these more realistic examinations of how zoning issues were decided at the local level, a number of courts began to argue that variance procedures should be conducted in a more quasi-judicial fashion—that is, to involve the application of statutory standards, due process, and judicial review—all supported by adequate record-keeping. In making the argument for a fairer method by which to award zoning variances, however, the courts frequently discovered that the zoning ordinances and amendments to these ordinances themselves often failed to meet common legal criteria for workable standards (such as clarity and consistency). These ordinances and amendments were often not related to any clearly laid out plan or findings; rather, like variances, the ordinances were often passed in an arbitrary fashion, in response to developers' pressures, or in a manner that resulted in special treatment.[61] Finally, the courts also became concerned with the tendency in some jurisdictions for the more controversial zoning decisions to devolve to the people themselves through referenda and initiatives. The courts questioned, in essence, whether an individual property owner could get fair treatment through a popular vote where mass opinion would not be shaped and guided by even the minimal amount of study, debate, and reflection that occurs in local governmental councils. Furthermore, some courts questioned whether specific zoning actions could be properly construed as a legislative act. They argued that these actions are more accurately conceived as quasi-administrative and judicial processes. According to this reasoning, such zoning actions would only be legitimate if they were taken in accordance with a legislatively authorized comprehensive plan. Piecemeal zoning or zoning that differed from the comprehensive plan would be suspect. Because the interests of the whole community would have to be taken into consideration in the initial comprehensive plan, only this basic precursor to zoning could be considered a legitimate legislative act. Because taking a popular vote or even a vote of the council on piecemeal zoning questions would tend to eventually undermine the comprehensive plan, this part of the zoning process, it was argued, should be addressed in a more judicial or administrative manner.

To take the special interest politics and irrationality out of zoning, reformers in the classic liberal tradition believed it would be necessary to: (1) set out a land-use plan that was comprehensive and clear enough to act as a standard (or general rule) for the development of zoning ordinances, amendments, and variances; and (2) institute a quasi-judicial process for applying the standard to particular cases. This reform suggestion is sometimes referred to as "plan jurisprudence" and was set out most explicitly in the case of *Fasano v. Board of County Commissioners*, where the court reasoned that it was possible to distinguish individual piecemeal rezonings from the adoption of general plans or land-use controls. Theoretically, the court argued, decisions about the general plan could reasonably be viewed as legislative processes because such decisions would typically involve a large number of interests and could take place under conditions that would allow reflection, bargaining, and compromise so as to achieve a generally defensible and legitimate outcome. The other, more parcel-specific zoning decisions, the court argued, should be subject to more judicial processes that examine the facts in light of standards set out in the comprehensive plan. Applying the Federalist's idea of the need for a large republic to constrain factions in legislative bodies, the court's reasoning in the Fasano case implicitly questioned whether local government decisions are truly "legislative" in nature.[62] Some other courts have followed the reasoning in Fasano. For example, the Ohio Supreme Court held that local ordinances that required referenda in rezoning cases were unconstitutional because they made the rezoning "dependent upon the potentially arbitrary and unreasonable whims of the voting public."[63] However, the U.S. Supreme Court reversed this latter decision, ruling that rezonings were indeed legislative acts that the sovereign people could reserve for themselves.[64]

As Carol Rose points out, however, the Supreme Court decision merely fueled the debate over plan jurisprudence because the decision basically left the unsatisfactory land-use situation intact: Developers engaged in factional and piecemeal conflict with neighborhood groups, public judgments were made in "haste and lack of consideration of fairness," and the winners were determined by the distribution of political clout in the immediate situation.[65]

While the courts have failed to address the problem of there being a "local exception" to what might otherwise be considered effective classic liberal institutions for land-use control, it is not evident that traditional corporatist institutions would be any more successful in this regard. As will be made clear in the discussion at the end of this chapter, land-use issues tend to defy easy delineation of interests around the typical categories of labor and capital by which corporatist governance is usually organized. The key point to make at this time about local land-use zoning is that, notwithstanding the existence of interest group liberalism, the traditional institutions designed to decide zoning issues when viewed in light of traditional liberal political theory seem to lack legitimacy. An obvious first step in a potential resolution to this situation would be to draw a clear line between broad-scope land-use issues that are amenable to legislative processes and those land-use issues that are more limited in scope and might best be addressed in a more judicial or administrative manner. As will be explained at the end of this chapter, this obvious step in the right direction, upon examination, has its own problems. It should be noted that in some regards there is evidence that policy development is moving in this direction. For example, there is a growing tendency for state and federal governments to adopt minimum standards for such things as watersheds, wetlands, and ground water protection, while allowing local governments to adopt more stringent standards if they so wish.

Factional Local Land-Use Politics Magnified: The Coming of Social Justice and Environmental Issues

While not all of the problems in the governance of land-use issues can be traced to the rise of interest group liberalism, the corruption of classic liberal ideals has surely magnified the problems of social injustice and environmental degradation caused by inadequate land-use controls. Interest group liberalism at the least has frustrated attempts by advocates for social justice to overcome the advantages of organized banking and real estate interests in the legislative crafting and administration of fair housing and lending standards.[66] Moreover, interest group liberalism helps explain why poor minority communities face particularly high barriers when mobilizing against environmental threats. It is not just that the poor have less free time and available resources, but that the dynamics of interest group liberalism translate these limitations into lower levels of access to legal, technical, and medical expertise, which in turn results in relatively weaker influence with the media and the political centers of power.[67]

Similarly, at the local level, the presence of interest group liberalism can explain in part how the larger role given to the interests of developers and real estate brokers in the planning and zoning and public use of property has often occurred at the expense of the larger public interest. The strategic siting of public facilities has long been recognized as a source of windfall profits (or in the case of a LULU, losses) for nearby property owners. Membership on public authorities provides private individuals with a share of this power to site facilities strategically. Also, while zoning might appear to be anathema to these interests, the ability to shift property from one zoning category to another is a prime source of land speculation profits. In the typical case, a development corporation will purchase a piece of property at the market price for property that is zoned for a certain level or type of development. Windfall profits are achieved by having the property rezoned. For real-estate interests, the organization of the market through zoning can potentially be much more profitable than a truly free market in properties—especially if real estate development interests are given easy access to the less visible policymaking and administrative sectors of local government. As Robert Ellickson concludes, "Zoning is a trough at which rentseekers of various breeds come to feed. Developers can enrich themselves by securing unexpected approvals from politicians willing to exchange zoning concessions for campaign contributions."[68]

One of the effects of interest group liberalism on environmental land-use issues has been to shift the ground of political decision making away from public institutions and to create what Greider terms a "politics of the rude and crude." The shift is in part a result of an awakening by those who have traditionally been the consumers of residential land rather than the developers of such land. These consumers were typically denied positions on para-public land-use control boards or development authorities, and such consumers were, until recent times or until a zoning change request occurred, often satisfied and made to feel secure in the stability of their neighborhood by the existence of a comprehensive land-use plan. More frequent zoning change requests combined with the realization that most comprehensive plans are an inaccurate guide to eventual development to awaken owners of residential property to the threat of unwanted development. Rude and crude politics has been particularly evident in the area of environmental land-use issues involving hazardous waste or industrial pollution. After Congress passed clean air and clean water legislation and set up the Environmental Protection Agency, there was a general expectation among most citizens that the government would come to the rescue of those whose lives, health, and property were threatened by these wastes and pollutions. However, as environmental laws proved to be hollow in content or to lack an enforcement component, or, worse yet, were handed over to industry-oriented boards and commissions, citizens' expectations were in many cases dashed. As disillusionment set in and citizens realized that democracy did not work as it was outlined in civics classes, but is instead driven by money and public image, people learned that their best recourse was to engage in the crude politics of confrontation, guerrilla theatre, and civil disobedience. This politics is "very rude and very crude," explains Lois Marie Gibbs of the Citizen's Clearinghouse for Hazardous Waste.[69]

The Citizen's Clearinghouse newsletter, *Everyone's Backyard,* chronicles the course of hundreds of local protest encounters, involving citizens chaining themselves to the entrance gates to landfills, blocking roads with stalled cars, buses and trucks, "blowing up" public hearings with protest chants, establishing hand-to-hand encirclements of waste-treatment facilities, and engaging in numerous other forms of civil disobedience. The movement leaders are quite frank about using tactics that are outside the system. As Lois Gibbs says, "If you work within the established system, doing the right thing, more often than not you will lose. The system is put together by the powers that be so they will win. To be outside means not to accept that we will lose."[70]

The tendency to participate in more crude or direct forms of politics is especially evident in cases where "environmental racism" is being alleged. Because minority communities tend to see sitings of toxic facilities as part of the larger, seemingly more intractable context of institutionalized racism, citizens in these communities often have little confidence that efforts to address LULU-type injustices through sanctioned political channels will have any more effect than such channels has had in the achievement of other civil rights goals.[71] Close observers of environmentalism in minority communities have noted that direct, extralegal action such as sit-ins and picketing of shareholder meetings is emphasized, while "legal expertise is decidedly de-emphasized," but nevertheless employed in such activities as releasing demonstrators from police custody.[72] One reason for the lack of emphasis on the more customary channels for creating change is that litigation demands a high level of resources, the ability to document one's case, and the ability to avoid the costs of postponing action. Most minority communities often do not have these resources and abilities. The fact that poor minority citizens are less likely to have a consistent family physician, more likely to have poor diets, and more likely to be exposed to toxins on the job, for example, makes it difficult to build a medical record that would provide evidence of harm caused by pollution sufficient to justify and succeed in litigation. Direct action by minority communities is in some respects the result of their relatively greater difficulties in using established tools of democratic and legal choice combined with the more dire nature of their situation.[73]

Perhaps the most important reason that environmental groups resort to the crude politics of direct action has been the comparative effectiveness of this strategy in many cases.[74] The direct-action NIMBY approach to LULUs began and has probably been most successful in more affluent, white communities. However, this very success probably put more pressure on businesses and governments to site LULUs in poor, minority communities as the path of least resistance. This process, in turn, likely raised the awareness in these communities of environmental injustice, leading to a correspondingly high level of direct action in these communities. One result of this dynamic of increasingly direct action on the part of all communities has been a substantial rise in the cost of siting potentially noxious facilities. When confronted with such tactics, industry and government are often unsuccessful in siting toxic facilities in the location they have chosen, or they are forced to pay compensation to those who are affected by the siting. Most recent attempts to open new hazardous-waste treatment facilities, for example, have failed, and many proposed industrial plants have been stopped, delayed, or moved to alternative locations or overseas. These siting failures have occurred not just in cases where the proposed facility would have failed to meet air or water quality standards or would have damaged habitat or degraded historical or natural features of the environment. Rather, failures to site waste-producing or treatment facilities have occurred even where the proposed facility could have ameliorated an existing pollution problem. Joseph Browder has noted that "for most projects, conflict will come not because of failure or inability to comply with legal requirements, but because of failure to understand the more ambiguous questions raised by the project's intrusion into the existing environment."[75]

What Browder's research suggests is that as citizens lose faith in the ability of government to protect them and began to practice a local environmentalism, the protest against waste treatment and other industrial facilities will begin to be based more on NIMBY-type reasoning than on a full understanding of environmental values for the larger geographic entity. Although Browder believes that the environmental community should not concede that whatever is not prohibited should be allowed,

> neither should it be assumed that environmental criticisms and strategies that were valid in the 1970s are necessarily effective in responding for developments planned in the 1990s. Requirements for cleaning up the abuse that created existing pollution problems may not provide sound guidance for working now to prevent future pollution, and may even frustrate the introduction of superior technologies, fuels, and systems for controlling dangerous waste.[76]

The rude and crude, NIMBY-oriented politics, which were highly effective for their time, Browder suggests, may in some cases be the enemy of the long-term good. He believes, for example, that unreasonable opposition to new manufacturing, energy production, and waste treatment projects in the United States could result in a number of undesirable results, including a reduction in investment in pollution-reduction equipment, a loss of U.S. leadership in the production of pollution-abatement and treatment equipment and industrial designs, and a reduction in the environmental community's influence on the direction of global economic development.[77] Although Browder does not mention it, unbounded rejection of new industrial facilities could also undo whatever collaboration the environmental community may have been able to establish with the representatives of labor. Additionally, some observers have noted that when NIMBY opposition makes it impossible to dispose of waste materials in carefully regulated facilities, "they are often disposed of in far more environmentally unsound, often illegal, ways and settings, i.e., dumped in back lots [or] stored in unsafe warehouses."[78] The success of each individual local NIMBY action, when aggregated across communities and states, generates increasing pressure on remaining potential sites as well as much higher total costs for locating essential facilities.[79] Browder's basic argument against rude and crude environmental activity is sound within the context of a consensus as to what constitutes an "essential" facility or level of facilities. Unfortunately, in many cases, no consensus has been reached as to whether a particular facility is actually essential. Also, it is rarely the case that people can be assured that the existence of new facilities with better technology for pollution control and reduction will result in the closing of other more polluting facilities or will simply result in having an additional, though more efficient, pollution-generating facility. Until there are effective forums for arriving at such a consensus and for negotiating ceilings for total allowable levels of pollution, direct action will continue to be an attractive and necessary means of influencing policy for many environmentalists.

Direct action can unwittingly undermine the public good in another way. As more governments and corporations become aware of the potential for being stymied in their siting efforts, they are working to preempt this possibility. One means of preempting the potential for direct community action against toxic sites is the use of compensation or buy-out schemes that create buffer zones or impact easements around proposed facilities. While compensation is better than no compensation from the "good policy" perspective of having polluters internalize the full cost of their operations, buy-out programs neither reduce the potential for toxic emissions nor take into consideration the impacts on community life as whole.[80] Rather, they represent in some fashion a divide-and-conquer strategy in which the LULU operator quiets the voice of nearby residents who would have the strongest legal case against the facility, while not having to compensate those residents whose case may be legally weaker. In the process, however, the buy-out program has weakened community life and identity or even eliminated whole parts of the community. As law professors Regina Austin and Michael Shill note, while "individual monetary settlements can threaten communal solidarity, there is no precedent for pursuing claims of harm to an entire group qua group."[81]

These legal scholars go on to suggest that the tendency for victimized groups to engage in more direct or crude political action rather than more traditional forms of civic politics is exacerbated by a legal system that separates redress into common law and statutory actions. Because these two types of action are distinct, a potential plaintiff in objecting to a LULU siting often has to choose (for example, because of lack of resources) between the two courses. From the plaintiff's point of view, however, these courses of action have their individual and distinct advantages and disadvantages. A common lawsuit, for example, might be appropriate where a nuisance is easy to detect and where the plaintiff has a need for damage compensations. However, the common law has few or no provisions for attorney fees, and the remedy involved will not necessarily lead to a restoration of the environment if other compensation is cheaper. On the other hand, lawsuits based on public law will often provide for restoration and attorney fees, but are less likely to provide for damage recovery.[82]

A Rude and Crude Corporate Response

The lawlessness that interest group liberalism generates does not lead to rude and crude politics in the environmental community alone. Rather, corporate and industrial interests have fought back with a crude politics of their own, one, moreover, that threatens basic constitutional rights to free speech and citizen protest. The tactic that is used is the "strategic lawsuit against public participation" or SLAPP suits. These are defamation lawsuits based on the common law of torts that developed as a means of protecting contracting parties from interference by third parties. According to libertarian legal scholars, the law of torts developed in two directions—the tort of interference with advantageous relations and the tort of defamation—for the purposes of protecting the disposition rights of private property. Case law in these areas suggests that trespass on property is not necessary to claim a tort. Rather, interference can be claimed when, for example, one trader fires a cannon between a rival trader and the natives with whom he is about to trade. In defamation cases, one's reputation is not protected in the abstract; rather, defamation protects advantageous relationships against interference due to misrepresentation.[83]

Tort law protection of property disposition (which for the most part developed prior to codification of political rights in the amendments to the U.S. Constitution) was designed to address the interference of one private party or commercial interest with another. In situations where basic political questions are addressed by legislators and settled by the enactment of positive law, the jurisdictional limits of tort law would be clear and acceptable to most parties. However, when political issues are not settled by positive law (or are only settled in a pseudomanner through hollow or vague law or devolved onto agencies, boards, or commissions that lack democratic legitimacy), the limits of tort law will not be clear. Instead, in rude and crude politics, industrial waste producers or treatment facility operators will twist the law of torts to their own rude and crude purposes. In most instances, SLAPP suits have been unsuccessful whenever they have been challenged in the courts. Judges generally have ruled that the alleged interference with trade, not being motivated by a rival commercial interest, is a protected form of political speech.[84] In many instances, however, SLAPP suits have been effective in their prime objective of stopping environmental protest. The threat of substantial economic loss has often been sufficient to deter protesters from exercising their political rights. The effectiveness of this strategy of applying the law of torts to political questions is another indicator of the lawlessness that can be generated by interest group liberalism. The law of torts was designed to apply to commercial, propertied interests that were motivated by their business investments and could usually afford the court costs. Typically, in SLAPP suits only a few defendants have identifiable property interests; most are engaged in the protest because of belief in more generalized harm. As Olson's logic of collective action suggests, such defendants will be unwilling to engage in the substantial individual risk and make substantial private investments that would be necessary to defend against the SLAPP suit. However, industrial and waste treatment businesses, with a more concentrated interest, lawyers on retainer, and deeper pockets, are positioned to use the law of torts in a strategic manner. The fact that this is an effective tactic and that there is, from a legal realist outlook, a slippage in the proper realms of law is another indication that the lawlessness generated by interest group liberalism is not confined to an invasion of the administrative sector alone. As with undue private interest influence on executive branch agencies, the misapplication of the law of torts suggests an inability to identify the appropriate realms and roles for the private and public sectors, respectively. Conservative legal scholars are in agreement about the general lawlessness of issues involving environmental questions about land use, but identify a different side of the public-private problem—one still rooted in situations generated by interest group liberalism, but one that sees environmentalists, not as victims of strategic lawsuits, but as unwarranted usurpers of public power. One of these scholars, for example, has complained that "we allow people to exercise the power of public office when it seems entirely a matter of private ownership claims being extended." The example given of this private assumption of public rights is the ability of private citizens to bring suit for punitive damages against a polluter and to "negotiate to have damages sent not to the Treasury but rather to the citizens' favorite environmental organization." The situation described here, in which private citizens exercise "on behalf of the public a kind of property claim," is another crossing of what was once a clear line separating public and private roles in a classic liberal society.[85] As private citizens use the courts for public purpose, they bypass the legislative branch in favor of an appeal to another branch—the judicial one—that in the classic liberal formulation would be shut off from bargaining and lawmaking by private interests (except for cases strictly involving private interests in conflict with each other). As suggested earlier, the motivation for interest groups to try to enter and influence land-use decision making in the judicial realm is particularly evident in the United States because so many land-use control issues in the United States potentially involve judicial questions.

Modern Politics, State-Planned Markets, and the Death of Property

Periodically, during our era of progressive, interest group liberalism, a suggestion is made that appeals to ideology are at an end.[86] Ideology can be replaced, it is thought, by the application of information, expertise, and cost-benefit analyses. In 1980, Thomas Gray suggested a similar end to the liberal (classic liberal and libertarian) ideology of property. As with most suggestions of this sort, the quip about the reports of one's death being vastly exaggerated is apt. Gray's argument is based on the insight that property as a natural right or a place of "sole and domestic dominion"[87] has essentially disappeared, being replaced with multiple forms of fragmented, abstracted, and intangible property that eased the process of capital accumulation and industrial development. Gray further argues that because of the death of property, "the specialists who design and manipulate the legal structures of advanced capitalist economies could easily do without using the term 'property' at all" and that property is less and less a "central category of legal and political thought."[88] For Gray and others, the difference between state regulation and property rights delineation is essentially one of semantics. Property rights-based markets, as Karl Polanyi argued earlier in this century, are planned institutions, just as state regulations are planned. As such, property will likely be structured along the lines of a utilitarian choice of a "mix of means." However, the foregoing discussion of property-based ideologies (and corrupted versions of these ideologies) suggests that ideologues will continue to use property as a central construct, and will in turn propose particular configurations of property relationships as being more likely than other configurations to promote preferred values. These ideologies of property and politics, moreover, will become more and more important as long as current governance structures for making land-use decisions prove unsatisfactory. While these structures are thought to be based on neutral, "scientific" and judicial analysis of information within a legitimate, classic liberal institutional system, the reality is substantially otherwise, leaving a large space for ideological debate.

Additionally, the "death" of property, like the death predicted for ideology, is premature because the idea of property as a place of individual dominion will continue to play a major role in social relations. It will continue to be the sign and symbol of opposition to state regulatory power, and will continue to be thought of as a shield protecting individual freedom from encroachment by either private or public intruders.[89] Given that law is ultimately based on shared political understandings,[90] the idea of property is likely to have a long life because most individuals (and even many legal theorists and policy specialists in their everyday relations with neighbors) have yet to relinquish the traditional idea of property.

One effect of the continued life of the idea of property can be found in the widespread "not in my back yard" sentiment that is typically generated in reaction to developers' proposals to site an unwanted or undesirable facility near one's property. The NIMBY movement may be simply one part of a large political landscape. However, if "urban politics is above all the politics of land use,"[91] and if, as Tip O'Neil has suggested, "all politics is local," then the politics of "not in my backyard" may be more important than many within-the-beltway pundits and policymakers would admit. As one observer has noted, the number of public officials, for example, involved in land-use planning, zoning, and other efforts to rationalize and balance property rights at the neighborhood level is probably greater than that for any other policy area.[92]

NIMBYs and the Dynamics of Global Capitalism

Within a political environment dominated by interest group liberalism and articulated by the dynamics of capitalism, NIMBY issues, moreover, are likely to proliferate—even when a well-articulated environmental rationale is missing.[93] This is the case because NIMBY issues are governed by what Sidney Plotkin has termed an expansion-exclusion dialectic.[94] Plotkin argues that the structure of land-use rights in capitalist states will tend to shift between establishing expansion rights that are necessary for capital circulation and growth and exclusion rights that are necessary for "fixing" or storing capital. This shifting of rights, for example, can be seen in the evolution of property rights. Feudal "bundles" of rights and responsibilities essentially locked capital into land; early capitalism reduced these bundles to a "fee simple" state, thereby facilitating easy exchange and enclosure of the commons, while protecting each estate as if it were its own kingdom. And industrial capitalism (in the name of economic development and jobs) broke down the strict walls of Blackstonian property and the libertarian interpretation of nuisance law so as to favor industrial expansion. The evolution of property rights and the resulting social conflict to this point can be easily interpreted in light of a Marxian analysis of production-based class divisions.

More modern land-use conflicts, however, are not easily explained by a focus on conflicts of production-based interests (such as capitalists versus workers). Instead, contemporary land-use conflicts tend to divide citizens (who may be capitalist or workers) in their capacity as neighbors and consumers of land against industrial and development interests. Instead of conflicts between two identifiable classes, these conflicts will tend to break down along a number of different, sometimes unpredictable lines, including national or global versus regional or local, producers versus consumers, and majority racial groups against minority groups.[95]

Traditional Marxist theory is unable to explain fully these types of conflicts.[96] Observers have noted, for example, that worker-citizens, generally having accepted that they will be unable to affect the course of developments in the global production system, have shifted their desires to shape economic change to the local level. Local land-use issues, particularly land uses that affect their residential property, are the battlegrounds for the most intense social conflicts in postindustrial capitalism.

To explain workers' identification with place-based, land-use issues rather than larger class interests, Plotkin points to the transformation of capitalism that took place during the 1930s and that resulted in the development of a social welfare state. This change, resulting in a general distribution of private and collective goods to working class citizens, has also changed the basis by which we should understand the generation of social conflict. Rather than understanding land-use conflict as a result of a conflict between ever more sharply defined production-based interests, the mass distribution of goods has shifted the ground of conflict to more consumer-based interests. The relations of consumption, Plotkin argues, tend to be local in nature and to center on the consumption of housing—the largest item in an average consumer's budget.[97]

By accepting the relations of consumption as distinct from those of production and as strong a source of social value, it is possible to explain many land-use conflicts as a split between powerful producers of development projects and sometimes (in cases of affluent consumers) equally powerful groups of consumers of neighborhoods and communities. The producers of development projects will tend to be seen as large-scale outside forces for economic development whose desire for efficient location of production facilities is frustrated by local action. In many cases, the interests of what Plotkin calls "national political elites" will join with these developers to overcome local opposition or will propose their own large-scale projects (such as airports, highways, hazardous waste facilities) in support of national economic expansion. At the local level, however, private tenure rights in housing will tend to fuse with local political rights over land-use policy in efforts to resist the intrusion of developers. This consumption-based theory of land-use conflict explains how, for the most part, the environmental movement has developed from an individual NIMBY outrage to a local expression of the desire to protect "everyone's backyard," but has failed, in some respects, to generate serious national-level opposition to the development interests.[98] The consumptionist theory of land-use conflicts can also explain the origins of social justice-oriented land-use issues. Although social welfare measures have generated substantial consumer property, the allocation of this property has been highly unequal. Hence, more privileged homeowners and tenants will resist the inclusion of less privileged ones, especially those with characteristics (such as racial or handicapped status) that might lower property values. Unlike the relations of production, which tend toward a bimodal distribution, separating owners from workers, those of consumption involve multiple domains. The production of subdivision housing that is standardized and designed to meet the consumption and mobility needs (both economic and geographical) of citizens within a single income class has made visible and magnified the potential for localized, consumer group-specific conflicts. Depending on how each land-use issue aggregates separate consumer-group domains, land-use conflicts can range from neighborhood-specific efforts to exclude a mental health care home to countywide or regional efforts to block the introduction of a hazardous waste landfill.[99]

Although consumerist theory can help explain the origins of land-use conflict, Plotkin suggests that there is still a need to have a more unified understanding of the relations between consumption and production, because consumption theory alone tends to "cope with the contradictions of class and consumption less by explaining them than by taking them as a given historical distinction."[100] Plotkin argues that an examination of the characteristics of private property, particularly its twin properties of expansion and exclusion, can help explain land-use policies and politics.

Plotkin's argument is generally as follows: In order for capital to circulate and perform its "creative destruction" functions, a substantial amount of social capital has to be fixed in place. This is the case because, as Stephen Cohen and John Zysman, the authors of *Manufacturing Matters*, suggest, finance capital ultimately must be based on real assets.[101] Landed property provides the "entrenched value" needed to support business activities that are themselves subject to high levels of competitive threat. The "immobility of land underpins the power of landowners to resist the competitive forces of devaluation and dislocation." The common-law property right of exclusion is the key to landowners' ability to resist devaluation and dislocation. Hence, the magnified expansion rights of property that occurred in the age of industrial capitalism had to have limits if capital was not to self-destruct. As Polanyi's work suggests, as a viable social system, even capitalism cannot accept a perfectly free market—or at least not one that is based on the expansion rights of property alone. The ability to exclude and temporarily lock in capital is an essential attribute as well.

As expansionary capital was collectivized through the recognition of corporate citizenship in the early industrial era, there was a need to balance the growth of expansionary rights with a similar growth of exclusionary property rights. Hence, a parallel collectivization of exclusionary rights can be seen in the development of land-use planning and zoning controls and the widespread use of restrictive covenants. This collectivization was aided by local business and labor groups who were interested in "controlling the flow of capital in and out of their community" and stopping or slowing the tendency of capital to seek areas with the lowest production costs or to eliminate non-competitive local business.[102]

Marxist theory readily explains the dynamics of the expansionist-production side of land-use conflict dynamics, while consumptionist theory is more effective in explaining the exclusionary side of this dynamic. Expansion rights involve the investment in abstract titles that can either be used to change the land for productive purposes or be sold to absentee owners who will perform this function. Exclusionary rights involve rights against unlawful trespass and rights against other neighboring property owners using their lands in ways that would be injurious to private parties or the community in general.[103]

Plotkin suggests that the counterpoising of expansionary and exclusionary rights is an economic necessity for capitalism in that "they stem from the contradiction between fixed and circulating capital." However, on numerous levels, he believes, these counterpoised rights are likely to collide and cause social conflict. The role of the state in this dynamic is to mediate these conflicts by adjusting the balancing between these two aspects of property (and of capitalism) and thereby balancing the social power of expansionist capital with the preservation of entrenched users living in specific communities. By adjusting the legal-social relations of property in a social welfare society, Plotkin argues, the state can maintain the social relations of production. However, the result of the more recent adjustments, Plotkin believes, has been the relegation of labor to an "exclusionary position." As a result, the dominant forms of social conflict will tend to pit exclusionary interests against expansionary ones.

Plotkin's theory affords two observations relevant to understanding conflicts over land uses. First, Plotkin brings to the foregoing critique of interest group liberalism the insight that interest groups in land-use debates do not simply form in a willy-nilly fashion; they are shaped by very basic legal structuring, especially around property rights. And the state is not simply captured by interests that turn to the state for support or that request that the state mediate private sector conflicts. Rather, the state, especially the judiciary, has a major role in structuring the interest relationships around an expansion-exclusion dynamic. However, this role is difficult to fulfill in any way that is consistent with classic liberal notions of clear standards. Plotkin writes:

> We can also suggest a second generalization about the nature of the state's role in land-use policy. Under the gun of the exclusion-expansion dialectic, the liberal principle of formal-general legal rules, predicable and obeyable in advance, must fall. The lack of clear standards in land-use law and policy—a

> lack which vastly increases the importance of political struggles in shaping the outcomes of land-use controversies—is determined not by the incompetence of judges but by the internal contradictions of landed property. In this field contradiction and conflict are endemic. They cannot be avoided by clear and consistent rules, nor by the "comprehensive" land-use policy dreamed of by managers and planners. No corps of legislators, not the wisest or the most scholarly, could author a consistent land-use law because the dominant institution of land use—private capitalist property—must harbor the capacity to expand and exclude all at once. Just as no army of administrators could build a jurisdiction wide enough to encompass all the externalities of capitalist land use because the problems are inherent in the contradictory functioning of the institution, not its scale. In the end, any policy in consistent support of expansion or exclusion rights would shatter half the expectations of capital. Thus has it been left to the law courts and local and regional administrations of capitalist governments to regulate, however awkwardly, the force and counterforce of capitalist property, to keep rights moving or to keep them from caving in on the rights of others."[104]

A second observation can be drawn from Plotkin's land-use conflict theory. Because of the centrality and unavoidability of the expansion-exclusion property rights dialectic in capitalist societies, the classic liberal ideal of having private interests represented solely by the legislature branch is clearly unrealizable. As discussed above, in classic liberal thought only the legislature is considered a legitimate arena for mediating private sector interests because it alone allowed for balancing multiple interests at one time and for allocations based on democratic strength. Also, intrusion of private interests into the judicial or executive branch would violate notions of due process and equal protection. If, as Plotkin suggests, the delineation of expansionary and exclusionary property rights effectively organizes interests into two large blocks, then the safeguards for democracy of having numerous interests represented in the legislature are effectively undermined.

Moreover, the dominant position of the judiciary in articulating these rights would place this branch in a more sovereign role than was originally conceived by the Founders. At a minimum, the narrow channeling of social conflicts into judicial structures can result in very basic decisions being made in an apolitical manner. The effect of depoliticizing land-use disputes is furthered by the multi-tiered nature of the judicial system. Land-use disputes that in principle should involve the mediation of numerous interests situated at various levels of society are typically decided in a more narrow fashion. Because these disputes arise land plot by land plot, and are tried in any one of thousands of local and state courts, it is impossible for the broad and multiple interests at stake in land-use policy to be effectively heard. When decision making about something as basic as our built and natural environments is so fragmented that only a few of the parties who potentially have an interest in the outcome can, for all practical purposes, give voice to their interest, the results are not likely to reflect the underlying public interest. While it is true that the harm that judicial decision making can do in the area of land-use policy is constrained by the narrow scope, plodding pace, and fragmented nature of the process, it is no less true that these features of the judicial process undermine the potential for systemic resolution of land-use conflicts.

The Managerial Response

As social conflicts embedded in landed property rights to expansion and exclusion have played out and as the courts' mediations have been ineffective in resolving conflicts or unable to discover appropriate judicial precedent for an adequate resolution,[105] there have been numerous attempts to create a higher-level managerial solution to locally focused land-use conflicts. State and national level land-use planning and environmental legislation and national fair housing, mortgage lending, and civil rights legislation and enforcement are representative of this effort. The basis for these attempts has been a belief that a more centralized planning and land-use decision-making would reduce the irrationality of hundreds of various local planning ordinances and judicial decisions. The variety of such ordinances and decisions, it was argued, added only mind-numbing complexity to decisions about siting industrial, waste treatment, and community care facilities. Moreover, the complexity of resolving disputes about land uses seemed only to grow worse as decision makers increasingly had to consider the preservation of greenspace, historic values, and ecological sustainability.

The difficulty with the administrative solution to land-use disputes is that it accepts as given the existing delineation of conflicting property rights and the existing organization of interests that spring from this delineation. Additionally, as argued earlier, in a political structure characterized by interest group liberalism, the administrative structure at higher levels of government is as likely or more likely to be captured by elite interests.[106] In a telling passage, for example, William Greider quotes Leon Billings, an environmental consultant and a staff director of the Senate Public Works Committee who was active in development of key federal environmental laws:

> "Adopting national air ambience standards in the Clean Air Act was the biggest mistake we ever made," he confessed. "Citizens-for-clean-air groups were beginning to get local governments to adopt tougher standards around the country, much tougher than anticipated, and industry wanted to get out from under these local and regional activists who were coming after them everywhere. The Clean Air Act brought the fight to Washington where industry could manipulate things much more cleverly."
>
> "The federal law short-circuited the activism. It took away the forum for local activists, and they had to become involved in much more technical

arguments, an arena where industry is strong and citizens are weak. Once policy issues become engulfed in the federal bureaucracy, the public loses the ability to influence these decisions because local electronic and print media simply lose interest in the issues. The story is suddenly distant and difficult to cover in local newspaper. There's no local agitation because it's now a 'national issue.' "[107]

CONCLUSIONS

The corruption of classic liberal ideals into real interest group liberalism is evident in all three branches of the classically designed federalist governance structure. The Progressive Era-inspired development of open-forum, information-grounded, rational politics left open the question of how information would be generated and rationality defined. Powerful interest groups were quick to answer the question and to create in conjunction with the growing number of agency-based public officials subgovernments where policy is formulated outside of full public inspection. Legislators' desires to avoid conflict and the technical complexity of policy areas supported this blurring of the private and public realm so antithetical to classic liberalism. Finally, the role of the judicial branch in organizing and balancing private production and consumption interests in a capitalist economy suggests that the classic liberal ideal of democratic policymaking has often been bypassed by judicial delineation of property rights on the margins of the political landscape.

Because classic liberal ideals have ceased to guide the daily operation of modern political institutions, and because these ideals have been particularly corrupted by the dynamics of interest group liberalism, other ideologies afford particular if divergent lenses on the social origins of contemporary land-use conflicts. Conservatives of a libertarian bent are particularly sensitive to the dangers of administrative management or regulation of property; they would favor a return to earlier judicial notions of property rights, specifically the Blackstonian notions of unitary rights, and would use the takings clause of the Constitution to declare land-use regulations, including most zoning, equivalent to public condemnations. By requiring just compensation for such regulatory takings, libertarians and conservatives would use the judicial system to favor expansionist property interests and limit exclusionary interests to only those situations where the public is willing to pay. While conservatives would use cost-benefit analysis to determine those few situations where such regulation might seem reasonable from the view of mainstream (read conservative) economic analysis, strict libertarians, like Richard Epstein, extending the logic of "takings" to include most taxation, would limit the collectivization of exclusionary property rights almost exclusively to those created by voluntary contracts among property owners.[108]

Although conservatives and libertarians disagree on the relative primacy of the nation-state and the individual, they agree on the tactic of using judicial processes and "original" Blackstonian interpretations of property rights to reaffirm the dominant position of expansionary interests. In general, this tactic has been unsuccessful, due to the dominant judicial philosophy of the Supreme Court since the New Deal. However, the recent appointments of more conservative justices to the Court have given conservatives and libertarians some reason for hope. Four recent Supreme Court cases, *First English*, *Nollan*, *Lucas*, and *Dolan*, have suggested that the Court is somewhat more likely to recognize the conservative-libertarian takings position. Simply put, in each of these cases, the court found that regulations that leave the owner with no economically viable use or that divest the owner of some essential aspect of property would constitute a compensable taking.[109] Some observers believe that the stance taken by the court in these cases represents the effective culmination of conservative efforts to make it easier for property owners to get compensated for regulatory takings (that is, for those that do not involve a physical invasion of the property).[110] Others believe that these decisions are in a long line of decisions that have attempted (most observers say, without success) to define when a regulation has, in the words of Oliver Wendall Holmes, "gone too far." Those who believe that the Supreme Court's decision in *Lucas* is consistent with earlier decisions and is not particularly revolutionary note that the Court would have still allowed a 100 percent taking of the economically viable use of a property if the government's regulation is based on traditional notions and standards of nuisance law.[111] The relatively unrevolutionary character of these decisions, and of *Lucas* especially, is also supported by a review of subsequent cases where *Lucas* is cited. This review suggests that the *Lucas* situation (involving a restriction of all building on a piece of coastal property for which David Lucas paid nearly a million dollars several years prior to the regulation) was an extreme case and that most reasonable environmental regulation would easily pass a takings analysis.[112] In the *Nollan* and *Dolan* cases, the Court has overturned attempts by local governments to exact some value from a property owner that was not expressly and measurably related to impact that the proposed use of the property would have on the well-being of the community. In the more recent *Dolan* case, for example, a local government had conditioned the granting of a owner's request to expand his store on the owner's relinquishing 10 percent of his property for use as part of a pathway for walkers and bicyclists. The Court noted that the local government had failed to prove that the existence of a foot and bicycle path would in any measurable way be needed or effective in alleviating the assumed increase in traffic that would be occasioned by the store's expansion. While *Dolan* represents an extension of the earlier *Nollan* decision, in which the Court declared it unconstitutional for government to exact a property right (an easement for walkers) that was unrelated to the impact of the proposed property use (the building of a residence on coastal property), it is still too early to understand how this 1994 decision will affect other related land-use control efforts. The conservatives' judicial tactics in land-use cases may not have been entirely successful to date, but the current trend seems to favor more protection of individual and indivisible property rights. Considering that more than half of the judges now sitting in federal courts are Reagan or Bush appointees, many of whom have been schooled in conservative-libertarian private property ideology, the tactic that Sidney Plotkin refers to as a "replay of the script of nineteenth-century legal changes in property law" is not entirely farfetched. If one accepts Madison's more comprehensive view of property and a basic belief in citizen sovereignty and democratic processes, the success of conservative judicial tactics designed to give the same protection to property rights that is given to other civil rights is hardly auspicious or in the mainstream tradition of democratic values.[113] Although conservative and libertarian property constructs and political tactics do not provide sufficient guide to NIMBY or LULU-type problems, libertarian scholarship has shed important light on the value and potential of informal relations among property owners, which Robert Ellickson has described as "order without law." These insights into the nature of voluntary collaboration are of great value even if citizens decide that some law, or less formally, rules need to be crafted.[114] This theme will be picked up in the discussion of collective governance of common pool resources in the chapters that follow.

Communitarians' insights into the problems of interest group liberalism are much more telling. Drawing on the work of Unger, Polanyi, and Plotkin, among others, and on the context of European corporatism, communitarian strategies for overcoming the weakness of interest group liberalism are oftentimes more realist in nature than those implied in other ideologies. That is, communitarians tend to assume that private interests are difficult to separate from public ones and that the state is inextricably intertwined in the very organization of private interests. Communitarians also draw on the Progressive and legal realist traditions to point out how in modern circumstances the cherished moral values associated with property rights are as much undermined by traditional, unified conceptions of property rights as they are protected. In particular, these realists have demonstrated that the private power of concentrated property, unmediated by public power, has resulted in insecurity, dependency, and loss of personhood rather than the security, independence, and integrity that property rights were originally believed to secure.[115] This realist critique of property, moreover, uncovered a level of complexity in modern life and relationships that was absent in the constitutional world of the Founders.

For the Founders and for most peoples living in agrarian societies, boundary-making in terms of a constitutional separation of institutional powers and moral spheres of action (such as public versus private) is "conceptually and morally easy" in large measure because property provided both a metaphor and a base for such boundary-making.[116] The rise of the modern business corporation and the multiple forms in which property has been unbound in order to meet the needs of economic development and the desire for more complex interaction have destroyed the relatively easy world in which boundaries could be established, understood, and respected in both property and political realms.

Whereas classic liberals would re-establish clear boundaries and rules of law in both the political and property realms, even ideologically neutral observers (who tend to take a realist and utilitarian position) agree with Frank Michelman that "the price of such high [rule of law] formality, in a dynamic and impacted world, is obtuseness."[117] This obtuseness, Michelman suggests, comes in the form of the inability of a few formal, simple, and abstract per se rules to also allow the development of plausible policy. When, for example, property is understood as an abstract concept that is separated from experience and from historical change, applications of earlier concepts of property can lead to difficulties. One difficulty noted in recent property law decisions has been termed the "takings paradox": Some government regulation (such as that in the *Loretto* case) that clearly violates a formal rule, such as the one against physical intrusion, but that results in only a small monetary loss is deemed a taking requiring government compensation, while government regulations that result in large monetary losses (such as in the *Penn Central* case) but that do not violate a formal rule are not understood as takings.[118]

Paradoxes of this type, communitarians and critical legal studies scholars suggest, are inherent in legal formulas that have the feel of a common understanding of property but that run up against the reality of the multiple forms, economic practices, property interests, and "communities of understanding" in postindustrial societies. Adherence to rules, these critics of formalism note, will tend to result in the kind of unfairness found in the takings paradox.

This paradox can perhaps be explained in part by reference to world system theory. In this theory, originally put forth by Immanuel Wallerstein, capitalist development has evolved in a way not conceived by Marx, such that whole nations in the developed "core" take on the role of capitalist owners, while those in the less developed "periphery" are continually in a subservient position, similar to that of workers in a traditional Marxist class analysis. In terms of property rights dynamics, world systems theory might suggest that "core" areas would be more likely to secure exclusionary property rights as a way of protecting existing assets and storing profits in relative safety. Alternatively, more peripheral areas would be predicted to be subject to strong pressure to secure expansionary property rights akin to those that evolved in the United States during the nineteenth century, but that have since been balanced by the development of more exclusionary rights. While development of data on property rights in Third World nations is beyond the scope of this work, the pattern of recent takings decisions in the United States conforms to the expected pattern. That is, the property right rule that the Supreme Court has adhered to with the greatest consistency in recent cases (such as *Loretto*) has been the right of physical exclusion. This development is in line with Plotkin's idea of the development of a consumerist domain and with the implications of world system theory (predicting that this right of exclusion—one protecting established property interests—would receive favor in the core industrialized nations, while the periphery nations would, under the pressures of global capitalism, give greater weight to expansionary property rights).

The argument in the first part of this book suggested that it is just these exclusionary rights—both as they have been individually exercised (such as through restrictive covenants) and as they have been collectivized into zoning ordinances—that have maintained in some measure the evils of racial, income, and disability segregation on the one hand and environmental degradation caused by urban sprawl on the other. William Fischel captures this argument in a nutshell. He suggests that the current "system of land-use controls . . . provides for too little development in suburban communities," which in turn forces "new development into rural areas, creating noncontiguous patterns that involve too much commuting and the loss of agglomeration economies, and confines low-income people to older housing in crowded central cities."[119]

The purpose of this chapter has been to outline some of the political and legal concepts and events that form the background for understanding how NIMBY and LULU issues might be approached. Although readers will draw their own conclusions as to how this review of contemporary problems in political, property law, and related governance issues should inform policymakers, my sense is that plausible new policy initiatives will likely evolve more from the communitarian and classic liberal approaches to these issues than from other ideological streams, but that policy analysts should also occasionally draw on the insights provided by conservative and libertarian thought in the construction of specific policies. My proposed narrowing of the ideological streams for public policy inspiration is based on the view that both communitarian and classic liberal approaches offer a reasonable middle course between the extreme claims of state or self.

The validity of a search for a middle way is also backed by the historical precedents and contemporary experiments in "social-republican property" and new research into common resource problems. Before exploring these potential alternatives to (or innovations on) classic liberal and communitarian ideologies, it may be worthwhile to explore briefly how contemporary academic disciplines have framed various understandings of land-use conflicts. As will be readily apparent, the distinctive disciplines will, because of their particularly limited fields of vision, tend to support or at least give sympathetic understanding to particular ideologies.

NOTES

1. Madison, James. (1986). "Federalist No. 10." *The Federalist Papers*. In *Classic Readings in American Politics*, edited by Pietro Nivola and David Rosenbloom. New York: St. Martin's.

2. Arendt, Hannah. (1965). *On Revolution.* New York: Viking Press, for a discussion of the difference between the French and American views of the role of virtue in democratic revolutions. See Aristotle. (1988) *The Politics*, edited by Stephen Everson. New York: Cambridge University Press for a discussion of the evolution of political forms.

3. O'Looney, John. (1992). "Fractured Decision-Making: Sunshine Laws and the Colliding Roles of Media and Government." *National Civic Review* (Winter-Spring, 1992).

4. Mosher, Frederick C. (1982). *Democracy and the Public Service*. New York: Oxford University Press.

5. Wilson, Woodrow. (1956). *The Wilson Reader.* Edited by Frances Farmer. New York: Oceana Publications.

6. Bettman, Alfred. (1946). *City and Regional Planning Papers*, Cambridge, Mass.: Harvard University Press, p. 46., cited in Nelson, Robert. (1977). *Zoning and Property Rights.* Cambridge, Mass.: MIT Press.

7. Greider, William. (1992). *Who Will Tell the People.* New York: Simon and Schuster. Greider provides evidence that the largest and most powerful think tanks in Washington are sponsored by the "who's who" of corporate America. Copyright © 1992 by William Greider. Reprinted by permission of the author.

8. Caro, Robert. (1974). *The Power Broker: Robert Moses and the Fall of New York.* New York: Knopf.

9. Bettman, *City and Regional Planning Papers*, p. 46.

10. Nelson, *Zoning*, p. 78.

11. Rosenthal, Alan. (1981). "Legislative Behavior and Legislative Oversight." *Legislative Studies Quarterly* 6:1:115-31.

12. Hilferding, Rudolf. (1981). *Finance Capitalism: A Study of the Latest Phase of Capitalist Development.* Boston: Routledge and Kegan Paul.

13. Kolho, Gabriel. (1977). *The Triumph of Conservatism: A Re-Interpretation of American History.* New York: Free Press. See also Phillips, Kevin P. (1984). *Staying on Top.* New York: Random House, 1984.

14. Ripley, Randall, and Franklin, Grace. (1984). *Congress, Bureaucracy, and Public Policy*, 3rd edn. Homewood, Ill.: Dorsey Press.

15. See generally, Greider, *Who Will Tell.*

16. Olson, Mancur. (1979). *The Logic of Collective Action.* Cambridge, Harvard University Press.

17. Lowi, Theodore. (1986). "The Public Philosophy: Interest-Group Liberalism." In *Classic Readings in American Politics*, edited by Pietro Nivola and David Rosenbloom. New York: St. Martin's, p. 279.

18. Ibid., p. 279.

19. William Greider suggests that tax, finance, and banking law that are generated from subgovernment processes may have effects that are more than marginal.

20. Lowi, "Public Philosophy," p. 279.

21. Ibid., p. 273.

22. Greider, *Who Will Tell*, p. 133.

23. Nelson, *Zoning*, pp. 81-82.

24. Ibid., p. 82.

25. Lowi, "Public Philosophy," p. 273.

26. Greider, *Who Will Tell*, p. 113; see also Reagan, Michael. (1987). *Regulation: The Politics of Policy*. New York: Little, Brown.

27. Greider, *Who Will Tell*, p. 118.

28. Ibid., p. 132.

29. Berle, Adolf A., and Means, Gardiner. (1968). *The Modern Corporation and Private Property*. New York: Harcourt, Brace & World.

30. Horwitz, M. J. (1977). *The Transformation of American Law*. Cambridge, Mass.: Harvard University Press; Schreiber, H. (1973). "Property Law Expropriation, and Allocation by Government, 1789-1910." *Journal of Economic History* 33:232-51.

31. Greider, *Who Will Tell*, pp. 331-35.

32. The term "bad boy" is often used interchangeably with "bad actor" and is justified on the basis that all known corporate violators of environmental laws have had men at the helm at the time of the violation.

33. Western Organization of Resource Councils. (1993). *Citizen's Guide to Bad Actor Laws*. Washington, D.C. (draft, October 1993).

34. Hansen, Mark C. (1990). "Smear at Justice." *The Washington Post*, April 8, A, 21:3.

35. Western Organization of Resource Councils. (1993). *Citizen's Guide to Bad Actor Laws*. Washington, D.C. (draft, October 1993).

36. Lowi, Theodore. (1979). *The End of Liberalism: The Second Republic of the United States*. New York: Norton.

37. Lowi, *The End of Liberalism*, chapter 3.

38. Olson, Mancur. (1982). *The Rise and Decline of Nations*. New Haven, Conn.: Yale University Press.

39. Offe, Claude. (1985). *Disorganized Capitalism*. Cambridge, Mass.: MIT Press.

40. Schmitter, Philippe, and Streeck, Wolfgang. (1985). *Private Interest Government: Beyond Market and State*. Beverly Hills, Calif.: Sage.

41. Cawson, Alan. (1985). *Organized Interests and the State: Studies in Meso-Corporatism*. Beverly Hills, Calif.: Sage.

42. Katzenstein, Peter. (1987). *The Semi-Sovereign State*. Philadelphia: Temple University Press; Allen, Christopher et al. (1987). European Politics in Transition. Lexington, Mass.: D. C. Heath and Co.

43. Allen, *European Politics*, p. 295.

44. Kesselman, Mark, and Krieger, Joel. (1987). "State Institutions." In *European Politics in Transition*, edited by Allen Christopher et al. Lexington, Mass: D. C. Heath and Co.; Barsoux, J. L., and Lawrence, P. (1991). "The Making of a French Manager." *Harvard Business Review* 69:4:58-68.

45. Lowi, "Public Philosophy," p. 285.

46. Much of the literature on industrial policy is an expression of the tension between public and private sector roles in the development of national economies. See Magaziner, I. C., and Reich, R. B. (1983). *Minding America's Business*. New York: Vintage Books; Reich, Robert B. (1983). *The Next American Frontier*. New York: Times Books; Rothwell, Roy, and Zegveld, Walter. (1981). *Industrial Innovation and Public Policy: Preparing for the 1980s and the 1990s*. Westport, Conn.: Greenwood Press; Teubal, Morris. (1987). *Innovation, Performance, Learning, and Government Policy*. Madison, Wisc.: University of Wisconsin Press; Zysman, John. (1983). *Governments, Markets and Growth*. Ithaca, N.Y.: Cornell University Press; Porter, Michael. (1990). "The Competitive Advantage of Nations." *Harvard Business Review* 68:2:73-96; and Council on Competitiveness. (1991). *Gaining New Ground: Technology Priorities for America's Future*, Council on Competitiveness, Washington, D. C. More recently, there has been a debate as to whether it is possible in an age of global markets to identify and separate for policy development purposes a national economy. See Reich, Robert. (1991). "Who is Them?" *Harvard Business Review* 69:2:77-90; and Thurow, Lester. (1992). *Head to Head: The Coming Economic Battle Among Japan, Europe and America*. New York: Murrow.

47. Wildavsky, Aaron, and Webber, Carolyn. (1986). A *History of Taxation and Expenditure in the Western World*. New York: Simon and Schuster; and Wanniski, Jude. (1989). *The Way the World Works*. Morristown, N.J.: Polyeconomic.

48. Jacobs, Jane. (1992). *Systems of Survival: A Dialogue on the Moral Foundations of Commerce and Politics*. New York: Random House, p. 195.

49. O'Looney, John. (1992). "Public-Private Partnerships for Economic Development." *Economic Development Review* 10:4:14-23.

50. A number of *Wall Street Journal* editorials during the fall of 1993 treated this issue.

51. O'Looney, "Public-Private Partnerships," pp. 14-22.

52. Madison, "Federalist No. 10, " In *Classic Readings in American Politics*, edited by Pietro Nivola and David H. Rosenbloom. New York: St. Martin's Press, pp. 29-38.

53. Pitkin, Hanna, F. (1967). *The Concept of Representation*. Berkeley, Calif.: University of California Press, pp. 195-196; Rose, Carol M. (1983). "Planning and Dealing: Piecemeal Land Controls as a Problem of Local Legitimacy." *California Law Review* 71:837-912.

54. See, generally, National Institute of Law Enforcement and Criminal Justice. (1979). *Corruption in Land Use and Building Regulation*. Washington, D. C.: U.S. Department of Justice; National Institute of Law Enforcement and Criminal Justice. (1979). *An Analysis of Zoning Reform: Minimizing the Incentives for Corruption*. Washington, D.C.: U.S. Department of Justice.

55. Rose, "Planning and Dealing," p. 855.

56. Ibid., p. 856. See also, Michelman, Frank. (1977-78). "Political Markets and Community Self-Determination: Competing Judicial Models of Local Government Efficiency." *Indiana Law Journal* 53:145-73.

57. Popper, Frank. (1981). *The Politics of Land-use Reform*. Madison, Wis. : University of Wisconsin Press.

58. Bassett, Edward M. (1940). *Zoning: The Laws, Administration and Court Decisions During the First Twenty Years.* New York : Russell Sage Foundation; Dukeminier, Jesse F., and Stapleton, Clyde L. (1962). "The Zoning Board of Adjustment: A Case Study in Misrule." *Kentucky Law Journal* 50: 273; and Dukeminier, Jesse F., and Stapleton, Clyde L. "Zoning Amendments and Variation, and Neighborhood Decline in Illinois." *Northwestern University Law Review* 48: 470-80.

59. Rose, "Planning and Dealing," p. 858.

60. Babcock, Richard F. (1959). "The Unhappy State of Zoning Administration in Illinois." *University of Chicago Law Review* 26: 509-38.

61. For a discussion and critique of the lack of a relationship between planning and zoning, see Harr, Charles. (1955). "The Master Plan: An Impermanent Constitution." *Law and Contemporary Problems* 20:353-66.

62. *Fasano v. Board of County Commissioners* (1973). 264 Or. 574, 507 P.2d 23.

63. *Forest City Enters, Inc. v. City of Eastlake* (1975). 41 Ohio St. 2d 187, 195, 324 N.E.2d 740, 746. Cited in Rose, "Planning and Dealing," p. 864.

64. *Forest City Enters, Inc. v. City of Eastlake*, 426 U.S. at 673-74.

65. Rose, "Planning and Dealing," p. 867.

66. Sander, Richard. (1988). "Individual Rights and Demographic Realities: The Problem of Fair Housing." *Northwestern University Law Review* 82:3:888-90.

67. Taylor, Dorceta. (1989). "Blacks and the Environment: Toward an Explanation of the Concern and Action Gap Between Blacks and Whites." *Environment and Behavior* 22:175.

68. Ellickson, Robert C. (1990). "Three Systems of Land-Use Controls." *Harvard Journal of Law and Public Policy* 13:1:73. Ellickson sees most zoning proposals as problematic. He also suggests that it is not only powerful developers who capture unearned rents from land-use regulation. Theatre supporters, unions, and professional housing advocates, he notes, have attempted to get unearned subsidies for their own causes.

69. Gibbs is quoted in Greider, *Who Will Tell*, p. 167.

70. Ibid., p. 168.

71. Austin, Regina, and Schill, Michael. (1991). "Black, Brown, Poor & Poisoned: Minority Grassroots Environmentalism and the Quest for Eco-Justice." *Kansas Journal of Law and Public Policy* 1:69-82.

72. Ibid., p. 75.

73. Ibid., pp. 76-77.

74. Ibid., p. 75.

75. Browder, Joseph B. (1989). "Siting Industrial Facilities in the Western United States." In *Public Interests in the Use of Private Lands*, edited by Benjamin Dysart III and Marion Clawson. New York: Praeger, pp. 99-114.

76. Ibid., p. 112.

77. Ibid., p. 113.

78. Delogu, Orlando E. (1990). " 'NIMBY' is a National Environmental Problem." *South Dakota Law Review* 35:198-219.

79. Ibid.

80. Austin and Schill, "Black, Brown, Poor," p. 77.

81. Ibid., p. 77. See also Lewis, Richard. (1986). "Destruction of Community." *Buffalo Law Review* 35: 365.

82. Austin and Schill, "Black, Brown, Poor," p. 77.

83. Epstein, Richard. (1990). "Property and Necessity." *Harvard Journal of Law and Public Policy* 13:1: 5-6; Peake's N.P. 270, 170 Eng. Rep. 153 (K.B. 1793); and (*Story v. Challends*, 8 C. and P. 234, 173 Eng. Rep. 475 (1873).

84. Lecture by Rob Remar at environmental law seminar, University of Georgia Law School, Athens, Ga., November, 1991.

85. Rabkin, Jeremy. (1990). "Private Property and Public Office." *Harvard Journal of Law and Public Policy* 13:1: 58.

86. Bell, Daniel. (1960). *The End of Ideology*. Glencoe, Ill.: Free Press. More specifically, see Gray, Thomas. (1980). "The Disintegration of Property." *NOMOS: Property* 69.

87. Blackstone, W. (1791). *Commentaries on the Laws of England*. London, England: Dawsons of Pall Mall, 1066. Reprint of the first edition with supplement.

88. Gray, "Disintegration," p. 73.

89. Krier, James. (1990). "The (Unlikely) Death of Property." *Harvard Journal of Law and Public Policy* 13:1: 75-83.

90. Schauer, Fredrick. (1990). "Property as Politics." *Harvard Journal of Law and Public Policy* 13:1: 61-66.

91. Peterson, P. E. (1981). *City Limits*. Chicago: University of Chicago Press.

92. Ellickson, "Three Systems," p. 69.

93. Browder, "Siting Industrial Facilities," pp. 99-114.

94. Plotkin, Sidney. (1987). "Property, Policy, and Politics: Toward a Theory of Land-Use Conflict." *International Journal of Urban and Regional Research* 2:3: 387-404.

95. Plotkin, "Property, Policy, and Politics," pp. 387-404.

96. Plotkin reviews a number of class analysis explanations of the primacy of land-use conflicts but rejects these explanations because the same Marxist theory is used to develop a number of different accounts of the same events, suggesting a lack of theoretical coherence.

97. Saunders, P. (1981). *Social Theory and the Urban Question*. New York: Holmes and Meier.

98. See generally, Greider, *Who Will Tell*, for a description of the failure of the environmental movement to achieve its national-level objectives.

99. See generally, Castells, M. (1984). *The City and the Grassroots*. Berkeley: University of California Press; and Boyte, H. C. (1980). *The Backyard Revolution: Understanding the New Citizen Movement*. Philadelphia: Temple University Press.

100. Plotkin, "Property," pp. 389-90.

101. Cohen, Stephen S., and Zysman, John. (1987). *Manufacturing Matters: The Myth of a Post-Industrial Economy*. Washington, D.C.: Carnegie Forum on Education.

102. Plotkin, "Property," p. 390. Also, Bluestone, Barry, and Harrison, Bennett. *The Deindustrialization of America*. New York: Basic Books, 1982.

103. Plotkin, "Property," pp. 389-95.

104. Ibid., p. 395.

105. For example, the Supreme Court's decisions related to segregation based on historically drawn rather than racially motivated school districts or to the validity of exclusionary zoning based on wealth differentials.

106. See generally, Popper, *The Politics of Land Use*; and Greider, *Who Will Tell*.

107. Greider, *Who Will Tell*, p. 171.

108. Epstein, Richard. (1985). *Takings: Private Property and the Power of Eminent Domain*. Cambridge: Harvard University Press.

109. First English Evangelical Lutheran Church of Glendale, 482 U.S. 304 (1987); *Nollan v. California Coastal Commission*, 483 U.S. 825 (1987); *Lucas v. South Carolina Coastal Council*, 112 S.Ct. 28886 (1992). See also *Columbia Law Review* Vol. 88. No. 8. for a series of articles on the 1987 decisions; Williams, Norman (1993) for a two-part series on the Lucas decision, "A Narrow Escape?" *Zoning and Planning Law Report*, (April-May 1993), pp. 113-20, and pp.121-28; and Merriman, Dwight. (1993). "No, Norman the Sky is Not Falling." *Zoning and Planning Law Report*, 16:137-141. (July-August 1993), for a reply to Norman's article.

110. Norman, "A Narrow Escape?," pp. 137-141.

111. Levison, Alex. (1992). "Introduction to the Takings Issue." Talk at the December 1992 Colloquium, San Francisco, Calif.: Sierra Club.

112. Merriam, "No, Norman," 137-141. Merriam suggests that environmentalists who wish to ensure that their proposed regulations are not struck down due to a "takings" finding should follow some basic strategies: (1) designate critical areas early and often; (2) stick to life safety issues, nuisance, and property restrictions as a basis for critical area designation (one of the reasons the prohibition of coastal building was found to be a regulation was the state legislature's inclusion of "the promotion of tourism" as one of its purposes); (3) never render a property valueless (Merriam suggests the use of special permits, cluster zoning, conditional uses, and transfer of development rights as strategies for maintaining some value in property); and (4) provide escape hatches in the form of variance exceptions to a regulation that threatens to render a property valueless.

113. Plotkin, "Property," p. 398.

114. Ellickson, Robert C. (1991). *Order Without Law: How Neighbors Settle Disputes*. Cambridge, Mass.: Harvard University Press.

115. Cohen. (1927). "Property and Sovereignty," 13 Cornell L.Q.

116. Michelman, Frank. (1988). "Takings: 1987." *Columbia Law Review* 88:8:1600-29; Nedelsky, Jennifer. (1990). *Private Property and the Limits of American Constitutionalism: A View from the Formation*. Chicago : University of Chicago Press.

117. Michelman, "Takings," p. 1628.

118. Radin, Margaret Jane. (1988). "The Liberal Conception of Property: Cross Currents in the Jurisprudence of Takings." *Columbia Law Review* 88:8:1667-96; *Penn Central Trans. v. New York City*, 438 U.S. 104 (1978); and *Lotto v. Teleprompter Manhattan CATV Corp.*, 458 U.S. (1982).

119. Fischel, William. (1988). "Introduction: Utilitarian Balancing and Formalism in Takings." *Columbia Law Review* 88:8:1582-83.

CHAPTER 4

Land-Use Control and the Idea of Common Pool Resources

Historically, land-use controls have arisen from various mixtures of ideological views of property rights in the context of historically specific problems, emerging sensitivities, and the dominant political forces and structures. Hence, in the beginning of the Industrial Revolution, a number of factors—the need for greater economic productivity to supply larger populations, the known benefits of enclosure, the lack of awareness about many pollutants, the expansion of political power to emerging capitalists, the rise of liberal ideologies and laissez-faire markets, and the judicial ability to revise traditional property rights that had favored exclusionary (or nuisance avoidance) property rights—combined to affect a change in land-use controls that favored development and the interests of industrialists over more residential or agriculturally based owners of property. Where previous chapters of this book have explored historical and ideological elements of land-use control, this chapter examines generic criteria for effective land-use control that might have prominence within any historical or ideological context. More precisely, this chapter explores some of the academic thinking in different disciplines about land-use governance. The chapter begins with a discussion of four key criteria for assessing specific land uses. It proceeds with an exploration of a particular area of policy studies—the governance of common pool resources—that is relevant to understanding the governance of a number of LULU issues, and concludes with a suggestion that if one understands human dignity and public happiness as valid types of common pool resources, certain implications for land-use governance follow.

VALUES AND THE DEVELOPMENT OF LAND-USE CONFLICTS

Although each of the ideologies outlined earlier represents a complex weave of a number of conceptual and normative threads, specific land-use conflicts in their immediate context can often be understood as disagreements about the application of four distinct values or criteria: environmental quality, efficiency, equity, and community viability.[1] Environmental quality is based on a study of the features in an ecosystem that allow for the long-term maintenance of life. Efficiency as a criterion is built on an understanding of the relationship between individual or group effort or investment and the potential for return, especially material return. Equity includes the twin (and often counterpoised) ideas of a justice-based equity, which would allocate resources according to one's contributions and merits, and the idea of an ethic of care in which benefits and opportunities are distributed broadly because of human dignity or status. Community viability is based on an understanding of those features (such as socialization, morality, law) that are believed to be fundamental to a social order.[2]

Thomas Gutterbock has suggested that from these four basic criteria, one can identify six potential types of land-use value-criteria conflicts: [3]

1. environmental quality versus efficiency (such as air pollution caused by vehicle exhausts weighed against decreased travel time)

2. equity versus community viability (for example, inequitable exclusionary zoning can result in a community of homogeneous interests)

3. environmental quality versus equity (for example, the denial of access to national parks by limiting transportation routes to the parks or the number of people allowed on trails can increase environmental quality)

4. efficiency versus equity (for example, the market efficiency of allocating space for social care or correctional facilities usually results in poorer neighborhoods assuming a greater share of the burden of social responsibility)

5. environmental quality versus community viability (for example, national or regional environmental regulations can often have the effect of reducing local autonomy in choosing or regulating land-use options)

6. efficiency versus community viability (such as the economic costs to individuals of community control of land use or exchange)

Gutterbock is quick to note that his typology is not exhaustive. In particular, it does not address tradeoffs within a particular criterion such as might occur in land-use proposals that would benefit one type of pollution (such as air) while negatively affecting another (such as water). More important, Gutterbock admits that the typology does not directly address the issue of how to balance individual and collective rights and benefits—the issue directly confronted in the contrast of individual versus collective ideologies discussed in Chapter 2.

What Gutterbock's typology does offer, however, is a somewhat systematic way of thinking about the potential tradeoffs involved in any one land-use issue. It also helps to frame the challenge to analysts, planners, and policymaker: that is, how is it possible, first, to design policy that will minimize or eliminate the tradeoffs of values, and second, to effectively order the decision-making process so that all the values are able to be expressed and realized to a degree that is appropriate in a sustainable democracy.

Both challenges involve conscious innovation. The first challenge demands substantive innovation in areas such as the creation of non-polluting fuels or industrial processes, the development of community planning that can promote greater community ties, while reducing inefficient and environment-degrading urban sprawl, the design of human-scale production facilities that can be part of viable communities rather than intrusions on community life, and so forth. A subset of these potential innovations will be treated in detail in the next chapter. The second challenge—how best to balance competing values—cannot be addressed directly. Rather, meeting this challenge requires that we examine current policy-making procedures with regard to land-use control and institute governance and procedural innovations that do a better job of promoting a workable balance of competing land-use values.

Additionally, Gutterbock's typology provides a guide of sorts to the problems caused by the lack of interdisciplinary approaches to land-use conflicts and a perspective on how academic disciplines might contribute to a better understanding of these conflicts in the future.

The Lack of an Interdisciplinary Frame

Examination of the four basic criteria that are most directly involved in land-use conflicts reveals that particular academic disciplines are substantively focused on different criteria. The "hard" physical and biological sciences analyze the components of environmental quality, the "semi-hard" discipline of economics is chiefly concerned with efficiency, and the "softer" social sciences of political science and sociology are concerned with equity and community viability issues, respectively. While all of the academic disciplines weigh "facts" that have normative implications, the normative implications of the facts discovered by physical and biological disciplines for the most part tend to remain hidden until they are understood within a social science-based frame of reference. Among the social sciences, however, there has existed a deep rift between economics and sociology. The discipline of economics assumes that because we are rational, utilitarian, self-interested, and cost-calculating creatures, it is possible to structure a set of legal rules and economic incentives so as to ensure that particular behavioral choices will be made, despite our emotional and moral orientations. Sociology takes the opposite tack and suggests that it is precisely the values and moral orientations that will shape how people react to specific incentives and structures and ultimately determine the viability of these incentives and structures. As an example, Gutterbock points to the relative ineffectiveness of desegregation laws and fair housing regulations to address the problem of residential segregation by race. Despite the fact that many minority citizens could afford to rent or purchase properties in more elite suburban communities, a more subtle de facto racism—a moral and cultural value held by people in both majority and minority races—has probably undermined the effectiveness of the pro-integration structures and incentives, Gutterbock argues.[4] The perceptual rift between sociology and economics has a direct parallel in the division between legal formalists and critical legal studies. Formalists, like economists, believe that a structure of laws and associated sanctions can be created so as to drive behavioral choices, for the most part, in a chosen direction. Critical legal scholars and others (such as Frank Michelman, Margaret Jane Radin) who might more accurately be described as sociologically oriented pragmatists suggest that abstract laws cannot possibly be tuned to the harmonies of specific communities and cultures and therefore cannot be effective. In this view, systems of self-regulating laws, like Polanyi's self-regulating market, break down because they cannot possibly be adapted to the shifting and nuanced social orders and values of real communities.

LULUS AND THE STICKY CASE OF COMMON POOL RESOURCES

Mediating between Sociological and Economic Views

Political science stands between and often mediates the sociological and economic views of the world, siding sometimes with one side, sometimes with the other, and sometimes generating a hybrid view. In particular, the policy side of political science is often concerned with translating sociological and economic insights into practical ideas for governance. In addition to mediating for practical purposes the economics-sociology rift, governance must also consider how particular understandings of environmental qualities are to be integrated into political decision making. The role of policy studies is to create an interdisciplinary frame for resolving social conflicts. Too often, political science, like the other disciplines, has tended to make the "all things being equal" assumptions required to carry out analyses and in the process has ignored crucial findings that lie outside the discipline.[5]

One emerging area of policy studies—the study of common pool resource problems—may have particular relevance to NIMBY and LULU issues. This is the case because common pool resource problems, though conceptually and geographically bounded, usually demand the explicit balancing of all four of Gutterbock's key land-use criteria. Common pool resources (CPR) are generally conceived to be a natural resource such as a fishery, water basin, grazing land, timber stand, or irrigation system. The key property of a CPR is that it is potentially replenishable or renewable as long as it is managed so as to avoid depleting or destroying the system or stock from which the resource units are drawn. However, when an area is over-fished, or too much water is drawn from a basin, or an irrigation system is not maintained, the resource flow from the CPR system or stock will dwindle or, in severe cases, become extinct. Those who draw resources from a CPR are often called appropriators, because they appropriate a part of the resource stream. However, if a CPR is to be maintained, there must also be persons whose role it is to provide for the replenishment of the stock of the CPR or restrict the flow from this stock so that the pool itself is renewed through natural processes over time. Without these providers securing or replenishing the existing stock, the incentives for individuals to appropriate more resources than is sustainable over time may be ruinous to the system. For common pool resouces to remain viable, the system providers or managers clearly must balance economic efficiency with environmental concern. Less obviously, the system managers must maintain the community of owners (who are typically both resource appropriators and providers). Because any one owner can potentially destroy a common pool resource, providing for a high degree of equity among owners is usually necessary in order to maintain trust in the fairness of the distribution of the resource.

While the study of CPR has generally concerned specific natural resources, the knowledge gained from case studies of water basins, common grazing lands and fisheries, and shared irrigation systems may have much broader application. In particular, an argument can be made that the institutions that make up civic and community life may be thought of as a type of common pool resource. Churches, clubs, families, schools, hospitals, and governing bodies all partake of the key characteristics of common pool resources: They can be relied upon for a stream of benefits that can be continually appropriated only if they are also replenished and renewed. While the study of community resources is hampered by numerous intervening variables that complicate analysis, natural CPRs, by providing a simpler and more concrete focus for study, have provided a sort of mini-laboratory for observing naturally occurring social experiments that can provide insight into larger social processes.

Natural CPRs, moreover, are important because they represent direct examples of living environmental systems that can continue to provide benefits as long as they are well managed. Hence, by examining a variety of CPR management systems and comparing the degree to which different systems are able to maintain a steady and reliable flow of benefits without degradation of the resource pool itself, one may be able to draw some conclusions about the viability of particular governance schemes for sensitive environmental resources.

CPR arrangements were once a general feature of Western, feudal land use. Much of the grazing land on feudal estates, for example, was owned in common by the serfs who were attached to the estate. Of course, ownership of these common lands involved a complicated fee arrangement that did not include alienation or exchange rights. The rise of markets for agricultural products and the first agricultural revolution (which dramatically reduced the need for agricultural labor) provided landed estate owners with a major temptation. By "freeing" serfs, enclosing the formerly common lands, and hiring professional managers and seasonal labor, they could reap substantial monetary payments in the new markets for agricultural products. The English Enclosure Acts and the "fee simple" idea of property provided the legal means for doing so.

While most CPRs were institutionally eliminated, some resources, such as fisheries and underground water basins that could effectively be appropriated by numerous owners or residents living in the neighborhood of the resource, could not be practically privatized. These resistant-to-privatization CPRs have continued to be considered anomalies by conservative legal scholars who argue for a "first possession" rule for the origin of property.[6] Because of these unique properties in the natural landscape, a number of CPRs have continued to exist in the West. For example, much of the grazing land in the Swiss Alps is managed as a common pool resource. Moreover, in many places of the world that have not fully experienced or have resisted the pressures of laissez-faire markets, or that need irrigation systems to sustain agricultural yields, CPRs are still common.

LULUs and the Tragedy of Common Property

The importance of CPR studies to environmental land-use issues was dramatized by Garrett Hardin's publication of his "tragedy of the commons" thesis in 1968.[7] Hardin relates how herdsmen shared a common grazing land for centuries without damage to the land because the number of animals being grazed on the land did not exceed the "carrying capacity" of the land both to feed the animals and to replenish the natural grasses. However, with increased population and more herders, increasing numbers of animals were put on the commons to graze. Eventually, because no one had property rights to exclude others, each user rushed to harvest as much of the resource as he could, leading to overgrazing and degradation of land as a replenishable resource.[8] In terms of Sidney Plotkin's expansionary-exclusionary rights dialectic, the tragedy of the commons occurs in large measure because expansionary rights in property are total, while exclusionary rights are nonexistent.

For the most part, Hardin's tragedy of the commons has been used as an argument by conservative economists for the transformation of commons into private property so that exclusionary rights would be added to the commons' open-ended use right.[9] However, Hardin's thesis ran into difficulty when a number of observers noted that many common pool resources or common properties had not experienced tragedies of the type that Hardin predicted. For example, Swiss alpine grazing commons have existed for hundreds of years and continued to exist during periods of severe population growth pressures, yet these commons somehow escaped the tragedy that Hardin predicted for common-use properties.[10] The explanation for the failure of Hardin's prediction lay in the fact that the Swiss common property grazing system and Hardin's commons were essentially two different systems. Two features were found to mark the difference between the two systems: The Swiss common property system included mechanisms for limiting the entry into the commons and for managing how this limitation would occur over time and under different conditions. Hardin's tragic commons had no such mechanisms. Since this discovery, economists have generally distinguished these two systems by referring to Hardin's "tragic" commons as "open access resources," and referring to those systems where exclusionary property rights are established but these rights are collective in nature as "common property resources."

Before exploring how common property resources might function in land-use situations, it should be noted that common pool resource situations have been generalized in two other models. A second model of the "tragedy of the commons" is found in a number of prisoner dilemma games. In these games, one can imagine two herders who are trying to decide how many sheep to graze on a plot of land that is commonly held. There is a limit, however, to the number of sheep that can be grazed successfully so that the sheep will survive and be available for market at the end of the season. For illustration, say this number is twenty. If both herders place ten sheep on the plot, both will earn the profits on ten sheep. If, however, one herder puts more sheep on the plot, that herder will receive more profit as long as the other herder does not also graze an excess number of sheep on the common land. If both herders put an excess number of sheep on the land, neither herder will make any profit because the land will be so overgrazed as to not support any sheep over the entire season. If the herders desire equality (instead of individual resource maximization) and if it were possible for the herders to communicate and trust each other, they might limit their shares of the land to save its carrying capacity for grazing. However, the prisoner dilemma model assumes that players are unable to easily negotiate binding agreements and therefore opt to graze an unlimited number of their own animals, believing this to be the dominant strategy. When both players choose this strategy, however, the result is less beneficial than if they had been able to mutually limit their use of the land.[11]

A third model of the "tragedy of the commons," Mancur Olson's "logic of collective action," has already been discussed.[12] This "logic" explains why the organization and communication needed to escape from a prisoner dilemma game is unlikely to occur. Olson argues that when a benefit (such as an open-access grazing plot) that will be common to a large group demands some collective action on the part of that group in order to realize the benefit, it is unlikely that such action will be taken "without coercion or some other device to make individuals act in their common interest." The problem, as Olson describes it, is that because all will gain whether they contribute to the action needed to realize the benefit, there is no incentive for individuals to contribute to the collective action. Instead, they can free-ride on the action taken by others. As more of the group realizes the possibility of free riding, the likelihood of any collective action being taken is diminished. Olson argues that not only do such free riders fail to abide by rules that would provide for collective benefits, but more important, they also frequently will not expend the resources necessary to carry on negotiations about these rules.

A Narrow Set of Policy Responses

All three of these models of common pool resource situations suggest that perfectly rational individuals, when faced with a common pool resource problem or the need for collective action, will produce outcomes that are essentially irrational. While these models provide powerful analytical tools for thinking about common pool resource problems, policy analysts have often used these models to prescribe a narrow set of policies for real world settings that are much more complex and less constrained than the models assume.[13] In particular, in dealing with numerous and diverse common pool resource problems, policy analysts have tended to choose one of two major policy options that seem to provide some resolution of the common pool resource issue.

"Bringing in the Centralized State" Response

On the one hand, these policy experts have called for bringing the state back in to regulate common pool resource usage (such as to coerce those who would exceed the carrying capacity of the land or deplete permanently the capacity of a basin to hold water to desist). Environmental problems have, until recently, been approached in this general manner.[14] As D. W. Ehrenfeld has argued, when private actors do not act to protect the public domain, regulation by external governmental agencies is needed.[15] Similarly, Ian Carruthers and R. Stoner conclude that without public control, economic efficiency in the development of a common property resource will not occur.[16]

One difficulty with bringing the state in to regulate common pool resources, Elinor Ostrom suggests, is that governmental agents often have very incomplete information about specific strategies that would be needed to induce those who are using a common pool resource to do so wisely. Ostrom illustrates this notion with a prisoner dilemma game in which she assumes that the state will be correct 70 percent of the time in applying a sanction to someone it believes is using a CPR in an improper manner. In playing out this game, she discovers that when the state is incorrect 30 percent of the time in applying its regulations, the equilibrium outcome of the game (the outcome in which each player has acted in a rational self-interested manner) has a lower value than in an unregulated game.[17]

The "Privatization" Response

While imposing central authority over a CPR is often not satisfactory, Ostrom argues that the other dominant policy option—privatization—is also often flawed. Proponents of creating a system of private property rights to solve the commons "tragedy" use economic analysis to conclude that these rights are needed to avoid the inefficiency of overuse of a CPR.[18] However, Ostrom counters that this analysis is often too abstract to be applied to naturally occurring CPRs. She argues that many existing CPRs cannot be divided in a manner that would allow for effective or efficient use. This is obviously the case with many nonstationary resources such as air, fisheries, or underground water, but it is also the case, under some conditions, with respect to resources such as grazing land. For example, if a common meadow is subdivided into private plots, each herder now has to invest in fences and monitoring costs to ensure his or her exclusive use. Additionally, if the weather varies considerably from year to year, the herder who possesses the plot where little or no rain has fallen is likely to overgraze and destroy the long-term capacity of the land. If this variation continues, over time much of the land will be in turn overgrazed by the herders whose land does not yield sufficient amounts of fodder during the year in which their plot is deficient in rainfall. While economists can argue that it is possible to set up insurance schemes to guard against the risks of variable weather, Ostrom reminds us that these and other schemes designed to overcome the temptation to over-graze tend to have high start-up and maintenance costs.

Are LULUs a Category of Common Pool Resource Issues?

Although caution must be used in attempting to extend a concept developed in one context to other settings or problem areas, a case can be made, I believe, for applying the finding from studies of common pool resource problems to NIMBY and LULU issues and problems. The case is particularly strong with regard to environmental LULUs of the type that may involve economic and other types of losses to individuals and the community at large as a result of pollution or incomplete disposal of waste. In these cases, a common pool resource analysis has been suggested by a number of scholars. Explanations for the abuse of common air and water resources as sites for waste disposal seem to follow an open-access, "tragedy of the commons" model. Other LULU-related problems that have been identified—urban sprawl (created by large-lot zoning attempts to keep out LULUs); segregation of residences by wealth, race, and disability status; and the imposition of large-scale developments on community life—represent more complex issues that are often the result of the combined system-effects of specific

LULUs (highways, waste disposal sites, and so on) and the attempts to control these unwanted uses. In extending the common pool resource analysis to these cases, it is necessary to identify the particular common property that is involved. If one takes a narrow view of property rights as applying only to rights in tangible property (or real estate), one would have some difficulty stretching the common pool resource idea to cover LULU-type issues. Nevertheless, one could make an argument that the spillover or externality effects of land uses are essentially types of common property. LULUs would be a type of negative property for those persons who are subject to the negative spillover effects. An argument to consider spillover effects as a type of common property, however, would be limited to those cases where it was impossible to privatize the spillover effect (or in economic language, internalize the externality costs). Based on this narrow argument, one could question whether the CPR concept was applicable to a significant number of cases. However, I believe it is possible to apply the CPR concept to LULUs on a much more universal basis. In this regard, the classic liberal idea of human dignity, specifically, James Madison's comprehensive view of property as involving much more than just landed or other tangible property, are important. That is, to the extent that the system for siting LULUs undermines human dignity and the chances for participating in a level of "public happiness" that was suggested by the Founders, an argument can be made that the governance of LULUs should be considered type of common property.

HUMAN DIGNITY AND PUBLIC HAPPINESS AS COMMON PROPERTY

While we all have individual property rights in such features of human dignity as living without threat of harm, being free to form and express opinions, to experience public happiness, and to realize our individuality, these individual rights also imply the existence of a common property in these rights. They are not just for some individuals alone, but are rights that are owned in common and that imply certain corresponding public duties. To enjoy these rights ourselves, we must take on the social responsibility to maintain this common property.

If we are to engage the power of the common pool resource metaphor in our discussion of the governance of NIMBYs and LULUs, a more exact specification of the parallels is needed. In a typical common pool resource situation, a vulnerable but potentially replenishable resource exists. If this resource (such as grass, fish, or water) is appropriated in a reasonable amount or manner, it will continue to be available in the future. However, if the resource is over-appropriated, as might occur with the overgrazing of a common meadow, the resource is depleted and can in some cases be destroyed entirely.

In a LULU situation, the person siting a LULU facility can be seen as appropriating a different, more intangible type of common pool resource or property. The property in question might best be described as human dignity or public happiness. The placement of a LULU, particularly in a neighborhood or community that has already been the site of numerous LULUs, represents a diminution of human dignity and of the potential for public happiness. Participation in public life depends on there being a quality of community and neighborhood life that can support such participation. This view of human dignity and public happiness as a sort of civic common pool resource that must be protected and replenished can help us think more concretely about the governance of LULUs. The chief implication of this view is that groups that require the existence of LULUs for their continued economic growth cannot wisely ignore the denigration of human dignity in the process.

A recent editorial that appeared in the *Atlanta Constitution* following a series of reports on "environmental racism" crystallizes the notion that particular distributions of LULUs are likely to involve an assault on the common property of human dignity.

> It is hardly news that in Georgia, most neighborhoods around factories and landfills are poor and black. . . . An analysis by the Associated Press has translated that everyday observation into hard statistics that show a direct correlation between the racial makeup of a community and the amount of pollution it is forced to accept: The blacker the neighborhood, the more pollution. These numbers are important because they provide at least a partial explanation for shorter lifespans, a greater incidence of cancer, lower birthweights, and other health problems among minorities. They also highlight a growing national debate around an issue described variously as environmental racism, environmental justice, or environmental equity.
>
> At the root of the issue is the recognition that a just society does not inflict cancer and other health and environmental problems on its poor and disenfranchised, while its affluent and powerful live in safe communities and reap the profits and benefits. (December 29, 1993)

The issue of the biased siting of facilities with high LULU values, the *Atlanta Constitution* editorialists go on to explain, is not one of conscious racism, but rather a problem of simple economics: Businesses (and governments) seek out the least expensive properties on which to site their unwanted facilities. The least expensive properties also tend to be those where nearby citizens who will be affected by the LULU have little or no access to political and other decision makers who can assist them. By way of totally unrelated market transactions, the affluent are able to escape the concentrated effects of these facilities.

Ideally, regulatory agencies would use their police powers to prevent the harmful effects of these facilities on the powerless populations that are most directly affected. However, when regulatory institutions are part of a governing system based on interest group liberalism, this expectation is undermined. Also, when system effects such as those described in the first chapter are involved, human dignity and public happiness can be diminished without any one actor or group playing a conscious role in the process. As can be predicted in an interest group liberalism governing environment, the chief regulatory agency charged with mitigating some of the harmful effects of biased siting of unwanted facilities, the Environmental Protection Agency, has itself engaged in biased enforcement of environmental laws. As the *National Law Journal* has reported, the Environmental Protection Agency has been much less aggressive in its response to environmental problems in minority communities than in white communities. As one example of this bias, the *Journal* reported that the average fine levied by the EPA for violating federal toxic waste provisions was six times higher in white neighborhoods than in minority communities.[19]

The benefits of particular LULUs may in fact be worth their costs in terms of a loss in environmental support for public happiness and human dignity. That is, not every LULU is a threat to human dignity. However, the systematic degradation and zoning of the built environment in terms that undermine its ability to support human-scale, citizen-to-citizen interaction, neighborhood life, social justice, and communication and understanding among persons of different races and income classes do represent a substantial threat to these values. While there is no plausible way to eliminate LULUs from the environment, there may exist alternative governance structures that can ensure a minimization of the losses involved and support more deliberative and democratic choices about the regulation and siting of LULUs. Moreover, even though some LULUs may represent a loss of these intangible values, the existence of strong deliberative and democratic governance structures can help restore some of the loss of human dignity and public happiness that certain LULUs may occasion.

Property, Human Dignity, and a Common Property in Ward-Sized Civic Space

The linking of a common property in basic human dignity to some rights (common or otherwise) in real property has a long tradition in American, especially early republican, thought.[20] The basic idea is that real property, especially landed property, provides the security necessary for individuals to be able to speak their thoughts without fear of being subject to expulsion from access to subsistence-providing land. That is, the independence and dignity of citizenship are dependent on some property ownership. This understanding was reflected in requirements, issued by most states in the early period of the U.S. republic, that citizens wishing to vote provide evidence of property ownership. While the link between property ownership and suffrage or other citizenship rights was eventually severed to expand the benefits of democracy to those who were not owners of real property, the logic of this link is still thought by many political theorists to be solid.[21] The link between property ownership and effective citizenship has also been reflected in proposals to provide freed slaves (i.e., new citizens) with sufficient property to support a level of self-reliance that is typically associated with citizenship (e.g., "forty acres and a mule").

While effective citizenship may be premised to a degree on the ownership of real property, the philosopher Hannah Arendt argues that the more intangible types of property rights that James Madison wrote about are perhaps even more important. Such property rights to human dignity and "public happiness," are, in Arendt's view, only realized when citizens have access to community and civic space. This civic space is important to democratic governance because it is where real opinion, as opposed to mass or corrupt opinion, is forged. Such civic space, Arendt's work suggests, represents a sort of common pool resource or property that must be maintained against the forces in the public sphere calling for state control and those in the private sphere calling for privatization of community space.

Although the Founders of the United States were fully aware of the danger of state tyranny or state-led corruption of democracy, Arendt's writings mark an important milestone in American political thought because she was one of the first social analysts to identify "the people" as the major source of corruption in republican forms of government. Most political theorists before her time and most of the Founders identified government and the governing elite as the sole source of corruption from which the people need to be protected by such measures as the separation of powers and a bill of rights. This sole concern with governmental corruption was historically suggested by the existence of corrupt monarchies and aristocracies prior to the modern republican form and in the artificial dichotomy these societies established between the ruler and the ruled. A focus on this history suggested to the Founders that the primary danger for republican government was in the expansion of public power at the expense of private interest. This tendency of the Founders to see only the danger posed by the existence of a governing elite and to ignore the threat posed by a seemingly innocent people, Arendt argued, was limited and short-sighted. She suggests that in a republic, "under conditions . . . of a rapid and constant economic growth, that is, of a constantly increasing expansion of the private realm—and these were of course the conditions of the modern age—the dangers of corruption and perversion were so much more likely to arise from private interests than from public power."[22]

According to Arendt, to counter the threat to republican forms of government posed by a rapid growth of the pursuit of private interests (or private happiness), it is necessary to develop space for the pursuit of public happiness. In Jefferson's phrase, such space would need to be created so that citizens could be "participators in the government of affairs." This right to pursue "public happiness,"[23] Thomas Jefferson believed, depended on the right of access to the public realm and to share in the public power. If Jefferson had gone only this far, we probably would now be thinking of him as the father of interest group liberalism. Instead, Jefferson enjoined his fellow Founders on every occasion to "divide the counties into wards."[24] Jefferson's call for neighborhood-level government, Arendt argues, was based on his realization that it was extremely dangerous "to allow the people a share in public power without providing them at the same time with more public space than the ballot box."[25] In essence, Jefferson would argue that the American experiment with the "knowledgeable-flexibility" method (to use Jane Jacobs' term) of maintaining the separate integrities of the public and private moral realms would depend on citizens having significant and ongoing experiences of public happiness and participation—not just occasional moments on election days.

For Arendt and Jefferson, moreover, these spaces for public action were necessary if real individual opinions were to exist. That is, they believed, contrary to current rational choice and market theorists, that real opinions are not things that exist a priori. Instead, real opinion can only be generated through substantial dialogue and interaction with other citizens. Without this dialogue, individuals would not possess truly formed opinions but would instead likely hold opinions that merely represented a weak reflection of mass opinion. In essence, true human dignity and individuality can be realized only in situations where, to use Albert O. Hirschman's metaphor, ample and important opportunities to use "voice" exist. For Jefferson, creating a space where citizens would have the opportunity to exercise their voices and to forge real opinions in dialogue with others meant that specific public forums for this propose had to be created. Moreover, these forums would have to be more than mere debating societies if they were to engage the energy of a wide spectrum of citizens. In this regard, Jefferson argued that government, specifically local government, should be divided into smaller and smaller units, down to the ward level, while at the same time distributing to each level of local government the functions it was competent to perform.[26] While Jefferson was somewhat vague as to the exact functions that these neighborhood republics should perform, he did argue that they would be a better way to "collect the voice of the people than the mechanics of representative government." [27]

Arendt suggests that Jefferson's idea of the ward system represented not merely a reform but rather an entirely new form of government. Jefferson assumed, Arendt writes, "that no one could be called happy without his share in public happiness, that no one could be called free without his experience in public freedom, and that no one could be called happy or free without participating, and having a share in public power." [28]

If we accept Arendt's and Jefferson's analysis—that new civic or public space is needed to support public happiness and to foster an understanding of public morality—then Karl Polanyi's work needs to be seen in a new light. If, as Polanyi argues, self-regulating laissez-faire markets in labor and land tend to destroy community, they are also likely to be destructive of the civic space that Arendt and Jefferson argue is so essential to effective democracies.[29]

Taken together, the insights of Ostrom, Arendt, Jefferson, and Polanyi offer a comprehensive rationale for establishing a certain degree of land-use control at a neighborhood level. That is, to secure common property rights to human dignity and public happiness, neighborhood "republics" need to establish and to have some authority over land-use issues. Ideally, this authority would be framed specifically around issues of human dignity and the protection of civic space. By reframing the authority over land use at the ward level, moreover, such neighborhood governments would become more than mere debating societies focused on abstract values; they would engage the energies of self-interested citizen in an ongoing process of civic education.

Prior to exploring this new land-use governance option in more depth, I propose in the following chapter to examine some the existing governance structures and policy tools that characterize the current approach to land-use conflicts. As a beginning point for this examination and as a means of tying the discussion of policy tools to ideologies explored earlier, I follow a typology of land-use conflict originally proposed by Thomas Gutterbock. This typology outlines some categorical approaches to land use conflicts. Two of these approaches or basic policy tools—a political one and a market-based one—are examined in some detail. In Chapter 6, I attempt to describe a specific theoretical and historical context for the emergence of alternative land-use control policies and governance structures.

NOTES

1. Much of the following discussion is based on Thomas Gutterbock's "Sociology and the Land-Use Problem." *Urban Affairs Quarterly* 15:3 (March 1980): 243-67.

2. Gutterbock credits M. Clawson (1971). *Suburban Land Conversion in the United States: An Economic and Governmental Process*. Baltimore: Johns Hopkins Press, as the source of the four key criteria.

3. Gutterbock, "Sociology," pp. 243-67.

4. Ibid., p. 256.

5. Ibid., p. 248, on the problem of disciplinary blinders.

6. Epstein, Richard. (1979). "Possession and Title." *Georgia Law Review* 13:1221-43.

7. Hardin, Garrett, and Baden, John. (1977). *Managing the Commons*. New York: W. H. Freeman.

8. For a summary of the theoretical refinement of Hardin's thesis, see Stevenson, Glenn. (1991). *Common Property Economics: A General Theory and Land Use Applications*. Cambridge, England: Cambridge University Press.

9. Demsetz, H. (1967). "Toward a Theory of Property Rights." *American Economic Review* 62:347-59; Johnson, O. E. G. (1972). "Economic Analysis, the Legal Framework, and Land Tenure Systems." *Journal of Law and Economics* 15:259-76; and Smith, R. J. (1981). "Resolving the Tragedy of the Commons by Creating Private Property Rights in Wildlife." *CATO Journal* 1:439-68.

10. Dahlman, Carl. (1980). *The Open Field System and Beyond: A Property Rights Analysis of an Economic Institution*. Cambridge, England: Cambridge University Press.

11. See Stevenson, *Common Property Economics*, pp. 8-38; and Ostrom, Elinor. (1990). *Governing the Commons: The Evolution of Institutions for Collective Action.* Cambridge, England: Cambridge University Press, for further explication of game theoretic models.

12. Olson, Mancur. (1971). *The Logic of Collective Action.* Cambridge, Mass.: Harvard University Press.

13. Much of the argument here follows Ostrom's work, *Governing the Commons*, pp. 1-122.

14. Heilbroner, R. L. (1974). *An Inquiry into the Human Prospect.* New York: Norton.

15. Ehrenfield, D. W. (1972). Conserving Life on Earth. Oxford, England: Oxford University Press.

16. Carruthers, Ian., and Stoner, R. (1981). *Economic Aspects and Policy Issues in Groundwater Development.* World Bank Staff Working Paper No. 496. Washington, D.C.: World Bank.

17. Ostrom, *Governing the Commons*, pp. 1-163.

18. See generally, Demsetz, "Toward a Theory of Property Rights"; Johnson, "Economic Analysis"; and, Smith, "Resolving the Tragedy. "

19. Lavelle, Marianne, and Coyle, Marcia. (1992) "Unequal Protection: The Racial Divide in Environmental Law." *National Law Journal* (Sept. 21) p. S2.

20. See generally, Harrington, James. (1977). The Political Works of James Harrington, edited by J. G. A. Pocock. Cambridge, England: Cambridge University Press.

21. Amar, Akhil Reed. (1990). "Forty Acres and a Mule: A Republican Theory of Minimal Entitlements." *Harvard Journal of Law and Public Policy* 13:1:37-44.

22. Arendt, Hannah. (1965). *On Revolution.* New York: Viking Press, p. 256.

23. Jefferson used this term in a paper he prepared for the Virginia Convention of 1774.

24. Letter to John Cartwright from Thomas Jefferson, June 5, 1824. Cited in Arendt, *On Revolution*, p. 257.

25. Ibid., p. 256.

26. Ibid., p. 257.

27. Ibid., p. 258.

28. Ibid., pp. 258-59.

29. Polanyi, Karl. (1957). *The Great Transformation.* Boston: Beacon Press.

CHAPTER 5

Policy Tools and Approaches to Land-Use Conflict

A FRAMEWORK FOR UNDERSTANDING AND DESIGNING POLICY RESPONSES

Because of their narrow focus, academic disciplines are rarely the source of politically satisfactory public policy. Nevertheless, such disciplines can sometimes shed light on particular aspects of a policy field. Thomas Gutterbock, a professor of sociology, for example, has conceived a useful framework for understanding how land-use conflicts emerge. Such an understanding can help us to organize our thinking about the governance of land-use issues. Gutterbock proposes a fourfold typology of approaches to land-use problems. This typology is composed of two dimensions: a "view of society" dimension that concerns the degree to which one is confident that society represents anything more than autonomous individuals, and a "causal approach" dimension that concerns the degree to which one believes that human beings are motivated by ideals and values rather than mere incentives and rewards. After describing this typology in more detail and explaining how it relates to our discussion of ideologies, I will return to these two basic dimensions and explore how they can provide a useful frame for understanding the contemporary debates over land-use governance and policy tools.

In the first dimension, the "view of social problems," Gutterbock distinguishes first between what he calls "system integration" and "conflict" views of social problems. System integration views identify social problems as "temporary disruptions among social units which are taken to be interdependent parts of a complex but functionally integrated social system." A system integration or unitary view of the social order is optimistic that genuine solutions of a win-win variety exist and can be negotiated in some forum. System integration views in a democratic society also suggest the possibility of a different type of democracy—what Jane Mansbridge has called "unitary democracy."[1]

Conflict-oriented views of a social problems tend to identify the problem situation as a "zero-sum" game in which some persons will benefit from the resolution of the problem while others lose. Win-win solutions are not generally available in some social problem areas. Moreover, conflict among groups with different interests will have to occur, and unless there is recourse to revolution, these conflicts will have a tendency to be perpetual. The approach to these types of problems in democratic societies involves traditional "adversary" procedures for determining which interests will prevail.

The second dimension of the typology concerns what might be called the dominant approach one takes to a social problem. Gutterbock and others have suggested that there are essentially two ways in which academics view problems.[2] One approach to social problems emphasizes "social structure" as the underlying cause of the problem in question. The other perspective emphasizes the role played by peoples' "values" as the more important basis for the existence and continuance of the problem. In many respects these contrasting perspectives mirror the rift between sociology and economics, where sociology generally accentuates the part that values play in problem development, while economics stresses more structural explanations.

One way of understanding and expanding on Gutterbock's typology is to examine how the ideologies described earlier might fit within the typology categories. Simply put, communitarians and conservatives believe that it is possible and desirable for society to be an integrated system where the whole is larger than the parts, while both libertarians and classic liberals view the individual as having distinct interests that cannot easily be subsumed into the whole. Categorizing ideologies on the second dimension is more difficult because each of the ideologies examined tends to promote both a set of basic values and preferred structures. However, it is possible, I believe, to distinguish whether an ideology implicitly assumes a particular social structure as a way of realizing a primary value or whether a primary goal can be realized within more than one social structure. In this respect, communitarians can be distinguished from conservatives, and libertarians from classic liberals. Specifically, communitarians' dedication to the primary goal of equality and the positive freedom found in community life has generally demanded that they give considerable consideration to particular structures, both political and economic. Without particular structures for neutral dialogue, equal votes, and the like, communitarian goals would not likely be reached. This, of course, does not mean that communitarians will necessarily agree on all aspects of the structure, only that most observers would tend to agree that a particular structure is needed to realize these goals. Conservative goals, on the other hand, demand a certain set of values, such as loyalty to the state and personal honor, but can often be realized within a number of different political and economic structures. Although contemporary conservatives support a market approach to most social disputes, this emphasis may be, as Robin Malloy has pointed out, more a matter of expediency than a consistent belief among conservatives that market-based approaches are an integral part of their ideology. As Malloy suggests, it may be that conservatives use market-based, cost-benefit analysis of policy options because this technique involves a considerable degree of subjective valuation in producing supposedly objective outcomes.[3] In a similar manner, as much as classic liberalism is associated with a federalist structure of public institutions and a reliance on free-market organization of the private sector, its primary goal of maintaining human dignity and freedom could easily demand a major restructuring of public or private institutions and policies to maintain the balance of public and private power that is necessary for realizing the primary goals of dignity and freedom. For libertarians, however, the primacy of individual freedom leads in more or less lockstep fashion to a structure of necessary political and property rights, which generally cannot be unbundled, reduced, or adapted to new circumstances.

Table 1: A Typology of Ideologies

	View of Society	
Dominant Approach to Problem	**Conflict**	**System Integration**
Structure	<u>Libertarian</u> Emphasis on structuring individual rights in the public and in the market; outcome value (e.g., individuals sold into slavery) is indeterminate.	<u>Communitarian</u> Emphasis on structuring equality relationships; outcome (e.g., the potential for "bad" groups) is indeterminate.
Value	<u>Classic Liberal</u> Emphasis on the value of individual human dignity for all and a balance of public and private power; structures can vary accordingly.	<u>Conservative</u> Emphasis on the value of the state, honor, and aggregate wealth; structure is less important because conservative rule and values can prevail within numerous structures.

Source: Adapted from Gutterbock. See Gutterbock, Thomas. "Sociology and the Land-Use Problem." *Urban Affairs Quarterly* 15:3 (March 1980), pp. 243-267.

Gutterbock's typology (see Table 1) fits neatly with and helps explicate the ideologies examined earlier. The typology is particularly useful, however, in helping to identify specific ways in which social problems such as those posed by locally unwanted land uses might be addressed and resolved. Given these two dimensions of causal emphasis, on the one hand, and views of the social order, on the other, Gutterbock generates four categories of social problems and potential resolution strategies.

Table 2: Social Problem Types and Potential Resolution Strategies

	View of Society	
Dominant Approach to Problem	**Conflict**	**System Integration**
Structure	Interest Group Conflict approach Solution: Accommodation (proportional benefits) or repression (winner take all)	Social Disorganization approach Solution: Reorganization
Value	Value Conflict approach Solution: Compromise or sacrifice of values	Cultural Lag approach Solution: Institution building

Source: Gutterbock, Thomas. "Sociology and the Land-Use Problem." *Urban Affairs Quarterly* 15:3 (March 1980), pp. 243-267.

Although the framework used in Table 1 and Table 2 is essentially the same, there is only a weak linkage between the typology of ideologies and the typology of approaches to social problems. That is, each ideology may at some time propose each approach. The choice of problem-solving approaches will depend on the particular problem being defined and addressed and on the political context in which policy innovations are being considered. A general case might be made that policy developed from a particular ideological perspective (Table 1) will tend to emphasize problem-solving approaches (Table 2) that fall outside that particular ideological category or cell as it is defined in Table 1. This would be the case because when a "problem" exists in a society that is founded on a particular ideology, it would be unrealistic to expect policy makers who share the dominant ideology to search for a solution to the problem that would involve questioning that ideology. For example, if a society is organized around and dominated by conservative principles, when conservative policy analysts look for policy options to a social problem, they may look to approaches that do not involve institution building. For conservatives to consider institution building as a problem-solving option would be to admit to the failure of the current institutions. Such a stance would, of course, be antithetical to what it means to be conservative. If the problem is crime by deviants in an otherwise conservative, law-abiding society, conservatives might suggest a change in the interest group structure so as to accommodate or repress the deviant group. Richard Nixon's twin policies of a guaranteed income and a tightening-up on the rights of defendants, for example, suggests the use of both these strategies. Alternatively, conservatives might propose that those who are acting in a criminal manner adjust or sacrifice their values. Still other conservatives might argue that the courts be reorganized so as to allow victims more of a say in criminal proceedings.

However, when an ideological group has little or no influence in society, it may tend to propose the policy options that will more directly bring its ideology into actuality. When faced with the communitarian policies of the former Eastern European states, the most plausible policy option for conservative outsiders was to emphasize conservative values of the family and wealth aggregation. In order to actualize these values conservatives proposed *institution-building* strategies centered around stock markets and legal systems. In a like manner, liberal outsiders would emphasize the development of liberal values, such as individual dignity, tolerance for differences, and civic freedom. Instituting these value in society traditionally controlled by party bureaucrats would involve the development of an ability to *compromise values*. Similarly, but in an obverse way, communitarians, who have had relatively little say in contemporary American politics, are the group that is generally the most likely to offer ideas and policy options for *reorganizing* the structure of the state and the market.[4] Also, to the degree that libertarians ideals have been overwhelmed by the social welfare state, the chief policy thrust of those who share this ideology has been to re-establish a structure for *accomodating* individual rights in property and *repressing* collective rights in property.

The following exploration of Gutterbock's four approaches should be seen in light of this dynamic context and the generally weak association between ideologies and the promotion of particular policy approaches. As scholars of the policy-making process have concluded, policy makers, for practical reasons, are most likely to follow a "garbage can" model of policymaking. According to this model, policy makers act as opportunists, taking from the random mix of agendas, policy ideas, and approaches to problems those that seem to fit the moment—attempting all the while to place an ideological slant on the policy options under consideration.[5]

The Four Approaches to Social Problems

The first category, characterized by a conflict view of society with an emphasis on structural causes of land-use problems, Gutterbock identifies as a "political economy" or "interest group" conflict approach. Much of Sidney Plotkin's discussion of the dialectic of expansionary and exclusionary property rights is based on this approach; also, some of the critical legal studies scholarship partakes of this view of conflict as a never-ending dialectic of different communities' understandings of basic ideas of fairness, ownership, gender roles, and so forth.[6] Within this "political economy" approach to social problems, two potential strategies exist. First, the dialectic can be broken by adopting a new non-capitalist system of property. In the era following the fall of socialism, this option appears to be particularly implausible. However, as will be discussed in the chapter that explores particular policy alternatives, the proposal for a natural resource/land tax along lines similar to those suggested by Henry George partakes somewhat of this strategy. Second, the dialectic can be repressed by formal rules that favor the dominant, conservative interest.

Proponents of the "value-conflict approach" to social problems share with the political economy school the view that conflict is inevitable, but are skeptical that structural changes would be effective in resolving the conflict. The value-conflict approach to social problems is most relevant to cases where land-use conflicts are based on ideological differences. The review of ideologies presented in Chapter 2 outlines a number of areas of potential ideological conflict. It should be recognized, however, that specific land-use conflicts can sometimes be resolved through a coalition of strange ideological bedfellows. This situation occurred, for example, in Portland, Oregon, when environmental "no-growth" advocates of a communitarian bent teamed with pro-growth developers to pass managed growth legislation. As Charles Lindblom has often noted, ideological opponents who would have difficulty agreeing on goals can, more often than one would suspect, agree on a similar means to two different goals.[7] As with the structural-conflict approach, the value-conflict approach does offer the prospect of easy problem resolution. To a certain degree, the value-conflict approach suggests that it may be necessary to wait for consciousness to change so substantially that it will not matter what structures are in place. For example, if every one practiced an ecologically correct morality, laws against pollution and waste would both be quickly passed and become unnecessary at the same time. A more likely event in the area of land-use law will be the continued trade-off among conservative, communitarian, libertarian, and classic liberal values, with no one ideological position gaining dominance and all consistent and potentially effective and utilitarian formulations being frustrated.[8]

Belief in this value-conflict approach can be found in Gregory Alexander's discussions of the values and limitations of group autonomy. Alexander argues against what he calls a strong form of group autonomy. In this form of autonomous communities or groups, value conflicts among groups are repressed because each community is totally independent from regulation or substantial influence by other communities or by a more overarching hierarchy. Alexander sees a danger in the strong from of group autonomy: that a tyranny of the majority will keep a community from formulating a conception of the good or that an individual community will short-circuit the conversation about the good by grabbing too much power. Instead of there being any one settlement of land-use issues through the invocation of formal rules, Alexander argues that the best that one can hope for is a legal system that provides a frame for open-ended dialogue and adjudication based on a reasonableness standard applied judiciously according to specific community contexts. For Alexander, the continuation of conflict is assumed to occur and the best that can be done is to create open-ended forums for mutual understanding and in which varied individual interests can be adjusted over time in light of the ideal of community itself.[9] Communitarians like Alexander must ultimately offer a structure, if only a procedural one, for realizing the twin but somewhat competing values of community integration (implying that a group with similar interests can form associations that exclude strangers) and "the community ideal" (which implies an integration of all the potential members of a community, including strangers).

The third approach, termed the "social disorganization approach" by Gutterbock, emphasizes the structural causes of problems but suggests that the social order can ultimately be integrated—if certain rule-oriented reorganizations take place. This approach suggests that Lindblom's observation about agreement on means—no matter what the ends—would apply in the problem situation being examined. Reorganizing the rules of land use can take a number of different forms, such as the realignment of property rights, the creation of tax incentives and regulatory controls, and the development of local, state, and regional planning bodies to oversee and manage land use. Because benefits would accrue from a realignment of the incentives and rules related to land use, conflicting interests in this "social disorganization" approach could, theoretically at least, be mollified.

Finally, Gutterbock's fourth approach, which he calls the "cultural lag" approach, "assumes that solutions are possible which will generate substantial collective benefits, but emphasizes the importance of new values rather than new structures or rules."[10] Gutterbock suggests that this approach is most appropriate in circumstances where society's shared value system has failed to keep up with changed circumstances. One can see evidence of this approach in legal realists' laments about the inadequacy of traditional, eighteenth-century or Blackstonian notions of property in an age of corporations, futures options, time-sharing, and numerous other forms of unbundled property.[11] As with the "value-conflict" approach, the cultural lag solution to land-use conflicts is thought to exist in consciousness-raising. Attempts to develop new land-use ethics that are more in line with contemporary circumstances and ecological understandings would be representative of the cultural lag approach. However, from within the cultural lag perspective, problems are thought to be resolvable in an integrative way. From this perspective, therefore, it makes sense to develop political, social, educational, and legal institutions that can accelerate the "catch-up" of social values to modern circumstances.

The *ordenung* process used in a number of European corporatist states represents one variation of the cultural lag approach to resolving social conflict. The German idea of *ordenung*, a concept without an exact English equivalent, describes the conscious organization of private sector actors in ways that promote communication and mediation among potential antagonists (e.g., labor and capital) and that afford state authorities relatively easy overview of the spheres of society. *Ordenung* essentially involves the organization of interests in a manner that promotes and sometimes mandates that groups educate each other. In return for being a willing vehicle for resolving social conflicts through education, the recognized groups are granted a privileged level of influence over public policy. *Ordenung* is thus a process that precedes planning, insuring that those who have the power to influence planning outcomes speak with an organized voice and have been exposed to the views of other organized interests.[12] Most European historians would suggest that because nations such as Germany, when compared with the United States or Britain, did not form until a latter point in the development of industrial social relations, these late developing nations tended to organize private sector interests in ways that differed substantially from those of the early nation-states. The organization of the state vis-à-vis these private interests would therefore reflect and enable social ordering of values more in line with contemporary situations.[13] While the *ordenung* process in European corporatist states represents one way in which institution-building can promote consciousness raising , Jefferson's ward- or neighborhood-level governments represent another institutional innovation—one with origins in classic liberal thought—that can also play this consciousness-raising and value reconciliation role.

FRAMING THE DEBATE: MARKETS VERSUS POLITICS, AND ADVERSARIAL VERSUS UNITARY POLITICS

Before examining the particular innovations in land-use policy or policy-ordering, it is worthwhile to explore in more depth two dimensions of Gutterbock's typology. These dimensions—causal emphasis, on the one hand, and the view of social order, on the other—form the current frame in which policy innovations, hybrids, and shifts must take place. As such, they deserve a more detailed examination. The debate as to causal emphasis or the dominant approach to problems (that is, value-based versus structural) is primarily centered on the question of whether a particular social problem can be addressed through a structuring of private actions (e.g., by manipulating the incentives that promote those actions or designing markets to have the same effect), or whether these problems also involve a sorting out of less tangible values. Such a sorting out of intangible values is only likely to be possible within a political frame. With regard to the causal emphasis dimension, the focus of the debate about environmental land-use controls has been on the role of the market versus that of the state. Advocates for free markets, for example, contend that once market structures and incentives are in place, and there is a means of enforcing contracts and private property rights, there is little or no need for further political action. Others who have studied the problems posed by the existence of locally unwanted land uses suggest that markets will never be able to address and sustain values that are not monetary in nature.

Whether one accepts or rejects the proposition that markets are self-regulating and capable of incorporating all the value dimensions that must be included in legitimate policy making, one must still debate the second of Gutterbock's dimensions: What is the proper view of social conflict? Within this second debate, the focus is on the attributes and potential effects of choosing among different political systems, mechanisms, and approaches. The choice in this second debate is chiefly between approaches that are adversarial in nature (that is, they assume that conflict is inevitable and ongoing) and those that are more unitary (they assume that interests can be integrated). That is, if one sees conflict as endemic, a call for adversarial mechanisms, such as pluralist legislatures or adversarial court system, is appropriate. In contrast, if the issue area holds some potential for social integration, more unitary approaches, such as mediation, consensus decision making, and neighborhood-level government, may be more appropriate.

In terms of LULU issues, the first set of debates tends to occur around the substantive policy questions of whether and how to regulate land use. These debates generally occur between two opposed factions: (1) market oriented advocates for deregulation who point to Houston's traditional lack of zoning ordinances as a primary source of economic growth and evidence that zoning can negatively affect land values[14] or can result in undesirable effects because of administrative difficulties;[15] and (2) advocates for increased regulation and planning who note that a number of social problems cannot be resolved without some comprehensive planning[16] and that properly designed land-use restrictions will not exacerbate problems such as the lack of affordable housing.[17]

The second set of debates concern the procedural question of how best to go about making the more substantive land-use policy decisions. The focus of this second set of debates is on legal and political theory. These debates often occur over the viability and desirability of such procedures as legislative or executive decision making, "plan jurisprudence," environmental impact statements, nuisance suits, and local versus state or national decision-making as the preferred means of establishing land-use policy.

In order to shed some light the first of these debates, the following reviews the strengths and weaknesses of using market and market-mimicking mechanisms, on the one hand, and regulation, on the other hand, to insure a balancing of key values in the use of land in the United States. In conducting this review, I have adopted

Gutterbock's four key values—efficiency, equity, environmental quality, and community viability—as the filters for identifying potential strengths and weaknesses. This review of the central substantive question in land-use policy is followed by a similar review of the basic procedural issues in the land-use reform debate. The purpose of both of these reviews is to lay a foundation for understanding how various mixtures of substantive and procedural land-use policies might affect the realization of important values.

LULUS FROM A MARKET THEORY PERSPECTIVE

The key issue in the causal emphasis debate is the degree to which the dominant structural mechanism of capitalist societies—the market—is an effective and efficient cause of human behavior and progress. Because some of the ideological assumptions of market theory have been discussed in the chapter dealing with ideology, I will not repeat the points made there. What is necessary to add to the discussion in Chapter 2 is a specific examination of how LULUs might be seen from a market theory perspective. After a brief discussion of how markets might generally meet or fail to meet Gutterbock's four land-use criteria, three aspects of market theory will be addressed: the information assumption, the many buyers and sellers assumption, and the lack of externalities assumption.

When economists compare markets with politics, one of the key positive attributes of markets is their superior ability to allow people to express accurately the intensity of their desires. That is, in contrast to political elections, where voters are only allowed to say yes or no to an often unsatisfactory set of choices, in market-based decision-making, consumers can precisely indicate through their "willingness to pay" the degree to which they would like to possess certain goods or experience certain services.[18] If the choices of goods and services are not satisfactory, the marketplace consumer can indicate dissatisfaction by refusing to participate in the current market (that is, she can "exit," in Hirschman's terms) while also potentially deciding to provide the good or service herself (that is, enter the market). Because of this close linkage between personal wishes and material effects, markets are thought to be more rational than politics in many respects.[19]

Markets and Gutterbock's Four Land-Use Criteria

Efficiency and Equity

With regard to Gutterbock's four primary criteria, there is little question that markets for the most part do tend to promote economic efficiency. Markets, however, are not particularly well-known for their equity-promoting qualities. Nevertheless, in one respect, it may be argued that markets support the promotion of equity values. In making this argument, however, it is necessary to understand that equity is not a one-dimensional value. Rather, equity can be understood as having two ethical sides, a justice ethic side and an ethic of care side. Equity from and ethic of care point of view demands that each person be cared for or treated equally in all circumstances that could potentially lead to major differences in the well-being of individuals or groups. In the justice ethic side of equity, the equity value is fulfilled by appropriating to each person their due in light of what they themselves have contributed to the greater good. By affording a high degree of rationality (in the sense of supporting a strong link between personal interests and actual choice of goods and services), an argument can be made that markets are also highly effective in promoting at least one side—the justice ethic side—of the equity criterion. That is, markets provide a fine-tuned mechanism for allocating rewards to those who are thought to have merited them due to their production of quality goods or services.

With respect to the other side of the equity issue—the ethic of care—markets appear to be neutral at best, but are more typically destructive of equity over the long run. However, the use of market solutions is often based on the rationale that the ability of markets to increase total wealth makes it possible to establish what might be termed baseline equity. That is, if markets can produce enough wealth for everyone to possess the basic necessities of life, everyone will have at least the basic tools for pursuing private happiness, and everyone will also be able to some degree to pursue the public happiness they desire as well.[20]

When examining any particular case of whether establishment of a market-like solution to a policy problem is appropriate, policy analysts will often apply what is known as the Kaldor-Hicks criterion.[21] This criterion states that the policy solution should be able to make at least some persons better off without making anyone worse off. Use of this criterion in deciding to employ market-mimicking policy tools would lessen, but not eliminate, the tendency for market-based policies to reduce equity.

Community Viability

With respect to community viability, the case for market solutions is weak in both the general respect and in the more specific area of supporting needed but unwanted land uses such as community care homes.

General community viability and social relationships: While Adam Smith was touting the many virtues of markets in his classic work on *The Wealth of Nations*, he was at the same time warning against a number of destructive effects of markets on the potential for community life, including: (1) the persistent potential for conspiracy among business interests to undermine the public interest; (2) the development of laws and government that promote the interests of the rich against those of the poor;[22] and (3) the destructive effects of market-driven divisions of labor on human capacities in general, and by implication, for community life as a whole. The community, and specifically government, Smith argues, must intervene to prevent this destruction:

> In the process of the division of labor, . . . a man whose whole life is spent in performing a few simple operations . . . has no occasion to exert his understanding . . . [and] generally becomes as stupid and ignorant as it is possible for a human creature to become. . . . In every improved and civilized society, this is the state into which the labouring poor, that is, the great body of the people, must necessarily fall, unless government takes some pains to prevent it.[23]

More recently, law Professor Joseph William Singer has analyzed how the laws that support the existence of markets define and affect social relationships in ways that are often destructive and not always fully understood. He constast the market approach to relationships with a more social relations approach. The free-market model, he suggests, places undesirable limits on the types of social relationships that can be addressed or mediated through legal analysis and resolution. This limitation occurs because commercial law focuses on agreements and entitlements defined by the state prior to the relationships occurring. Furthermore, the law characterizes these rights as fully articulated upon entry into contracts, and focuses on the questions of ownership and the initial promise (in, for example, an employment contract). This limited focus, Singer suggests, narrows the scope of the moral community and undermines the implied rights, duties, privileges, and immunities that grow up around social relationships over time. In contrast to the free-market model of property, he suggests that the social relations approach

> encourages us to see people as situated in various relationships with others that continue over time; describes social relations as comprising a spectrum from short-lived relations among strangers to continuing relations in the market, to intimate relations in the family; comprehends rights as emerging out of understandings that develop over the course of relationships rather than as being fully articulated at clear decision points; and encourages us to ask questions about the relationship.[24]

If one accepts Singer's contentions and the implications of Adam Smith's work, a case can be made that the application of laissez-faire policies across the board, that is, without consideration of the context of relationships, can undermine social and community relations, and ultimately community viability.

Viability of community care: Market-like proposals to address the problem of narrow NIMBY attitudes blocking the siting of facilities that are essential to community and civic life (such as group homes, half-way houses, personal care homes, and so on) could, theoretically speaking, provide a greater level of efficiency in the siting of these facilities and overcome or mitigate the fears of

LULU resisters by providing incentives and compensation to nearby residents who might otherwise object to the siting. Unfortunately, many of the most essential LULUs are public or non-profit facilities. The operators of these treatment and rehabilitation facilities are typically lacking in the resources needed to participate in such a market-mimicking compensation scheme. Most important, public and non-profit sponsors of such facilities cannot easily pass on the increased operation costs (such as for buying the development or zoning rights) to their consumers or otherwise adjust to market forces. Moreover, in some cases these public and non-profit developers may be limited by law or administrative policy in their abilities to enter into negotiations or compensate other parties for the purposes of acquiring a suitable site.[25]

Environmental Qualities

The relationship between markets and environmental qualities is also troublesome. Two basic rules for the maintenance of environmental qualities might be formulated as: Life "does not use up the forces that maintain life" and "there must be a natural balance between reproductive and destructive forces."[26] Traditionally, self-regulating markets have not effectively met these conditions. Nevertheless, it is important to lay out the case for market-based solutions to environmental problems.

Market-Based Approaches to Environmental Values

Market advocates rightly argue that disregard for environmental qualities may largely be a matter a tragedy of the commons. That is, because much of the natural world—air, water, and underground resources in particular—has not been organized as private property and, as such, has no guardian owner to protect it against open-access exploitation, it is vulnerable to exploitation. The solution, market advocates suggest, is not fewer markets and less private property, but more. With particular regard to natural resources, advocates suggest such market solutions as a system of charges, deposits, and refunds for pollution waste disposal. For example, polluters would purchase a permit or "right to pollute" a certain amount by providing the government a deposit that would be refunded (in part or in whole) after the polluter had proven that the waste had been effectively treated, stored, or removed. Such a system could then become more self-regulating and efficient once the permits themselves could be transferred among potential polluters. These transferable pollution permits would be more economically efficient because different factories often have different cost structures for reducing pollution. A company facing only minimal costs for reducing pollution would have an incentive to reduce its noxious emissions far below what might otherwise be allowable by whatever level of permit it had already purchased. This would be the case because it would be able to sell its pollution permit at a price that would be higher than the cost of its pollution-reduction action. Other companies that owned factories with higher cost structures would find it cheaper to purchase a pollution permit than to pay the price of pollution control technologies. By government's setting the price of permits at a level sufficient to reach overall pollution-reduction goals, the public, in theory, would be able to get clearer air, water, and land, while placing only the minimal level of burden on private industry.[27]

With respect to the problem of NIMBY sentiments threatening to halt essential but unwanted land uses, a number of market-like policy proposals have been made (see Chapter 7 for a more detailed description of some of these proposals). Generally, these proposals would give legal sanction to mechanisms, such as contract zoning and compensation auctions for LULU sitings, to compensate groups, neighborhoods, and municipalities that would agree to accept a LULU. Establishing these mechanisms would help rationalize a process that has become highly irrational and that has led in some cases to a siting gridlock in which even LULUs that might provide net environmental benefits are rejected.

Objections to Market-Based Approaches to Environmental Values

However, from a environmental perspective these mechanisms still pose a number of problems. In particular, market-mimicking mechanisms for siting particular facilities, say, toxic waste disposal plants, are by themselves unable to address or support the full range of environmental values in the siting process. Such a procedure would be most likely to identify land areas (and community zoning rights) that for various reasons—their rural location, their lack of other economically viable uses (such as marshlands), the economic needs of the owners—are priced cheaply in the market for LULU siting. Other values, even economic ones such as transportation costs, and especially environmental values such as soil and groundwater protection, are less likely to enter the market pricing mechanism or to be validated in the ultimate selection of facility sites. As one observer has noted, "It would be a fortuity beyond belief if a market produced site for a waste disposal facility, for example, were also a suitable site for that facility from the standpoint of . . . overall environmental protection—so fortuitous, in fact, that it almost never happens."[28]

While market-based solutions to environmental quality issues promise a high degree of efficiency, even the advocates of these solutions recognize certain technical limits or problems. For example, Richard Stewart, a strong advocate for the development of marketable pollution permits, admits that such a system would be inappropriate for control of some pollutants such as pesticides that "elude workable quantification" or others, such as toxic chemicals, that have "threshold" effects (that is, where the harm is only evident when the chemical is concentrated within a particular area).[29] In fact, a system of marketable permits could magnify the harm in threshold-effect cases because it would likely result in facilities with high pollution-control costs buying the majority of permits, thereby intensifying the presence of the toxins in particular localities.

The unanswered question regarding market-based solutions to environmental quality issues is the degree to which ideally configured markets can achieve environmental values. That is, would these markets achieve desirable results if they were organized in a comprehensive fashion and perfectly articulated the exclusionary property interest in environmental qualities such as clean air, water, and land or the continued presence of natural resources such as forests and minerals? Market theory suggests that as a particular resource (such as forests or wildlife) approaches exhaustion, it becomes relatively scarce. Scarcity raises the market price for the resource in question, resulting in a decrease in demand and an intensified search for substitutes. Both of these tendencies should, it is believed, relax the pressure on the resource, allowing it to be replenished.

This scenario presents a few difficulties. First, the increased price of a resource may not result in a drop in demand sufficient to result in adequate relaxation on the resource. The continued demand for rhinoceros horns or the flesh of endangered species, despite major increases in market price (not to mention severe legal sanctions), provides some evidence of this possibility. This example also illustrates the second problem: There may be no adequate or acceptable substitute for the resource in question. This problem becomes important because markets are sometimes unable to recognize or correctly price environmental scarcities. Inaccurate pricing occurs for several reasons beyond the obvious one that we often lack adequate data about ecological complexities and environmental dangers.[30] Markets tend to represent the near-term and foreseeable interests of property owners. This is the case because a stream of future benefits is generally considered to be worth less than currently consumable resources. As a result, most persons are thought to discount the future stream at some rate. This discount rate is then actualized or built into the interest rate that one must pay to obtain resources in the present that will be paid for with interest in the future. Observers of markets, however, have noted that at most assumed discount rates (such as those that are built into money markets), the future at some point is essentially considered to be without value. Hence, without some intervention in these markets, there is a risk that resources available for future generations may be heavily depleted. Because future generations are not able to bid on the value of these resources, their more highly valued current use could dictate a rate of current consumption that endangers the resource.

A further market-based discounting of environmental qualities may occur because the division of labor that free markets promote probably magnifies the "environmental stupidity" of individual property owners. That is, if, as Adam Smith suggested, the division of labor renders people incapable of "any just judgement concerning many of the ordinary duties of private life," how much more likely would this division render us incapable of imagining, understanding, and acting on issues, such as those involved in maintaining environmental quality, that demand a large intelligence and an eye toward public duties?[31]

Finally, as Elinor Ostrom has suggested in her discussion of common pool resources, market-based fragmentation of land ownership can result in a sort of sequential degradation of land-related resources. Herders, for example, who expect a certain yearly profit from their animals may overgraze their own land when rainfall does not arrive in expected quantities. Over time, a sequential overgrazing may take place—one that might have been prevented if these herders had shared and managed the whole of their land, allowing a shift of all the animals to the pasture areas that received sufficient rainfall.

Abundant and Cheap Information

Disregarding for the moment the inequality that market-based decision making generates whenever there is a severely unequal distribution of income, wealth, and other resources, there is still another hurdle that market mechanisms must overcome before they can achieve the kind of efficiency that is attributed to them. For markets to allocate values efficiently and to "clear" in the way they were designed, those who enter the market must have access to abundant and cheap information. More simply stated, the information assumption about markets suggests that for consumers to accurately gauge their willingness to pay, they must also have a very accurate sense of what they will be getting with their purchase of particular goods or services. When information is not cheap and abundant, it becomes difficult for people to organize exchanges or to imagine accurately how the terms of such exchanges or contracts will play out over time. Economists suggest that in these cases, parties to a contract will experience high transaction costs in addition to the normal market costs of the goods or services in question. If transaction costs are high enough, even exchanges that would normally be profitable become questionable.

A field of economics is now dedicated to the issue of transaction costs.[32] Those who work in this field (transaction cost economists) note, for example, that certain types of goods and services that are more complex, uncertain, involve more untested, new, or high technology, are of a long-term nature, and involve assets that are more specifically dedicated in terms of markets or geographical location will tend to have higher transaction costs. The costs are involved in monitoring the terms of the contract to see that one is receiving the benefits that one expected when the contract was first negotiated. Expanding on transaction cost theory, it is possible to observe that in many ways the purchase of landed property within a particular community involves a high level of transaction costs. That is, the purchase of an individual piece of property provides little or no guarantee that one's expectations about that community's future quality of life will be fulfilled. As this uncertainty reaches unbearable levels, transaction costs again rise correspondingly: Home buyers (and potential sellers) spend inordinate amounts of time investigating different communities in which to live, reading and comparing subdivision ordinances and restrictive covenant deeds, considering the purchase of easements, the potential of nearby land for industrial siting, and so forth.

Robert Nelson has suggested that the fluidity and uncertainty of current zoning practices often make transaction costs for individual residents and developers much higher than they might otherwise be. Nelson argues that naturally occurring economic development will pressure neighborhoods toward a "transition" from lower-valued to higher-valued use. If current zoning represented a truly permanent barrier to development, such pressure could be resisted. However, for reasonable development purposes, it may be inevitable that a neighborhood undergo transition. However, because current zoning stands in the way of seller and buyers making property exchanges, parties wanting to deal face the transaction costs involved in changing the zoning—usually against the wishes of existing neighbors. When such changes inevitably occur, they usually do so in a haphazard way that does not allow for equitable compensation to all the owners of property in the area.[33]

The theory of transaction cost economics suggests that as the cost of monitoring agreements (that is, transaction costs) among participants increases, the ability of the market to consider adequately these costs diminishes. Depending on the level of transaction costs involved, either hierarchies in the form of corporations (such as neighborhood associations) or public associations (such as local governments) will become the more efficient organizational design. When transaction costs are minimal, markets are efficient; when these cost become moderate in degree, hierarchies become more efficient; when they are especially high, collegia become the most efficient organizational design.[34]

The rapid economic growth that has resulted in the development of LULU issues in communities across the nation has probably increased the degree of uncertainty and the level of transaction costs in the market for residencies in a corresponding fashion. This tendency provides a economic explanation for the sequential development of the three types of land-use orderings that help reduce the transaction costs of consumers. These are, first, the informal ordering of social norms that arise over time and that rely on common understandings of the proper use of land.[35] Second, private organizations and mechanisms, such as neighborhood associations and restrictive covenants, can lower transaction costs in a voluntary fashion. These developments are aided by the delineation of Blackstonian property rights and the existence of a common-law system for ordering these rights: That is, when groups of property owners agree to relinquish their individual rights to a corporation, the law will assist them in interpreting the terms of these transaction cost-reducing corporate charters. And third, cases where transaction costs continue to be high, a collective means of regulating development that is backed by positive law can be established. Euclidian zoning ordinances that delineate separate areas for various grades of commercial, industrial, and residential use is the most prevalent example of a collectivist strategy for reducing transaction costs.[36] In this respect, transaction cost economics can explain in some measure the increasingly frequent use of zoning that observers of land-use policy have noted.

Of the two types of NIMBY/LULU issues—environmental and social—that are addressed in this book, one can identify factors that might exacerbate transaction costs and therefore push policy toward greater reliance on collectivist solutions. With respect to environmental issues, the key forces pushing up transaction costs are the high-tech and uncertain nature of potential pollution-control technologies. The nature of these technologies works to increase transaction costs in several respects. First, the understanding of these technologies is generally limited to experts of various types, effectively isolating the average citizen from an understanding of the situation and the potential trade-offs. For example, if citizens living near a polluting LULU knew that it is possible to join together and assist, at a reasonable cost, the polluter in purchasing the latest pollution-control equipment and thereby substantially reducing their exposure to noxious elements, these citizens might be willing to do so—if the transaction costs involved in laying out the terms of the contract between them and the polluter were not too high. (A contract would be needed to specify that the polluter would not, for example, increase production, and therefore the level of overall pollution, after the introduction of abatement technologies.) However, because knowledge about pollution-abatement technologies is not usually available to informal groups, the potential for this market-based solution to the problem is less likely to occur. Moreover, because most industries exist in a competitive and potentially destructive market, they often have few or no incentives to acquire or invest in knowledge of emerging pollution-reduction technologies. Second, transaction costs are increased due to the uncertain and often delayed or long-term nature of most environmental effects. Toxic effluents may or may not have negative effects on particular individuals; that is, the effects of pollution tend to be statistical probabilities, not certainties, and these effects are often years in the making. As such, parties to contract negotiations for setting particular levels of acceptable pollution are often uncertain about the level needed to ensure safety. The costs of gathering information to reduce such uncertainty can be considerable and can often doom what might otherwise be a valuable understanding between a locally unwanted land use and those who live near the LULU.

Uncertainty and delayed effects increase transaction costs in cases of human service-type unwanted land uses as well. As with many environmental toxins, the negative effects of social service LULUs tend to be somewhat unquantifiable. These effects tend to be of a type that legal scholars call "demoralization effects." That is, while it is difficult to measure, we know that children who grow up in impoverished neighborhoods that are filled with LULUs and TOADs tend to experience demoralization effects over and above the effect of poverty and family background. Also, the economic prospects of adults in such LULU-intensive neighborhoods tend to be negatively affected, if only in subtle ways. Such demoralization effects, moreover, often act indirectly through other effects, and they involve long-term incubation periods and an "overdetermination" prior to the emergence of the effect. These are the situations that engage social scientists in debate as to the magnitude and circumstance of the effects in question. The research on and debate over the spatial mismatch theory (that is, the theory that hypothesizes a negative effect on the job prospects of workers who are forced by circumstances and zoning to live apart from the more economically viable areas of a city) provide an example of the difficulty bringing certainty to individual choices as to the true value of particular residential or business sites.[37] When experts, even after substantial study, are unable to pin down the real values (as opposed to spot market values) of particular locational decisions, how will average citizens fare in this uncertain and high transaction-cost environment? Similarly, while the existence of negative "neighborhood effects" on the social, intellectual, and moral development of children is generally not disputed, assessing the magnitude of these effects presents one of the major challenges to social science research.[38] Common-sense evidence for these effects can be seen in the everyday search of parents for the neighborhoods that represent the feeder districts for the best schools. While the merit of good schools is not totally dependent on neighborhood effects, educational research suggests that the value of good schools is effectively enhanced by neighborhood features and opportunities.[39]

While the uncertainty of future nearby land uses can increase the costs of securing the benefits of property ownership and reduce the ability of persons to negotiate contracts on their own that can secure these benefits, a number of land-use policies and practices have nevertheless evolved for the purpose of securing such benefits. Unfortunately, some of these policies and practices, while promoting the value of security, undermine other important values. For example, a number of policies and practices—from the informal norms and biases of purchasers of homes, to property-based associations and covenants and corporate Levittown-type developments, to government-sponsored zoning ordinances—have created a pattern of homogenous, income and race-segregated residential development. Such a pattern of land uses reduces transaction costs in the market for homes, but this reduction in transaction costs comes at what many would consider a larger social cost of its own. In fact, each time we allow these mechanisms to differentiate the housing market into more definable and secure properties, we implicitly discount many of the systemic and long-term costs of increased social segregation. As chaos theory suggests, in complex systems there are points at which small changes can result in a disintegration of the system itself. Some observers would argue that just this type of process is taking place within the communities most disadvantaged by the increased differentiation and lowered transaction costs in the market for residential property.[40] When the magnitude of system-disintegration effects cannot be easily measured (and is even disputed by some social scientists), there is little to induce the average citizen to address these effects, especially when the culture is primarily concerned with facilitating (through a reduction in transaction costs) specific transactions in the private market for land.

Although an understanding of system effects could lead to greater overall utility, information to support collective action is not cheap. Rather, until the social science research data, which typically confirm thoughtful common-sense understandings, are processed in what Thomas Jefferson and Hannah Arendt might call "opinion-creating forums," they are likely to remain inert. Only upon processing do these data become information in a form that can lead to effective policymaking.

Buyers and Sellers

A second feature of LULU markets—the lack of many buyers and sellers—also increases transaction costs and can lead to market failure. Economic theory suggests that for markets to function in the efficient manner that is theorized, there needs to exist a number of buyers and sellers in each market. When there are too few sellers, monopoly-type inefficiencies are believed to exist; when there are too few buyers, monopsony-type inefficiencies occur. In either case, there is a potential for one party—buyers in the case of monopsony and sellers in the case of monopoly—to gain an unfair (in terms of market inefficiencies) advantage. To guard against these chances for "opportunism," parties to a market or contract, particularly if they expect this contract will last for a period of time, will be forced to incur a (one-time or continuous) monitoring cost. The monitoring cost of ensuring that the other party will not use its advantageous position to cheat on terms of the bargain is another form of a transaction cost.

One of the difficulties in untangling LULU issues is identifying who the buyers and sellers are in these situations. However, it seems reasonable, but not immediately obvious, to identify the current property owner as the "bidder" in a market for a LULU uses. That is, although by definition a LULU is unwanted in the local community, there also exists a subset of the community of property owners who desire to use (or sell their property to someone who will use) their property for a LULU facility. This subset of owners is willing to bid (in the form of an asking price for their property) on the prospects of a LULU development because a LULU will be more profitable than the current use. For any particular LULU, the number of "bidders" for the facility or use is likely to be constrained for a number of reasons: the existence of covenant and zoning restrictions, a potential bidder's ownership of other property in the area in question (because the value of this other property would be reduced by a LULU siting, this potential bidder would be discouraged from making an offer), the informal norms against invading or disturbing existing neighborhoods, the existence of even higher valued uses for other properties, and the limitations of the environmental qualities of the land itself (such as lack of access, topographical and drainage features, and so on). Most important, because land is a good that is naturally limited in terms of quantities and qualities, the number of bidders for any one LULU development may be limited.

Although there are a number of forces keeping the number of bidders for LULUs down, another peculiarity of LULU-type markets—its "the lady or the tiger" quality—tends to force an increase in the number of bidders. That is, once the initial universe of bidders has been determined, the nature of the market is such that persons owning properties surrounding or nearby a potential LULU will be tempted to join the market. This is the case because if neighbor A is the successful bidder for the LULU, neighbor B will likely bear many of the external costs of the development, while neighbor A (the successful bidder) will acquire a higher-than-average price for their property and, using the proceeds, escape the negative effects of the LULU by moving to another neighborhood. The nature of this type of LULU market is especially evident in depressed neighborhoods. Many of the properties in these neighborhoods are owned by absentee landlords who have little expectation of being able to sell or rent their property. In some cases the property has been abandoned by the owner, who is reluctant to pay property taxes on land that cannot produce enough revenue, or he has no expectation of such to justify paying these fees. Where neighborly norms and NIMBY solidarity might have helped to keep resident owners from becoming LULU bidders, for these absentee owners in disintegrated neighborhoods, there is likely to be a rush of bidding to see who can escape the "sinking ship" neighborhood.

As Karl Polanyi's work suggests, the market for land is different, especially in the case of a LULU. When one enters a market for most goods or services, there may exist a temporary limit in the good or service being produced for market. However, as the demand for the good or service increases, the supply will also tend to increase as old producers expand their capacity and new producers enter the market. With respect to land, this relationship does not exist; in Lockean terms, there is not always "good enough and plenty" left over for others, especially after a LULU has been sited.

Market Externalities

As suggested earlier, NIMBYs and LULUs are perhaps most appropriately viewed as complex instances of market externalities. That is, land uses by one owner tend to have substantial effects external to the person or persons who initiate or voluntarily partake in the land use. The external effects are complex because in any given case of a land use, there is likely to be a mix of both positive and negative externalities. Such facilities as elementary schools, for example, appear to provide positive externalities for a neighborhood as a whole, but have a concentrated negative impact on residents in the immediate area of the school.

Market theory suggests that market failure exists when there are substantial externalities involved in market transactions (such as the purchase of land for the purpose of placing a landfill or other LULU on the site). When market failure exists, there are three potential courses of action. First, the market can be dissolved in favor of public provision of a good or, in the case of LULUs, in favor perhaps of not providing the "good," such as a hazardous waste dump. Second, the market can be structured so as to provide definitive property rights to those who are external to the transactions of the market. This is sometimes known as the Coaseian solution, after Ronald Coase, who argues that once property rights are fully apportioned, property owner can negotiate among themselves efficient solutions to externality problems. Currently, nuisance laws provide such rights to those who can prove a direct harm resulting from someone's use of his market or property rights.[41] Third, the public can regulate the market through numerous devices such as permits, licenses, mandatory controls and limits, and so forth.[42]

Cultural Values as a Way of Reducing Transaction Costs

When transaction costs become too high or markets fail, there exist both long- and short-term alternatives. The long-run alternative is to address the underlying value system that is leading to a breakdown in the market. As Adam Smith taught us in a famous passage, the market is a mechanism that does not depend on the generosity of the butcher or baker for our subsistence; rather, it works because it relies on their self-interest. However, Smith was quite aware of the negative consequence of market orientation and called for public education, and particularly education in "moral sentiments."[43] Such education, especially as it promotes the values of trust and honesty, can effectively lower transaction costs and build norms that provide a sort of self-correction to behavior that would have potential negative externalities. In this way, market failure could be reduced. Additionally, the reduction of transaction costs through the building of trust can have numerous positive economic effects even where socialization for trust is not directed at market externalities per se.[44]

Although long-run "value education" and collegium-building solutions have a sort of romantic feel about them and do not seem to involve so much coercion on the part of the state, we should be reminded that consciousness raising is generally a more difficult, though perhaps a more long-lasting, approach than changes in political structures or market incentives. The history of contemporary education suggests, moreover, that moral education in a free society is hard to secure; it is most often overwhelmed by the cultural values that emerge from the economic structure of supply and demand of communications and entertainment in a mass market context.[45] Less free societies can create more effective systems of moral education, but still often have to wait a generation to reap the results of these systems. Only totalitarian societies, such as China during the Cultural Revolution, can hope to effect short-term changes in social mores of a substantial nature.

Additionally, an argument can be made that cultural explanations of phenomena such as the level of transaction costs or the willingness to engage in pollution evident in different societies may explain too little. In many cases the cultural values that appear to be mediating market experiences and behavior in one society, but not another, may be simply the cumulative effect of policy-based structures and incentives.[46]

While most policy analysts tend to downplay long-term values-education strategies alone, many will argue the importance of reforming legal and political structures as a complement to monetary or other immediate incentives for behavioral change. Among those who study social welfare policy, for example, there is a definite split between culture-of-poverty theorists and those who are more market-oriented. Both sides might agree, however, that education in values can be affected in some measure by structural elements in public policy of one type or the other.[47]

In the short run, the only recourse to market failure is reliance on various forms of positive law and regulation. However, as the description of contemporary interest group liberalism presented in an earlier chapter suggests, political systems also fail. The following reviews some of the strengths and weaknesses of major political-system approaches to LULU issues.

POLITICAL APPROACHES TO LULU ISSUES (VIEW OF THE SOCIAL PROBLEM)

Some of the difficulties with political approaches to LULU-type issues have already been touched on. We have seen how a number of political forces, events, structures, and behaviors undermine plausible efforts to govern LULUs. Such things as the "logic of collective action," discrimination in the siting of LULUs, the uneasy basis for zoning, constitutional and other legal and cultural constraints on decisions affecting real property, and general legitimacy problems posed by interest group liberalism have combined to make political governance of land-use issues one of the most complex and difficult of areas in which to form a coherent set of political procedures and approaches to governance. The purpose of the following discussion is to examine in a little more detail the specific institutional features of two categories of political approaches suggested by Gutterbock—conflict- or adversary-based approaches, and integrative, or unitary approaches. As with the discussion of markets, the features of these institutions will be reviewed in light of the four key criteria—equity, efficiency, environmental quality, and community viability—for evaluating land-use policy making.

At the root of all comprehensive planning of LULU siting is the notion that political processes can effectively aggregate or transform individual interests into the public interest. As Jane Mansbridge has suggested, this aggregation or transformation generally involves one of two basic short-term decision making processes:[48] (1) an adversarial process involving majoritarian, tradition-based, or hierarchical decision making, and usually resulting in the assignment of winners and losers; and (2) a unitary process requiring participatory dispute resolution and the consent of all the parties that will be subject to the costs and benefits of the decision.

In addition to making different assumptions about whether people's interest conflicts unitary processes in a democracy also differ from adversarial ones with respect to participants' status, decision rules employed, and the level of intimacy. Although unitary approaches to democracy do not demand or assume, as adversarial ones do, that every participant have equal power to protect their interests—this is unnecessary when interests are held in common—they do demand that participants have equal status.

Whereas adversarial processes use a majority vote decision rule, unitary approaches involve decisions based on consensus. Consensus or unanimity protects the rights of the minority in a group to be heard, and consensus can often be reached whenever full and free discussion is likely to reveal an underlying common interest or whenever the group values mutual friendship more than the outcome of any particular decision. Adversarial approaches, however, use majority rule decision making because it is thought that the persons who are attempting to make decisions are neither friends nor have common or reconcilable differences. Assuming that each decision is an isolated case and no common interest can be found, majority rule in this respect is thought to provide the greatest good for the greatest number.[49]

The other key feature of unitary approaches or unitary democracy is face-to-face contact through which persons have opportunities to discuss, challenge, negotiate, and compromise. The assumption is that this process will bring people who originally might be far apart in their opinions to some point of mutual interest or agreed truth. The jury system is based, for example, on this assumption. The parallel, but opposite, feature in adversarial approaches is the secret ballot. The assumption in this decision mechanism is that knowledge of one's interests is fully formed and fairly immutable.[50]

The division between adversarial and unitary democracy, Mansbridge points out, is substantially different from the traditionally recognized division between direct and representative democracy. Both adversarial and unitary democracy have both direct and representational forms. That is, even though unitary democracy is generally associated with such direct democracy examples as town meetings, the principles of unitary democracy—consensus, face-to-face communications, and equal status—can characterize deliberations of representative bodies, while the principles of adversarial democracy—aggregation of interests and majority rule—often characterize how issues are settled in direct democracies.

Advantages and Disadvantages of Unitary and Adversarial Approaches

In the following discussion of the advantages and disadvantages of political approaches to land-use issues, I have divided these approaches into essentially adversarial and essentially unitary ones. The inability to strictly categorize particular processes or mechanisms, such as traditional judicial decision making, as either unitary or adversarial is due to the fact that some of these mechanisms use a combination of approaches. In judicial decision making, for example, judges will often attempt to use unitary approaches of face-to-face contact and consensus-building negotiations among the parties prior to recognizing that disputants' opinions ultimately conflict, and consequently asking a jury to decide (that is, vote on) the issue. A similar process of using majority rule only as a last resort can be seen in other essentially adversarial processes. In the following discussion of adversarial and unitary approaches, I have made somewhat of a purist division, including processes that are not fully unitary in the adversarial process category. Other authors have taken a different approach, suggesting, for example, that administrative or judicial decision making is often unitary in nature. My reasons for differing on this point are sometimes due to a broader look at the processes in question. In judicial processes, for example, even when justices on, for example, an appeals court panel come to a consensus among themselves through a face-to-face process, the result for the litigants is essentially a zero-sum, winner-take-all decision. Alternatively, with respect to administrative processes, I have included these in the adversarial approach category because the participants in these processes, though often interacting in a face-to-face manner, are usually not of equal status.

ADVERSARIAL APPROACHES

Legislative, but Majoritarian Processes

Equity

Just as markets logically seem to fulfill the efficiency criterion, majoritarian legislative processes will logically engage and fulfill the equity criterion more than they will the other land-use evaluation criteria proposed by Gutterbock. Because legislative processes usually require a degree of open debate, public consideration of issues, and compromise, these democratic processes are more likely to be able to make reasonable trade-offs between strict justice understandings of equity and more "ethic of care" understandings of equity.[51] Conceptually speaking, majoritarian processes are those that at a minimum provide for the inclusion of all citizens and equality in voting and, in a more comprehensive view, also involve ideas about effective participation, control over the agenda, and numerous minority rights that make these equity-fulfilling elements more realizable in specific settings.[52]

Efficiency

Because of these features, majoritarian processes can more legitimately explore the larger issues (such as property rights, human rights, environmental security) involved in land use than other approaches that do not have engage the traditional loyalty that Americans give to the majority-rule principle.[53] As the earlier discussion of interest group liberalism indicated, democratic theory has hardly been realized within the current circumstances for political representation and accountability. More generally, political scientists have noted that few citizens have any idea as to how their representatives have voted on any issue.[54] However, even if one were to assume that the maldistribution of power generated through interest group liberalism could be controlled and political accountability of representatives could be tightened considerably (such as through the reform of campaign and think-tank contributions suggested by William Greider), majoritarian voting processes may still result in inefficient representations of citizens' desires. Such faulty representation can occur because voting as a mechanism for deciding among numerous alternatives involves some methodological problems as well as a degree of inherent irrationality. Methodologically speaking, the division, statement, and sequencing of a spectrum of choices can be crucial to the final decision. Moreover, as Kenneth Arrow, a Nobel prize-winning economist, has suggested, even an extended series of votes will not guarantee that there will be a rational linkage between voters' desires and the actual outcomes of the vote.[55]

Environmental Quality

In terms of environmental quality, the key question might be whether majoritarian processes would bring the kind of broad intelligence that is focused on the long term as well as specific technical expertise needed to formulate and address many environmental issues. Grieder's view of the relative success and momentum of local environmentalists when compared with national-level environmental protection efforts suggests that small-scale majoritarian processes might be more effective than large-scale majoritarian processes that have been corrupted by interest group liberalism. Sidney Plotkin's view of the tendency of local political units to guard the exclusionary interests of property owners against the expansionary interests of global capitalism supports this thesis. Frank Popper's review of land-use politics is less sanguine in this regard. He tends to see local land use as being dominated by development interests no matter how the majoritarian process is structured. In contrast, Joseph Browder, writing more recently, sees a local majority of environmentalists as being successful in blocking new industrial sitings, but in ways that may be foreclosing development of superior technologies for pollution control. That is, majoritarian approaches may be generating new values, but not enough new intelligence to go along with those values. Richard Stewart makes generally the same point when he argues that democratic accountability and environmental protection are hardly served by public debate on complex technological issues. However, Stewart does seem to believe that majoritarian approaches and public debate can be effective ways of establishing overall levels of acceptable environmental risk, while allowing the market for pollution permits to establish how specific polluters will employ technology to address their part of the risk. Joel Mintz, however, is skeptical that a marketable permit system for pollution control would reduce the demand for legislators to comprehend and address the technological complexity of environmental policymaking. He says, for example, that even under a market system, legislators would have to take into account "the relative environmental impact of various levels of pollutant discharges, the implications of different alternatives with respect to energy consumption, and the relative economic costs of all options."[56]

Community Viability

In terms of community viability, majoritarian processes, as suggested above, have a high degree of legitimacy, at least when contrasted with market-based or executive, or judicial approaches. This is true in environmental as well as other areas.[57] However, this legitimacy can often be based on short-run, expedient coalitions needed to form temporary majorities. These coalitions can fall apart after a key vote, resulting in less than adequate legitimacy. Moreover, and perhaps most important, majoritarian decision making—as with all of the adversarial processes—tends to create winners and losers. The game-like competition of majoritarian approaches can result in rigid coalitions of legislators who collude more for the purpose of winning in legislative combat than for the purpose of developing rational, interest-linked policy.

A special legitimacy problem of local legislative control of land use is examined immediately following this review of adversarial processes. The key point to be made in this regard is that local legislative bodies do not encompass large enough populations and a large enough breadth of issues so as to afford a sufficient and on-going clash and bargaining of interests. As such, these bodies are less likely to engage in the kind of thoughtful deliberation and balancing of interests that is central to the realization of democratic ideals.[58] Hence, as legitimacy is undermined, so too is community viability.

Judicial Approaches

Much of the earlier discussion of property rights definitions and allocations, judicial notions of formalism and realism, and the debate over controversies such as "general rules versus standards" spoke to the issue of how judicial processes might affect community viability, equity, and efficiency. More specifically, the discussion of Robert Nelson's critique of the "legal fiction" of zoning pointed to the weaknesses of attempting to solve emerging and unique problems within the constraints of legal precedents and traditional concepts and doctrines. I will not repeat these discussions here, but will only make a few general points about how judicial approaches might affect realization of the key land-use criteria.

Judicial approaches tend to be used when legislative approaches do not prove satisfactory to one or more parties. In these cases, residents who are protesting the siting of a LULU can sometimes choose among or combine three tactic. In addition to calling for a review of zoning ordinances, judicial approaches to LULU issues include recourse to a nuisance suit (with either injunctive or compensatory remedies) and requests for a judicial review of environmental impact statements. Because the issue of zoning has received extensive treatment, my discussion will focus on the latter two judicial tactics.

Nuisance Law

First, one of the obvious advantages of judicial approaches is that they can be used in conjunction with market approaches to establish, to a certain degree, a self-regulating system for land-use decision making. I am referring, of course, to Ronald Coase's suggestion that the common law, properly understood, can form the basis for an efficient market for handling negative externalities in land uses.[59] That is, as long as the law clearly assigns liability to one of two neighbors whose land uses conflict and as long as there are no transaction costs, the Coase Theorem tells us that the outcome will be economically efficient. The common law of nuisance traditionally was able to provide such clear-cut assignment of rights. However, when at the turn of the century the courts started to weigh the costs and benefits of allocating land-use "spillover" rights, certainty and clarity of rights were lost. As a guide for deciding disputes, the liability rules that emerged from a series of nuisance suits by residents against industrial defendants provided fewer sharp, bright lines and rather more confusion. In attempting to look beyond disputing parties and toward the overall social consequences of granting remedies or injunctions to plaintiffs, the courts have consistently articulated inconsistent decisions. Some of this inconsistency is the result of variations in the contexts of the individual disputes. However, Denis Brion, in a recent review of chestnut cases from nuisance law, suggests that the inconsistency in nuisance decisions may be systematically biased against plaintiffs. Brion argues that these nuisance plaintiffs, being risk-adverse, also tend to be poorer than risk-taking entrepreneur developers. In cases where a plaintiff is requesting a damage remedy, the judicial process will favor defendants who tend to have greater resources, superior knowledge of its operations, and superior access to experts. Also, though Brion does not say so, defendents are often able to escape liability because of the difficulty plaintiffs have in proving causation. Brion concludes that in avoiding the issue of wealth distribution, "judicial analysis falls substantially short of thoroughness . . . and that in granting at most a damage remedy, the court in effect allows the defendant to expropriate a substantial part of the plaintiff's wealth, an expropriation that tends to exacerbate the inequality in wealth distribution that prevails in society."[60] In terms of the division of property rights into expansionary and exclusionary interests, Brion's argument suggests that with respect to nuisance law at least, the expansionary interests are systematically given the upper hand.

A second advantage of judicial decision making would be its tradition and stated goal of objectivity and neutrality, equal protection, and due process in decision making. In contrast to majoritarian approaches, in which political passions, procedural manipulations, public-opinion pressures for action, and the like can undermine due deliberation, an exchange of ideas, and openly debated, judicial approaches give greater credence to these values and in this sense help increase the level of community viability in the sense of the overall "ideal of community."[61] Additionally, the heightened attention to these procedural values is likely to provide a greater hearing, testing, and weighing of complex scientific and technological knowledge and understandings. This general feature of judicial processes—though not always realized in particular cases—would have obvious advantages in attending to the environmental quality criterion as well as potentially realizing efficiency values in cases where cost-benefit analyses are used to enlighten rather than close off judgment.[62]

Environmental Impact Statements

The judicial approach to decision making about LULUs has been institutionalized in the use of environmental impact statements. While these statements are most frequently required where environmental values, strictly speaking, are at stake, some states and municipalities have begun to require an assessment of the social impacts. Such social impact statements might be required where the LULU in question is thought to have general impacts of an environmental nature. For example, an impact statement might address the social effects of a landfill on a neighboring community. In other cases, such as those provided for in New York City's new charter, the local government is required to assess the social impact of facilities such as group homes, where environmental values, strictly speaking, are not in question.[63]

While environmental impact statements are required of public agencies and private developers who are attempting to site facilities, judicial review of these statements for their comprehensiveness is the basis for their potential legitimacy as public policy tools. As such, environmental impact statements can work to suggest to potential opponents of a LULU that they have been heard by an impartial representative of government and therefore need not continue their protest in a more volatile or crude fashion. However, judicial review for comprehensiveness is not the same as review of the accuracy of the substance of the findings. In most cases, judicial review examines only whether the steps in the impact statement process have been followed. Consequently, it provides the parties in conflict only a rather shallow sense of having had their day in court. When an impact statement has been generated in a competent and fair manner, it also provides valuable insight into the costs and benefits of a proposed land use. However, if the statement has met all the procedural elements but is the result of incompetent or seemingly competent but biased analysis, courts are generally limited in their abilities to address these substantive issues.[64] In sum, as environmental impact statements are currently structured, they do not take full advantage of the potential strengths of the judicial approach. However, if judges were allowed to address the substantive issues, the legitimacy of such judicial activism would no doubt be questioned.

One method for infusing greater legitimacy into judicial review of environmental impact statements would be to employ juries as part of the review process. When fine-tuned procedures for advancing judgment through knowledge are combined with a jury system, the judicial approach would appear to further reinforce community viability, though perhaps in a narrow sense. That is, despite the long tradition of the jury system, jury decisions and awards are still the subject of substantial questioning in the community at large. Overall, however (and especially in an age where interest group liberalism has seriously undermined the legitimacy of other branches of government), judicial approaches that include juries have particular advantages in terms of community viability and equity. In light of the corruption wrought by interest group liberalism, the system of random selection of juries, bypassing organized interest group influences, may in some respects be seen as lending a greater legitimacy to the judicial approach than to others.

Juries have traditionally been used to establish the need for and level of damages to be awarded to plaintiffs (typically neighborhood residents) who sue LULU owners (typically developers), charging that developers have violated nuisance law in the building or operation of facilities. Although juries are theoretically best suited to determine the amount of damage that a neighbor has suffered in being forced to give a nuisance easement to the LULU developer, there are a number of practical and other considerations that make damage determination more than a little difficult. First, juries cannot refer to any objective valuation of a nuisance easement. Because there is little or no trade in such easements, no established market value can be referenced. Second, there is little guide for juries (or judges, for that matter) to provide compensation for the loss of security (or demoralization cost) that occurs when property rights are eroded at the initiative of another private owner whose use constitutes a nuisance. Such private "takings" are thought to involve a considerable erosion of security in property over and above the erosion that public eminent domain proceedings occasion. Third, some of the value in the plaintiff's or neighbor's property will be subjective. Some of this subjective valuation is generally understandable and easily provides grounds for a jury's empathy.[65] But the special character of plaintiffs in nuisance cases—the fact that they tend to be risk-adverse—may undercut the potential for a full evaluation of damages. Risk-adverse plaintiffs are likely to value their property much higher than either defendants (who tend to be risk-takers) or juries (who are relatively risk-neutral). That is, even more than usual or more than juries, the plaintiff in a nuisance suit, being highly risk-adverse, will likely value what she possesses more than the dollars offered in compensation for her acceptance of the nuisance.[66] Fourth, juries are likely to see the nuisance suit brought by the plaintiff as part of a game in which the plaintiff overstates the full range of subjective losses that awarding a nuisance easement has caused.[67] Fifth, juries (and judges) may not be able to evaluate adequately how a nuisance easement will affect a person's entitlement in property that is part of an integral community habitat. That is, if a person's property forms a basis for his identity in a cohesive community, no objective or market valuation of the loss of such property can be made. Echoing Karl Polanyi, law Professor Denis Brion writes: "Market value connotes price; price connotes trade. The value of community cannot be traded, however, to an outsider. The outsider cannot buy into the community. At most, he can hope eventually to become a part of it."[68] In summary, including juries in a judicial approach to land-use disputes can offer some increase in overall legitimacy, but cannot remove biases that are built into current understandings of nuisance law.

General Disadvantages of the Judicial Approach

However, there are a number of general disadvantages to the judicial approach as well. One of the difficulties encountered by this approach is the legitimacy issue. As Simon Rifkin has put it, "By what authority do judges turn courts into mini-legislatures?" More practically, "How can government by non-elected, lifetime officials be squared with representative democracy?"[69] As Adam Smith intimated in his discussion of property, to the degree that the judicial system follows the common law of property and is restricted from taking a more comprehensive view of property, it acts as an institution designed to protect those who have property, while ignoring those who are without. Morton Horwitz's conclusion to his history of the development of American law is pointed in this regard. He writes that "by the middle of the nineteenth century, the legal system had been reshaped to the advantage of men of commerce and industry at the expense of farmers, workers, consumers, and other less powerful groups in society."[70] This tendency for a system bias against ordinary citizens is particularly evident with respect to the issue of standing in many land-use cases. William Whyte, the author of *The Last Landscape*, describes how in many cases, citizens who wished to use the courts to protect existing municipal park property against the ravages of public purpose development or highway construction could not do so because they did not personally own the land in question. Because municipalities are considered creatures of the state, for example, the state would not have to even consider the wishes of the local municipality itself, much less those of a subset of citizens. Whyte has suggested that legislation be crafted to provide citizens some standing in cases such as these.[71]

As a general point, the problem with judicial proceedings, as is commonly noted, is that it is based on a specific set of adversaries who tend to represent only a subset of the potential interests involved in the outcome of the case.[72] Furthermore, because of the narrow case-by-case process and the slow movement of judicial decision making when there is a potential for appeal, this approach can compromise all of the four key criteria whenever there is a need for broad-based treatment of an issue or whenever a particular value is linked to timeliness. Classically, issues of equity ("justice delayed is justice denied") are believed to be affected by this tendency; however, cases where environmental qualities such as the survival of an endangered species are at stake also can be severely affected by the lack of timeliness in the judicial approach.

A different type of time-related problem can occur as a result of reliance on a judicial approach. When the judicial approach to clarifying common-law property rights that are in dispute results in the emergence of new property rights, these new rights are not necessarily congruent with the public interest. In fact, there may be a potential for the accumulation of private contracts and understandings to result in a diminution of communities as viable environments for individuals who are not party to these contracts or agreements. This potential is magnified by the existence of legal entities—corporations—whose interests do not expire at the end of a period of time (which would remand properties back to individual persons) and whose interests are often of an absentee nature or at least not dependent on viable communities. Essentially, the problem I am describing would occur as property owners sell nuisance easements of various sorts to other owners who might wish to pollute, make excessive noise, or emit obnoxious odors. Over long periods of time, corporations could acquire easements of this sort to such a substantial degree that there would be few places where one could choose to live without a constant level of nuisance. Although this danger would appear to be fanciful, corporations as legal entities with an endless lifespan have only existed for a little over a century. Moreover, some naturalists suggest, for example, that already it is nearly impossible to find any place in America that is not affected on a daily basis by the industrial and transportation noise produced by corporations.

Executive/Administrative Approaches

Theoretically speaking, executive branch processes are only adversarial in a secondary or indirect sense. That is, administrative approaches are designed to carry out the wishes of the majority as defined by a legislative assembly. Once the legislative branch has decided an issue, the executive branch is supposed to be unified in carrying out this decision. However, as astute observers of political processes have noted, there are several moments within the political process when executive approaches can be thought of as adversarial in nature, such as during the problem definition, agenda setting, legislation drafting, and especially during the rule writing and enforcement stages of the political-legal process.[73] This tendency for the executive branch and the various bureaucracies to become a secondary battleground for interest groups has been exacerbated by the corruptive tendencies of interest group liberalism. But notwithstanding these degenerative influences, in administrative decision making, in an age when bureaucracies are large enough to include a diverse set of personal and professional perspectives and favored practices, internal conflict is probably unavoidable.[74] [75] Additionally, in contrast to the early spoils system for filling bureaucratic posts and ensuring hierarchical control through implicit loyalty to executive orders and policy, the reformed "civil service" bureaucracy can often elude orders from elected officials, and it can develop and implement policy with only the most cursory level of oversight or control from these supposedly more sovereign parts of governments.[76]

As the rise of corporations without sunset limits has affected the pattern of landed property rights (and consequently land-use practices themselves), so too has the rise of bureaucracies with effective lifespans that are much longer than the democratic assemblies and executives that are elected to "run" them affected the distribution of political power. A number of political theorists of the public-choice school have suggested that one result of the rise of the bureaucratic state has been a variety of "political failures" that represent in some measure the parallel of "market failures." Political failures, the theory suggests, occur in the bureaucracies and among elected officials because persons in these positions are human and therefore prone to look after their own interests. However, instead of only doing so within their capacity as private sector actors, where such behavior is expected, public officials and personnel attend to their own interests, public choice theorists suggest, by masking these interests in the guise of the public interest. This corruption of the public interest occurs in a number of ways, including the tendency of public officials to establish and maintain ineffective or unnecessary programs that will provide them with "credit" from interested publics. Housing programs will, for example provide specialists in housing, planning, and environmental control with jobs, contracts, status, and power.[77] Public choice theorists also point to the tendency of program managers to increase their status, political power, and compensation by increasing the size of their budgets and program authority—whether or not these actions would provide commensurate benefits to the public.[78]

One of the difficulties in discovering whether "political failure" has occurred is due to the inappropriateness of judging public sector operations by the standards of private sector ones. That is, it is not usually fair to judge public agency operations by the efficiency criterion alone. As numerous observers have noted and as Gutterbock's four land-use criteria specifically suggest, public sector bureaucracies often have to balance a number of different values.[79] As such, specific structural contexts, personnel training regimens, and overall social and organizational values may precipitate or prevent political failure. For example, Christopher Leman's study of the difference between Canadian public sector management of forest resources and U.S. private sector corporate management suggests that the priority that Canadian regional authorities placed on revenue generation tended to result in more intensive and less sensitive (to environmental values) logging and forestry management practices than was the case in the comparable private sector forestry industry in the United States Leman's findings would seem to support generally a public choice perspective on environmental land management. He also discovered such "political failures" as the refusal of Canadian provincial governments to assent to federal government regulation. (A similar case has been made in the United States that many government agencies, such as the Departments of Defense and Energy, have eluded regulation by other agencies charged with this task.) Leman also notes that public sector insulation from market forces can lead to exploitation of forest resources even in instances where the market would not support logging. This occurs when governments subsidize logging operations by providing the infrastructure of forest roads that are necessary to make the operations profitable.

On the other hand, some of the factors at work in forestry land-use problems do not suggest a failure of the public sector per se. For example, Leman believes that much of the U.S.-Canadian difference is due to differences in the two markets. In the United States, he argues, the market supports forestry regeneration efforts, whereas in Canada this is much less the case. Additionally, one of the differences he notes—that American private sector operations are more heavily influenced by professional foresters than are their Canadian public sector counterparts—suggests that, contrary to "political failure" theorists, this particular public bureaucracy has not become too bloated and overrun by professional interests, but rather the opposite: the governmental operation was perhaps too lean. Leman also cites the good record of U.S. governmental agencies—in contrast to the more inactive Canadian agencies—in preventing environmental harm on private lands.

Leman's conclusion is instructive with respect to the debate between public-choice theorists who emphasize political failure and advocate large-scale privatization, and policy analysts who tend to see market failure as the more serious land-use problem: "Institutions clearly matter for forest regeneration, but public and private approaches alike can produce the desired results, while failures can be found in both nominally public and nominally private organizations."[80]

In comparing administrative processes with other political adversarial approaches, however, administration likely has an advantage with respect to the application of expertise and practical experience. Bureaucracies more than judicial or legislative bodies, maintain a corps of professional planning experts and associated resources. As a result, bureaucracies can call on their institutional memory for rapid and fairly accurate policy evaluation. Moreover, through the use of executive orders, elected executives can often make and implement decisions in a faster, and to that degree more efficient, fashion than would be the case with either of the other adversarial approaches or with the unitary approach to be discussed below. This potential for efficiency is, of course, masked in situations dominated by the interest group processes that Greider, Lowi and other critics of the current state of the union describe.

A disadvantage of administrative processes for development of land-use policy is that decisions resulting from administrative rulemaking tend to be top-down or undemocratic in nature. Even where citizen participation in rulemaking is mandated, the lack of procedural decision-making rules (as exist in judicial deliberations) or representational rules (as exist in majoritarian decision making) undermines the legitimacy of these processes in the eyes of the community. Again, the forces of interest group liberalism exacerbate this situation.

Finally, administrative processes, like the other adversarial approaches, tend to create winners and losers. Additionally, however, administrative decisions can often leave disputants in a land-use controversy feeling as if they are all losers. Reaction in the logging and environmental communities to the recent decision by the Clinton administration to set a specific limit on logging in the Pacific Northwest might be said to typify community-level responses to administrative decision making: Both groups felt that the decision was not a good one and both vowed to continue to fight for their interests.

A review of the advantages and disadvantages of administrative processes would be incomplete without referring to the debate among economists about the costs and benefits of the markets versus those of regulation and economic planning (implicitly carried out by public administrators). While the extreme positions of economic laissez-faire and state socialism have receded in the economic policy debate, the more "meso" issue of regulation versus deregulation mirrors in a number of ways the debate about land-use planning. It is notable, for example, that movements to regulate or deregulate aspects of the economy tend to come in waves of enthusiasm followed by dissatisfaction and movement toward the other policy pole.[81] Recently, for example, cracks have occurred in the movement toward deregulation of markets in areas such as air transportation, securities, and savings and loan institutions. As a consequence, the design of regulatory policy in these areas has re-emerged, but not entirely drained the energy from the deregulatory movement.

There have been three basic responses to the appearance of failure in deregulated markets. Among true believers, the failure of deregulation is attributed to the timidity or ineptitude of initial deregulation efforts. Policy advisers correctly note that some of these markets were deregulated in such a manner as to promote high levels of risk-taking among participants. Risk-taking was promoted because in the savings and loan industry, for example, the profit side of the enterprise was deregulated, while the loss side remained regulated and insured through government guarantees against depositors' losses. Because of this insurance, savings and loan administrators had little incentive other than standards of practice to exercise due caution. Removing the government interference in this market, true believers in deregulation argue, would correct for the failures of deregulation that are currently coming to light.

A second response to the failure of deregulation has been to reject deregulation totally and call for a return to either government provision or much higher levels of government regulation or control. Proponents of this re-regulation (or industrial policy) response suggest that the government has a role to play to make sure that in the airline industry, for example, profits are sufficient across the board to pay for long-term reinvestment in new equipment or maintenance of existing vehicles. In addition to providing strategic support for the airline industry in the global marketplace, such manipulation of the market, it is argued, would also prevent any short-term disruptions in supply of airline service that might occur as a result of cutthroat competition eliminating the viability of particular routes or air transport suppliers.

Understanding the economic effect of land-use regulations has been more difficult because the goals related to land-use control tend to be more diverse and the arguments for and against regulations often are based more on ideology than any particular utilitarian consideration. A recent study by Ira Lowry and Bruce Ferguson, however, sheds some light on the effect of one major type of land-use regulation—development or growth management regulation—and the affordability of housing. Lowry and Ferguson looked at land-use regulatory effects on housing markets in three growing metropolitan areas—Sacramento, Nashville, and Orlando. After examining the types and degree of regulation, these researchers were able to determine that Sacramento was the most tightly regulated market. Planners there used three types of regulations—restrictions on development, impact fees, and costly and uncertain review processes—in ways that effectively limited the supply of housing so that growing demand caused housing prices to rise substantially. At the opposite end of the spectrum, Nashville could generally be characterized as a city without substantial growth-management regulation. Orlando could be said to lie somewhere between the highly regulated Sacramento and the generally deregulated Nashville. Orlando's regulations included impact fees and development reviews (to determine if the development was compatible with regional plans and available infrastructure support), but not outright development prohibition on land that would otherwise be suitable for development. As supporters of deregulation would have predicted, both of the regulated cities, Orlando and Sacramento, experienced increases in housing costs, with the increases in the Sacramento being much greater than those in Orlando. However, contrary to predictions by deregulation proponents, during the study period from 1980 to 1990, "the median price of existing homes in Nashville rose by 55 percent, compared to 45 percent in Orlando—despite the much weaker demand for housing in the Nashville area."[82] This finding suggests that the middle way between extensive regulation and full deregulation may be the most appropriate policy design. Lowry and Ferguson attribute this negative effect of deregulation to a boom and bust cycle of development that occurs as developers, in rushing to cash in on an increase in market demand, build more capacity than is needed. The unregulated market in housing, they suggest, can be fueled by speculation, leading to wasteful overbuilding that can hurt the developers and the final consumers of housing. They speculate that perhaps there is a happy medium between too much and too little regulation. They suggest that a slowing of the permit process in Nashville, for example, might have benefited developers and housing consumers in the long run.[83]

Administrative processes are most clearly called for in situations where state regulations might have an opportunity to create net social benefits. With respect to the NIMBY syndrome undermining society's capacity to establish and maintain essential facilities, some policy analysts have called for broad-based federal regulation of LULU siting processes. In one such regulatory proposal, it is suggested that the federal government require each state to develop "reasonable, rational, and completely above-board site selection criteria that have a technical validity and at the same time make sense to the average citizen."[84] The author of this proposal goes on to suggest that states also need to severely limit the role of voters in approving or disapproving the site selected, while providing the parties affected by the NIMBY-type use of nearby land with compensation. Also, unlike market-mimicking proposals for the siting of LULUs, regulatory procedures would not allow communities to "buy in" or "buy out" of the selection process. While the sentiment behind such a proposal for regulatory relief from the NIMBY syndrome is understandable, the potential for administrative processes to meet effectively the criteria of making siting decisions in a "reasonable, rational and above-board" fashion may, as I suggest below, be unrealistic. Such proposals, while strengthening the power of the state against powerful private interests (such as the affluent communities that do not allow LULUs but that nevertheless benefit from having others accept LULUs), often end up, for practical purposes, placing an inordinate amount of new power in the hands of the central government. The author of one of the proposals for federal and state regulation of the NIMBY proposals, for example, calls for "the state to acquire, and when necessary, to resell, presumably with appropriate conditions, any site identified as suitable for a NIMBY-type activity or facility."[85] Extending the state's power of eminent domain for purposes and in situations that are only quasi-public would, for most citizens, probably require a high level of proof that this was the only or the best means of addressing the NIMBY problem.

Adversarial Approaches, Zoning, and Comprehensive Planning

As theories of federalism and this brief review of the advantages and disadvantages of the three essentially adversarial processes suggest, no one process is likely to be appropriate in all or even some instances. As was argued earlier, legislative land-use decision-making politics are suspect at both local and national levels. Whereas well-organized and resource-rich interests are able to form effective political "factions" at both levels, the mechanisms by which these interest groups achieve their goals and the particular sorting out of winners and losers may differ at the two levels. The national interest groups attempt to achieve their goal through the marshaling of "sponsored information" and dogged infiltration of the bureaucracy. As corporate resources are key to winning in this arena, interest groups with expansionary goals and a desire to gut environmental or social regulation will tend to be favored. At the local level, where influencing elected officials or winning referenda is the key to success, there is a greater balance between expansionary and exclusionary interests, with the balance in contested situations being decidedly against minority interests that may have no leverage as part of any coalition. "Here," Carol Rose writes, "a quickly assembled majority for, let us say, residential zoning and a short 'amortization' of existing uses may totally defeat owners of gas stations[86] or grocery stores—without the threat of the losers' political retaliation later."[87]

James Madison's innovative argument in *The Federalist Papers*—that extended republics can support a more general balancing of private interests overall and a greater potential for the emergence of a public interest—would suggest that although national-level decision making in an interest group liberalism environment might be subtly influenced by well-funded and tightly organized groups, such a pattern of corruption is perhaps fixable. However, if Madison is correct, local governments are perhaps inherently subject to majority interest groups dominating public decision making and tyrannizing minorities. As was described earlier, this tendency has led a number of legal theorists to propose substitution of "plan jurisprudence" or various mixtures of judicial and administrative processes for the more typically legislative processes and deliberations that are currently used to decide local land-use issues. These more judicial and administrative processes, the reform advocates believe, can help reduce the role of popular and powerful interest group pressures and the tendency toward haste and partial judgments that are endemic to local government councils' attempts to make piecemeal land-use decisions.[88]

Implementing the plan jurisprudence approach is dependent on a pre-existing comprehensive land-use plan that can act as a standard by which individual land-use cases are decided. Successful implementation might also be dependent on local office holders being able to switch easily from legislative to judicial/administrative roles. Critics of the plan jurisprudence approach, however, have questioned whether it is realistic to expect that these preconditions for a plan jurisprudence solution exists or can be put in place. That is, it may not be possible for plan jurisprudence to solve the problem of factions or special interests dominating local land-use decisions.

Carol Rose has reviewed a number of arguments in this regard, including: (1) the lack of elected local officials having a secure tenure in office—a feature that the authors of *The Federalist Papers*—believed to be a prerequisite for impartiality and insulation from political pressure;[89] (2) the lack of elected local officials having the land-use planning expertise that the traditional doctrine of administrative law suggests might be a substitute for judicial stature and tenure in the process of arriving at a correct decision;[90] (3) the fact that the political expertise of elected officials is likely to undermine whatever substantive land-use expertise they might have or acquire; (4) the clash between the judicial prohibition of ex parte contacts between the decision maker and the involved parties, and the political expectation that such contacts and the informal solicitations of citizens' views are part of the elected representative's role;[91] (5) the difficulty in elected officials claiming impartiality; and (6) the impossibility of identifying those situations (which might involve only a few people or a small plot of land) that call for judicial/administrative processes rather than legislative ones. Making this distinction is unlikely to be feasible because even the most general planning processes and ordinances can favor certain citizens and harm others. More specifically, most local land-use decisions, even those at the broadest level, have a potentially harmful effect on minorities, suggesting the need to invoke a judicial/administrative procedure in all cases.

Additionally, even if it were possible to craft a legitimate, interests-balancing, comprehensive plan, Rose questions whether such plans can, in fact, act as a judicial standard. She makes three arguments in this respect. First, she argues that traditional planning doctrine wrongly assumes that deliberations related to the adoption of a general land-use plan (the plan that precedes the zoning of particular parcels of property) will generate sufficient as well as impartial information or that these deliberations will be conducted in a neutral manner. In fact, it may take a concrete proposal to zone or rezone a particular piece of property to generate the broad-based public attention and participation required to legitimize any governmental decision. Typically, Rose argues, it takes such specific, highly visible zoning acts to create the incentives for the public to be willing to exert sufficient energy to collect information, focus arguments, and engage in a level of debate that would sanction the deliberations and decisions that result. That is, the act of creating a general but unenforceable land-use plan would not be sufficient to promote a full and open airing of the implications of the plan and the energetic representation of all the interests involved.[92] If this is the case, general-level planning usually will not afford the sort of active citizen participation that modern planning has traditionally relied on for its legitimacy. Rose concludes that "because some emotional involvement is a necessary part of attentive decision making, the price of basing a decision on an advanced plan may be that a vague, abstract, or incompletely aired 'advisory opinion' is substituted for an overheated decision."[93] The implication of Rose's analysis is that construction of general-level plans may provide few or no benefits, while occasioning substantial cost.

Second, Rose suggests that modern planning doctrine, while recognizing the flaws of traditional doctrine and calling for a planning "process" rather than an "end-state depiction" of goals, cannot support the ideal of plan jurisprudence. It is unable to do so because such judicial/administrative processing of zoning and rezoning claims demands the end-state conception of planing. Planning-as-process, she argues, does not suggest or generate a standard by which a judge can determine whether an individual rezoning decision can be reconciled with the plan. The absence of pre-existing standards essentially undermines the case for treating decisions as quasi-judicial in the first place, Rose points out. An end-state plan is needed as a point of reference for legitimate judicial decision making. Without such a point of reference, plan jurisprudence probably has less legitimacy than outright political bargaining.

Third, Rose notes that plan jurisprudence is unlikely to be an effective policy because local politicians (like their counterparts at the national level) have generally been successful in avoiding the development of clearly articulated general plans or rules for translating these plans into specific regulations. To avoid immediate conflict, local politicians will often craft vague plans and rules. In this regard, officials have looked favorably on a number of old and new planning tools that provide for a great deal of flexibility and room for bargaining, case-by-case negotiation, and political compromise. In addition to the expanded use of traditional tools such as variances and conditional use permits, Rose notes that devices such as "floating zones," "planned unit developments," and "development rights transfers" all provide further evidence that localities have no fixed plans for development.[94] Local politicians are likely to be quite inventive, Rose reports, in maintaining local ad hoc control. For example, when court decisions (based on the *Fasano* case) required local jurisdictions in California to conform their zoning decisions to their general plans, these jurisdictions changed their master plan instead of altering their zoning regulations to match the existing plan. Subsequent legislation limiting changes in the master plan to three times a year only resulted in a saving up of individual piecemeal changes and the adopting of ever vaguer plans, rather than conformity to the spirit of plan jurisprudence.[95]

Rose rightfully concludes that attempts to force local governments to act in ways that comport with outdated notions of planning (such as attempts to posit an explicit and desired end-state) and that require unrealistic changes in the customary relationships between politicians and their constituents are likely to backfire. Specifically, she predicts that these efforts are more likely to generate "false and evasive plans and false and evasive escapes therefrom" rather than the realization of a quasi-judicial ideal.[96]

Perhaps, Rose speculates, instead of relying on attempts to analyze, categorize, and constrain local land-use decisions in terms of classic liberal safeguards that are built into the three adversarial approaches (that is, the legislative, judicial, and administrative), we should consider an alternative tradition and approach. Rose suggests consideration of a greater degree of citizen participation in mediation and other dispute-resolution processes. Rose proposes the use of more unitary approaches to land-use issues and conflicts. The next section explores some of the advantages and disadvantages of this alternative political approach—unitary democracy—that was described briefly at the beginning of this discussion of political approaches. As suggested, these unitary approaches are built on the idea that social integration is sometimes a feasible goal.

The alternative tradition of unitary democracy clearly provides a potential way out of the paradox that local government presents to classic liberal thought—that much local government decision making inescapably undermines the potential for realizing essential safeguards of a classic liberal polity. Paradoxically, while we ordinarily think of local or small-scale democracy as more pure than large-scale democracy, it is in fact more difficult at the local level to establish a sharp separation of powers, a wide-ranging clash of interests, and a sharp line between public and private roles—essential attributes of classic liberal institutional arrangements.

SOCIAL INTEGRATION OR UNITARY APPROACHES

American politics and policymaking have been dominated by the Founders' belief that "men are not angels" and that the problem of irreconcilable "factions" will continue to exist and to require continual management.[97] In contrast, other political traditions have variously emphasized the potential development of a "general will" or the "will of the people" as something that is greater than the sum of its parts or than the "winning" policy in an adversarial process.[98] As originally formulated by Rousseau, unitary decision-making approaches assume that there is a "correct" resolution arising from the shared values of those participating in the process. For Rousseau, this resolution could be achieved "if one takes away from [all particular] wills the pluses [of a common interest] and minuses [of a selfish interest] that cancel one another, the general will remains as the sum of the differences."[99] Although Rousseau's vision of a general will has not been fully implemented in any state, versions or adaptations of unitary approaches to issues exist in a number of national cultures, such as Japan's, to a greater extent than in the United States.

Perhaps because of the relative national success of American political processes in terms of political stability and economic growth, political theorists advocating alternatives to adversarial approaches have found only a limited audience.[100] However, as U.S. economic dominance has slipped, more Americans have become willing to look at other nations' approaches to public and private sector operations, problem-solving, and organizational conflict-resolution strategies. On the whole, such strategies as self-managed teams, quality circles, interorganizational collaboration, and mediated conflict resolution seem to partake of a different—more unitary—approach to governance in general.[101]

Unitary processes require participatory dispute resolution and consensus-building among all the parties that will be subject to the costs and benefits of the decision. The key to these types of approaches is often the joint development and widespread distribution of information. With enough information, appropriately structured, it is often possible for people to be able to ground their negotiations in their real interests rather than in their preset opinions or information-poor, debating "positions." Because interests tend to be more broadly defined than positions, there is often room to satisfy more than one interest at once.[102] In this respect, unitary approaches may often depend on the created or discovered potential for persons with different goals to agree upon similar "means."[103]

Unitary Processes: Are They Realistic?

Unitary processes and decision making, David Lampe notes, are often criticized because it is believed that they are unrealistic, requiring the individual to identify with the community as a whole, rather than simply participate in the community.[104] Although unitary processes of negotiation and consensus building have been advocated most strenuously by those (such as in the human relations and culture-theory schools of organizational behavior) who view organizations as largely cooperative and unitary systems, the value of negotiation and consensus-building approaches (as opposed to voting, market, or command systems) has not escaped those who see organizations essentially as fields for subgroup conflicts.[105] That is, some observers of organizational systems who believe that conflict is essentially unavoidable still hold out the possibility that cooperative *coalitions* of separate individual interests (or interest groups) can form.[106]

However, as Mancur Olson's "logic of collective action" suggests, collective action in the public interest is often problematic because of the free-rider problem. Olson concluded that in large groups it would be necessary to provide "selective incentives" such as punishments for free riders or rewards for cooperators) if collective action in the public interest is to occur. However, these incentives themselves require the existence of a central authority acting in the public interest. As such, a second-order problem arises: A central authority is itself a public good that demands collective action to create and maintain.[107] Olson suggested that groups up to a medium size might be able to take collective action on a conditional cooperation basis (for example, "I'll cooperate if you will"). In contrast, Robert Axelrod has argued that a conditional cooperation strategy (that is, tit-for-tat), when combined with mechanisms such as the "reputation" of the participant, might be able to extend collective action to larger groups.[108] Finally, Elinor Ostrom's review of the ethnographic studies of collective action around common pool resources suggests that, contrary to Olson's pessimism about collective action, systems evidencing collective or collaborative behavior can emerge and remain relatively stable over long periods of time. These systems, Ostrom argues, represent something that is different from either state control or an individual ordering through private contracts. It should be recognized, however, that although decentralized, collective-action collaboratives for the appropriation and replenishment of common pool resources represent a different type of ordering of land use than either the state or individual ordering, the type of decision-making approach used within these collaboratives is not always unitary. That is, these collectives, like larger democratic governments, will often use voting (or weighted voting), rather than only bargaining and consensus, to decide intra-group issues.[109]

While critics complain that unitary processes are often plagued by the high level of demand that they put on people's time and energy and the overall slowness of the process, proponents of the use of unitary processes suggest that the more traditional adversarial approaches are even more costly in this regard. A few proponents, for example, have noted that "the costs of delay and contentiousness, measured in dollars, human suffering, environmental destruction, or any other terms are a terribly high price to pay for our inability to address the legitimate concerns of those upon whom the burdens of regulation are visited."[110] Specifically, these proponents suggest that negotiated resolutions of environmental (or other) disputes generally reduce the risks of "winner-take-all" litigation, reduce court costs, legal, fees and inflationary delays, increase the efficiency of the outcomes, and increase the likelihood of achieving an agreement that will not be broken or form the basis for further conflicts or costly appeals.[111]

As agencies regulating environmental, social services, and other land-use issues have become more sophisticated, they have increasingly turned toward the development and use of unitary, negotiation-based approaches to NIMBY land-use problems. These approaches include various principles and mechanisms such as public participation, mediation, negotiation, compensation, mitigation, and selective incentives.[112] In some respects, the decision to use a unitary approach may be being driven by the public's lack of faith in the both the traditional public mechanisms (law, court decisions, and administrative regulation) and the invisible hand of the private market.[113]

Use of these approaches, however, has drawn criticism from a number of directions. Although classic liberals would typically see few problems in voluntary agreements that are often the product of unitary approaches, they would object both to compulsory negotiations and to the fact that, to the extent that these agreements have the force of law, they potentially represent the substitution of general rules by hundreds of specific rules. Potentially, that is, equal protection can be undermined by unitary processes. Although unitary approaches are most congruent with communitarian ideals of neutral dialogue, a number of more leftist critics of unitary processes have argued that implementation of these approaches in a society or specific situations characterized by large differentials in wealth and power would lead to outcomes that are undesirable. Additionally, critics without ideological portfolio have noted that the public's ability to process the technical information that is needed to understand a number of environmental land-use issues is probably fairly low.[114] This deficiency is magnified by the lack of certainty in the environmental sciences about the potential costs and benefits of any specific set of policies or technologies.[115]

Proponents of unitary approaches are not unaware of these criticisms but counter that skilled collaborative problem-solvers are ethically bound to conduct negotiations in ways that are inclusive of all interests, balance the power among the parties to the mediation, and educate parties as to potential technical considerations. Moreover, such skilled mediators can propose that the disputants craft contingent agreements that, for example, allow activities to be conducted on a temporary basis subject to the gathering of further information, such as on the environmental or social effects of the activity.[116]

Additionally, recent evidence on the use of unitary, citizen participation processes suggests that even though a specific, institutionally powerful agency or industrial interest might propose use of a negotiated process with the idea of controlling the terms of the process, local communities will often turn the process to their own ends. For example, in a recent attempt to place a radioactive waste site, a community that was the target of those wishing to locate the waste facility was able to use the mediation process to question and to attempt to change the institutional relationship and negotiation framework that the siting agency had assumed would be under its control. In the process the community was able to establish a more coherent and objective view of the information related to the proposed facility.[117] It may be that one of the strengths of unitary processes is that they are able to establish a secure area for discussion and deliberation and can therefore reduce the need for "rude and crude" politics.

Alternatively, communities have set up their own unitary processes for dealing with land-use issues. Dayton, Ohio, for example, set up a Well Field Protection Program, supplying in the process some organization to citizen and local government concerns about land-use sources of water contamination. This award-winning program combined citizen action (information gathering and distillation) with a professional advisory function to provide impetus for regional cooperation in addressing water contamination problems in the most cost-effective and informed way.[118]

While a few progressive communities have developed the mechanisms for a unitary process, most continue to use adversarial processes, with only the minimum of citizen participation required by due process or regulatory mandates.[119] Although unitary decision-making processes might be preferable, the number and complexity of LULU-type items on local government agenda, the lack of familiarity with and skills in unitary (or dispute-resolution) processes, and the unwillingness of public officials to relinquish their authority to what appears to be an ad hoc process with regard to these decisions has dictated against the use of this approach.[120]

Unitary Processes: Are They Corrupting?

In addition to the charge that unitary processes are not realistic or feasible, it is also argued that these cooperation-based approaches potentially corrupt personal autonomy and citizenship. The argument in this regard is that in attempting to find the will of the community, people will be coerced into abandoning their own beliefs and will begin to accede to the pressures for conformity and "group think."[121] Because of this tendency toward communitarian conformity, Benjamin Barber attempts to distinguish what he calls "strong democracy" from "unitary democracy." While both approaches share the value of equal participation, strong democracy is less concerned with achieving a unitary resolution to conflicts than it is with the creation of an educated "political community." In this regard, strong democracy is less a process for social integration than it is for cooperative education. Jane Mansbridge is also aware that unitary democracy's consensus rule may often be too demanding and unrealistic in situations where interests truly conflict. In these situations, Mansbridge and Barber would both likely suggest that after a certain period devoted to "democratic talk," mutual education, and the discovery of a common interest, without satisfactory effect, it might make sense to use a more consociational decision-making rule, specifying that benefits be divided "in proportion to the numerical strength of the competing factions"—rather than either by consensus or winner-take-all, majority rule.[122]

An Illustration of the Combining of Adversary and Unitary Approaches

Albert Matheny and Bruce Williams' review of the public decision-making approaches, both adversarial and unitary, that have been used in the siting of hazardous waste facilities in Florida illustrates how the different approaches are commonly combined.[123] Their review begins with a description of how Congress, using adversarial approaches, developed and passed the Resource Conservation and Recovery Act. This legislation essentially failed to allocate the NIMBY-type costs or specific environmental risks to particular communities. Instead, the responsibility for these hard choices were devolved onto the Environmental Protection Agency. Matheny and Williams identified the EPA as engaging in more unitary or consensual decision-making process within its internal operations with respect to this issue area. This unitary process, however, was not effectively used during all phases, and was especially not used to integrate EPA's interests with those of local communities.

Although the EPA is mandated to include opportunities for public participation in its rule-making processes, Matheny and Williams' description of the approach used in developing rules and decisions related to the Resource Conservation and Recovery Act suggests that while the letter of this mandate is perhaps being followed, the spirit is not. In particular, they discovered that the EPA tended to build its decisions around technical information of both the controversial and non-controversial type, and as such, gave only pro forma consideration to the potential for various interests in the community (or communities) to be reconciled.

As a consequence of Congress's failure to forthrightly allocate the costs and benefits of LULU disposal facilities on the legitimate basis of representative government or devolve the issues onto another process—such as "strong democracy"—that could lay some claim to legitimacy, the process proved to be unsatisfactory in terms of its perceived legitimacy. The dominant sense of those in the communities selected for a hazardous waste facility was one of being betrayed by processes that were "political" in nature. This sense of betrayal occurred even though the EPA could reasonably claim that its decisions were a combination of technical criteria and community input. While the EPA is currently in the process of setting standards for the placement of hazardous waste facilities that would restrict the placement of such facilities over groundwater recharge areas or wetlands, such technical criteria for eliminating some sites will not resolve the problem of choosing among the remaining potential sites.

COMBINING POLITICAL AND ECONOMIC APPROACHES—THE CASE OF ZONING

A review of the various political and economic approaches to land-use issues does not provide policy analysts with any easy answers to the difficult question of how to promote or maximize equity, efficiency, community viability, and environmental quality. Most proposals that suggest using a particular policymaking process or decision-making technique will ignore one or more of the values that should be considered or discount these values at a high rate. The result has often been simplistic and ultimately unsatisfactory policymaking. The story of traditional zoning and the proposed political- and economic-oriented means of dealing with the externalities of zoning provide a case in point.

As a result of the dominant use of the adversarial process, many zoning and other land-use decisions result in what one commentator has called private gains and public losses.[124] The maldistributive effect of many of these decisions has been documented in a number of areas, including: the supply of low-income housing,[125] segregation by age or income,[126] [127] the freedom to pursue an alternative lifestyle,[128] the siting of solid and toxic wastes in minority neighborhoods,[129] housing for the elderly,[130] as well as living arrangements for the retarded, [131] the mentally ill,[132] and juvenile offenders. Simply put, when adversarial processes are used, those who are homeless or transient, of low income, from a minority ethnic or racial group, mentally or emotionally disabled, or of an age when political mobilization becomes difficult tend to lose out. The very citizens who most need to mobilize to protect their neighborhoods and communities appear to be the least likely or least able to do so.[133]

The Failure of the Free Market Alternative

While zoning ordinances, when combined with adversarial decision-making processes, seem to benefit some groups at the expense of others and promote private benefit at public expense, the lack of such ordinances or other regulatory mechanisms—what might be termed the free market alternative—appears to be no more desirable or effective.[134] In particular, the free market alternative does not seem to result in a fair distribution of the burden of LULUs or the shouldering of social responsibilities. For example, despite its lack of zoning laws, Houston's siting of solid waste facilities was not random, as might be expected. Instead, these facilities were likely to be found in or near African-American neighborhoods and schools. Robert Bullard, who studied the siting pattern, concluded that lack of zoning contributed to Houston's black neighborhoods becoming the "dumping grounds" for the area's solid waste.[135] Significantly, redevelopment activities within Houston's inner city have contributed to a recent shift toward a more pro-zoning sentiment in the community.[136] Similarly, efforts to create regulation-free (or -reduced) enterprise zones have raised questions and concerns about the equity and efficacy of associated development, the displacement of existing small businesses, and the representation of neighborhood interests.[137]

Wrestling with Externalities: The Social Costs of Unequal Siting of LULUs

While zoning ordinances create a new property of sorts (or secure an old one), they do so in a manner that is in some cases anathema to the basic American tradition of inclusiveness. In other cases, these ordinances should be considered fiscally suspect because they involve costs (or as economists term it, externalities) that have not been included in the price of the property. For example, when people purchase property whose worth is increased because of the security value of restrictive zoning, their gain does not take place in isolation. Rather, when people purchase property whose value is increased because it is free of LULUs, they generally do not pay to compensate those who cannot afford to move into areas that are so well protected by land-use control. Purchasers of LULU-free properties also do not usually pay for the added social services that are needed to address the relative disintegration of neighborhoods where LULUs are concentrated. While siting of LULUs in poorer neighborhoods is not the primary cause of neighborhood disintegration, it is surely a contributory cause and one that deserves further study. The siting of LULUs in these neighborhoods, moreover, is probably more destructive proportionately because of these neighborhoods' already weakened condition. Even though some LULUs may bring a limited number of jobs to depressed neighborhoods, it is more likely that these undesirable land uses will tend to discourage the kind of general business development that would be necessary to lift these neighborhoods out of depression or at least stem their decline. The continued flight of mainstream businesses and neighborhood leadership to distant suburbs has been identified as a major cause of social decay in inner city neighborhoods,[138] the same neighborhoods in which LULUs appear to have the most chance of being located. These deteriorating neighborhoods now account for the largest proportion of public assistance and social service costs. Even when the economy in general is growing, in these isolated, decaying neighborhoods, the effect is often not felt.[139]

While it is difficult to quantify the exact level of benefit, it seems to be the case that those who have benefited the most from the establishment of new property rights (such as zoning that would exclude most LULUs) have often not borne the social costs associated with these private benefits.[140] As economists will tell us, unless these associated "externalities" are included in the price of the property, the market for these properties will be skewed toward much greater consumption than would otherwise be the case (if the external costs were included in the purchasing and operating price of property ownership).

Internalizing External Cost: The Political Estimation Approach

There are several ways to respond to the tendency of zoning to create new exclusionary property rights that benefit some while indirectly making the living environment worse for others and potentially exacerbating the aggregate social costs of community care and environmental quality. One response would be to estimate the externality costs of creating a property right that did not exist before and to include these costs in the price of properties. Hence, one would still allow narrowly restricted zoning practices, but would, for example, raise ad valorem taxes on these new or more secure properties in proportion to the estimated social costs involved in shifting unwanted development toward other neighborhoods or areas. Imposing impact or development fees is another example of such an approach.[141] Unfortunately, there are several problems with this approach beyond some constitutional ones that will be discussed in the last chapter. First, as the logic of collective action would suggest, small, well-organized interest groups would be more likely to receive special consideration when it came to establishing both the estimate of social costs and the tax rate that would apply as a result of this estimation. The logic of collective action (that large-scale collective action is relatively ineffective) suggests that evaluating the effect of every new property right would provide myriad opportunities for special interests to receive special treatment without a great deal of public scrutiny.[142] The technology of estimation would likely be beyond the understanding of the general public such that genuine disinterested review would be as impossible as it would be unlikely, given the number of new property cases that would occur over time.

A second problem with this "internalization of external cost" is related to the difficulty of cost estimation. While the benefits of new property are often experienced in the present by small groups of private individuals who can easily get a sense of the utility that the new property will provide them, the social costs of the new property: (1) are diffuse in nature so that no one person or small group of persons experiences these costs; (2) only become apparent over a long period of time; and (3) are borne chiefly by persons unable to estimate their losses, link their losses to the establishment of a pattern of LULU sitings, or communicate their loss to those who are able to change things.

As a result of these characteristics, it is also quite unlikely that the potential savings of internalizing external costs would necessarily be used to benefit or recompense those who had paid the costs. Instead, it would be more likely that these savings would be poured back into the general fund or used to provide public infrastructure to more privileged properties. Hence, while the "internalization of external cost" approach is attractive on the surface, since it appears to provide a market-like solution to the problems associated with creating some new property rights, the political reality dictates against creating this type of market-correcting solution to the problem of new property externalities.

The problem with the "internalizing-externalities" or "impact fee" solution is that these mechanisms generally require a centralized agent to estimate the external cost of new property rights. While these estimates may sometimes be made in a fair and equitable manner, more often than not they will be made through an adversarial process that results in winners and losers. While a unitary decision-making process at the community level might result in more acceptable solutions psychologically, this process tends to provide unique solutions. The potential variance among these solutions could result in outcomes as inequitable as those arising from adversarial processes.[143]

Internalizing External Cost: The Free Market and Organized Market Estimation Approaches

Some policy analysts believe that it may not be necessary to rely on governmental decision-making mechanisms to correct undesirable side effects of new property creation. Instead, they argue that the correction of problems associated with market mechanisms may be accomplished through further refinements in these mechanisms. Two approaches to this have been suggested.

The first market mechanism approach, and one that is most in line with free market economics, would simply involve continuing to use and refine the property tax system. Currently, property owners pay some of the cost of the negative social externalities resulting from exclusionary zoning in the form of property and other taxes that go to support social services and public infrastructure. Property tax financing could be refined by more heavily taxing those whose property increased rapidly in value due to factors unrelated to the owner's improvements and by taxing more lightly properties whose value tended to stagnate or decline. Such a land-tax policy was first proposed by the American economist, Henry George, whose ideas have recently been resurrected and applied to land-use environmental issues.[144] While a land tax could be applied in such a way as to compensate those who have been harmed by LULUs, such a tax would likely work against the goal of securing neighborhoods and communities. While compensating those whose land values are damaged due to undesirable development (by taxing more heavily those whose land has increased in value), the land tax approach would tend to promote the highest market-value use and thereby undermine those who desire a certain degree of control over the built environment. In this manner, the land tax would promote a greater degree of justice in that it would deny the unearned gains of those who had enough power to institute exclusionary zoning ordinances that favored their interests. In addition to the rough justice that such a tax would establish, proponents of land tax policies typically focus on the potential of such policies to promote dynamic economic growth, especially when they are combined with an elimination of zoning ordinances. However, in their cost-benefit calculations, proponents of such land taxes typically ignore the economic and other value that residents and business owners experience as a result of being secured against dramatic changes in the built environment. The value of the security that zoning implies is not just a consumption value; rather, it is also affords a different type of incentive for economic investment. Such security, for example, might induce owners to build high-quality facilities that are built to last for centuries rather than for a single decade. Currently, a considerable dead weight loss often occurs when developers build cheaply and then quickly replace facilities in order to take advantage of a change in zoning. With a land tax in place, property owners would have one less reason to believe that the built environment will maintain certain qualities, and they would have one more reason to believe that they will be unable to control how that environment will change. In such a situation, some owners would take advantage of the uncertainty to promote major improvements in the value of their property (e.g., by developing a commercial enterprise in a residential area). However, other owners would will likely react to increased uncertainty by withdrawing from desirable investments in their property. Without tests of various land tax policies, it is impossible to predict exactly how and to what degree each of these likely effects would occur.

A second market approach would involve the development of an organized market in which LULU developers offer payment to communities that in turn allow the siting of a LULU in their jurisdiction. The amount of the payment would be determined by the community in question being the first to accept an offer made at auction by the LULU developer. The amount of the offer would continue to increase until some community believed that the value of the payment was greater than the cost associated with the LULU.[145] Because the purchasing of LULU development rights at auction is an open process that leads toward an equilibrium price of development rights, it might be preferable in this sense to isolated negotiations with individual communities for these rights. Such an open auction process would seem to provide some fair level of compensation for the placement of an unwanted facility. Unfortunately, since these auctions identify communities that are more desperate for funds (or, on the positive side, more aware of the overall public interest in fulfilling necessary social and ecological obligations), they are not likely to result in an equitable distribution of community responsibilities related to caring for the down-and-out or storing waste materials. In fact, even though such auctions would steer the siting of LULUs toward those who would gain the most (all else being equal) at the least expense to government or industry, the outcome would nevertheless continue the pattern of uneven distribution of the burdens associated with LULUs. Additionally, as studies in city development and residential racial segregation suggest, there likely exists a number of "tipping points" at which a neighborhood or community's development will become characterized by one particular form of growth.[146] As argued earlier, once a certain section of town has become the site for a number of social service agencies, half-way houses, and community living homes, the ability of such neighborhoods to resist further siting of such institutions is weakened. As political decision makers search for the point of least resistance, they are likely to hit upon these already weakened neighborhoods, with predictable results.

Although development of an organized market in LULUs and using auctions for siting LULUs have some desirable features (such as identifying those communities that are likely to see a greater benefit-to-cost ratio for accepting a LULU), such auctions, like most free market mechanisms taken by themselves, do not have any built-in limits over time, especially where less wealthy and less organized neighborhoods are pitted in marketplace bargaining against highly organized communities with substantial resources. As long as neighborhoods are segregated by income and education, and the distribution of family incomes remains highly unequal, the likely outcome of creating an organized market for LULUs will not be substantially different than is the case in current political decision making: Communities that are poorer, less well-informed, and less organized will end up with the great majority, if not all, of the LULUs. The organized market for LULUs may nevertheless be marginally more desirable than current political decision making because: (1) it makes explicit the power relationship that is currently hidden within the adversarial and interest group-dominated decision-making processes; and (2) it affords those communities or neighborhoods that do enter into negotiations with LULU developers a chance to gain some resources in return. Under current political decision making, such resources are informally distributed to communities or areas within a community that escape the siting of a LULU. In terms of basic equity considerations of the "ethic of care" variety and community viability criteria, however, the organized market for LULUs fails because it tends to lead to a placement of sites in areas where they will likely tip the long-term balance against the residents and communities who are forced to bid in the auction.

CONCLUSIONS

This chapter has reviewed a number of political and economic approaches to land-use issues and attempted to explore the potential of each of these approaches to fulfill four basic criteria that are commonly applied in thinking about and deciding land-use issues. Additionally, this chapter examined a specific land-use policy—zoning—in light of the potential of economic- or politics-based mechanisms to mitigate the negative side effects of zoning policies.

Some of the political and economic proposals and processes suggested for dealing with the current failures of zoning (or other land-use siting processes) hold some promise in that they represent an improvement over current methods for deciding land-use issues. Moreover, some of these proposals may represent healthy hybrids of approaches that could lead to more effective prevention of both "market failure" and "political failure." However, the examination of some of the political and economic mechanisms used in land-use policymaking (such as the hybrid of different political approaches used in the development and implementation of the Resource Conservation and Recovery Act) suggests that not every hybrid approach is either a real hybrid or a healthy one.

NOTES

1. Mansbridge, Jane. (1983). *Beyond Adversary Democracy*. Chicago: University of Chicago Press.

2. Gutterbock, Thomas. (1990). "Sociology and the Land-Use Problem." *Urban Affairs Quarterly* 15:3:243-267.

3. Malloy, Robin Paul. (1991). *Planning for Serfdom: Legal Economic Discourse and Downtown Development*. Philadelphia: University of Pennsylvania Press.

4. Bruyn, Severyn T. (1987). *Beyond the Market and the State*. Philadelphia: Temple University Press.

5. Cohen, Michael, March, James, and Olsen, Johan. (1972). "A Garbage Can Model of Organizational Choice." *Administrative Science Quarterly* (March):17:1.

6. Rose, Carol M. (1985). "Possession as the Origin of Property." University of Chicago Law Review 52:73-88; and "Women and Property: Gaining and Losing Ground." *Virginia Law Review* 78:421-59.

7. Lindblom, C. E. (1979). "Still Muddling, Not Yet Through." *Public Administration Review* 39:517-25.

8. Radin, Margaret Jane. (1982). "Property and Personhood." *Stanford Law Review* 34:957-78.

9. Alexander, Gregory. (1989). "Dilemmas of Group Autonomy." *Cornell Law Review* 75:55-61.

10. Gutterbock, Thomas. (1980) "Sociology and the Land-Use Problem." *Urban Affairs Quarterly* 15:3:262.

11. Baker, C. Edwin. (1986). "Property and Its Relation to Constitutionally Protected Liberty." *University of Pennsylvania Law Review* 134:741-55.

12. Reinders, J. E. (1975). "Ordening as a Preparation for the Planning Policy of Today." *South African Journal of Sociology* (September 12):89-102.

13. See generally, Gerschenkron, Alexander. (1962). *Economic Backwardness in Historical Perspective*. Cambridge, Mass.: Belknap Press of Harvard University Press; Goldthorpe, John H. (1984). "Introduction." In *Order and Conflict in Contemporary Capitalism*, edited by John H. Goldthorpe. Oxford, England: Clarendon Press, pp. 1-14; and

Gourevitch, Peter. (1986). *Politics in Hard Times*. Ithaca, N. Y.: Cornell University Press.

14. Vaillancourt, Francois, and Monty, Luc. (1985). "The Effect of Agricultural Zoning on Land Prices." Land Economics 61:1:36-42.

15. Dalton, Linda. (1989). "The Limits of Regulation: Evidence from Local Plan Implementation in California." *Journal of the American Planning Association* 55:2:151-68.

16. Golith, Robert, and Betancur, John. (1988). "Where Downtown Meets Neighborhood: Industrial Displacement in Chicago, 1978-1987." *Journal of the American Planning Association* 54:3:279-90.

17. Miller, Thomas I. (1968). "Must Growth Restrictions Limit Moderate Priced Housing?" *Journal of American Planning Association* 52:3:319-25.

18. See generally, Arrow, Kenneth. (1984). *Individual Choice under Certainty and Uncertainty*. Cambridge, Mass.: Harvard University Press; and Arrow, Kenneth. (1970). *Social Choice and Individual Value*. New Haven, Conn.: Yale University Press.

19. See generally, Arrow, *Individual Choice under Certainty and Uncertainty*; and Arrow, *Social Choice and Individual Value*.

20. For an elaboration of this argument, see Murray, Charles. *In Pursuit: Of Happiness and Good Government*. New York: Simon and Schuster.

21. Use of an alternative criterion, known as the Pareto criterion, would allow for an easier justification of market policy solutions because this criterion states that for a policy solution to be acceptable, it need only be able to prove that the size of the total pie will increase, making it theoretically possible to compensate persons who are harmed by the implementation of the policy solution. Adam Smith, though unaware of the Pareto criterion by name, in his *The Theory of Moral Sentiments* (1976). Oxford, Eng.: Clarendon Press., implicitly rejects the use of such a criterion. Smith writes: "In the race for wealth and honours, and preferments, he may run as hard as he can, and strain every nerve and every muscle, in order to outstrip all his competitors. But if he should jostle, or throw down any of them, the indulgence of the spectators is entirely at an end. It is a violation of fair play, which they cannot admit of" (p. 162).

22. See Smith, Adam. (1976). *An Inquiry into the Nature and Causes of the Wealth of Nations*, edited by E. Cannon. London: Metheun, pp. 23-44. "Civil government, so far as it is instituted for the security of property, is in reality instituted for the defense of the rich against the poor, or of those who have some property against those who have none at all" (p. 256).

23. Ibid., pp. 302-303.

24. Singer, Joseph W. (1988). "The Reliance Interest in Property." *Stanford Law Review* 40:611:614-63.

25. Delogu, Orlando. (1990). " 'NIMBY' is a National Environmental Problem." *South Dakota Law Review* 35:206.

26. These rules are drawn from George, Henry (first published 1879; 1979). *Progress and Poverty*. New York: Schalkenbach Foundation, pp. 133-34, 196. See Backhaus, Jurgen, and Krabbe, J. J. (1991). "Henry George's Contribution to Modern Environmental Policy." *American Journal of Economics and Sociology* 50:4:485-501.

27. See generally, Mintz, Joel. (1991). "Economic Reform of Environmental Protection: A Brief Comment on a Recent Debate." *Harvard Environmental Law Review* 15:85:149-64.

28. Delogu, "NIMBY," p. 207.

29. Stewart, Richard. (1988). "Controlling Environmental Risk Through Economic Incentives." *Columbia Journal of Environmental Law* 13:161.

30. See generally, Latin, Howard. (1985). "Ideal Versus Real Regulatory Efficiency: Implementation of Uniform Standards and 'Fine-Tuning' Regulatory Reforms." *Stanford Law Review* 37:1267-332.

31. Smith, *Wealth of Nations*, p. 303.

32. See generally, Ouchi, William G. (1980). "Markets, Bureaucracies, and Clans." *Administrative Science Quarterly* 25:129-41; and Williamson, O. E. (1985). *The Economic Institutions of Capitalism*. New York: The Free Press.

33. Nelson, Robert. (1977): *Zoning and Property Rights*. Cambridge, Mass.: MIT Press.

34. Ouchi, "Markets," pp. 129-41.

35. Ellickson, Robert. (1991). *Order Without Law: How Neighbors Settle Disputes*. Cambridge, Mass.: Harvard University Press.

36. Ellickson, Robert. (1990). "Three Systems of Land-Use Controls." Harvard Journal of Law and Public Policy, 13:1:67-74.

37. O'Sullivan, Arthur. (1993). *Urban Economics*. Homewood, Ill.: Irwin Press.

38. For example, in a review of the existing literature on risk factors, Joy Dryfoos (1990. *Adolescents At Risk*. New York, Oxford University Press) has identified neighborhood disintegration as one of the major factors underlying a host of social problems including juvenile delinquency, teenage pregnancy, substance abuse, and school failure.

39. See generally the works of James Coleman (e.g., Coleman, James. (1990). *Equality and Achievement in Education*. Boulder, Co.: Westview Press.); also, Clark, Reginald M. (1990). "Why Disadvantaged Students Succeed: What Happens Outside School is Critical." *Public Welfare* (Spring), 48:2:17-23.

40. Mead, Lawrence. (1992). *The New Politics of Poverty*. New York: Basic Books. Although Mead describes the social disintegration of underclass neighborhoods, he attributes this disintegration to a breakdown in local social and cultural norms of work abetted by the welfare system. He does not directly address the land-use policy origins of the segregation of neighborhoods as a contributing factor.

41. Smith, George P., and Fernandez, Griffin W. (1991). "The Price of Beauty: An Economic Approach to Aesthetic Nuisance." *Harvard Environmental Law Review* 15:33:53-83. The authors present an argument for extending traditional nuisance law regarding aural and olfactory nuisance actions to aesthetic or visual situations. They point out that the:

> traditional distinction of visual versus aural and olfactory interferences with the enjoyment of property lacks sufficient justification. Instead, the courts should resolve conflicts emanating from unaesthetic uses of land through a balancing test which incorporates the same "objective" standard courts use in cases involving allegedly unreasonable sounds and smells, that is, what the surrounding community considers unreasonable. This objective standard, combined with an analysis of the economic

consequences of the injury suffered and the relief sought, provides a sound basis for the adjudication of aesthetic nuisance cases. (p. 55)

42. These options are obviously variations on two of the options presented above—the negotiated private property rights option and the public regulatory option—for ordering markets when transaction costs get too high. The informal ordering option is not listed because market failure by definition occurs when informal options have been exhausted.

43. Smith, Adam (first published 1759; 1976). *The Theory of Moral Sentiments*, edited by D. D. Raphael and A. L. Macfie. Oxford, Eng.: Clarendon Press.

44. O'Looney, John. (1991). "The Organizational Basis of Innovation in Developed States." Unpublished dissertation, University of Georgia. See also, Landes, David. (1970). *The Unbound Prometheus*. Cambridge, England: Cambridge University Press; Johnson, Chalmers. (1982). *MITI and the Japanese Miracle*. Stanford, Calif.: Stanford University Press; Etzioni, Amitai. (1988). *The Moral Dimension: Toward a New Economics*. New York: The Free Press; and Lodge, George C., and Vogel, Ezra. (1987). *Ideology and National Competitiveness*. Boston: Harvard Business.

45. Recent debate in the United States over the public regulation of violence on television can be contrasted with the customary regulation by most other nations of violence and other features of video broadcasting.

46. For a more extended argument of this point, see Tilly, Charles, ed. (1975). *The Formation of National States in Western Europe*. Princeton, N.J.: Princeton University Press. Also see Kuttner, Robert. (1987). *The Economic Illusion*. Philadelphia: University of Pennsylvania Press; and Westney, D. Eleanor. (1987). Imitation and Innovation. Cambridge, Mass.: Harvard University Press.

47. See generally Murray, Charles. (1984). *Losing Ground: American Social Policy 1950-1980*. New York: Basic Books; and Mead, Lawrence. (1992). *The New Politics of Poverty*. New York: Basic Books. Murray and Mead are both conservative social theorists, but they differ substantially as to whether the root cause of contemporary poverty is result of a deterioration in civic and cultural structures or the lack of the right economic incentives.

48. See generally, Mansbridge, *Beyond Adversary Democracy*, pp. 3-23; Also see Benjamin Barber (*Strong Democracy: Participatory Politics for a New Age*. Berkeley, Calif.: University of California Press, 1984) for a third decision-making model, which he terms "strong democracy." Strong democracy involves a process of self-education and participation. As a result of this process, the individual learns to associate with the community and to reconcile their private interests with the public good. While this third decision-making model can produce viable and desirable outcomes in the long term, the educational process involved suggests that this model will generally not be effective in the short term.

49. Mansbridge, *Beyond Adversary Democracy*. Mansbridge argues, however, that the assumption about each decision being an isolated and indivisible case is rarely true. Rather, she suggests, there often exists a way to divide the costs and benefits of the issue in question, whether through turn-taking, log-rolling of votes on future issues, or dividing up the time in which a particular groups' desires will have the effect of law. Using a Benthamite calculus that assumes that those who have little will gain more happiness by every additional unit of benefit than will those who already have a lot, Mansbridge reasons that discovering ways to divide up a benefit proportionally among the population will result

in greater overall happiness. She argues that majority rule in many cases should perhaps be replaced as often as possible by proportional outcomes (pp. 266-67). See also Barry, Brian. (1979). "Is Democracy Special?" In *Philosophy, Politics, and Society*, Fifth Series, edited by Peter Laslett and James Fishkin, Oxford, Eng.: Blackwell.

50. Mansbridge, *Beyond Adversary Democracy*, pp. 292-302.

51. Wilson, James Q. (1993.) "On Gender." *The Public Interest* 112:3-24.

52. See generally, Dahl, Robert A. (1956). *Preface to Democratic Theory*. Chicago: University of Chicago Press; and Schumpeter; Joseph A. (1942). *Capitalism, Socialism, and Democracy*. New York: Harper and Row.

53. See generally, de Tocqueville, Alexis. (first published in 1835; 1956). *Democracy in America*. New York: Mentor Books, pp. 112-13.

54. Hurley, Patricia, and Hill, Kim Q. (1980). "The Prospects for Issue Voting in Contemporary Congressional Elections." *American Politics Quarterly* 8:446.

55. See generally, Arrow, *Individual Choice*; and, Arrow, *Social Choice.*

56. See generally, Greider, *Who Will Tell*; Stewart, "Controlling Environmental Risk." Plotkin, Sidney. (1987). "Property, Policy, and Politics: Toward a Theory of Land-Use Conflict." *International Journal of Urban and Regional Research*, 2:3:387-404. See specifically, Mintz, "Economic Reform," p. 160.

57. Sagoff, Mark. (1989). *The Economy of the Earth*. New York: Cambridge University Press.

58. See generally, Rose, Carol. (1983). "Planning and Dealing: Piecemeal Land Controls as a Problem of Local Legitimacy." *California Law Review* 71:872.

59. See Note 42 in Chapter 1.

60. Brion, Denis J. (1988). "An Essay on LULU, NIMBY and the Problem of Distributive Justice." *Environmental Affairs* 15:437-503.

61. Alexander, "Dilemmas of Group Autonomy," pp. 50-61.

62. Toker, Anne S. (1991). "Admitting Scientific Evidence in Toxic Tort Litigation." *Harvard Environmental Law Review* 15:165-179.

63. Been, Vicki. (1993). "What's Fairness Got To Do With It? Environmental Justice and the Siting of Locally Undesirable Land Uses." *Cornell Law Review* 78:1001-87.

64. Margulies, Peter. (1992). "Building Communities of Virtue: Political Theory, Land Use Policy, and the 'Not in My Backyard' Syndrome." *Syracuse Law Review* 43:977-78.

65. Radin, "Property and Personhood," pp. 957-78.

66. Brion, "An Essay on LULU," pp. 437-563. Also, see Mishan, E. J. (1961). "Welfare Criteria for External Effects." *American Economic Review* 51:594-603.

67. Brion, "An Essay on LULU," p. 478.

68. Ibid., p. 481.

69. See Simon Rifkind, as quoted in Crampton, Roger C. (1982). "Judicial Law Making and Administration." In *Current Issues in Public Administration*, 2nd. edn., edited by Frederick S. Lane. New York: St. Martin's Press, p. 154. The second quote is from Crampton (p. 154).

70. Horwitz, Morton J. (1977). *The Transformation of American Law, 1780-1860.* Cambridge, Mass.: Harvard University Press, pp. 253-54.

71. Whyte, William H. (1970). *The Last Landscape.* New York: Anchor Books.

72. This dilemma is especially evident when a plaintiff in a product liability suit agrees to settle with a defendant, who may still be producing the product in question, and the plaintiff agrees as part of the settlement not to disclose any information to the public. In these types of cases, the public interest in removing harmful products from the market is ignored in favor of the interests of the two private parties.

73. See generally Kingdon, John. (1984). *Agendas, Alternatives, and Public Policies.* Boston: Brown, Little; and Cohen, March, and Olsen, "A Garbage Can Model of Organizational Choice," pp. 1-25.

74. Wilson, James Q. (1975). "The Rise of the Bureaucratic State." *The Public Interest* 41.

75. Mosher, Frederick. (1968). Democracy and the Public Service. Oxford, England: Oxford University Press.

76. Rosenthal, Alan. (1981). "Legislative Behavior and Legislative Oversight." *Legislative Studies Quarterly* 6(1):115-3; and Cronin, Thomas. (1980). "Presidential-Departmental Relations." In *The State of the Presidency*, edited by Thomas E. Cronin. New York: Little, Brown and Co.

77. Niskanen, William. (1971). *Bureaucracy and Representative Government.* Chicago: Aldine-Atherton. See Ellickson, "Inclusionary Housing Program," pp. 83-90, for a critique of inclusionary zoning. Ellickson argues that the benefits of these policies will more likely accrue to "professional housers" than to those who are in need of housing. See also Stewart, "Controlling Environmental Risk," p. 154, where Professor Stewart charges: "Our environmental regulatory system . . . has grown to the point where it amounts to nothing less than a massive effort at Soviet-style central planning of the economy to achieve environmental goals."

78. Wildavsky, Aaron B. (1982). "Budgeting as a Political Process." In *Current Issues in Public Administration*, 2nd edn., edited by Frederick K. Lane. New York: St. Martin's Press, pp. 339-48.

79. See generally, Rainey, Hal G. (1991). *Understanding and Managing Public Organizations.* San Francisco, Calif.: Jossey-Bass Publishers. See also, O'Looney, John. (forthcoming). "Inter-Organizational Transformation in the Public Sector: The Case Against "Running Things Like a Business." *Journal of Applied Social Sciences.*

80. Leman, Christopher. (1988). "A Forest of Institutions." *Land Rites and Wrongs: The Management, Regulation and Use of Land in Canada and the United States*, edited by Elliot Feldman. Boston, Mass.: OGH Pub., p. 188.

81. This tendency probably has its origins in the cycles of "shifting involvements" of the public's interest in government activism that Albert O. Hirschman has noted. Hirschman, Albert O. (1982). *Shifting Involvements: Public Interest and Private Action.* Princeton, N.J.: Princeton University Press.

82. See Lowry, Ira S., and Ferguson, Bruce W. (1992). *Development Regulation and Housing Affordability.* Washington, D.C.: Urban Land Institute. p. 155.

83. Ibid., p. 155.

84. Delogu, "NIMBY," p. 213.

85. Ibid., p. 217.

86. Rose, Carol. (1983). "Planning and Dealing: Piecemeal Land Controls as a Problem of Local Legitimacy." *California Law Review* 71:872.

87. Ibid., pp.837-81. Also, *Standard Oil Co. v. City of Tallahassee*, 183 F.2d 410, 413 (5th Cir.), cert. denied, 340 U.S. 892 (1950) (eight-month amortization period for nonconforming gas station upheld).

88. Rose, "Planning and Dealing," p. 867.

89. See generally, Hamilton, Alexander. (1961). "The Federalist No. 78." *The Federalist Papers*, edited by J. Cooke. New York: New American Library, pp. 524-29.

90. Sabatier, Paul. (1975). "Social Movements and Regulatory Agencies: Toward a More Adequate—and Less Pessimistic—Theory of 'Clientele Capture.' " *Policy Science* 6:301-302.

91. *Neuberger v. City of Portland.* (1980). 288 Oregon 585-90, 607 P.2d, 722-26.

92. Janis, Irving., and Mann, Leon. (1977). *Decision-Making.* New York: Free Press.

93. Rose, "Planning and Dealing," pp. 876-77.

94. Ibid., p. 879. See also, Babcock, Richard. (1966). *The Zoning Game.* Madison, Wisc.: University of Wisconsin Press; Krasnowiecki, Jan. (1965). "Planned Unit Development: A Challenge to Established Theory and Practice of Land Use Control." *University of Pennsylvania Law Review* 114:73-77; Costonis, John. (1973). "Development Rights Transfers: An Exploratory Essay." *Yale Law Journal* 83:75.

95. Rose, "Planning and Dealing," p. 880.

96. Ibid., p. 881.

97. See generally, Hamilton, Alexander, Madison, James, and Jay, John. (1961). *The Federalist Papers,* edited by J. Cooke. New York: New American Library, but especially "Federalist No. 10."

98. Rousseau, Jean Jacques. (first published 1762; 1935). *Social Contract.* G. D. H. Cole, trans. New York: Dutton.

99. Quote from Rousseau found in Arendt, Hannah. (1963). *On Revolution.* New York: Viking Press, p. 73.

100. Mansbridge, *Beyond AdversaryDemocracy*, pp. vii-xii.

101. See generally, Gray, Barbara. (1989). *Collaboration.* San Francisco: Jossey-Bass Publishers; Bartlett, Christopher, and Ghoshal, Sumantra. (1990). "Matrix Management: Not a Structure, a Frame of Mind." *Harvard Business Review* 65:4:138-45. Boyett, Joseph, and Conn, Henry. (1991). *Workplace 2000: The Revolution Reshaping American Business.* New York: Dutton Books; Carkhuff, Robert. (1988). *The Age of the New Capitalism.* Amherst, N. H.: Human Resource Development Press; Carpenter, Susan L., and Kennedy, W. J. D. (1988). *Managing Public Disputes.* San Francisco: Jossey-Bass Publishers; Fisher, Roger. (1981). *Getting to Yes: Negotiating Agreement Without Giving In.* Boston: Houghton Mifflin; Jacob, Rahul. (1992). "The Search for the Organization of Tomorrow." *Fortune* 125:10:92-98; National Institute for Dispute Resolution (NIDR). (1991). *Community Dispute Resolution Manual: Insights and Guidance from Two Decades of Practice.*

Washington, D. C.: NIDR; and Shipper, Frank, and Manz, Charles. (1992). "Employee Self-Management Without Formally Designated Teams." *Organizational Dynamics* 20:3:48-61.

102. See generally, Fisher, *Getting to Yes*.

103. See generally, Lindblom, "Still Muddling."

104. Lampe, David. (1992). "The Politics of Environmental Equity." *The National Civic Review* 81:1: 27-35.

105. For a view of the human relations school, see Mayo, E. (1933). *The Human Problems of an Industrial Civilization*. New York: Macmillan. For a view of participative management ideas, see Likert, R. (1967). *The Human Organization*. New York: McGraw-Hill. For a view of cultural-based ideas in organizations, see Ouchi, W. (1981). *Theory Z*. Reading, Mass.: Addison-Wesley. For a more conflict-based view of negotiations, see Bacharach, Samuel B., and Lawler, Edward J. (1981). *Bargaining*. San Francisco: Jossey-Bass.

106. Bacharach, Samuel B., and Lawler, Edward J. (1980). *Power and Politics in Organizations*. San Francisco: Jossey-Bass.

107. See generally, Olson. *The Logic of Collective Action*. Also, Oliver, Pamela. (1980). "Rewards and Punishments as Selective Incentives for Collective Action: Theoretical Investigations." *American Journal of Sociology* 53:1-8.

108. Axelrod, Robert. (1984). *The Evolution of Cooperation*. New York: Basic Books. For a more detailed analysis of voluntary versus selective incentives approaches to collective action, see Heckathorn, Douglas D. (1993). "Collective Action and Group Heterogeneity: Voluntary Provision Versus Selective Incentives." *American Sociological Review* 58:329-350.

109. Ostrom, Elinor. (1991). *Governing the Commons: The Evolution of Institutions for Collective Action*. New York: Cambridge University Press; and Stevenson, Glenn. (1991). *Common Property Economics: A General Theory and Land Use Applications*. Cambridge, Mass.: Cambridge University Press.

110. Susskind, Lawrence, Bacow, Lawrence, and Wheeler, Michael. (1983). *Resolving Environmental Regulatory Disputes*. Cambridge, Mass.: Schenkman Publishing, p. 1.

111. Ibid., p. 2.

112. Peele, Elizabeth, and Ellis, Richard. (1986). "Beyond the 'Not-in-my-Backyard' Impasse." *Forum for Applied Research and Public Policy* 2:3:68-77; Sorenson, John, Soderstrom, J., and Carnes, S. (1983). "Sweet for the Sour: Incentives in Environmental Mediation." *Environmental Management* 18:287-94.

113. Hirschhorn, Joel. (1984). "Siting Hazardous Waste Facilities." *Hazardous Waste*, 1:3:423-29.

114. Lampe, "Politics," pp. 27-35.

115. Susskind et al., *Resolving*, p. 1.

116. See, generally, Moore, C. (1986). *The Mediation Process: Practical Strategies for Resolving Conflict*. San Francisco: Jossey-Bass; National Institute for Dispute Resolution, *Community Dispute Resolution Manual*.

117. See generaly, Peele, Elizabeth. (1989). "Innovative Process and Inventive Solutions: Nuclear Waste Packaging Facility Case Study." In *Public Interests in the Use of Private Lands,* edited by Benjamin Dysart and Marion Clawson. New York: Praeger.

118. National Civic Review Staff. (1992). "Grass-Roots/Local Environmental Action." *National Civic Review* 81:1:36-42.

119. As David Lampe has reported, the rationale for deciding against implementing a unitary dispute-resolution process is that "the public's ability to process technical information related to the location of toxics is generally estimated to be low" (p. 29). See Lampe. (1992). "The Politics," pp. 27-35. It should also be noted that while this rationale for not using unitary processes for the siting of mental health homes or half-way houses is less apt, unitary dispute-resolution mechanisms are also rarely used in these decisions. The unwillingness of public officials to relinquish some of their authority to the general citizenry and the relative newness and unfamiliarity of unitary and ADR (alternative dispute resolution) processes may explain in part the relatively uncommon use of these processes.

120. For a review of experiences using negotiations in environmental land-use disputes, see generally Susskind et al., *Resolving.*

121. Barber, Benjamin. (1984). *Strong Democracy: Participatory Politics for a New Age.* Berkeley, Calif.: University of California Press.

122. Mansbridge, *Beyond Adversary Democracy*, pp. 266-67.

123. See, Matheny, Albert R., and Williams, Bruce A. (1988). "Strong Democracy and the Challenge of Siting Hazardous Waste Disposal Facilities in Florida." *National Civic Review* 77:4:323-41.

124. Proudfoot, Stuart B. (1979). "Private Gains and Public Losses: The Distributive Impact of Urban Zoning." *Policy Sciences* 11:2:203-26.

125. Goetz, Edward. (1991). "Promoting Low Income Housing through Innovations in Land Use Regulations." *Journal of Urban Affairs* 13:3:337-51.

126. Neiman, Max. (1980). "Zoning Policy, Income Clustering and Suburban Change." *Social Science Quarterly* 60:3-4:666-75.

127. Doyle, M. (1977). "Retirement Communities: The Nature and Enforceability of Residential Segregation by Age." *Michigan Law Review* 76:1:64-104.

128. Ritzdof, Marsha. (1988). "Not in My Neighborhood: Alternative Lifestyles and Municipal Family Definitions." *Lifestyles* 9:3:264-76.

129. Bullard, Robert. (1990). *Dumping in Dixie* Boulder, Colo.: Westview Press.

130. Traxler, Herbert. (1983). "Share-a-Home: Economics and Logistics of Unrelated Elderly Living as a 'Family.' " *Journal of Applied Gerontology* (December):2:61-69.

131. Boyd, Penelope. (1980). "Strategies in Zoning and Community Living Arrangements for Retarded Citizens: Parens Patriae Meets Police Power." *Villanova Law Review* 25:2:273-316.

132. Budson, R.D. (1978). *The Psychiatric Halfway House: A Handbook of Theory and Practice.* Cambridge, Mass.: Harvard Medical School.

133. David Lampe, in "Politics," pp. 33-34, suggests that black churches and civil rights organizations have had some limited success in mobilizing around LULU issues, but that linkages to environmental organizations that could increase the political clout of minority

groups have been weak. See also Hutcheson, John D., and Prather, James. (1988). "Community Mobilization and Participation in the Zoning Process." *Urban Affairs Quarterly* 23:3:346-68.

134. Fort Collins, Colorado, is often touted as an example of where the lack of typical zoning ordinances has nevertheless resulted in positive land-use development. However, in Fort Collins, growth is strictly regulated through negotiated planned developments. Developers are willing to enter into such negotiations because of the city's control over utility hook-ups.

135. Bullard, Robert. (1983). "Solid Waste Sites and the Black Houston Community." *Sociological Inquiry* 53-2-3:273-88.

136. Bullard, R. (1984). "Endangered Environs: The Price of Unplanned Growth in Boomtown Houston." *California Sociologist* 7:2:84-102.

137. Clarke, Susan. (1982). "Enterprise Zones: Seeking the Neighborhood Nexus." *Urban Affairs Quarterly* 18:1:53-71.

138. Nicholas Lemann (1991. *The Promised Land: The Great Black Migration and How It Changed America.* New York: Knopf) describes how the migration of business and other leaders in the minority community to the suburbs left many inner cities in weakened condition and contributed to the creation of a culture of poverty. Joy Dryfoos (1990. *Adolescents At Risk.* New York, Oxford University Press) has identified neighborhood disintegration as one of the major factors underlying a host of social problems, including juvenile delinquency, teenage pregnancy, substance abuse, and school failure.

139. Mead, Lawrence. (1992). *The New Politics of Poverty.* New York: Basic Books.

140. Proudfoot, "Private Gains," pp. 203-26.

141. For a discussion of balancing growth with development costs see DeGrove, John M., and Metzger, Patricia, eds. (1991). *Balanced Growth: A Planning Guide for Local Government.* Washington, D.C.: International City Management Association.

142. See generally, Olsen, *Logic of Collective Action.*

143. Substantive justice requires that solutions to similar disputes be substantively similar. Unfortunately, this is not guaranteed in alternative dispute resolution or unitary processes. For example, suppose citizens in two neighborhoods enter into negotiations with two solid waste disposal developers to estimate the impact costs of locating a waste facility in the neighborhoods. Suppose, additionally, that in the first neighborhood, the negotiation is led by a neighborhood member who is a lawyer specializing in environmental law and who has donated her time, while in the second neighborhood the person representing the neighborhood's interest is semi-literate and ignorant of relevant ordinances, rights, and case law. While the resulting negotiated outcomes are both likely to be satisfactory to the parties involved, the substantive "deal" for the neighborhood is likely to be much better for the first neighborhood.

144. This could include a high tax on extraction of mineral or other natural resources that exist independent of an owner's improvements. See, Backhaus, Jurgen and Krabbe, J. J. "Henry George's Contribution to Modern Environmental Policy, Part II, The Theory Applied," *American Journal of Economics and Sociology* 51:1:115-27.

145. Inhaber, Herbert. (1992). "Of NIMBYs, LULUs, and NIMTOOs." *Public Interest* (Spring):107:52-64.

146. Jacobs, Jane. (1966). *The Life and Death of Great American Cities.* New York: Viking Press.

CHAPTER 6

Generating Policy Innovations in Land-Use Control: Some History and Ideas

As the literature on common property resources suggests, both the free-market, deregulatory policy option and state regulatory, or political, approaches to the management of these resources often result in less than equitable or satisfactory outcomes. The purpose of this chapter is to explore the legal and ideological background of potential policy alternatives to the standard laissez-faire versus regulatory options for land-use control. It will be argued that two such sets of alternative policy approaches exist: one set of options involves "framing" a market for development rights; the other set of options involves a "reframing" of political institutions so as to better channel and mitigate the effects of private power. In essence, this chapter will lay the basis for arguing that it may be necessary in part to draw from both policy approaches. As will become apparent in the following chapters, this will involve reframing our political institutions in ways that support a new market in environmental control or development rights. In terms of policy innovations, these two alternatives represent different sides of the same coin—the development of hybrid public-private or political-market approaches to land-use issues. In this respect, policy innovation in land-use issues may differ little from innovation in other issue areas. For example, a number of observers have noted that the history of scientific, technological, and industrial development is a history of three evolutionary patterns of: (1) the refinement and differentiation of these two organizationally and ethically separate modes of behavior (public and private); (2) the discovery that specific areas of human activity under specific circumstances (such as basic science during a period of cutthroat industrial growth) might best be organized chiefly through one of the modes (for example, the public mode); and

(3) the transference of ideas and techniques that were originally developed within one realm (public or private) but that were found to have favorable effects when adapted for use in the other realm.[1] If innovations in other policy fields follow those that are thought to exist in the field of industrial and economic development, it is likely that key policy innovations are to be found in subtle but important reordering of the roles and responsibilities of the private and public sectors, respectively.

SOCIAL POLICY INNOVATIONS AS PUBLIC-PRIVATE HYBRIDS

Jane Jacobs's recent work on the moral foundations of the public and private spheres of activity provides an appropriate starting point for thinking about social policy innovations as a hybrid of public and private sector approaches.[2] As noted earlier in this book, Jacobs argues that two fairly universal moral syndromes exist: a "taking" or public moral syndrome that has traditionally been followed by a "guardian" class, and a "trading" or commercial moral syndrome traditionally followed by private sector actors. Jacobs suggests that nearly every society has created ways of separating the guardian from the commercial realms. Typically, this separation is accomplished through a training or socialization of the persons who will move in these realms. That is, persons who will be entering the commercial sphere of activity will be taught the precepts of the commercial moral syndrome, while those who will engage in guardian functions will be socialized in the values of the public moral syndrome. According to Jacobs, the commercial syndrome includes such value imperatives as: shun force, come to voluntary agreements, compete, respect contracts, be efficient, promote comfort, use initiative, and dissent for the sake of the task, among others. The public or guardian moral syndrome includes value imperatives of an entirely different type, such as: shun trading, exert prowess, be loyal and respect hierarchy, deceive for the sake of the task, dispense largess, treasure honor, and make rich use of leisure.

Jacobs argues that almost every culture has taken pains to separate commercial from guardian morals and to socialize people in ways that would reinforce the use of the appropriate morality in the appropriate circumstances. This universal pattern of moral development took place because all societies found it necessary for survival and growth to separate private- and public-oriented activity. For example, she suggests that the guardian or "taking" moral syndrome arose first in hunting-based societies (where one took one's sustenance from the natural world) and then developed even more coherently around the need for internal and external security. The guardian value of deception, for example, is needed in both hunting and military strategies, while the value of prowess (or a monopoly of violence) is useful to enforce military discipline and avoid internecine battles among feuding clans or groups. In contrast, values like honesty, respect for contracts, and initiative have historically been associated with effective trading. Separately and in proportion, the moral syndromes can help support each other. For example, effective trade can provide the wealth necessary to support armies that can, in turn, provide the peace and security necessary for trade. Alternatively, as Paul Kennedy has recently pointed out, when one moral syndrome becomes dominant, it can stifle activity in the other sphere.[3]

Jacobs, however, takes the argument about a virtuous balance of public-private power in a somewhat different direction. First, she argues that the differentiation between guardian and commercial moral syndromes is one that grew out of very specific demands put on society. She suggests, moreover, that because many of these demands remain the same today, the clear ethical boundary between the two realms will most likely need to be retained to a large degree in contemporary societies.[4]

Second, and uniquely, Jacobs suggests that as circumstances change or as society evolves in reaction to changed circumstances, it will often use or reconfigure existing organizational or ethical systems in new ways. She compares this process of social evolution with what Stephen Jay Gould has termed "co-opted epiphenomena" or the tendency of evolved animals to use old structures for new purposes (for example, birds now use wings, which originally evolved to provide temperature control, to fly). Such innovations in social structures and values, however, tend to breach the sharp line that has historically developed to separate activities that fall appropriately under private sector ethics and those that are more readily categorized as public in nature. In some cases, Jacobs argues, this breaching of the boundary between guardian and commercial realms has led to what she terms "syndrome-friendly" inventions. These are innovations that provide benefits without doing any systematic harm to respective syndromes themselves. One example of such an invention, Jacobs notes, is the emergence of a new form of credit, one that uses "lending circles" in which all members of the circle guarantee each other's loans. This political innovation enables commercial banks to lend to individuals whose loan-risk level is considered too high. Another syndrome-friendly innovation is a government-supported office that helps identify businesses that need to purchase business inputs and matches them with local providers of these inputs. This innovation involves public officials in an activity that is normally performed by private business. More important, because this activity has traditionally been performed according to the guides of the commercial moral syndrome exclusively, the performance of the same activity by public managers makes new demands on the public sector's moral system. That is, if public officials are to accomplish their new mission, they will have to take on some of the values of the commercial moral syndrome, such as the value of initiative.

The history of public administration, moreover, tells how a number of operational mechanisms and management tools have been borrowed from the private sector with substantial benefit. Everything from performance budgeting and productivity and operations analysis to, more recently, total quality management, strategic planning, and "entrepreneurialism" has been adopted from private sector experiences and adapted and implemented (with varying degrees of success) in public organizations.[5] Similarly, though acknowledged less often, is the fertilization of commercial practice by the concepts and structures originating in the public sector. The popularity of books describing business management in terms of the "art of war" or in terms of political structures such as federalism that are thought to be relevant to modern corporate governance testify to the fact that the hybridization (of public-private values and ideas) is not simply a one-way street.[6]

Unfortunately, the search for syndrome-friendly innovations is not without danger; oftentimes, hybrid innovations can have the effect of undermining or perverting the basic functioning of one or both moral systems. Jacobs provides a number of examples of such systematic corruption: when armies such as those in charge of the Nazi death camps "pick up industriousness from the commercial syndrome" leading to "a factorylike business of murder and genocide;"[7] and when the Mafia's private sector commercial enterprises are operated according to selective guardian values of prowess, loyalty, hierarchy, and control, while ignoring the guardian value of "shunning trade."[8]

Although Jacobs is unclear as to exactly how or when one can expect a breach of the boundaries between the syndromes to lead to systematic corruption, she suggests that whenever a massive breach occurs or whenever one syndrome does not leave room for the other, the breach is likely to be corruptive. With regard to the ideological stances described earlier, Jacobs's study might suggest that those at the ideological extremes of the continuum between individuals and the state—libertarianism and conservative ideologies—would, almost by definition, be most likely to support or maintain a major breach or imbalance in the moral syndromes. Persons living within a libertarian society, that is, would be likely to apply a set of commercial moral values to situations that demanded more guardian values; similarly, persons living in a truly conservative society would be likely to apply the more command-and-control guardian values and mechanisms to situations that, strictly speaking, were commercial in nature.[9] In both situations, the imbalance between the realms of public and private power would likely lead to systematic corruption—or the use of one coherent set of moral standards in numerous situations where their application is inappropriate. Such corruption is based on the collapse of whole categories of values (such as efficiency in the production of consumer goods or honor in ones' relations with others) and the narrowing of opportunities for human happiness.

If one accepts the idea of systematic corruption as a viable threat, it would be prudent in the search for plausible innovations to limit the inquiry to those instances that are likely to be more syndrome friendly rather than systematically corrupting. In terms of inspiration from ideologies, this logic could be interpreted as suggesting that only communitarian and classic liberal ideologies be explored as the basis for possible syndrome-friendly hybrids. This is the case because each of these ideologies has: (1) maintained a tradition that recognizes a need for balance between public and private power; (2) shown respect for (though to somewhat differing degrees) both individual liberty and group autonomy; and (3) identified the public realm as a place for achieving some individual values. These ideologies, of course, differ with respect to which they posit that the individual can be identified prior to her entry into community life or to the degree that market-based choice is preferred to political choice. However, in contrast to conservative and libertarian ideologies, which leave little room for compromise and demand little in the form of a balance among competing values, communitarian and classic liberal ideologies are open to compromise and demand some balancing of private and public realms and of differing groups' ideas of the good or the right.

Perhaps the greatest difficulty in attempting to craft reasonable hybrids of classic liberal and communitarian ideologies lies in the need to find some principles for mediating between the primacy of values (human dignity and freedom) in classic liberal ideology and the primacy of structures (those necessary for equality) in communitarian ideology. Additionally, as Gutterbock's typology suggests, it is necessary to mediate between a view of society as an arena for conflict and one that sees society as a place for friendship and harmony.

Perhaps the most effective way of understanding the nature of fortuitous hybrids is to examine the ways in which the public realm can be organized within a basically democratic polity, and specifically to examine how this organization has implications for the shape of the market. While abstract organizational models will not generate concrete policy by themselves, the expansion of our repertory of models can increase our policymaking flexibility as well as our ability to evaluate particular policies, structures, and institutions in light of a full range of options.

Many of the elemental dimensions of governance and policy choice have been discussed earlier in this essay: formal rules versus standards, public sector "voice" dominance versus market "exit" dominance, unitary versus adversary approaches, direct versus indirect democracy, and large-scale versus small-scale political units. However, at least two key dimensions in the menu of elemental organizational governance choices have not been adequately explored. One dimension, the purposeful organizing of political interests versus allowing interests to be organized solely on a voluntary basis, has been touched on in the discussion of the contrast between American interest group liberalism and European corporatism, but it is in need of some further elaboration. The second dimension, the framing of social markets versus the regulation of free markets, has yet to be examined. I propose to address these dimensions, especially the social market one, in a somewhat theoretical and historical manner initially. Then I will provide some social market examples of potential policy options for LULU-type problems. In particular, I will suggest that certain governance models—known as social-democratic and social-republican models, respectively—represent hybrids of the more pure communitarian and classic liberal ideologies examined early in this work. I will also suggest that these hybrid governance models address in some measure the two governance dimensions—the organization of representation and level of regulation—that need further exploration prior to engaging in innovative land-use policy development. This exploration will, I believe, lay some groundwork for a general land-use governance model that could represent a potentially syndrome-friendly hybrid of existing governance options. Such an exploration may also help us to identify the features of such policy hybrids that might represent fertile grounds for corruption. In the final chapter, I will present an example of such a general land-use governance model or framework and some suggestions for addressing the governance of the specific land-use issues noted in the beginning of this book.

The dimensions of framed versus regulated markets and organized versus unorganized politics can be located in the space between classic liberal and communitarian ideologies. Generally speaking, in terms of the market dimension, classic liberals very reluctantly agree to regulate markets in a minimal way and according to general rules in order to protect human dignity, and communitarians reluctantly agree to establish highly constrained markets for the limited purposes of allocating resources among groups. Essentially, these ideologies have opposing views of the market's place in society. In describing the dimension of framed versus regulated markets, communitarians can be seen as attempting to frame markets to fit the needs of the group, while classic liberals regulate the market so as to allow for each citizen to have a measure of human dignity. In terms of the historical movements, however, flag-bearers of specific communitarian ideologies (communist and socialists) often constrained the market out of existence by calling for a nationalization of property. On the other hand, the gradual commodification of land and labor (for example, based on changes in the fee-system of property and the elimination of feudal servitude) coupled with the forces of economic growth and large-scale corporate organization, have allowed market power to overrun societies based on classic liberal principles. Moreover, the rise of a corrupted version of liberalism—interest group liberalism—has resulted in a morass of complex, detailed, and often ineffective regulation.

The historical record, however, is not entirely devoid of ideas and practices that draw their strength from a hybrid of communitarian and classic liberal ideals, while simultaneously addressing some of their respective weaknesses and historical degenerations. More particularly, these hybrid approaches directly challenge classic liberal notions of property without resorting to the institution of state property or classic socialism. In discussing these alternatives, one can identify two streams of hybrid approaches that parallel the two organizational dimensions mentioned above.

SOCIAL-DEMOCRATIC HYBRID

One stream, variously called corporatism, cosociational democracy, social democracy, or organized capitalism, attempts to address the problems associated with the industrialization-driven rise of concentrated private sector power by organizing and recognizing a few broad and important interest groups in society and ensuring that these groups obtain a roughly proportional share of the resources and benefits of political power. In addition to the organized representation of interest groups in administrative policymaking already discussed, social democracy typically provides for proportional representation of political parties in national and regional legislatures, the substitution of multi-interest councils for single offices or head of state, the rotation of offices among representatives of key groups, the establishment of separate interest group-governed institutions such as schools, and the taking of turns with respect to the seats of political power.[10]

Generally, social democratic societies enact policies that reduce the ability of individuals in their private capacity to control disproportionate shares of economic and political resources. Empirically speaking, the effects of such policies are reflected in the relatively high rates of voting and the relatively even distribution of income and wealth in these societies.[11] Social democracy, moreover, appears to be somewhat effective in resolving social tensions in multicultural societies without demanding acculturation into a melting-pot society.

However, in addition to ignoring the unorganized or emerging interests, social democracy is generally complacent about the scale, scope, and organized power of well-established institutions. For example, by managing large blocks of corporate stock in addition to regulating the flow of commercial loans, German merchant banks have historically been able to exercise considerable power over numerous corporations, yet the market for opening a bank of this type is not open to all; only a few chosen bankers who meet very high capital reserve tests and the approval of the government are allowed into this business. The result of this conscious organization of social interests is a system that not only allows for large-scale power and concentration of resources, but encourages these institutional characteristics.[12]

SOCIAL-REPUBLICAN HYBRID

The second hybrid—built around the distinction between framed and regulated markets—also has a variety of names, such as economic democracy, social-republican property, or common property collectives, depending on the author or context in which they are being discussed. However, the distinctive feature of these hybrid systems, according to William Simon, is that the holding of property by private individuals is conditioned on: (1) "the holder bearing a relation of potential active participation in a group or community constituted by the property;"

and (2) some limits to the potential for inequality among the members of the group or community.[13]

The social-republican hybrid represents a selective combination of classic liberal and communitarian ideas on how a just and democratic society ought to be organized. The republican end of the hybrid is based on the classic liberal ideal of participation and equality in the public sphere, while the social end of the hybrid is based on the notion that participation and equality are necessary in the economic realm as well. The hybrid itself is drawn from two historical movements —republicanism and market socialism—with each representing a somewhat different critique of classic liberalism and corporate capitalism. However, in historical perspective, the differences have been minimal, in the nature of "group image" or variations-on-a-theme differences, while in most important respects agrarian Jeffersonians, Knights of Labor, French followers of Pierre-Joseph Proudhon, and radical republicans of the Civil War era all shared similar themes and all advocated what could be described as a hybrid of classic liberal and communitarian ideologies.

The two most prominent ideas in this tradition have been that economic inequality cannot be allowed to go so far as to undermine democracy and that traditional representative and adversarial means of participation unnecessarily limit the scope of personal expression and development. Both the republican and social market movements emphasized and valued the small-scale, local, and face-to-face relationships and sought to control the tendency of accumulated wealth to corrupt public decision-making or to create situations of extreme dependence in the private sphere.

The chief means of achieving these social-republican goals, according to Simon, was to create a new type of social-republican property. This new property would include only productive resources or capital property, not personal or residential property, and would involve control of this property by workers in a "participatory workplace subject to important obligations to the larger society."[14] Simon has identified two policy means by which social-republican property has traditionally been created. The first policy set includes restraints on the transfer of property that act to keep the control of property in the hands of active or potentially active participants in the community. Such restraints help to prevent transfers of property that might lead to increasing disadvantage, but they also act to safeguard some level of property-based independence of those in the community. Simon cites a number of alienation restraints that tend to act in this manner, including: those placed on Social Security benefits, the residency and usage requirements found in the Homestead Act of 1862, and those found in Western state waters laws that require continued use in order to maintain ownership. Additionally, social-republicans have tended to promote policies that favor one type of property ownership—land ownership—that is inherently more difficult to transfer than the more liquid financial property. Because land is relatively immobile, it is believed that ownership of this type of land will more likely result in participation and investment in the community. The same prejudice against making mobility easy (and therefore community difficult) was expressed in social-republican objections to slavery. That is, slave property, when compared with landed property, is relatively mobile, making it easier for slave owners to "treat land as a variable cost, cultivate extensively, and then move on as soil productivity declined, without developing local attachments" or investing in local communities or the public infrastructure that makes community life viable.[15] This criticism of slavery and other forms of excessive mobility has a certain parallel in Albert O. Hirschman's notion that "exit" should not be made too easy if people are to be induced to use "voice" to improve the community organization.[16]

Social-republican movements have also frequently proposed policies that would reduce the ability of any one or small group of individuals to accumulate property in quantities far out of proportion to that owned by average citizens. In addition to noting James Harrington's proposal for requiring an equal division of property to heirs at death, Simon has identified a number of more recently proposed and enacted accumulation restraints, including: the Homestead Act's limits of the number of acres that might be acquired per claimant, the Federal Reclamation Act's limits of the number of acres that one person could use as a basis for claiming access to federally subsidized water, the American partnership law presumption of equal rights of control and income in the absence of contrary agreements, and the cross-securing (or cross-collateralization) of credit by members of credit or labor unions or by members of cooperative housing associations (that is, where "individual owners typically pledge their ownership interests as security for their neighbors', as well as their own debts").[17]

Perhaps the most persistent type of accumulation restraint that has its origins in social-republican movements is the idea of restraining corporations' abilities to aggregate resources from distant, absentee owners. In addition to seeing the corporate form as a source of monopoly that exploits local business suppliers and consumers, social-republicans criticize this form of ownership because the absentee owners are believed to be less sensitive to the potential for negative effects of business operations on community life or environmental qualities. In essence, the argument is that because absentee owners would not themselves experience the negative externalities of such legally accepted nuisances as "acceptable" pollution, they would not support reasonable efforts to eliminate them.[18] Robert Ellickson's recent examination of how social norms develop as a means of controlling undesirable behavior supports the social-republican perspective on absentee ownership. One of the key elements in the development of such norms, Ellickson observed, is the expectation of a long-term relationship. Without this expectation, Ellickson discovered, appeal to community norms is likely to be without force, resulting in a need to create and call on the force of law.[19]

It is important to note how social-republican property differs from both the socialist and the social-democratic traditions. Although social-republican property places an emphasis on a rough equality in material relations, the commitment to this equality is qualified and mediated by a decentralized institutional structure and a unitary political culture. As Jane Mansbridge has pointed out in her study of unitary democracy, in many instances of unitary political cultures it is often not necessary to achieve an exact equality among participants; rather, a rough equality of respect is sufficient: "Like friendships, unitary democracies are composed of equals, not because the members, out of envy or rapacity, want to tear down the prominent and share their goods, but because potential superiors and inferiors alike gain from stressing the ways in which they are equal." The face-to-face nature of small-scale institutions when combined with consensus decision-making tends also to limit the need for strict economic leveling that many socialists believe is necessary as a precursor to or continuing pillar of democracy.[20]

The social-republican vision of society shares a great deal with the social-democratic one in that both represent a hybrid of sorts of classic liberal and communitarian ideologies, and in this respect, attempt to combine egalitarian and individual liberty concerns in their ordering of a democratic polity. The difference between the two hybrids is the degree to which they attempt to frame and restrain (in size and scope) rather than tax and regulate the institutions of production and exchange. The social-democratic hybrid tends to limit its policies for reducing inequality to some provisions for education and equal opportunity and a taxing of inheritance. Social-democratic policies do not restrain owners of capital from forming ever-larger corporations or generally from acting as full and legal entities in the political realm. Whatever ills are created by this system (such as unemployment, large-scale intrusions on community, or pollution) are believed to be resolvable either through post hoc regulations of specific problems or through an industry-specific (or in European societies, a nationwide) organization of the interests of workers and capitalists through collective bargaining.[21] Out of such bargaining and the economic surplus, those who are harmed by mega-sized institutions adjusting to new market circumstances can be provided a safety net of essential services or monetary compensation.

The social-democratic system of regulation differs from classic liberalism in its tendency to: (1) promote numerous specific rules about representation, turn-taking, and the like; (2) enact a substantial number of detailed, post-hoc regulations (though less than is the case in interest group liberalism) rather than a few, typically a priori, general rules; and (3) attempt some organization of social interests beyond mere citizenship. Finally, social democrats would claim that their relative sympathy for large-scale enterprise and concentrated capital is more realistic and efficient than the social-republican vision of a small-scale, owner-managed enterprise.[22]

Social-republican property has, of course, received the greatest degree of criticism from libertarian and conservative critics, who argue that it is highly inefficient. This criticism is based on the assumption that social-republican property undermines free markets and therefore is, ipso facto, inefficient. The recent literature on national competitiveness has generated a number of arguments that social-republican property might not be as inefficient as these critics, or as market theory, would predict. The volume of this literature makes it impossible to convey in this limited space the nuances of these arguments. However, it should be noted that, in general, advocates for social-republican property (or "economic democracy," as it is often called) argue that this type of property can improve productivity and overall happiness by: more closely aligning workers' individual interests and satisfactions with those of the entire productive community,[23] reducing the amount of short-term profit-taking and increasing long-term investments,[24] increasing the willingness of owners to see their property as something to be worked rather than traded,[25] increasing the tendency of owners to value their property for its own sake rather than for what they think others might give them for it,[26] increasing workplace teamwork and firm-specific human capital,[27] increasing the efficiency of shopfloor governance, and the effective introduction of technology.[28]

The objections to social-republican property are also numerous and represent a combination of those that are made with respect to unitary political approaches (for example, that they are costly in terms of time and complexity and subject to group coercion) and others that are more specific to particular worker ownership or productive capital situations (such as, the heterogeneity of labor specialization works against the development of common interests and outlooks,[29] the concentration of workers' wealth in specific production property does not provide for adequate diversification of workers' wealth,[30] and the tendency, because of the need for an influx of capital, for worker-owned properties to shift back to investor-owned or become capital-starved)[31].

OPERATIONALIZING SOCIAL-REPUBLICAN PROPERTY: COLLECTIVE ACTION AROUND COMMON POOL RESOURCES

The essential features of one particular instance of social-republican property—collective action around the management of common pool resources—have been described in an earlier section of this book. The suggestion was made that locally unwanted land use could be seen as something akin to the inverse of a common pool resource, something that might be termed a common pool detriment. As with common pool resources, there is a strong potential for tragedy as people systematically concentrate LULUs into small areas, making that area increasing unlivable.

Also as suggested earlier, because it is the nature of certain resources such as water basins and fisheries to have the potential for tragic outcomes, most policy analysts have suggested either privatization or state regulation or nationalization of the resources. Yet collective management, sometimes over a period of centuries, of common pool resources has in many cases successfully prevented the predicted tragedy. In other cases, however, collective management has been less than successful in fully preventing Hardin's "tragedy of the commons."

Elinor Ostrom, Robert Wade, and others have studied numerous cases of collective action to manage common pool resources. Drawing on the work of these scholars, it is possible to enumerate contextual features that tend to be associated with the success of collective action around common pool resources. Based on her study of a number of successful and failed CPR institutions, Ostrom speculates that there are at least seven basic design principles at the base of long-enduring common pool resource institutions for collective action. These are listed in Table 3. Under some of these generic principles, I have included some additional conclusions based on Robert Wade's studies of collective action in the management of common pool resources.[32]

Table 3: Design Principles Illustrated by Long-Enduring CPR Institutions

1. Clearly defined boundaries: Individuals or households who have rights to withdraw resource units from the CPR must be clearly defined, as must the boundaries of the CPR itself.
   — the smaller the boundaries, the greater the CPR's success.

2. Congruence between appropriation and provision rules and local conditions: Appropriation rules restricting time, place, technology, and/or quantity of resource units are related to local conditions and to provision rules requiring labor, material, and/or money:
   — the higher the cost of exclusion technologies (e.g., fencing, or in the case of LULUs, the cost of zoning), the better chances of success.
   — the greater the overlap between the location of the common pool resource and the residence of the users, the greater the success.
   — the more vital the resource for survival, the greater the success.

3. Collective-choice arrangements: Most individuals affected by the operational rules can participate in modifying the operational rules.
   — the smaller the number of users, the greater the chance of success.
   — the more powerful are those who benefit from retaining the commons, and the weaker are those who favor enclosure or private property, the better the chance of success.
   — the better developed the arrangements for discussion, the greater the chances for success.
   — the extent to which users are bound by mutual obligation, the greater the chance of success.

4. Monitoring: Monitors, who actively audit CPR conditions and appropriator behavior, are accountable to the appropriators or are the appropriators.

— the more the users already have joint rules for other purposes than the management of common pool resources, the better the chances of success.

— the more noticeable the rule breaking by free riders, the better the chance of success.

5. Graduated sanctions: Appropriators who violate operational rules are likely to be assessed graduated sanctions (depending on the seriousness and context of the offense) by other appropriators, by officials accountable to these appropriators, or by both.

6. Conflict-resolution mechanisms: Appropriators and their officials have rapid access to low-cost local arenas to resolve conflicts among appropriators or between appropriators and officials.

7. Minimal recognition of rights to organize: The rights of appropriators to devise their own institutions are not challenged by external governmental authorities.

Source: Adapted from Elinor Ostrom's *Governing the Commons*, p. 90; and Robert Wade's "The Management of Common Property Resources: Collective Action as an Alternative to Privatisation or State Regulation," (1987) *Cambridge Journal of Economics* 11:95-106.

Full exposition of these principles of institutionalizing collective action is beyond the scope of this book. It is important to note, however, that a comparison of these principles with LULU problems suggests that the governance of many LULU issues might be plausibly addressed by collective choice mechanisms instead of through either state control or the privatization of the entire bundle of property rights. However, it should also be pointed out that a number of the context features that would tend to make collective choice governance successful with respect to LULU-type issues are not currently in place. The following section explores how specific features of the LULU context might support or fail to support the principles undergirding successful collective action.

A. Features of LULU issues that potentially fit with collective choice governance.

1. Boundaries: Many LULU issues can be defined as having relatively clear boundaries. That is, particular LULUs tend to have very specific and geographically limited effects. An exception to this generalization would be land uses that involve air pollution of a type whose major effects were far downstream from the pollution source. However, LULUs of different types tend to have different effective boundaries. Elementary schools, for

example, may have a LULU effect of less than a block, while large-scale industrial waste disposal facilities or prisons may have a more community-wide effect. Even in these cases, however, the size of the major impact of the facility is likely to be limited more to the size of a neighborhood.

2. Congruence with local conditions: The increase in NIMBY and LULU issues in recent decades suggests that these issues are indeed important to citizens. Furthermore, movements against LULUs are generally highly localized in ways that would tend to lead to an overlap of the location of the "common detriment" with the residences of those who could potentially take collective action.

3. Collective-choice arrangements: Those who are in favor of creating or maintaining protections against the "common detriment" represented by LULUs tend to have substantial power. This power has two sources: the traditionally common law power of exclusion and the power to collectivize this exclusionary right through the passage of local zoning ordinances. This power, however, is often subject to and overwhelmed by the substantial countervailing powers of expansionary capitalism.

4. Monitoring: Collective-choice arrangements for LULUs would be fostered by the fact that potentially unwanted land uses often, especially when they require zoning changes or permits, are visible to nearby residents prior to their implementation.

5. Conflict resolution mechanisms: While low-cost conflict resolution mechanisms such as neighborhood mediation programs are not available in all communities, a substantial development of alternative dispute resolution techniques and programs has occurred during the last couple decades. This development suggests that further expansion that would directly support collective action around LULU issues would not present extensive difficulties. Because these conflict resolution mechanisms tend to support bargaining and side payments, their implementation could also tend to establish a mechanism for graduated sanctions against LULU developers.

B. Features of LULU issues that currently do not fit with collective choice governance.

1. Boundaries: Currently, the boundaries for the governance of many LULUs (such as county- or municipal-sized districts) are much larger than the "common detriment" effect of the LULU itself. That is, the powerful interests within the jurisdiction can direct the costs of LULUs away from

their residences or other properties while still enjoying the benefits that the LULU facility can provide.

2. Congruence with local conditions: A major factor in current land-use control governance working against the potential for across-the-board collective action to govern LULUs is the fact that the costs of enclosure (or privatization of LULUs) is much greater for some than for others. That is, because land ownership is currently highly privatized, with sufficient wealth one can escape LULU effects through private means (such as the purchase of large plots of land or negotiation of restrictive covenants) or public ones (organization for passage of restrictive zoning). Those with fewer economic or political resources will have more difficulty with either strategy.

3. Collective-choice arrangements: In general, as Jane Mansbridge's study suggests, the "arrangements for discussion" in most American communities and neighborhoods have atrophied since the heyday of the New England town meeting in the eighteenth and nineteenth centuries. Collective choice has more generally been effected through more adversarial and representative systems that tend to strictly limit rather than encourage open-ended discussion. Additionally, the chances for success of collective action around LULU issues is also lessened by the small extent to which residents in most American communities are bound by mutual obligation. As outlined in the first chapter, a number of features of the modern urban landscape dictate against mutual obligation, including: (1) the division of places of production from residences has resulted in fewer persons in a neighborhood being mutually obligated co-workers in a business; (2) the commodification of features of the economy such as care of children and the elderly that used to be produced at a more neighborhood level through informal mutual assistance;[33] (3) the hypermobility of citizens; and (4) the commodification of residential housing and developments such that individual residences and whole subdivisions are financed and planned in such a way as to promote liquidity and resale value rather than long-term commitment to a community (as evidenced by personalizing individual residences and investing in neighborhood organizations).

4. Monitoring and conflict resolution: While there exists a substantial degree of monitoring of collective-choice arrangements, most of this monitoring, as Ellickson has suggested, is of a high-cost, formal regulatory nature.[34] This monitoring involves thousands of professional planners, zoning and development inspectors and specialists, zoning commissions and variance boards, local government decision-makers, and land-use lawyers and judges in the process of making numerous detailed and piecemeal decisions that

often involve several layers of appeal prior to a final decision. Implementation of collective-action processes and institutions for monitoring the common detriment property involved in LULU situations would likely mean that the current costly apparatus for monitoring choices would have to be substantially pared down and reformed.

Size and the Problem of Collective Management Institutions

Both the theory and practice of social-republican property and collective management of common pool resources run into what has been called the paradox of decentralization.[35] That is, although citizens generally feel more effective in being able to influence and shape the policies and decisions of a smaller unit of government than a larger one, they are simultaneously aware that larger governments tend to have a more substantial effect on their lives because they are able to make more collective choices. Elinor Ostrom implicitly addressed this paradox when she included an eighth design principle for common pool resources that are parts of larger systems. This principle, one that she calls "nesting," suggests that the appropriation, monitoring, conflict resolutions, and governance activities related to common resources (or in the case of LULUs, common detriments) can effectively be organized in "multiple layers of nested enterprises."[36] If Ostrom is correct, then one of the key questions about governing in an age of NIMBYs and LULUs becomes: How can we determine the range of land-use control issues that should be decentralized and the degree of decentralization that would be appropriate? Answers to this question, of course, have major implications for whether a social-democratic or social-republican approach to land-use control policy would be preferable. Jane Mansbridge provides some guidance in answering this question. She writes:

> Deliberate decentralization of political decision to the smallest possible units would obviously increase the role of small polities in citizens' lives, but economic and ecological interdependence means that such decentralization is sometimes prohibitively costly. As a strategy, for increasing citizens' chances of protecting and furthering their interests, decentralization works best when the scope of the decision need not be broad and when accuracy, speed, and adaptability are at a premium.[37]

Earlier it was argued that the scope of many land-use control decisions should probably be broader than is typically the case with respect to land plot by land plot decisions made in judicial settings. Because such decisions typically do not involve the full set of community interests, they have often led to a cascade of private land-use changes that, when taken as a whole, undermine the potential for a more satisfactory mix and arrangement of land uses. Yet, at the same time, if ample citizen participation in the decision making is supported, the scope of most land-use decisions does not necessarily need to be broader than the local community or neighborhood that will be directly affected by the decision. Land-use control decisions that affect the sustainability of a large natural environment, of course, represent an exception to the decentralization principle. In this latter case, the scope of the land-use decision should be broad enough to ensure that the value of the natural ecology remaining functional can be fully considered by all those who are potentially dependent on it or who have an interest in its survival. Generally, however, if we assume that most land-use decision making can remain at the local level, we can also conclude that social-republican approaches to managing LULU situations would likely be more appropriate than social-democratic ones.

Establishing social-republican property involves not only managerial issues (such as those related to discovering the most effective form and scale of such property), but also what William Simon refers to as a problem inherent in the dialectic between internal and external equality. This problem occurs, for example, when those inside a collective-management institution use their policymaking power to exclude outsiders from benefits (as in exclusionary zoning) or attempt to foist the major costs of their decisions on those who live outside the local or neighborhood polity (such as through siting unwanted developments on the edges of a jurisdiction, thus placing much of the LULU-associated costs onto the adjacent jurisdiction). As Simon notes, however, this problem of internal and external equality is not limited to social-republican property, but is pervasive in industrial democracy. However, the tendency of collective institutions to create equality at the expense of outsiders presents an especially serious barrier to realizing the vision of social-republican ideals. In addressing the problem of exclusion, Simon suggests a few policy options: (1) a more centralized government can regulate the choices as to who will be admitted to the collective institution; (2) the more centralized government can constrain the degree of expansion of the collective institution; or (3) the centralized government can subsidize new competing institutions. Simon warns us, however, that even though policy options are available for addressing the exclusion problem, these approaches can "threaten the vitality of social-republican institutions." "The critical task," he writes, "is to design constraints on exclusion without excessively impairing the autonomy and security necessary for such institutions to flourish."[38]

SYSTEM EFFECTS AND FEDERAL RESCUE OF POOR POLICY

The exclusion problem, unfortunately, can be exacerbated as well as ameliorated by policies of a more central government. The full effects of policies such as rent control, inclusionary and exclusionary zoning, and interdistrict school segregation are often not immediately clear to the proponents of these policies or to local or state government officials who create these policies. In some instances, the full system effect of such policies are not felt by local and state officials because the federal government has put in place a number of programs, funds, and resources that are designed to offset the harm of ineffective or counterproductive land-use policies. Robin Paul Malloy, for example, makes this argument specifically with respect to rent control policies. These policies, he says, help a specific group of people living in the rent-controlled apartments found in cities that enact rent control ordinances, while putting substantial costs on other citizens and growth-management pressures on outlying areas. The result of rent control is to reduce the amount of housing available in the rent-controlled city (because landlords have a disincentive to invest in rental housing), forcing tenants who might otherwise live in the city to live in surrounding areas. These would-be city tenants now must commute to work, putting pressure on existing highways and increasing traffic, noise, and air pollution. As these pressures grow, surrounding areas are forced to pay the cost or find some way for the rent-controlled city to pay for the cost of its policies. The potential for a healthy political clash, however, is undermined by the federal government's provision of revenue to pay for the negative effects (or externalities) of the rent-control policy. Payments for road construction, mass transit, auto pollution control, and the like, Malloy suggests, essentially spread the costs of the rent-control policy among the nations' taxpayers, while the benefits remain concentrated among those few citizens who are lucky enough to live in rent-controlled apartments.[39]

Given the tendency for local autonomous groups to generate policy options that direct the benefits toward those within the group while directing the cost toward those outside, it would be fair to conclude that policies that are designed to enable local communities or neighborhoods to exclude the negative environmental effects of expansionary, "absentee" capitalism must also control the potential of these autonomous communities to be socially exclusionary. Although the development of policy options for LULU problems might proceed along lines that "seek out the integral features—the meaningful, technical, ecological, and morphological interrelationships—in landscapes, ecosystems, urban form,"[40] and the like of each segment of human habitation, as Ernest Sternberg suggests, it will nevertheless be necessary in the development of hybrid policy innovations to keep an eye on the balance between local autonomy and the universal ideal of social justice.

In this chapter, I have suggested that two historical traditions—social-democratic and social-republican—represent potentially "friendly" hybrids of more mainstream political and ideological traditions. The social-republican tradition, moreover, was found to have substantial similarities to collective-choice governance mechanisms that have been successfully employed in the management of common property. Drawing on recent studies of successful collective-choice institutions and following the argument that LULUs are a special type of common property—I examined the potential for using collective-choice arrangements to govern LULU issues and identified a key problem in this regard: the tendency of collective choice governance toward exclusionary values.

In the following section of this book, I will review some concrete alternatives to the traditional way in which we make decisions about locally unwanted land uses.

NOTES

1. See, generally, O'Looney, John. (1991). "The Organizational Basis for Innovation in Developed States." Unpublished dissertation, University of Georgia; Phillips, Kevin P. (1984). *Staying on Top.* New York: Random House, 1984; and Porter, Michael. (1990). "The Compctitive Advantage of Nations." *Harvard Business Review* 68, 2 (March-April): 72-95.

2. Jacobs, Jane. (1992). *Systems of Survival: A Dialogue on the Moral Foundations of Commerce and Politics.* New York: Random House.

3. Kennedy, Paul. (1989). *The Rise and Decline of Great Powers.* New York: Vintage Press.

4. Many of the specific policy suggestions found in David Osborne and Ted Gaebler's influential *Reinventing Government* are built around a similar argument for a proper sorting out of the functions that are best performed by the public and private sectors. See, Osborne, David, and Gaebler, Ted. (1992). *Reinventing Government.* Reading, Mass.: Addison-Wesley.

5. Landau, Martin. (1969). "Redundancy, Rationality, and the Problem of Duplication and Overlap." *Public Administration Review* 29:346-58, argues for overlapping organizational structures rather than neat divisions into specialty bureaus. Bender, Jonathan B. (1985). *Parallel Systems: Redundancy in Government.* Berkeley, Calif.: University of California Press, supports building competition into bureaucratic organizations.

6. For example, the popularity in the business community of Musashi Miyamoto's *A Book of Five Rings* (Woodstock, N.Y.: Overlook Press, 1982), and Sun-tzu's *Art of War* (New York: Oxford University Press, 1971). For the influence of the concept of federalism see, Handy, Charles. (1992). "Balancing Corporate Power: A New Federalist Paper." *Harvard Business Review* 70:6:59-73.

7. Jacobs, *Systems of Survival*, p. 80.

8. Ibid., pp. 93-100.

9. It is also feasible that the opposite corruption might occur, namely, that libertarians, who have to learn guardian ways in order to survive, might begin to apply these values where they do not apply.

10. See generally Lijphart, Arend. "The Netherlands: The Rules of the Game," and other articles in McRae, Kenneth (ed). (1974). *Consociational Democracy.* Ottawa: McClelland and Stewart.

11. See generally, Orren, Gary R., and Verba, Sidney. (1985). *Equality in America.* Cambridge, Mass.: Harvard University Press. Almond, Gabriel A. and Verba, Sidney. (1963). *The Civic Culture.* Boston: Little, Brown.

12. See generally, Gourevitch, Peter. (1986). *Politics in Hard Times.* Ithaca, N. Y.: Cornell University Press.

13. Simon, William. (1991). "Social-Republican Property." *UCLA Law Review* 38:1335-50.

14. Ibid., p. 1340.

15. Ibid., p. 1344.

16. Hirschman, Albert O. *Exit, Voice, and Loyalty: Responses to Decline in Firms, Organizations, and States.* Cambridge, Mass.: Harvard University Press.

17. Simon, "Social-Republican Property," p. 1347.

18. Ibid., p. 1347.

19. Ellickson, Robert. (1991). *Order Without Law: How Neighbors Settle Disputes.* Cambridge, Mass. : Harvard University Press.

20. Mansbridge, Jane. (1983). *Beyond Adversary Democracy.* Chicago: University of Chicago Press, p. 28.

21. Simon, "Social-Republican Property," pp. 1349-50.

22. Ibid., pp. 1349-50.

23. Keynes, John Maynard. (1936). *The General Theory of Employment, Interest and Money.* New York: Harcourt, Brace, p. 150.

24. This is a generally recognized problem with forms of capitalism that allow for a too easy flow of investment in and out of companies. Such a "quarterly earnings" perspective, critics suggests, keeps companies from making the kind of long-term investments in research and development that are the key to economic success. Critics of economic democracy argue that this tendency to capitalize and secure future income streams may represent as much of a problem for social-republican property as it does for systems with highly developed capital markets. See generally, Kuttner, Robert. (1987). *The Economic Illusion.* Philadelphia: University of Pennsylvania Press; Drucker, Peter F. (1991). "Reckoning with the Pension Fund Revolution." *Harvard Business Review* 69:2:106-14; and Williamson, O. E. (1985). *The Economic Institutions of Capitalism.* New York: The Free Press.

25. This tendency is reflected in modern corporate take-over practices that are aimed at earning money through breaking-up existing assets rather than working them. Robert Reich has criticized this "paper entrepreneuralism" from a competitiveness perspective because it draws important talent and resources away actual productivity. See Reich, Robert. (1993). *The Next American Frontier.* New York: Times Books.

26. Keynes, *General Theory*, pp. 155-58. Also, see Fowler, Edmund P. (1992). *Building Cities that Work.* Montreal, Canada: McGill-Queen's University Press, for a discussion of the tendency of people to buy and live in houses that meet average market needs rather than personal needs.

27. The lack of investment in workers' training is an oft-cited factor in explanations of relative economic decline. While the Japanese have created cultural expectations of long-term employee relationships and the French have established a social-democratic payroll tax to encourage worker training, America has generally left this social good to the market. Transaction-cost economics tends to dictate against easy market solutions because it is difficult for employers and employees to develop air-tight contracts that protect employers from employees who take their expensive training to a competitor. See generally, Simon, "Social-Republican Property," pp.1391-93; Also, see Aoki, Masahiko. (1984). *The Co-*

operative Game Theory of the Firm. New York: Claredon Press. Simon's article, for instance, suggests that social-republican property would tend to make it in everyone's interest to invest in worker's training.

28. Weiler, Paul C. (1990). *Governing the Workplace: the Future of Labor and Employment Law.* Cambridge, Mass.: Harvard University Press; Allen, Christopher S. (1988). "Trade Unions, Worker Participation and Flexibility: Linking the Micro to the Macro." *Comparative Politics* 22, 3 (April 1990):253-72; and Hoerr, John. (1991). "What Should Unions Do?" *Harvard Business Review* 69:3:30-45. These articles generally discuss an important governance role for unions that is substantially different from the standard role that American unions have played in the last four decades. Instead of limiting their concerns to wages, hours, and work rules, more effective unions with respect to the common interest of labor and capital would be involved in, and therefore support rather than sabotage, a host of issues that are currently considered the prerogatives of management. Social-republican property, it can be argued, would lead naturally to this new type of union role.

29. See Simon's discussion of the work by Henry Hansmann, in "Social-Republican Property," p. 1394.

30. Simon, "Social-Republican Property," pp. 1397.

31. See *Wall Street Journal.* (June 3, 1994). "Study Commends Worker Participation, But Says Labor Laws May Be Limiting." A, 2:2, for a recent review of the fate of various types of worker-own companies. The key to success appears to be less a matter of ownership per se than a high level of involvement and participation by workers in improving company productivity.

32. Ostrom, Elinor. (1990). *Governing the Commons: The Evolution of Institutions for Collective Action,* Cambridge, England: Cambridge University Press, p. 90. Also, see Wade, Robert. (1987). "The Management of Common Property Resources: Collective Action as an Alternative to Privatisation or State Regulation." *Cambridge Journal of Economics* 11:95-106.

33. Cahn, Edgar S. (1992). *Time Dollars.* Emmaus, Penn.: Rodale Press.

34. Ellickson, Robert C. (1990). "Three Systems of Land Use Control." *Harvard Journal of Law and Public Policy* 13:67-74.

35. Mansbridge, *Beyond Adversary Democracy,* p. 279; also, Lincoln, James R. (1976). "Power and Mobilization in the Urban Community: Reconsidering the Ecological Approach." *American Sociological Review* 41:1-15.

36. Ostrom, *Governing the Commons,* p. 90.

37. Mansbridge, *Beyond Adversary Democracy,* p. 279.

38. Simon, "Social-Republican Property," p. 1413.

39. Malloy, Robin Paul. (1991). *Planning for Serfdom.* Philadelphia: University of Pennsylvania Press, pp. 56-59.

40. Sternberg, Ernest. (1993). "Justifying Public Intervention without Market Externalities: Karl Polanyi's Theory of Planning in Capitalism." *Public Administration Review* 52:2:100-109.

CHAPTER 7

Policy Options

In this chapter, I examine some specific policy options for siting unwanted land-use facilities. Each of these policy options represents an attempt to craft hybrid policy in the sense that the ideological sources of inspiration and justification are found in more than one ideological stream. In particular, the policy options examined tend to represent ideological combinations of classic liberal and communitarian perspectives. The first type of policy option to be examined—the development of a more formal process by which LULU developers and LULU communities can negotiate and bargain—represents only a small, and not entirely satisfactory, shift away from a classic liberal reliance on the market. The second type of option—a framework policy for a social market in development rights—is a more complete hybrid. In fact, this second type of option represents a combination of the features of social-republican and social-democratic approaches (which are themselves hybrids of classic liberal and communitarian ideologies) to policy issues. In this sense, the second type of policy option represents a hybrid of a hybrid.

Within the second type of land-use policy option, I examine several proposals that advance the art of land-use policymaking, but that are still unsatisfactory as mechanisms for addressing LULU problems. Finally, I suggest a sample framework policy that draws on earlier proposals for new systems of land tenure, but that more adequately addresses the full array of LULU-siting and burden-sharing issues. The policy proposal I present represents only one example of framework-type policies, and perhaps a flawed one at that. However, the purpose of setting forth a specific proposal is not to convince policy makers that there is a single, best-of-all land-use control policy; rather, it is to stimulate thinking about the details of policymaking in this area and to advance the state of the art in developing framework policies. Framework policies, in this respect, represent an attempt to frame or contain the effects of a free market in property rights so as to support community, equity, and environmental qualities, while not losing a great deal of efficiency. In this sense, framework policies represent an attempt to bring a greater balance of values and interests to the way we shape the built environment. Whether framework policies offer a syndrome-friendly refinement of the current approach to land-use control and to the current configuration of the public and private realms and roles can be determined only by an empirical testing of specific policy options. As a prelude to such a test, however, I will present in the chapter after this one a number of potential legal, political, practical, and ethical objections to the "sample framework policy" outlined in this chapter. However, prior to presenting the difficulties of a specific policy approach to the governance of LULUs, it is necessary to address a number of more general objections that have been raised with regard to policies that would distribute the burdens of LULUs more evenly among citizens or communities.

In preceding chapters, I examined some existing or proposed policy approaches that were linked to specific political mechanisms. In the discussion of adversarial approaches, I examined the strengths and weaknesses of: regulatory activities, judicial review of environmental impact statements, the use of common law nuisance suits, and the use of lawsuits in the enforcement of public law. In the discussion of unitary political approaches, I explored some of the advantages and disadvantages of mediation and other alternative dispute resolution mechanisms. I will not repeat these discussions here, but instead refer the reader to these sections. The following discussion centers specifically on policy options that offer more comprehensive approaches to the problem of unequal or unfair siting of LULUs.

MODERN SITING TECHNOLOGIES: MORE INTEGRATIVE, BUT STILL UNSATISFACTORY

Recently, some policy analysts have proposed some variations on the policy notion of establishing a simple auction market among communities for LULU development. Some of these policy variations, it should be recognized, partake of elements of both a political (basically communitarian) and an economic (basically liberal) approach to land-use issues. That is, even though the LULU-auction mechanism is market-mimicking, it is also based on the idea of legitimizing a collective property right (that is, the right of the community to sell to a developer LULU-siting authorization). However, proponents of this option also recognize that it formalizes the rights of developers to negotiate with communities. In this latter regard, it can be said that this option does a good job—perhaps too good of one—of dealing with the problem of property rights being so exclusionary as to limit needed development. That is, developers who represent the expansionary rights of property are given an opportunity to bargain directly with communities in ways that would not be deemed appropriate in a classic liberal society. In the classic liberal society, that is, individual property owners either would or would not (depending on the general rule) be able to use or sell their property for LULU purposes. The auction mechanism, perhaps combined with a community-wide mediation session on the environmental impact of the proposed development, would essentially allow communities to make each LULU development contingent on such things as environmental safeguards, side payments, provisions for jobs, and the like.

Stephen Swallow, with others, recently offered a specific approach for siting noxious facilities that integrates technical, economic, and political considerations in a three-stage process.[1] Swallow and others make the key assumption that the benefits of the facility to the region outweigh the costs that are imposed on any specific community or property owner where the LULU will be sited. Working from this assumption, they argue that during the first stage of the siting process, an agency such as the Environmental Protection Agency would certify that all the proposed sites meet certain minimal technical standards. This expert-driven process, the policy proponents explain, would result in a "long list" of sites that generally meet the standards of health, safety, and engineering efficiency as understood by a panel of experts in these areas. During the second stage of the siting process, sites would be evaluated for their social suitability. An attempt would be made to identify the effects of a possible siting decision as well as an understanding of the public preferences for tradeoffs among these impacts. One potential preference, for example, might be local compensation for the impact costs. In this stage, issues such as the loss of wetlands, impacts on open space and recreational use of lands, historical and archaeological characteristics, traffic, land acquisition and development costs, effects on costs of other business functions, and aesthetic impacts would be considered.

The key to this second stage is the development of a ranking scheme that assigns to each site characteristic a weight reflecting the relative importance of the characteristic to the community. For example, loss of an acre of wetlands might be weighted as 1.0, while an increase in traffic that results in a 5 percent increase in driving time might be weighted as 1.43. The challenge, as the authors note, is to develop a system of weights that provides a reasonably good approximation of public preference. These authors suggest that a modified polling process (similar to that used to develop or test a concept's or instrument's face validity, but one used by panels of citizens rather than committees of experts) would likely be sufficient to develop an adequate weighing scheme.[2] Alternatively, some researchers have developed elaborate surveys that outline numerous potential paired comparisons of various values that might be affected by the siting of a noxious facility. In one type of paired comparison, survey respondents are asked to choose between two sites that are similar in all respects but for one tradeoff characteristic (such as two acres of woods versus a half-acre of wetlands). By analyzing a sufficient number of these trade-off choices, researchers believe that it is possible to estimate the difference in utility between development of one site versus development of another.[3]

The outcome of the social suitability stage of the siting process is a short list of "socially preferred" sites. They argue that the social suitability stage they propose is the "primary tool by which the proposed approach improves on the efficiency of the site selection process." Finally, in stage three, Swallow and his colleagues propose using a combination of the inverse auction proposed by Herbert Inhabler, among others, along with a referendum process for determining the appropriate bid (for compensation) that the community will accept.[4]

Policy options like the one proposed afford a number of benefits, but they do not provide a fully satisfactory realization or integration of the four basic or touchstone values—equity, efficiency, community viability and environmental quality—by which policy options are likely to be judged. The benefits include an explicit recognition of the need to protect very basic environmental qualities. One suspects that in doing so, long-range economic efficiency would also be promoted, even though in the short run, exclusion of environmentally sensitive sites might present some economic costs. The second stage of the process, moreover, appears to give explicit recognition to, and provide a plausible measurement of, social values that are aligned in large measure with the "community viability" criteria. Again, the use of econometric measures of trade-offs and "willingness to pay" provides some assurance that community viability is achieved in a way that is economically efficient. Finally, the compensation mechanism that is assumed to occur in cases where the proposed developer must bid for the right to place a facility in specific communities provides some recognition of the need to address the equity issue in the siting of LULUs. The inverse auction, moreover, results in bids that are economically efficient from the point of view of the allocation of resources.

In other respects, however, the policy option offered by Swallow and others is less than fully satisfactory, especially from an equity criterion perspective. First, and to repeat an earlier criticism, without other policy mechanisms in place (such as constraints on the unequal distribution of income), auction markets will not solve the problem of external social costs being generated by the concentration of LULUs within select neighborhoods or community areas.[5] Because poor communities will tend to have a greater need for income, they will be more tempted by the proposed compensation. Meager as it might end up being, it is more than these communities now receive for accepting LULUs. Yet, precisely because of their great need, these needy communities are likely to place a much higher discount rate on the potential for long-term or future damage to the environment, community viability, or human health.

A similar process can be seen in the development of the weights by which social suitability is thought to be identified. The weights are developed in the abstract by a community or a number of communities as a whole. However, the impact of siting of facilities is often much more geographically specific. It is not that the estimation of public preferences is skewed by this fact; rather, it is the result of using these weights that leads to skewed outcomes. For example, the public will generally agree that placing a noxious facility next to another noxious facility will likely be more socially suitable than placing such a facility next to a park or a place of natural beauty. When this discovery is translated into suitable sites, however, it is likely to mean that a number of suitable sites will be discovered in poor neighborhoods that border existing noxious facilities, while few suitable sites will be discovered in more "preferred" areas where the wealthy have been able to preserve features such as open space, natural beauty, and historic qualities. Hence, what appears to be a perfectly neutral process is likely to systematically choose poorer communities, and poorer neighborhoods within communities as the most socially suitable site. While it can be argued that the poor essentially "agreed with the decision-making criteria, and explicitly in stage three with the decision itself," the process hardly meets the highest standards of social justice.

Along these same lines, simply because a community as a whole agrees to the siting of a noxious facility does not mean that the specific community of persons being negatively affected by the facility agrees with the decision. Of course, the compensation provided through the inverse auction process could reimburse those affected by the loss, but there is no guarantee that this compensation is adequate because the persons most directly affected were not given any special power with respect to being able to accept or reject the proposed compensation.

Finally, although the integrated siting process proposed by Swallow and others suggests a number of valuable techniques that might be transferred to other LULU siting issues, as it is currently conceived, this process may have limited potential as a policy option for treating such LULU issues as the siting of community care homes, the intrusion of large-scale industrial plants or businesses that are not necessarily noxious in the ordinary sense, the need for stable multiple-use land development, or even the placement of schools within a community.

FRAMEWORK POLICIES IN THE REGULATION-DEREGULATION DEBATE

Two Responses to the Failure of Regulation and Deregulation

As the Lowry and Ferguson study (reviewed in Chapter 5) of land-use regulation suggests,[6] it may be beneficial to search for policies that lie between the extremes of a full deregulation or re-regulation response. Such alternative policies would borrow some of the reasoning from the two dominant responses and suggest that, while the levels of supply and demand need to flow freely (as market advocates would argue), there also needs to be a way to: (1) check speculation and boom-bust cycles; (2) ensure that all the external social costs in the decision to locate a LULU are considered; and (3) ensure that the most powerful interests in a community bear their share of unwanted development. In European social market economies, these alternatives have often been identified as "framework" policies. A framework policy, ideally, promotes smooth and steady adjustments in markets while respecting social investments and community life. Often such framework policies are what comparative political economists refer to when they describe social market economies. However, in a larger sense, framework policies refer both to policies that frame the arena in which individuals will function in supply and demand relationships and policies that create or authorize networks of institutions (or collective-choice arrangements) that mediate between citizens and their governments.[7] The social-democratic and social-republican ideologies and practices described in the previous chapter suggest two possible streams of inspiration for framework policies. In the following discussions, the term "framework policy" will be used to denote those policies (generally derived from both social-republican and social-democratic thought) that identify who can be a market participant (individuals or institutions) and the scale of the market (neighborhood, community, regional, state, national or global), while the term "organized market," which is a sort of a subform of framework policies, will denote those policies (generally drawn from social democratic thought) that address only the scope of the market (see Table 4).0

Building market frames or organizing markets requires a high level of sensitivity to the public interest as a whole, while acknowledging and respecting the power of markets to improve the lives and fortunes of individuals. Framework building is different from re-regulation in that, while frameworks shape and sometimes limit the scope and scale of markets, they allow, and indeed encourage, free play of market forces within the defined framework. Framework policies, as opposed to traditional regulatory policies, are not designed to encourage or discourage the choice of particular goods and services; instead, they are used to create a market for a good or service that may not exist without the framework.

Some, but not all, zoning ordinances and standard setting policies are classic examples of framework policies in that they help create a market that might not otherwise exist. In the case of zoning, the market for residential property, for example, is improved if the purchaser is assured that a polluting industry is not likely to set up shop next door. Zoning laws in this regard create a new property right even as they limit rights to resell or use the property for commercial purposes. As Hernando de Soto has shown in his book *The Other Path*, establishment of property rights is essential to the creation of a market and motivation to improve property.[8] Without some zoning-like protections, residents would be less likely to invest in their properties to any great extent as they would be fearful that, for instance, a landfill might be placed next door, thus reducing the value of their investment. With zoning protection, however, property owners feel secure that their investment will not be lost because of a neighbor's incompatible property use.[9] The ability of historic preservation ordinances to increase property values is only the latest example of how policies that frame property rights can help create or define a new property and a new market (for historical sites), and thereby increase the value of existing property.[10]

Table 4: Policy Approaches for Addressing LULU Problems

	Traditional Regulation	Free Markets	Organized Markets	Framework Policies
Decision-Making	Political a. through adversarial processes b. through unitary processes.	Individual market participants make the decision (e.g., state purchases property for detention center from land owner willing to sell).	Purchasers of LULU development rights are an organized entity (e.g., an incorporated community or neighborhood jurisdiction)	Purchasers of LULU development rights are individuals, but the scope of development is restricted by political (or framework) decision makers, while sub-jurisdictions such as neighborhood-level institutions are authorized to conduct auctions or shape the nature of the proposed development. Neighborhoods adopt unitary approaches to collective action, but also allow auctions for development rights.
Level of Restrictions on LULU Land Use Rights	Micro-level restrictions (e.g., cannot purchase rights to develop land for unzoned use).	No restrictions	Level of restrictions depends on the market power of neighborhoods or community institutions	Macro-level decision-makers place restrictions on the number of LULU developments that can occur within any one neighborhood (i.e., set a scale frame). Within this frame, a neighborhood-sized market for such development exists and is unrestricted.

Table 4: Policy Approaches for Addressing LULU Problems

	Traditional Regulation	Free Markets	Organized Markets	Framework Policies
Who Benefits?	Often the most powerful locally organized interests, usually the organized business interests.	Individuals with sufficient wealth to live in protected, high-priced areas and selected individual property owners who sell their property to a LULU developer (and who do not currently live or expect to live in the LULU affected area).	Neighborhoods or communities with both a high level of wealth or resources and a high level of organization.	Neighborhoods that already have a higher than equitable share of LULUs; individuals with sufficient wealth to purchase development rights or the right to be free from a neighborhood-level LULU; impacted neighbors who receive the added value from the auctioned LULU development right; and the public, which receives the benefits of more workable neighborhoods that are better able to socialize children and secure individual well-being.
Potential Means of Dealing with External Social Costs	LULU location decisions are adjusted on a case-by- case basis by elected representatives responding to constituent pressure.	An estimation of the social cost is made by analyzing property value variations due to LULU impacts and property taxes are adjusted upward on those owners who live in areas that are found not to bear their share of social costs.	Organized social units enter into inverse auctions (where LULU developers keep bidding until the first community accepts a bid). Members of the community are expected to consider social costs in their reactions to particular bid levels.	Social externality costs are distributed equally across small-scale jurisdictions; within these micro-jurisdictions, individuals and organized social units may be able to use unitary or negotiated processes to further refine the distribution of or further alleviate external social costs.

Updating the Framework over Time

Unfortunately, understanding the difference between framework policies and more debilitating regulatory policies is not always easy. While many zoning ordinances have framework qualities, many other such ordinances and policies cross the line and become highly regulatory, skewing consumer choices among goods and affecting the efficiency of how goods and services are allocated to different uses. Additionally, over time policies that were once framework policies can become highly regulatory due to changes in the technological or social environment. For example, the use of zoning ordinances to create residential property that is protected from commercial intrusion has in many American cities resulted in lifeless suburban zones that force excessive, inefficient use of automobiles and isolate age and income groups as well as our personal lives from more public- and work-oriented spaces. While many of these ordinances were designed to protect residences from factories that have traditionally been noisy, polluting, and large-scale, they have also excluded modern, small, quiet, non-polluting workshops and offices from becoming part of multiuse neighborhoods. As more work occurs in these light service industries, the original rationale for some of these zoning laws has been lost. Similarly, some zoning ordinances have been structured so narrowly as to isolate rich from poor (through lot size and building size requirements), old from young (through single-family zoning and restrictions on "granny flats"), and renters from owners (through restrictions on subletting or single-family restrictions). [11]

Framework Policies: A Tree with Many Branches

Because hybrid policies tend to have multiple sources of ideologically based inspiration, the second type of hybrid policy—implementing frameworks for either or both land-use markets and land-use politics—has been operationalized in more than a single manner. Below, I discuss three existing proposals for framework-like alternatives to the traditional system of land-use governance:

1. An auction-like mechanism for the siting of LULUs that is dependent on equal initial positions of those participating in the action, rather than on the economic power that usually determines the outcome of LULU-type auctions.
2. A policy proposal put forth by Robert Nelson that is similar in some respect to the ideas put forth by Swallow and other advocates of the community auction for LULUs, but is designed to address more adequately the problem of within-community equity. Nelson's alternative has strong roots in communitarian ideas for neighborhood-level governance and in social-democratic efforts to organize markets.[12]

3. Another alternative, put forth by Douglas Kmiec, that takes a different—more classic liberal in some ways and more social-republican in others—approach to developing a framework for land-use governance. [13]

Unfortunately, in the latter two of these framework-like governance systems, equity issues with regard to the siting of LULUs appear to be only an afterthought, and while equity is a primary consideration in the first of these proposals, pragmatic considerations make use of this policy unlikely. Hence, following the discussion of these examples of framework-like policies, I outline a sample or draft framework approach that is fashioned to address equity issues as well as a broader range of LULU problems—not just the placement of obviously noxious facilities, but also problems related to the segregation of residential, business, and waste disposal land uses and the disruptions caused by systematic cycles of development and decline in the built environment.

An Equal Initial Position Auction

The chief impediment to market-mimicking mechanisms for the distribution of LULUs among communities is the essential unfairness or inequality in initial positions of the communities participating in the bidding. Affluent communities can always escape hosting a LULU by out-bidding poorer communities. Drawing on Ronald Dworkin's work on the meaning of equality, law Professor Vicki Been has suggested that an auction mechanism using an equal distribution of "vetos votes" would represent, in fairness terms, a substantial improvement over the typical LULU auction mechanism.[14] Been describes the equal initial position auction:

> For example, suppose there are five communities of equal population and land area and there are fifteen LULUs, ranging from a home for juvenile delinquents to a low-level radioactive waste dump. Each community would be allocated ten veto chips. [Each community's share of currency could be based upon the community's population, land area, or some other measure.] The auctioneer would begin by announcing that a particular LULU would be randomly distributed among the communities, but the highest bidder could remove itself from the eligible pool. If community A bids two chips to avoid it, B bids three, and C bids four, C "wins" the veto, paying four of its chips to disqualify itself from the selection process. Communities A, B, and D and E are still eligible, unless one wants to bid again. Suppose that A and E each again bid two, and B bids three; B is then eliminated, and so on, until none of the eligible communities wishes to veto the LULU. It is then randomly distributed among them. The process repeats for the next LULU. Once

a community spends its ten veto chips, it is eligible for all remaining LULUs. The auction ends once all LULUs have been distributed.[15]

While the equal initial position auction would seem to provide a very viable solution to the LULU burden-sharing problem, Been notes a number of practical barriers to implementing this solution. Some of these barriers, such as the need to define neighborhood, and the need to decide whether a neighborhood that is responsible for generating a need for the LULU should receive less veto power than other neighborhoods, represent ethical and implementation barriers that plague most LULU burden-sharing schemes. One barrier to implementing the equal initial position auction, however, is somewhat unique to this scheme and may be insurmountable. That is, this auction model requires that the participants have knowledge of the number and type of LULUs that will be sited in the future. Projection of this type seem to be beyond the current capabilities of planning departments. As Been suggests, "Unless auction prices factor in the potential for error, those neighborhoods that 'buy' LULUs that never materialize will receive a windfall compared to those that 'buy' LULUs that do materialize."[16] Also, to result in a fair distribution, this auction model, like the more common auction schemes, would require that all participating neighborhoods have an equal knowledge of the risks that particular LULUs represent and would require the design of a cost-effective auctioning mechanism. Finally, even though this auction model might be adequate to address problems related to an initial distribution of LULUs, it would require substantial adaptation if it were to be able to handle LULU policymaking where there may already exist an unequal distribution of LULUs. Unfortunately, the current problem situation is one characterized by such an unequal distribution of LULUs.

Several other features of this initial position auction policy should be noted. First, the policy has an appealing feature—its ability to consider the potential of communities having different tastes in LULUs—that should be considered in designing other LULU burden-sharing policies. However, another feature of this proposal—its take-it-or-leave-it proposition—does not allow for the kind of flexibility that one would desire in a LULU-siting policy. That is, instead of a community having to decide to accept or reject particular LULU sites (under threat of having to accept other sites), it might be valuable if the policy could allow some negotiations between the community and the LULU site developer as to particular features of the proposed facility or land use. The auction proposal is less than ideal in this regard.

A Classic Liberal-Oriented Framework Policy with a Henry Georgian Twist

Douglas Kmiec's analysis of the existing system of zoning sums up a number of the criticisms of zoning made in this book.[17] Kmiec complains that the existing system is "procedurally unfair" because it favors a self-selected group of neighbors over the larger interests of consumers or specific landowners; is "distributionally unfair" because it benefits some property owners while harming others; is "inefficient as a mechanism for internalizing harmful spillovers" because the costs of setting up and administering the system of controls often outweigh the value of the protection that is achieved, especially when the land market itself can often achieve a major portion of this protection without the administrative costs,[18] or when the specific standards make it impossible to experiment with more creative solutions such as clustered development; is "inflexible" because it is based on generalized prohibitions that do not allow for development of particular mixed-use facilities with desirable attributes if the use is generally prohibited (such as an apartment complex that preserves open space); and is "uncertain"[19] in that zoning changes can undermine the value of investments made on the basis of existing standards.[20]

Kmiec proposes a modified market alternative to the existing system of zoning that addresses most of the problems he lists. Kmiec's alternative land-use governance system is based on the idea that there are two basic policy options for controlling the degree to which individuals can use zoning to foster their own interests: Either directly authorize neighborhood-level control or expressly prohibit it. Kmiec chooses the latter option and attempts to design a "free enterprise development system" for eliminating the role of neighbors beyond an initial framework-setting process in which "land-use intensity" ratings schedules, maximums, and other general policies would be set. Kmiec's scheme also includes a modified version of Henry George's single tax on land.[21] Along the lines Henry George suggested over a hundred years ago, Kmiec would require developers to pay for the "unearned increment" of the increase in value of the land that occurs because of their higher-than-baseline intensity use of the land. The system would work as follows:

> After land-use intensity schedules had been developed for four basic types of projects—residential, commercial, industrial, and mixed-use—owners of undeveloped land, all of which is now zoned as open space/agricultural, would select the desired intensity of use for the development project they propose. The schedule would indicate a maximum density (such as a floor-space-to-land-available ratio) permitted for each type of development, and as long as a developer's project was within that maximum, the project would be approved. That is, the public would not get a chance to challenge any specific development, but would only be allowed to set overall intensity-of-use schedules and community-wide maximums. However, the framework part of Kmiec's alternative is based on the Georgian twist: That is, the developer would have to pay the difference between the land value prior

> to the newly permitted intensity of use and the value after the more intense-use development had been built.

As part of the scheme, the public would be obligated to provide the public infrastructure necessary for the development to reach the chosen intensity of use. The public would be allowed, however, to keep the difference between the costs of the added infrastructure and the total revenue that was collected from the developer (that is, the amount of exaction would not be limited to what is needed to address the specific impact of the development).

Kmiec's plan eliminates the temptation for corrupt bargains because developers decisions to build will not depend on the potential of a zoning change, but only on whether the investment can pay for itself over and above the unearned or speculative value of development that is inherent in the existing system of zoning. Under Kmiec's alternative policy, there is no public windfall or wipeout to be conferred by zoning decisions—only the rational choice of individual developers acting within the market. However, it should be noted that while Kmiec's plan can broadly be categorized as classic liberal in character, it also represents a framework policy of sorts because it implicitly retains collective control over development, by zoning all undeveloped land as agricultural/open space, while allowing a free flow of supply and demand about specific development decisions.

Douglas Kmiec has laid out an innovative framework policy, one that leans heavily on classic liberal ideas of general rules, individual choice, and a recognition of the need to reduce the passage of specific rules that favor particular individual interests. Kmiec attempts to address the corruption of classic liberal ideals that has taken place because interest group liberalism has allowed private interests to affect public decisions beyond the legislative arena. He suggests that by taking all but the most general decisions (that is, how much overall growth and intensity of growth will be allowed) and the traditionally recognized nuisance regulations out of the hands of public decision-makers, thereby leaving the specific decisions about development to the market, the potential for corrupt bargains between public officials and private interests is eliminated. Kmiec argues that his alternative system would not encourage corrupt behavior because it would leave nothing for public officials and developers to bargain over.

While Kmiec's proposal has a number of highly innovative features and addresses most of the problems with the existing system of zoning, this policy option is weak in two respects. First, it does not address the issue of equity or the fairness of the siting of existing or future LULUs. As such, the implementation of Kmiec's proposal would probably do little to reduce the accumulative and concentrated effect of LULUs (both environmental and social) on neighborhoods where less affluent and minority citizens reside. Kmiec does recognize that "neighbors have used zoning to foster their individual interests rather than public policy," but coming from a classic liberal perspective, he fails to fully recognize that some groups of neighbors have been consistently more able to foster their interests better than other groups of neighbors. This more communitarian insight would suggest a somewhat different policy alternative from that proposed by Kmiec. Because Kmiec does not recognize the possibility that free markets in land, even those from which unearned and speculative profits have been eliminated, can result in agglomeration effects of the sort that lead to social injustice and environmental racism, his solution to the LULU problem is ultimately unsatisfactory. Loosely speaking, Kmiec's alternative system generally represents an innovation in the classic liberal tradition; however, because he includes the Georgian twist of exacting the unearned increments of land use "rents," Kmiec's alternative also has social-republican qualities. As a particularly creative alternative in these respects, many of Kmiec's ideas have been incorporated in the sample framework policy developed below.

A second weakness of Kmiec's proposal is its assumption that a general or comprehensive land-use plan—one that at a minimum outlines four very basic land-use zones—can meet the tests for democratic legitimacy. All the arguments that Carol Rose and others have made against "plan jurisprudence" and the idea that objective, legitimate, and consistent land-use planning can occur and will be used to guide zoning decisions also apply to Kmiec's assumptions. In essence, while Kmiec goes a long way toward radical reform of current zoning policies, he does not question the assumption that a general land-use plan will result in some broadly defined zones. Essentially, Kmiec retains the logical and legal structure of zoning, but he changes substantially the scale at which zoning occurs and the procedure for attaining development rights within these broadly defined zones.

A Somewhat Communitarian Alternative

If Kmiec chooses to eliminate the role of neighbors in land-use decision making, Robert Nelson has taken the opposite tack to the problem of private interests in the development of land-use controls; that is, he suggests that neighborhood associations be given full authority over development decisions within the neighborhood.[22] Nelson argues that even though zoning is legally based on nuisance law and government's police powers, most zoning has gone far beyond these "legal fictions" and is conducted in accordance with the expressed desires of residents for greater residential amenities. By eliminating the legal fictions and devolving a full set of land and environmental control rights directly to neighborhood groups, a new collective property right is created with some particular advantages. First, such a system of collective exercise of control over neighborhood quality would provide for greater certainty among residents that their neighborhood would receive the protections that traditional zoning is thought to provide but that occasionally does not, because of arbitrary zoning changes or political manipulation of variance procedures. Second, the private, but collective, tenure of rights to development provides a check on governmental police powers that under current zoning practices appear to have few limits. Third, along the lines suggested by Mansbridge and others, neighborhood control over land use would support democratic values and education as well as a bulwark against the movement toward "huge, dehumanized scale in social organization."[23] The fourth, and for Nelson, most important advantage of neighborhood ownership of development rights is that such a tenure scheme would provide a mechanism—the sale of neighborhood zoning rights—for neighborhoods to change in ways that are orderly and that provide for the protection of residents against arbitrary and piecemeal deterioration of residential amenities. Ordinarily, as pressures and monetary incentives for development build, they become too strong for some neighbors to resist. The key problem with traditional zoning, Nelson suggests, is that customary agreement among neighbors about protecting neighborhoods against unwanted land uses breaks down during periods of transition. The local government zoning administrators at this point "are subject to intense developer pressures, to conflicting pressures from individual neighborhood residents, and sometimes even to large bribe offers."[24] Establishing collective and sellable rights to development can remove many of the problems associated with transition by allowing neighborhood associations to control directly the scope and timing of the transition and by allowing developers to negotiate directly a purchase price for development rights to the entire neighborhood area. This procedure would substantially reduce the high transaction costs that currently characterize exchanges of property in the context of neighborhood transition. Also, allowing such negotiations would enable neighborhoods to avoid the piecemeal neighborhood disintegration that takes place as individual residents break ranks and sell their property to developers, leaving remaining residents worse off and with even greater temptations to get their share of development profits while they can. As Nelson points out, this piecemeal development dynamic results in both an ad hoc distribution of rewards and punishments for land owners, depending on when they sell their property, and highly disordered and visually unintegrated and unappealing developments.

Nelson's new tenure system of collective rights to development can be categorized as a social market type of ideological hybrid of communitarian and classic liberal concepts. As with social markets or social-democratic mechanisms, Nelson's innovation is to organize new ownership rights around socially defined groups. Also as with social market organization, once the group property or control rights are established, the market is otherwise free to develop. The specific organization of social rights, unfortunately, can sometimes leave certain groups unrecognized and without market power or other protections against market forces. When this occurs, social markets can create new inequities as they alleviate old ones. Nelson's new tenure system, while offering a number of desirable features, does not effectively or fully address the equity problem posed by the tendency for LULU-type developments to be concentrated in less affluent neighborhoods. Hence, many of the arguments made against the inverse auction system for the siting of LULUs within communities can also be made against Nelson's new collective tenure system—a system that basically establishes collective rights to development at the neighborhood level, rather than community level.

A major difference between Nelson's new tenure system and the sample framework policy to be presented below is that Nelson is much more sanguine about the "unavoidability" of neighborhood decline. Whereas he sees declining neighborhoods as serving some basic social purposes (for example, they provide "cheap housing, . . . places for garages, filling stations, and other such uses that have to be located somewhere")[25] and as being unaffected by zoning-based attempts to halt the process of decline, the framework policy presented below is designed with the specific purpose of halting such neighborhood decline.

REFINING THE FRAMEWORK FOR GOVERNING LULUS

While an equal distribution of neighborhood market power (enabling a free but fair market for LULU development rights) may be beyond political feasibility and require a degree of economic leveling that would be rejected by all but the most dedicated communitarians, creation of a social-republican type of framed market could provide a politically viable means of ensuring that the external costs of LULU siting decisions are not borne disproportionately by the poor and unorganized. That is, by limiting the market for LULU-like development rights to those who reside in the affected neighborhood and by placing a total (but movable) cap on such developments, the power of concentrated, absentee capital to overwhelm a single area with numerous LULU developments can potentially be restrained. As long as a neighborhood has more than its fair share of LULUs, further developments of a LULU type would have to be directed to those neighborhoods that have not reached the designated ceiling for LULU developments.

While distribution of market power provides naturally for fair pricing in a market (that is, it provides for a sort of built-in governance of the market), a framed market is one that involves a sort of social or artificial governor on the market. Such a governor-like mechanism can take a number of forms. Jane Jacobs, for example, has suggested that to stop the cancerous-like growth in mono-use development (the type of development that may raise property values at first but that eventually leads to decline), cities might want to institute a limited set of development rights that could be auctioned off to developers in a particular area. The limitation would be based on the proportion of buildings that were over a particular age, and would result in each area maintaining a certain percentage of old, lower-rent buildings. As development in one area reached its limits, developers would be forced to focus their efforts on another, more neglected area.

While the metaphor of the frame or governor to a market engine might suggest a number of specific regulations that could be enacted, framework policy experience in European states, especially Germany, indicates that instead of government simply setting a standard or rule (such as prohibiting buildings over 30 feet high), it is often more valuable to establish or authorize mediating or para-public institutions that can create and adapt standards to particular circumstances. Unfortunately from the standpoint of democratic values, European para-public institutions, which tend to be large scale and sometime unrepresentative of all the interests in society, may not provide the best model for controling the expansionary tendencies of capitalism. Neighborhood-sized institutions nested within more regional, state, and perhaps national levels of neighborhood councils and generally operated on principles of unitary democracy might be a better model for American framework policies. With respect to addressing the LULU problem, these institutions would be charged with balancing property rights with responsibilities and externality costs.

A Draft Framework Policy for LULU Problems

The primary policy assumption made in developing the following framework is the elimination of nearly all other zoning restrictions with perhaps the exception of a category of heavy industry that cannot be economically reduced in size or impact to a more human scale. At its simplest, a framework for the market in unwanted land uses should involve:

1. Development of a system of generalized weights or "LULU credits" based on public preferences for avoiding particular types of LULUs.

   The term "credits" is used in the sense that under this policy, neighborhoods will get credit for having taken on the burden of being a host to a LULU. In developing such a system, one could adapt one of the methodologies suggested by Swallow (such as ranked comparisons). However, the focus of the system of weights would be different; instead of coming up with measurements, as Swallow suggests, of the value of particularly desirable features in the existing environment to determine how those features might be affected by the siting of particular LULU facilities, the system of generalized LULU credits or weights would be used to determine how the public would generally assess the impact costs of different types of LULUs that might be located adjacent to their residence. The overall purpose of developing this system of LULU weights would be to get people to compare the impacts of different types of LULUs regardless of how particular LULUs might affect particular environmental features. The creation of a common and abstract scale for weighing the impacts of LULUs is not meant as a means of ignoring the issue of "particular" LULU impacts being unique; other parts of this sample framework policy are designed to allow a flexible response to unique or particular LULU impacts. Rather, building a system of LULU credits is designed to allow for the establishment of a type of rough justice between and among neighborhoods with respect to burden sharing.

Because one of the purposes of this framework policy would be to begin to allow mixed-use development, but also to stabilize such development before it transforms a favorably located, single-use residential area into a single-use business area, the system of generalized weights would be developed for all purposes that exceeded a basic single-family type of development. That is, multifamily housing, apartments, offices, small businesses and institutions, and even large-scale industrial and transportation developments would be included in the system of weights. The likely outcome of this process would be a range of LULU-type weights that might extend from 1.0 for additional "granny flats" to 3.0 for an elementary school, to 4.0 for a typical small business, to 30.0 or more for a large-scale industrial site or sanitary landfill, with even higher weights for toxic waste disposal facilities. The system of weights would be developed independently of any proposed use for the weights in deciding on the placement of particular LULU facilities. People would generally choose their preferences behind a "veil of ignorance" with respect to the particular LULU-siting situations they might face in the future.[26] As this rating system will apply to future sitings of LULUs, most neighborhoods, not knowing the potential for their being a site in the future, would likely be able to agree on a rating scale.

2. Establishing, defining, and authorizing a number of neighborhood or even sub-neighborhood-size jurisdictions.

This step in setting up a framework for regulating LULU development is probably the most important in that the preferred governance rules from an equity perspective for actual LULU siting might differ, depending on the nature of the group that is created through the drawing of boundaries. For example, suppose that boundaries are drawn in such a way as to minimize the differential between the wealth and incomes of those who will reside in the neighborhood-sized polity. Given the dominant residential land-use pattern described by Fowler—of residential areas developed and segregated by income levels—this type of boundary drawing is not unfeasible. Considering this homogeneous neighborhood situation, within-the-neighborhood, market mechanisms for deciding on LULU sitings (given the other features of the framework described below) would not unduly undermine equity values. All residents would be able to use their dollar votes in an equitable manner to indicate their desire to acquire LULU development rights, or alternatively, LULU avoidance rights. However, if neighborhood boundaries are drawn in such a way as to provide a mix of residents with different income levels, the market mechanism could lead to substantial equity problems along the lines of those described in the above discussion of the inverse auction among communities for LULUs. Additionally, an argument could be made that the entire framework policy approach would be voided if boundaries were drawn in such a way as to include a mix of residents with different income levels, because this would most likely disguise the fact that most LULU-type facilities are located adjacent to poorer residents in the community. Once this fact is disguised through a sort of LULU gerrymandering, the effect of the framework policy (to limit new LULU development to areas that do not already have a disproportionate share of such development) is muted. One way of avoiding this problem would be for the more macro-level of government that is responsible for the design of the framework to require that the basic LULU jurisdiction be relatively small (for example, having a contiguous population of less than 300 people). Given the dominant pattern of residential housing, such a small size would likely result in a population with a fairly even distribution of wealth and income. Moreover, such a size would support the development of a face-to-face, unitary democracy approach to LULU problems within the neighborhood.[27]

To address the problem of spillovers between neighborhood-sized jurisdictions, it might make sense to have the geographical area in which LULU developments will be counted, rated, and "credited" to particular neighborhoods (see feature 4 below) be more extensive than the neighborhood jurisdiction itself. That is, for the purposes of determining whether or not a particular neighborhood was being subjected to more than its share of negative impacts from LULUs, a boundary line might be drawn, for example, a half-mile outside the neighborhood boundary line. One result of doing this would be to reduce the incentives for other neighborhoods to site all of their LULUs at the neighborhood boundaries, rather than across the jurisdiction as a whole. The incentive structure would work in this manner because siting LULUs only at the edges of a neighborhood would result in that neighborhood "sharing" its "LULU credits" with another neighborhood. This is not desirable within the sample framework policy because the policy tends to reward relative neighborhood position with respect to LULU burden-sharing, rather than a neighborhood reaching some sort of absolute standard of burden-sharing.

3. Designation of the "governors" and "users" of LULU development rights.

A second key feature of boundary drawing with respect to the governance of LULU-type "common detriment," is the designation of those to be included in the decision making about LULU developments or who will be using potentially purchasable development rights. It is at this point that social-democratic and social-republican approaches to framework policies diverge. While social-democrats would tend to designate the owners of residential property as the only legitimate members of the governance body, social-republicans would likely differ on this score. That is, they would probably invoke the principle of "the holder [of a governance right] bearing a relation of potential active participation in a group or community constituted by the property"[28] and declare that only members who are legitimate residents in the neighborhood would be citizens of the neighborhood-level LULU-governance polity. Generally following the logic of innovative compromise, one might propose a hybrid of these two rules: allowing both sets of parties or interests to be members of the governance body, or structuring the rules such that only actual residents were allowed to participate in certain decisions, only owners in other decisions, and resident owners, non-resident owners, and renters in other decisions.[29]

4. Calculating for each neighborhood a LULU-development score or LULU rating that indicates the current aggregate level of LULU sitings within each particular jurisdiction.

This operation could be easily conducted by institutions with sophisticated geographical information systems (GIS) that are capable of identifying all the relevant features and factors associated with land use, including but not limited to size of lots and facilities, topological, geological, and hydrological features of the land, and facility pollution emissions and diffusion patterns.[30]

5. Setting a cap and other "regulators" on the development of LULUs.

The cap feature of the framework would essentially forbid the siting of any more LULUs in neighborhoods that have accumulated more than the maximum set of LULU points or weights. Newer LULUs would have to be placed in neighborhoods that have a lower level of LULU points. To further direct development toward those neighborhoods that currently have the least amount of LULU development, two approaches are feasible: (1) set the cap annually such that only the neighborhoods with the least amount of LULU development are included in the category of neighborhoods eligible for development; or (2) set up a sliding scale fee system that will make it more costly to develop in neighborhoods that are approaching the development ceiling.

Although the overall framework policy is designed to achieve a greater equity in terms of sharing the social and environmental burdens of modern life, it is possible to design the framework policy such that it also supports the achievement of other goals. For example, by designing some separate "caps" or "governors" that set proportional limits for different types of developments (such as offices, schools, small stores, gas stations, or waste disposal facilities) in addition to the overall LULU-development caps and governors, the framework could be adapted to guide more directly facilities development toward more multiple use.[31]

The existence of such caps would provide an additional incentive for communities to follow the lead of Ventura, California, in conducting and using pollution reduction audits.[32] Such audits inventory whether a company is doing all it can to reduce emissions and waste. As development is stymied in certain areas because of a cap that is linked to pollution levels, there would exist incentives for developers to encourage such companies to take the pollution control steps that are available to them. As development in capped areas became more desirable, developers might themselves begin to foot some of the bill for pollution control.

6. Framing a set of governance rules for deciding how development rights will be allocated among those who wish to develop their property.

Framework policies, unfortunately, do not eliminate the need to choose between market or auction-based allocation rules or political rules such as various types of unitary or adversarial approaches to decision making. As suggested in guideline 2 above, setting up a within-jurisdiction market for the remaining LULU development rights would be a plausible governance rule option for neighborhoods whose residents generally hold equal economic power in a potential market. In this instance, persons wanting to sell their property to an agent for a LULU would bid with other property owners for this right. In these cases, moreover, it would be possible to use the proceeds from the auction to compensate those whose properties were most severely affected or devalued as a result of their proximity to the LULU.

In situations where economic power is not roughly equivalent, the market approach to neighborhood governance would obviously involve some trade-offs with respect to the equity criterion. However, because the market was framed at a neighborhood level, the reduction of equity due to market allocations would be far less than in an unorganized market.

Although neighborhood districts in the current land-use environment could probably be drawn in such a way as to create roughly equivalent economic power among the residents, this would not be the case in some communities. More important, it would not be the case in a more ideal society where income and economic power would be generally irrelevant to choice of residential location. Also, as the framework governance scheme began to have its intended effects over time, fewer and fewer neighborhoods would likely be characterized by income homogeneity. In these instances, it might not be the best policy to presume a social-democratic market solution to LULU siting problems. Instead, one might want to consider a more social-republican property solution. This solution would collectivize at the neighborhood level LULU development rights and would use unitary approaches to decide how these rights might be allocated. While unitary approaches often break down at the community-wide level and become mere window-dressing at levels above the size of a small township, the key assumptions and features of unitary democracy (common interest, equivalent status, consensus, face-to-face discussion) would seem to be realizable in neighborhood governance around land-use issues. The divergence between the interests of absentee landlords and resident tenants might present a counter-example to this generalization. However, given the realities of the current land-use environment, the places where this divergence of interest are most obvious are likely to be the same places that either have reached or are soon likely to reach the near-term LULU development ceiling. Even if one assumes the opposite —that areas with a high rate of absentee ownership would also have a high level of LULU development rights left after implementation of the sample framework policy—it is not necessarily the case that unitary processes will fail. It may be that residents and absentee landlord can come to some agreement about the most "desirable" pattern of potential LULU development that will involve, all things being equal, a win-win pattern of benefits and costs. Additionally, unitary approaches do not preclude the use of market mechanisms. Some of the more fruitful purposes of a unitary approach might be related to designing means to mitigate the effects of LULUs and using the resources raised in the development rights auctions to do so.

Although unitary democracy approaches seem to fit the LULU governance framework situation being described here and would probably go some ways toward meeting what Jane Mansbridge describes as our hunger for a more soulful way of aggregating interests,[33] we should also be cautioned against choosing this governance rule based on the assumption that land-use interests will be harmonious, even at the neighborhood level. Only experience will determine if a more adversarial, majority-rule approach might not be needed to achieve the desired purposes.[34] Robert Nelson has suggested the use of multiple tiers of decision-making rules: Essentially, higher levels of consensus or super-majority votes would be needed for more severe types of land-use control.[35]

7. Using the ad valorem tax system to support the framework.

As the framework has been outlined so far, several practical problems quickly surface. The purchase price of development rights in wealthier neighborhoods is likely to be substantially higher than is the case in poorer neighborhoods. As a consequence, developers of LULU-type facilities will still gravitate toward the neighborhoods with the lowest development rights prices, leaving wealthier neighborhoods still free from assuming their fair share of the social burden of unwanted land uses. One method, suggested above, of dealing with this problem would be to place a sliding scale fee on the auction purchase price of development rights in neighborhoods approaching the development ceiling. The closer a neighborhood was to the ceiling, the higher the transaction fee. However, the more general use of ad valorem taxes might have a similar effect. The proposed framework is based on the assumption of the elimination of most zoning restrictions. Within the framework policy option, the traditional basis for ad valorem taxes—evaluation of the highest and best use—might continue to be used, but in a somewhat different manner. That is, in addition to properties being assessed on the basis of their current value and use, the neighborhood as a whole would be assessed for the value of LULU development rights. Areas that are currently LULU-free and being taxed at a rate implying that their highest and best use is single-family residential would be forced to pay substantial "development rights property" taxes for as long as properties in the neighborhood remained LULU-free. Additionally, the neighborhood could not use traditional exclusionary zoning to keep out unwanted development. Neighborhood residents and owners could, of course, outbid potential developers and retain for themselves the development rights. In doing so they might delay the day of reckoning, but hardly for long, because a rise in the bidding for development rights in a neighborhood results in a corresponding rise in the ad valorem taxes on development rights. That is, the more neighborhoods attempt to exclude LULU-type developments, the costlier it becomes.

This process, however, would seem to result in another problem. Many of the potential developers for community care institutions are state agencies that currently argue that they cannot afford to maintain a system of community care institutions even in the areas where land and housing are at rock bottom due to the deterioration of the neighborhood. How, then, they might ask, can they afford to bid for development rights in wealthy neighborhoods? It should be admitted, first of all, that a major part of this problem is due to the lack of state commitment of adequate resources to community care. General tax revenue, then, offers one possible solution. However, the framework could potentially deal with this problem as well. For example, proceeds from the sliding-scale fee system, most of whose users would be businesses, could be directed toward support for community care institutions. Additionally or alternatively, it might make sense to appropriate a percentage of the proceeds from the sale of development rights. One might not want to tax the proceeds from the sale of development rights in neighborhoods where there was already substantial

LULU development because these proceeds could be used to help maintain the neighborhood polity and to provide compensation for those most severely affected by new LULUs. However, in relatively LULU-free neighborhoods, a partial tax on these proceeds could be used to help community care organizations afford development rights in these neighborhoods. With the right sliding scale fee and tax on development rights system, it might be possible for LULU development processes to take on a self-regulating character. That is, the more macro-level of government need not interfere with the general process of LULU siting except where the siting would affect two or more jurisdictions.

8. Encouraging broad-scope neighborhood development through: (1) technical assistance and subsidies to neighborhood-level corporations that would support collective action on LULU development issues, broadly conceived; and (2) similar supports for neighborhood development in general conflict resolution, community development, and policymaking skills.

The literature on collective management of common pool resources suggests a number of features of successful collective choice institutions that would likely be encouraged by the proposed framework policy (see preceding chapter for a list of these features). For example, the policy calls for:

- delineation of clear neighborhood boundaries
- generally small-sized areas for collective choice
- a high degree of overlap between the location of the common good (or in the case of LULUs, "common detriment") and the collective choice boundaries
- the elimination of exclusionary mechanisms such as zoning and laissez-faire markets that would undermine the actualization of development rights as a common good
- a strengthening of the power of those who would benefit from retaining the common property and a relative weakening of those who would favor complete privatization
- a strengthening of the bonds of mutual obligation through the use of unitary decision-making processes
- the strengthening of incentives for neighbors to monitor the collective choice arrangement. In essence, the system rewards neighbors who uncover developments that have not been legitimated by a purchase or allocation of development rights. The incentive consists of everyone having to pay ad valorem taxes on unused development rights. Hence, residents have an incentive to look for illegitimate development because discovering it can lead to a reduction in their taxes. They also have an

incentive to consider allowing in the neighborhood legitimate and needed, but unwanted developments such as community care facilities.

However, in addition to these collective choice-supporting features of the framework policy, there is probably a need for a more macro-level of government to provide, at least at first, some support for and facilitation of:

- "arrangements for discussion." For example, providing funds for neighborhood-level civic centers, group facilitation, group decision technologies and the like.
- support for low-cost conflict-resolution mechanisms such as neighborhood dispute resolution centers, skilled mediators, and negotiations training. Support could come in the form of the provision of outside mediators or could involve the use of planners in mediator roles.[36]
- support for neighborhoods taking on "other tasks than simply the management of the common pool" detriment of LULUs. Such tasks include neighborhood watch, neighborhood recycling centers and composting, neighborhood coordination of police protection and patrols, and so forth. Additionally, the proposed neighborhood government associations could act like existing homeowner associations, assessing residents for common improvement of garden, street, lawn, and recreation areas and for neighborhood activities, if the community decided to provide these associations with such authority. These associations could be authorized to collectively control minor changes in properties as is the case with established historical districts and architectural design districts.[37]
- support for "educative republicanism." Educative republicanism is concerned with bridging private and public concerns and improving the deliberations about the common good by ensuring an infusion of fresh ideas and perspectives and reducing barriers, such as professional jargon, to such dialogue. With respect to LULU siting controversies, educative republicanism would call for some structured means of engaging neighborhood groups, citizen consumers (of community care or the products of an industrial site), and professional care givers or site developers. The purpose of creating such educative structures in addition to the neighborhood collective is to provide an antidote to neighborhood self-interest and to the distortions that are evident because of people's natural tendency to value risk-aversion above the potential for gain.[38] The combination of neighborhood self-interest and the relative saliency of risk aversion can often overcome reasonable siting proposals. For example, this combination will often win out against proponents of community care facilities, such as persons seeking services, their families, and professional caregivers, because the latter groups are joined only by a diffuse desire for a new benefit rather than a concrete risk to the values they currently

possess. Educative republicanism would suggest, for instance, that neighborhood associations act as advisory councils for supportive care facilities in the neighborhood. The New York legislature has considered measures to require such advisory committees for community residences housing persons with mental disabilities.[39] Having neighborhood groups engage in small-group dialogue with citizens in need of care and their care givers has been shown to promote a greater understanding of multiple perspectives and needs, to reduce the "us-versus-them" dynamic driving conflicts over facilities siting, and to mitigate the tendency of neighborhood groups to view persons with special care needs as different or as a threat to safety and property values.[40] Proponents of an educative republican approach to NIMBY problems related to the establishment of community care facilities suggest that fair-share provisions and distance controls similar to those in the sample framework policy proposed herein are needed as a basis for commitment to community care because such commitment tends to disappear when market forces, the political power of affluent neighborhoods, and professional biases act to create systematic inequities in the siting of unwanted facilities and the perception that such inequities will continue in the future. Standards that check overconcentration of LULUs are needed to ease the fears and perceptions of residents that cooperation with the siting and design of a community care facility will simply lead to further sitings. Such "nose of the camel" fears are not unwarranted, as studies of siting decisions by experts suggest that such decisions tend to favor the position that is most available.[41] Continual placement of facilities low-income neighborhoods that do not have the power to resist or in neighborhoods that have accommodated such sites in the past becomes the path of least resistance. Consideration of the long-term consequences of unequal siting of facilities will not be given its due attention as long as siting decisions remain exclusively in the hands of LULU-development organizations.[42] To provide a forum for consideration of long-term interests, proponents of educative republicanism suggest mobilizing authentic voices of citizen consumers of services to counterbalance professional or insular neighborhood voices. They also call for linking entitlements to civic obligations so as to tell a more compelling story of mutual benefit in the establishment of a necessary LULU. For example, Peter Margulies suggests that citizens whose families live in a particular neighbor be given priority to community care beds available in that neighborhood. In return, neighborhood residents would have a greater sense of civic obligation to volunteer in community programs.[43]

NOTES

1. Swallow, Stephen K., Opaluch, James J., and Weaver, Thomas F. (1992). "Siting Noxious Facilities: An Approach that Integrates Technical, Economic, and Political Considerations." *Land Economics* 68:3:238-301.

2. For an example of the development of a weighted criteria system, see Keeny, R. L., and Nair, K. (1977). "Selecting Nuclear Power Plants in the Pacific Northwest Using Decision Analysis." In *Conflicting Objectives in Decision*, edited by E. E. Bell, R. L. Keeney, and H. Raiffa. New York: John Wiley and Sons. Also, there are a number of parallel processes used by economists to measure what is sometimes termed the shadow price or the "willingness to pay" for features that may not have a specific market value.

3. Opaluch, J. J., Swallow, S. K., and Weaver, T. F. (Forthcoming). "Evaluating Impacts from Noxious Facilities: Including Public Preferences in Current Siting Mechanisms." *Journal of Environmental Economics and Management.*

4. Kunreuther, H. and Kleindorfer, P.R. (1987). "A Compensation Mechanism for Siting Noxious Facilities: Theory and Experimental Design." *Journal of Environmental Economics and Management* 14:4: 371-83. Also, Inhaber, Herbert. (1992). "Of NIMBYs, LULUs, and NIMTOOs." *Public Interest* (Spring):107:52-64. For a discussion of the use of community enforcement of property rights though a referendum process, see: Mitchell, R. C., and Carson, R. T. (1986). "Property, Protest, and the Siting of Hazardous Waste Facilities." *American Economic Review: Papers and Proceedings* 76:2:285-90.

5. Although establishment of such constraints has sometimes made it to the political agenda (as evidenced by the number of proposals to increase the earned-income credit or to re-establish progressivity in the tax code), proposals that distribute income explicitly tend to be designated as "welfare" or denigrated as "socialistic," and have in recent decades fared poorly in the legislative arena.

6. Lowry, Ira S. and Ferguson, Bruce W. (1992). *Development Regulation and Housing Affordability*. Washington, D.C.: The Urban Land Institute, p. 155.

7. For a discussion of framework policies and the new institutionalism, see Allen, Christopher. (1989). "The Underdevelopment of Keynesianism in the Federal Republic of Germany." In *The Political Power of Economic Ideas: Keynesianism Across Nations*, edited by Peter A. Hall. Princeton, N. J.: Princeton University Press, pp. 263-289.

8. De Soto, Hernando. (1989). *The Other Path: The Invisible Revolution in the Third World.* New York: Harper & Row.

9. While this might suggest that property owners in cities or counties that do not have zoning would experience a decline in property values, because of mechanisms such as restrictive covenants, large-scale planned developments, or restrictions on utility hook-ups that act in a manner similar to government zoning, this potential reduction in the value of property affected by incompatible development may not be visible. Also, because the wealthy and the educated, politically active classes are most likely to participate in these non-zoning, property-protection schemes, the negative impact of the state's failure to create legal protection for specific property uses will tend to fall on the poorer, least educated, and least politically active parts of the community, as Robert Bullard has noted. See, Bullard, Robert D. (1990). *Dumping in Dixie*. Boulder, Co.: Westview Press. Additionally, some of the negative impacts of unrestricted development tend to occur most dramatically in the long

term or after the "bubble of development-associated rising property values" is burst.

10. A study of property value changes in areas protected by historic preservation ordinances in Athens-Clarke County, Georgia found that while values in other areas of the county increased only slightly or in some cases declined during the period of the study, values in the historic preservation areas increased considerably, often by over 70 percent. See Athens-Clarke Heritage (1992). "Property Values in Historic Athens-Clarke." (Unpublished report). Athens, Ga.: Athens-Clarke Heritage Foundation.

11. Duane, Andres, and Plater-Zyberk, Elizabeth. (1992). "The Second Coming of the American Small Town." *Wilson Quarterly* 16:1:19-32.

12. Nelson, Robert. (1977). *Zoning and Property Rights*. Cambridge, Mass.: MIT Press. Also, Nelson, Robert. (1979). "A Private Property Right Theory of Zoning." *The Urban Lawyer* 11:4:713-732.

13. Kmiec, Douglas W. (1981). "Deregulating Land Use: An Alternative Free Enterprise Development System." *University of Pennsylvania Law Review* 130:28-130.

14. Been, Vicki. (1993). "What's Fairness Got To Do With It? Environmental Justice and the Siting of Locally Undesirable Land Uses." *Cornell Law Review* 78:1001-85.

15. Ibid., p . 1053.

16. Ibid., p. 1055.

17. Kmiec, "Deregulating Land Use," pp. 28-130.

18. Ibid., pp. 28-130.

19. The "uncertainty" problem in zoning has generated a movement among developers to pass legislation that would provide "vested rights" in development once a developer had signaled an intent or made investments of a particular magnitude. Such vested rights would prevent the "wipeout" of an investment in trust that zoning would not change prior to realization of the investment. See, Hagman, Donald and Juergensmeyer, Julian C. (1986). *Urban Planning and Land Development Control Law*. St. Paul, Minn.: West Publishing. Also, *California Government Code* §§65864-65869.5

20. Kmiec, "Deregulating Land Use," pp. 28-130.

21. George, Henry. (1925). *Progress and Poverty*. New York: Doubleday; Sterk, Steward E. (1988). "*Nollan*, Henry George, and Exactions." *Columbia Law Review* 88:1731-51; and Backhaus, Jurgen and Krabbe, J.J. (1991). "Henry George's Contribution to Modern Environmental Policy." *American Journal of Economics and Sociology* 50:4:485-501.

22. Nelson, Robert. (1977). *Zoning and Property Rights*. Cambridge, Mass.: MIT Press. Also, Nelson, Robert. (1979). "A Private Property Right Theory of Zoning." *The Urban Lawyer* 11:4: 713-732.

23. Morris, David, and Hess, Karl. (1975). *Neighborhood Power: The New Localism*. Boston: Beacon Press, p. 5.

24. Nelson, *Zoning and Property Rights*, p. 176.

25. Ibid., p. 95.

26. See generally, Rawl, John. (1971) *A Theory of Justice*, Cambridge, Mass.: Belknap Press of Harvard University, for a discussion of the use of thought experiments involving a veil of ignorance. Rawls suggests that these experiments can provide a great deal of

insight into what a just society might look like.

27. Mansbridge, Jane. (1983). *Beyond Adversary Democracy*. Chicago, Ill.: University of Chicago Press, pp. 278-87.

28. Simon, William. (1991). "Social-Republican Property." *UCLA Law Review* 38:1335-1415.

29. Robert Nelson has described in some detail how such a sorting out of interests might be accomplished. See generally, Nelson, *Zoning*, pp. 208-13.

30. The Vinson Institute of Government of the University of Georgia, for example, has established a Geographical Information System division that is in the process of mapping numerous land-use features. Depending on the type and depth of the data bases from which the systems draw information and on the flexibility of the system structure itself, it is possible to use these systems to aggregate LULU weights to the level suggested in the draft framework.

31. Tucker, S. N. (1980). "Mixed-Use Area Development Control." *Urban Studies* 17:287-97.

32. Personal conservation with Laurie Fowler, director of Georgia Environmental Policy Institute, Athens, Georgia.

33. Mansbridge, *Beyond Adversary Democracy*, p. 301.

34. Mansbridge is clear on this point. Although she obviously sees a need for more unitary approaches in a number of policy areas and finds that adversary approaches can have a subversive effect on the potential for positive feelings about unitary approaches, she also cautions against the spread of a romantic idea of unitary approaches being applicable to all or even the majority of cases. Maintaining viable unitary approaches, she believes, depends on "rejection both of the cynical doctrine that interests always conflict and of the credulous assumption that they can always be harmonious" (p. 298).

35. Nelson, *Zoning*, pp. 176-220.

36. Risen, Barry A. (1984). "Resolving Local Land-Use Disputes: A Collaborative Approach." *Berkeley Planning Journal* (Spring): 91-111. For use of planners as mediators, see Forester, John. (1987). "Planning in the Face of Conflict: Negotiation and Mediation Strategies in Local Land-Use Regulation." *Journal of American Planning Association* 53:303-14.

37. Nelson, *Zoning*, pp. 173-214. Nelson outlines some of the potential policymaking structures that would allow neighborhoods to move in and out of different levels of collective authority.

38. Quattrone, George A., and Tversky, Amos. (1988). "Contrasting Rationale and Psychological Analyses of Political Choice." *American Political Science Review* 82:219-27.

39. New York S. 4699, 215 Regular Session, 1992.

40. Margulies, Peter. (1992). "Building Communities of Virtue: Political Theory, Land Use Policy, and the 'Not in My Backyard Syndrome.' " *Syracuse Law Review* 43:945-96. Also, Sandler, Allen, and Robinson, Rick. (1981). "Public Attitudes and Community Acceptance of Mentally Retarded Persons: A Review." *Education and Training Mentally Retarded* 16:97-101.

41. Margulies, "Building Communities," pp. 972-73.

42. Ibid., p. 975. The first priority of organizations is to deal with pressing problems, therefore delaying the development of long-term strategies. See Allison, Graham T. (1971). *Essence of Decision: Explaining the Cuban Missle Crisis*. Boston, Mass.: Little, Brown.

43. Margulies, "Building Communities," p. 993.

CHAPTER 8

Features, Qualifications, and Objections to the Proposed Framework Policy

This chapter explores in more detail the features of the land-use control framework policy presented in the preceding chapter. The first part of the chapter attempts to assist the reader in thinking about how framework policies relate to other land-use planning mechanisms such as performance zoning or transferable development rights. In this part of the chapter, I also examine how framework policies might work at different geographic or jurisdictional levels to address problems that are best handled either at a more micro or macro level than assumed in the sample framework policy presented in the previous chapter. The second part of this chapter focuses on a number of objections that might be raised to the implementation of framework policies for land-use control. I attempt, first, to respond to the general objections that are commonly made to any progressive burden-sharing scheme, and, secondly, to address practical, legal, and ethical questions that critical readers could raise with respect to implementation of framework policies for land-use control. In a third part of this chapter, I revisit an issue—residential segregation by race—that is only minimally addressed by the sample framework policy. I conclude the chapter with a discussion of an American "bias toward bigness" in our productive and political structures and of how neighborhood governance structures might help correct this bias.

FRAMEWORK POLICIES AND THE BROADER PICTURE

In the outline of a sample framework policy presented in the preceding chapter, I argued that the creation of neighborhood-level collective choice would be considerably advanced by allocating the governance of spillover land-use rights to such neighborhood governance mechanisms. Moreover, the legitimacy of neighborhood collective-choice forums would likely be furthered by their assuming the responsibility for governance of land-use rights. Providing neighborhood associations with real power is one way to ensure that those who need to be at neighborhood meetings or mediated dispute resolution forums actually participate. Those who study and practice in the field of alternative dispute resolution have long recognized that the most difficult part of making effective use of these more unitary approaches to governance is "getting people to the table."[1] However, in the preceding chapter I also suggested that the simple allocation of these rights to neighborhood associations (within the framework guidelines) may not be sufficient to provide for workable and legitimacy-creating collective choice at the neighborhood level. As Elinor Ostrom's research suggests, there probably needs to be multiple occasions for the use of the arts of citizenship and neighborhood decision making.

The policies set out in the preceding chapter are based on the idea that a community can define, limit, and direct "undesirable" development in ways that are more precise than the mere distinction between a piece of property being zoned or not zoned for a particular use, and in ways that allow customization of necessary LULUs to individual, neighborhood, and community tastes. Experimenting with and refining these policies should lead to a situation in which the creation of a property right to develop or exclude certain facilities and land uses will not result in social costs as high as they now are. With respect to property use, for example, it would likely be the case that most residential neighborhoods would not object to limited amounts of land devoted to non-polluting and quiet uses, whether for office, institutional, or community care facilities, as long as these uses did not transform the character of the neighborhood from a family-focused, residential nature to an institutional or commercial character.

Framework Policies and Performance Zoning

Readers who are familiar with the concept of performance zoning will likely notice some basic similarity between it and framework policies. Performance zoning is a technique for setting performance standards (for example, so much traffic impact, noise, and so on) rather than districts of specific uses (such as office, residential, institutional) to guide development in ways that will protect the public's health, safety, and welfare. The sample framework policy assumes a basic performance zoning idea, namely, that any use that meets the minimum performance criteria for, say, a neighborhood-type zone, will generally be permitted.[2] However, framework policies add to the basic performance zoning concept a proviso that can be stated as: "Any development that meets the performance standard is permitted unless there is already an excessive number of LULU developments in the neighborhood that in the aggregate would undermine a basic level of residential amenity." The ethical rationale for this proviso is that all residents of a community should bear their fair share of the burdens of civilized life. Because adequate human habitation is essential, there is a need to protect the habitat of society's least privileged citizens from being degraded due to the environmental and social consequences of development. Finally, performance zoning is not concerned with the establishment of neighborhood institutions that can give voice to individual interests and help shape development in ways that are more sensitive to local needs and ideals.

Framework Policies as Two-Level Decision Making

One feature of this policy proposal is that it represents a two-stage or two-level framework for making decisions related to siting LULUs. In the first step, the more macro-jurisdiction (such as a county government) establishes overall ceilings for particular types of development in a residential area. To promote multiuse development, separate ceilings might be enacted that would pertain to the number (or percentage) of community care, half-way houses, commercial, office/institutional, or multiresident developments that would be allowed in each area. However, a total ceiling based on a weighted rating of LULU developments overall would also be set. By setting overall ceilings on LULU development, the macro-jurisdiction in effect creates a new property by protecting the overall character of the residential neighborhood. These overall ceilings also work to stem the social losses created when the affluent or powerful are able to institute highly restrictive zoning and escape their share of necessary LULUs, while the less affluent are left with a disproportionate and debilitating share of such facilities.

In the second step, the more micro-jurisdiction (such as a defined neighborhood) is given ownership of what could be called limited development rights. These micro-communities or neighborhoods would realize the value of the right to develop property in ways that are of higher value than would be the allowed under traditional zoning schemes by selling this right at auction. Neighborhood organizations could also be allowed to build into the sale of development rights the ability to repurchase these rights. This repurchase right (or right of first refusal) would enable the community as a whole to steer development in particularly desirable directions.[3] For example, the community might decide to actively recruit particular developments (such as a developmental day care center or workshop for the disabled) or even sell development rights at a subsidized cost to especially desirable developers. Existing property owners or others could bid on these development rights with the proceeds from the auction being split among all property owners in the neighborhood or put in trust to compensate adjacent owners upon occasion of the siting of a LULU. The auction could be set up so as to allow one to purchase the development rights of adjacent properties such that it would be possible to veto or shape future development of nearby property. Blocking or preventing development, however, would have its costs. As development rights are privatized, the owners of these rights would have their property re-evaluated for tax purposes. Those who owned commercial, institutional or other development rights of higher than residential value would pay higher taxes than those who did not own such rights.

Regional Frameworks

The sample framework policy outlined here is designed to address LULU development within jurisdictions of the size of a county or metropolitan area. However, in most circumstances it would be necessary to negotiate a similar framework at a more regional or even state or multi-state level. This would be the case because dispersion of LULUs within a limited area, such as a city in which LULUs are already more concentrated than in the surrounding suburbs, could be a futile endeavor, since this practice could simply lead to the most affluent city dwellers moving to the suburbs to escape having to share LULU burdens.

Extending the framework-policy logic of burden sharing to broader jurisdictions has some appeal, especially if appropriate nesting of decision-making bodies could be achieved. Negotiating some limits on the siting of high-impact LULU developments in states or regions that already more than a proportionate share of such developments might be difficult for two reasons: First, the scale of the framework would tend to work against using unitary approaches. Second, because of state sovereignty, incentives would have to be provided to induce the more LULU-free states to participate. And third, because state-level frameworks would most likely be concerned only with the high end of the scale of "avoidance" preferences (e.g., toxic waste dumps) rather than with the entire scale (e.g., including office complexes and schools), the potential for all states to achieve uniquely satisfying patterns of development would be limited. Although developing framework policies at a broader jurisdictional level would not be easy for these reasons, they may not be impossible especially if states negotiate these policies in conjunction with negotiations on other policy issues that could allow for some issues trading among states or regions.

Also in regard to a regional framework, the system for setting a ceiling on such developments should probably consider the difference between LULUs that represent a within-area responsibility and LULUs that represent an importing of responsibilities from other areas. For example, we can imagine a case where, say, a specific region of the country has already accepted an aggregate LULU impact that is higher than the proposed ceiling. Now assume that this region needs a new landfill to dispose of waste that is entirely generated within the bounds of the region. Whereas under the sample framework policy other regions might be obligated to accept development of such facilities (unless they are otherwise banned), it might be appropriate to require that LULUs that provide region-specific benefits be exempted from the framework, allowing in this case for landfill development to take place within the region that otherwise already has exceeded the LULU development ceiling. Other LULU developments that provided more nationally dispersed benefits would be treated within the framework policy.

Comparison with Current Zoning

Because the right to develop property for uses other than the dominant (in this case, residential) use is limited, individual property owners who have developments occur on nearby property can be seen as being in both a better and a worse position than they would be under current zoning policies. They are better off because they can be assured that the commercial or other "intrusion" will not go any further than it has (or will under the "cap"). This is of particular benefit to individuals who desire to live in their residence for prolonged periods of time. They would seem to be worse off in the sense that they will generally be unable to develop at will their own property for commercial purposes. However, they are not ultimately worse off in that if they really want to develop their property (or sell it for this purpose), they can still do so—if they are willing to purchase the unused development rights at the original auction/negotiation for these rights or from those who now possess these rights.

Ownership of Property Adjacent to a LULU

At the level of individual owners of property, however, there would likely be an objection to commercial intrusion on adjoining property, especially if the earlier owner of this nearby property were to gain substantial profit from the sale of the property while the neighbor is left paying the costs associated with living next to a commercial or community care facility. The individual property owner who has a LULU on adjoining property may suffer a loss that is greater than other residents of the community. That is, while all residents would receive an equal (or proportional) share of the earnings from the auction of development rights, the resident who is closest to the LULU may have contributed more (in terms of nuisance costs) to the total neighborhood gain than the other residents. There are three potential solutions to this problem. One, the political solution, would involve a unitary decision-making process that required the consent of all or nearly all the affected parties to a development rights purchase. A second, market-referenced solution would involve tracing relative changes in the value of this resident's property vis-à-vis other comparable residents' property. Owners whose property declined in value relative to their neighbors' could be compensated (such as from the funds raised through the auction of LULU development rights). However, it is also feasible that particular developments (bakeries, well-landscaped properties, quality day care centers) would lead to relative increases in the value of nearby properties.[4] Finally, a further "fair share" or fixed density policy could be enacted within a neighborhood such that no one or small group of residents within an area would bear the burden of LULUs.[5]

Urban Sprawl and Open Space?

While the sample framework policy does not directly address the need to protect open space and reduce urban sprawl, framework policies indirectly support these values in three ways. First, because framework policies essentially eliminate zoning as we know it, they also work to reduce some of the sprawl that has been caused by ability of higher income residents to use zoning to subsidize the consumption of land. That is, without zoning, the logic of urban economics, a logic that favors concentrated development (because of economic agglomeration effects and the tendency of higher land values near the center of the city to demand a denser use), would be more free to work. Second, framework policies also work to increase multiuse development, which, theoretically at least, should reduce the need for highways, commuting trips, and attendant pollution. Even though explicit support for multiuse development can also work against the logic of urban economics, and thus undermine some of the first framework policy effect, the overll effect of these two tendencies should be to reduce urban sprawl.

Finally, because framework policies explicitly establish broad-scope development rights, these policies can work well with the most promising policy mechanism for protecting open space—the transfer of development rights (TDRs). The fit between LULU framework policies and TDRs would essentially work as follows: If a more macro-level government deemed that is was important to create a green belt around an urban area or community, it could, first, reduce the annual LULU-development quota (the level of development that will be allowed across all neighborhoods) below the level of expected development in the city for that period. Next, this macro-level local or regional government could distribute TDRs to property owners in the green belt area. A green-belt owner could not use the TDRs themselves, but could only sell them to neighborhoods or developers who agree to use them for development in areas where such development is acceptable. For developers to be able to place LULU-type facilities in the zone that allows development zone, they will first have to purchase such development rights from the owners of these rights (whether in the neighborhood in question or from the green-belt owners of these rights). If one wanted to support neighborhood-level control over these TDRs, it would be possible to give neighborhoods the rights of first refusal in the sale of the TDRs.

GENERAL OBJECTIONS TO LULU BURDEN SHARING

There are a number of different types of qualifications and objections that might be made to framework policies for environmental control. In the following, I address four major types of qualifications and objections: general objections to burden-sharing schemes, objections to the practicality of framework-type policies, potential legal questions related to the implementation of framework policies, and, finally, the ethical issues that are raised by such policies.

Vicki Been has recently chronicled four types of general objections to LULU burden-sharing schemes.[6] She suggests that schemes to distribute LULU burdens more equally (or to provide compensations for the burden) must first confront the issue of causation. That is, it could be that when most LULU facilities were sited, those groups that currently seem to be unfairly burdened were not the designated victims of a siting decision. Instead, it could merely have been the case that poor and minority groups moved to the host area because of the availability of low-cost housing (for example, after creation of more desirable housing in the suburbs made available cheap housing in central city areas where more LULUs in the form of abandoned factories were located). While there may be substantial truth in the lack of direct causation between siting decisions and unfair LULU burdens, Been suggests that most theories of fairness do not depend on a finding that siting decisions were intentionally made to disproportionally affect certain groups.

The second general objection that Been raises concerns the probable impact of policy making to address LULU burden-sharing. This objection, which she calls the "mobility objection," is based on the idea that even if policies were enacted for the purposes of more fairly distributing the burden of LULUs, they would be ineffective because wealthier residents would simply move away from existing affluent neighborhoods to new ones whenever the LULUs that they are required to experience as part of a burden sharing policy became too burdensome. As property values in the existing affluent neighborhoods declined and affluent residents left, lower-income persons would take their place, thus re-creating the pattern of disproportionate LULU sitings. In responding to the mobility objection, Been notes that continual relocation can be quite costly and even futile if LULU burden-sharing policies require all neighborhoods to participate. Furthermore, she points out that the negative impact of LULUs on surrounding property values is not typically substantial. These impacts would likely be much less substantial if LULUs were more equally distributed, because some of the negative impact on property values is traceable to the fear that the LULU-siting process will continue to result in ever more concentrated sitings of LULUs. Finally, Been suggests that the mobility effect might be quite slow in operating, such that the "advantages of a fair distribution over the short run might outweigh the potential long-term futility of the program."[7] This would especially be the case if it can be shown that government has a moral obligation to site LULUs in a fair manner.

The third general objection to LULU siting policies that Been raises concerns the notion that LULUs are only one part of an aggregation of burdens and benefits that neighborhoods experience. A neighborhood that includes a number of LULUs may also host a number of desirable land uses and facilities (such as parks, libraries, or museums) that are as beneficial as the LULUs are detrimental. While such a balancing of LULUs against desirable land uses might in fact be the case or nearly the case in many instances, Been suggests that in certain rather obvious instances the opposite is the case, and that there exist no benefits to offset the unfair siting of LULUs. Also, Been points out that although fair legislative processes for aggregating burdens and benefits might work in most instances, some small groups that are unable to organize, log-roll, and join coalitions may require further protection in the form of policy constraints on siting decisions.

Been's final general objection—that the burden of living near a LULU is no different from other values and should be allocated by a free market mechanism—has been examined in detail in an earlier chapter. Been's counter to the free market objection draws on a similar argument stressing that allocations of LULUs may represent a type of merit good exception to the presumption that markets are superior mechanisms for the allocation of values.

POLITICAL VIABILITY

Although it can be argued that market framing of the type outlined here would involve some redistribution of income (because those who wanted to use their property for a LULU or sell it to a LULU developer could not do so unless their neighborhood was deemed eligible), this type of hidden redistribution is much more viable politically than the type of highly visible welfare, public assistance, or income transfer payments that would be necessary for individuals, neighborhoods, or communities to achieve parity with other individuals, neighborhoods, or communities with respect to market power in the LULU-development auction proposals.

The kind of market framing identified here would essentially involve a redistribution and decentralization of political power—away from the center, which has been dominated by the interests of the business community. While the national business and corporate interests might fight the redistribution of power, at the local level, the business community would likely be split between local and small-scale business interests and those that are tied to national-level interest through franchise agreements or direct ownership. While the latter group would resist enactment of a framework policy, the more local business interests might find it attractive. Moreover, the idea of decentralization of power would likely be attractive to most consumer interests and neighborhood groups, even though it would result in some more affluent neighborhoods having to bear a greater share of LULUs. That is, the attraction of having more control at a lower level of political action (within a neighborhood market) would likely be strong enough to convince many citizens that a framework policy involving more neighborhood control and liberty in return for greater responsibility would in many cases be better than the current situation, in which one is subject to the whims of "experts," variance boards, and numerous other forces beyond one's control.

Additionally, establishing a framed market for LULUs could appeal to Americans' sense of a need to strengthen democracy, to re-establish civic responsibility, and to move beyond a client-service state.[8] In this light, the idea that all groups and all neighborhoods should rightfully share in the care of the needy and the disposal of their own waste speaks to the basic American values of self-reliance, self-government, and social responsibility.

Although an appeal can be made to the ideal of civic responsibility, critics could argue that the enactment of the sample framework policy would result in the generation of forces and incentives designed to promote greater social integration of and diversity in neighborhoods. Such diversity could in turn result in greater conflict, as neighborhood residents ceased to be all of one class and interests became less homogeneous. Traditional theories of unitary democracy would suggest that such conflicts of interests would make it more difficult to establish and maintain unitary democracy approaches and institutions. Similarly, conventional views of citizen participation, suggesting that the more affluent neighborhoods would be more active in neighborhood-level politics, would imply that as neighborhoods became more diverse, participation by the affluent might be adulterated. Recent research in neighborhood-level citizen participation, however, suggests that these traditional and conventional views may be mistaken, and that participation of residents to improve neighborhood conditions is heightened by a certain amount of social conflict, discord, and diversity. Matthew Crenson's study of neighborhood politics concludes that individual attempts to produce public goods in consultation with neighbors are more evident in somewhat poorer neighborhoods—no matter what the social status of the individual actor.[9] Crenson is not saying that the affluent are less likely in similar circumstance to take informed direct action; he is suggesting that both poor and rich will be more likely to take such action when they are living in the same diverse neighborhood. That is, high-status residents are more likely to participate in producing informal public services when they are living among residents of lower social status. While these higher-status individuals will benefit from their political actions, so will the neighborhood as a whole. Crenson's research, moreover, suggests that out of the social discord of diverse neighborhoods come efforts to forge neighborhood identity and a heightened sensitivity to inconveniences and aggravations in the neighborhood environment. Such neighborhood identity and sensitivity, in turn, prompt residents to identify what is bad and what can be improved. Crenson's findings support Jane Jacobs' theoretical ideas about the role of diversity and mixed-used development in the creation of viable communities. They suggest that the tendency of framework policies to promote social integration of neighborhoods and a consequently higher level of social discord within neighborhoods may have net benefits.

While the sample framework policy is intuitively attractive in an age that appears to be moving toward greater community control, localism, particularism, and pluralism,[10] it should be recognized that its implementation depends in large measure on more macro-level governments creating the frame within which neighborhood can be allowed a certain amount of free play. The essence of this "frame" is the delineation of specific requirements that neighborhoods would have to meet as part of their collective responsibility. Up to 1993 there have been only a few legislative and administrative efforts at providing a frame for allocating social responsibility among communities. The greatest percentage of these efforts have centered on the provision of low-income housing. For example, in the early 1970s, the Dayton, Ohio, area regional planning commission, among others, devised plans to distribute 14,000 units of federally subsidized housing units among the various jurisdictional units in its area. Massachusetts went as far as passing a Zoning Appeals Law (nicknamed the "Anti-Snob Zoning Law") that created a system of state oversight of local zoning decisions that might negatively affect development of low- and moderate-income housing. The appeals board that was set up under this legislation is specifically directed to consider the amount of low- and moderate-income housing that exists in the community. Appeals from developers who desired to place low-income housing in communities where low- and moderate-income housing already exceeded 10 percent of total housing would receive less favorable a hearing than developers who wanted to place such housing in communities that had less than this proportion of low- or moderate-income housing.[11]

While this type of legislation partakes of the general desire to create a framework for social responsibility, it hardly represents a model for framework policies. The appeals process envisioned by the Massachusetts Zoning Appeals Law essentially follows the traditional model of discretionary change and piecemeal zoning that has rightfully been criticized as provising neither certainty nor protection against corruption and unequal treatment across cases.

Additionally, these prototype LULU burden-sharing schemes were limited to one type of unwanted land use—low-income housing—and were designed to spread the burden of providing for this type of housing across communities, but not across neighborhoods. As such they would hardly affect the problem of unequal burden sharing that occurs within a single jurisdiction (that is, the differences in the intensity of LULUs between affluent and nonaffluent communities). Ideally, both levels of the problem of unequal LULU burden sharing would be addressed. The sample framework policy addresses this issue more directly.

The issue of sharing the "burden" of community care facilities has generated a number of other schemes for LULU burden sharing.[12] Municipalities in New Jersey, for example, can refuse the siting of a group home if the number of residents in existing homes exceeds 0.5 percent of the city's population. Wisconsin and Oregon have similar statutes that link the acceptance of new group home facilities to the county's population or the population of persons needing care in the jurisdiction in question.[13]

More recently, Congressman John Lewis (D-Ga.) has offered a bill, the Environmental Justice Act, to stop the introduction of toxic chemical facilities in 100 areas that already contain the highest total weight of toxic chemicals in the country, if the concentration of chemicals in these areas are also shown to cause an adverse health impact.[14] Similarly, in response to studies of environmental injustice in the placement of toxic and noxious waste-producing facilities, the Clinton administration has issued an executive order requiring federal agencies and other recipients of federal funds to monitor the effects of their actions on environmental health in minority communities. The executive order will require measurement and record keeping of the impact of individual pollutants and the total and cumulative impacts of all pollutants that affect a particular area.[15] Numerous state statutes require some consideration of the social impacts of land-use developments, and legislation proposed by Congressman William Clinger (R-Pa.) and Senator John Glenn (D-Oh.) would require that environmental impact statements related to waste treatment and disposal facilities include information about demographics of the host community and the existence of other such facilities in the community.[16]

The increasing frequency with which policies promoting fair burden sharing of LULUs among jurisdictions are reaching the agenda setting and policy passage and implementation stages suggests that these issues may create a basis for redesign of our governance institutions along the lines of a greater infusion of framework-type structures. Unfortunately, most of the proposals for sharing the burden of providing for low-income housing, group homes, and environmental treatment facilities among jurisdictions have been focused on only one of these burdens at any one time. As such, the implementation of any one of these policies has done little to protect vulnerable neighborhoods from the siting of other types of LULU facilities. That is, even though a statute might protect a neighborhood from further development of group homes, it would have little to say about the siting of a waste treatment facility, prison, or toxic chemical facility. Similarly, as Vicki Been has noted, passage of the Environmental Justice Act of 1992 would do little to prevent a neighborhood from being overburdened by community care or social service facilities.[17]

While most attempts to govern LULU siting decisions have been piecemeal in nature, in 1989 New York City adopted provisions in a new city charter that were designed to address the issue of the sharing of both LULUs and their opposite—locally wanted land uses, such as parks or other desired public facilities and services. These provisions required the establishment of criteria for locating, expanding, and closing city facilities such that there would evolve a "fair distribution among communities of the burdens and benefits associated with city facilities, consistent with community needs for services and efficient and cost-effective delivery of services and with due regard for the social and economic impacts of such facilities upon the areas surrounding the sites."[18] The new city charter also requires the publication of a statement of need that would identify all proposed additions, expansions, and closings of city facilities and provisions that would allow citizen comments on the statement of needs as well as allowing borough presidents to suggest alternative sites or lodge protests based on the fair share criteria. What is unique about the new city charter is the explicit recognition of neighborhoods as the appropriate geographical unit for assessing the totality of facilities-siting effects on quality of life. That is, in deciding to site a new city facility in a particular neighborhood, consideration must be given to "how the neighborhood's character will be adversely affected by the concentration of such facilities" and with the facility's compatibility to existing facilities and programs in the neighborhood.[19]

Although the new New York City charter represents a significant advance in policymaking, its effects on the overall problem of governing LULUs may not be substantial because the charter provisions regulate only the siting of city facilities. In addition, specification of other criteria, such as cost-effectiveness and community needs for services, provides significant room for maneuver, political manipulation, and decision making by experts. As Vicki Been notes, "The criteria fail to specify how distributional concerns are to be weighed against other concerns. Many of the factors listed as relevant to the siting decision will probably favor the siting of LULUs in already burdened neighborhoods."[20] That is, the cost-effectiveness criteria will lead to sitings in low-income neighborhoods where site costs are lowest, and the community needs or assessibility criteria will favor siting social service LULUs in neighborhoods that already have more than their share of these and other LULU facilities. In sum, while the New York City charter is a step in the right direction toward a more satisfactory governance of LULU issues, it is less than ideal.

Overall, the political viability of framework-like policymaking of a type that is more sophisticated and more tightly designed than the New York City charter is probably limited most directly by the complexity of the policy design and the degree to which these policies are viewed as a radically different way of ordering property rights. That is, our experience has generally been that property is either owned outright by individuals or by government. Establishing neighborhood-level property rights (or more specifically, development rights) will demand substantial adjustments in our ordinary conceptions of property. Hence, even though framework policies likely would receive strong support from persons whose neighborhoods were under immediate threat and from persons and organizations in the civil rights and environmental communities, this support may not be sufficient to overcome the inertia of traditional ideas about property. Moreover, this inertia is likely to be especially evident among persons whose property is already protected, perhaps because they already live in a "walled community" or perhaps because their residence is out of the way of any proposed development. Finally, persons who live in LULU-free areas, who also are generally more affluent and politically powerful than those in LULU-concentrated areas, would be ambivalent at best about a framework-like policy. Those who were most privileged in these respects, moreover, would likely be active opponents because such policies would force a degree of burden sharing that had not been mandated previously.

LEGAL AND PRACTICAL VIABILITY

Takings and Exactions

A number of legal issues need to be addressed in an assessment of the framework policies suggested for LULUs. The more negative is the obvious question of whether a framework-type policy would be considered a "takings" under the Fifth Amendment. On the one hand, a plausible argument can be made that framework policies of the type described would not constitute a takings under the traditional interpretation of this clause of the U.S. Constitution. That is, the Supreme Court has allowed regulations having even more substantial effects on the value of property (that is, effects on the magnitude of reducing property values by more than 75 percent) without holding that these regulations constituted a taking. Generally, as long as the regulation serves a valid purpose and does not leave the property owner without any reasonable use, the court has been reluctant to identify the regulation as a taking. Because the sample framework policy begins with the assumption that development for minimal residential use is an option available to all owners, the takings issue would seem to be a moot one.

However, the sample framework policy also includes a modified Henry George-type mechanism for exacting the unearned rent value of land ownership. While such mechanisms have generally been recognized as economically more efficient than traditional zoning in a theoretical sense and as involving no more substantial problems with fairness than would be the case with any other tax, they have nevertheless been criticized on a number of implementation grounds.[21] One criticism of such schemes is that they would essentially eliminate planning. That is, in a regular Georgist mechanism, the community would take bids for the development rights and would be unable to promise any stability to any potential developer. Another developer could bid on adjoining property and develop the property in ways that lower the value of the first developer's investment. A number of responses can be made to this assertion. For example, a plausible argument can be made that traditional zoning, which is supposedly able to provide such promised protections to developers, actually provides little more than short-term protection and the provision of notice for potential changes in zoning. More particularly with respect to the sample framework policy, planning is substantially protected at the neighborhood level by neighborhood associations' control over development rights. Once a developer becomes a "neighbor-owner," she is a accorded rights to participate in the governance of land use in the neighborhood. Also, as the framework policy works against excessive concentration of LULUs within any one neighborhood, it provides another layer of protection. This protection against concentrated LULUs admittedly does not protect against the potential for any and all changes in land use as is the case with traditional zoning. However, this surface-level uncertainty about individual pieces of property does not alter the fact that framework policies would probably provide much greater overall certainty that an area would not undergo unplanned or disorderly transitions that are inherent in current zoning arrangements.[22]

A second argument made against Georgist exaction schemes is that they would increase rent-seeking by non-owners; that is, they would foster the tendency of non-owners of property to try to persuade a third party, such as the state to allocate to themselves (the non-owners) the rents that would normally accrue to the owner.[23] Typically, rent-seeking by non-owners will occur when residents in a community attempt to get the state to restrict development on unoccupied land, thereby providing these residents (but non-owners of the undeveloped land) the benefits of greater open space and less traffic, while laying the cost of the restrictions on the owners of the undeveloped property.[24]

A system of exactions, law Professor Steward Sterk suggests, would increase rent-seeking behavior because it would create a "cost-free pot of money up for grabs by any interest group." As such, many more citizens than is usually the case will tend to get in the act of trying to extract funds from those who would propose to develop their property. In the current non- or limited-exaction situation, Sterk notes, only the landowners, nearby neighbors, and local government officials are involved in zoning actions that might result in a substantial benefit to the parties. With fewer persons involved, it becomes easier to bargain about the proposed land-use control. Because "both bargaining costs and costs associated with rent-seeking are dead-weight social losses,"[25] reducing the number of interested persons should reduce these losses. Commonly proposed Georgist exaction schemes, as Sterk suggests, would open the gates for more groups to engage in rent seeking. However, the sample framework policy is less likely to do so for several reasons. First, the framework establishes a single private party—the neighborhood association—as having the primary right to economic rent, but also having the primary responsibility for paying taxes on the unused part of these rights. To the degree that such rights to the economic rent are returned to the neighborhood residents as a group, the expansion of rent-seeking to the entire community is limited. Whether returning some of these rents to the community at large (so as to support placing community care institutions in high- cost areas, for example) would increase rent-seeking behavior substantially is a matter for empirical inquiry to determine. However, it might be possible to place some "regulator-type" limitations on the tendency for groups in the community at large to seek an ever greater share of economic rent. That is, a legal standard similar to the "nexus" standard for takings could be established to limit the larger community's share of unearned economic rents. For example, the larger community might be allowed to extract from the sale of development rights only the portion needed to provide for public infrastructure needs caused by the development (as is the case under current "nexus" requirements) and for a portion of the land-acquisition rights needed to locate community care institutions in the area. The remaining rent would be assigned to the neighborhood.

A final criticism of Henry George-type systems for exacting unearned rents is that such systems tend to undermine the formal rule of law.[26] Sterk, for example, believes that because such systems typically make all rents public, there is a lessening of incentives for private actors to attempt to restrain governments that make arbitrary decisions that, for example, would violate due process and equal protection standards. For Sterk, official arbitrariness in a Georgist world would come in the form of government asking developers for too little or too much money for permits or in treating individual developers differently. In the sample framework system, however, it is the neighborhood itself that would be setting the price for development permits in that jurisdiction and that would be receiving a substantial portion of the rents. Because neighborhoods must pay taxes on the unused development rights, there exists an automatic restraint on the tendency of neighborhoods to set their prices too high or too low.

While a modified Henry George-type system of exactions established within a framework for governing LULU development might not violate criteria for efficiency or overall moral hazard, numerous states have enacted either constitutional or other legal limits on exactions or land-use taxes that would, under current circumstances, likely restrict the implementation of such a system.[27]

The "Nexus" Requirement

A final "takings" issue is related to the feature of the framework policy that provides for the selling of zoning or development rights to recapture the unearned increment of development. Generally, the courts have demanded that there be a "nexus" or strong relationship between the requirements placed on potential developers (such as impact fees, provision of new roads, sewers, water lines, and so on) and the actual impact of the development.[28] The exception to this general principle is the explicit power of some communities to tax or levy fees. Such taxes are considered legitimate when property owners receive a benefit (such as protection against excessive LULUs or neighborhood control of many land-use aspects) and when no particular owner is singled out to bear the burden of the tax. In these cases, the courts will generally allow such fees unless they are confiscatory.[29] As suggested above, however, it might make sense to keep a modified nexus requirement with respect to the allocation of the funds generated by the sale of development rights between neighborhoods and the larger community.

Limitations on Classes of Commercial Activity

The second potential legal objection to the proposed framework policy is based on the general hostility of courts to the use of zoning in ways that would restrain trade or explicitly limit the number of any class of commercial activities in a designated area.[30] However, this hostility is not universal. In many instances, as long as a community has been able to provide a reasonable basis for the classification of property or for the cap on the number of properties of a particular type, the limitation has been upheld by the courts. For example, in *Stone v. City of Maitland*, the courts upheld the restrictions placed on the number of gas stations that could be located in a particular area. In other cases, the courts have allowed communities to develop regulations that distinguish between retail stores and shopping centers, or between chain stores and those that are not part of a national or regional chain.[31]

Reserved Powers

A third legal issue concerns the degree of delegation of regulatory authority to the resident owners in a neighborhood jurisdiction. The key issue in this respect is whether a community government can give away what might be considered "reserved powers" of this government. In specific cases, the major concern for the courts has been whether the delegation of authority included standards to ensure that neighborhood property owners would not simply be acting capriciously for their own interests. The key Supreme Court cases in this regard, *Cussack Co. v. Chicago* and *State of Washington v. Roberge*, provide some guidance. In *Cussack*, the court upheld an ordinance that prohibited the erection of a sign without the consent of a majority of the property owners, while in *Roberge*, the court invalidated an ordinance that would have required the property owners' consent to construction of an old-age home. In essence, the court distinguished between developments that could be considered a nuisance or near-nuisance from those that might simply be considered an annoyance.[32] The sample framework policy was not designed to make such distinction, and indeed is based on the idea that too much of any particular use can create a sort of generalized nuisance in the form of irrational land use, heightened pollution, and social injustice. A survey of state courts rulings, moreover, suggests that there may be a great deal of judicial discretion involved in deciding what will be considered a nuisance. For example, while old-age homes are not considered to be a nuisance, apartments in single- or even double-family residential zones have been deemed to be.[33] The plan for determining the nuisance value of particular types of uses set forth in the sample framework policy would seem to provide a more justifiable basis for determining the nuisance value of particular land uses and the potential for agglomeration effects of particular uses that individually would not seem to pose a nuisance.

Because the rights to LULU developments in the sample framework are allocated to neighborhood owners as a type of collective property right, one that is taxable like other property rights, the framework policy might in fact be exempt from the kind of review that courts make in cases where regulatory powers, rather than property rights, are delegated to neighborhood groups. Additionally, the framework in some senses assumes the creation of new legal jurisdictions based on state enabling legislation. If this were to occur, the issue of improper delegation would be a moot one, because the state would essentially be creating numerous new local governments, though of a less than comprehensive type. Even if states did not create new types of legal institutions, however, the tendency of state courts has been to allow a delegation of zoning-like authority to neighborhood residents when uses are generally prohibited throughout the jurisdiction unless consent from the residents is obtained. (However, these courts, have typically prohibited the delegation of such authority when the land-use in question is generally permitted in a jurisdiction, but could be prohibited by neighbors who have been delegated this authority for a specific subsection of the jurisdiction).[34] While the sample framework policy calls for a delegation of authority to neighborhoods, such a devolution of authority could easily be accomplished in the "typically prohibited, but permitted with consent" manner that state courts generally have allowed. However, this ad hoc devolution of power to neighborhood-sized areas would be more effectively and securely accomplished through the use of state enabling legislation.

Residential Mobility

A fourth legal concern—the potential for the framework policy to limit the right to travel or the right of residential mobility—is one that is relevant to all growth- control measures. Because the sample framework policy would allow landowners to build single-family residences in areas that were otherwise restricted with respect to LULU developments, it would on the face of it not restrict the constitutional right to travel. In fact, one of the major purposes of the framework policy would be to break down some of the exclusionary features of current zoning practices. However, the argument over the right to residential mobility could be made with respect to the tendency of framework policies to limit the construction of low-income multifamily residences in areas that already have more than their share of LULU development. To date, however, the Supreme Court has refused to rule that exclusionary zoning based on income or wealth is a violation of the constitutional right to travel. Only when a municipality's land-use ordinance has the intent and effect of restricting the rights of racial minorities to travel are the federal courts likely to strike down the land-use controls in question.[35]

ETHICAL VIABILITY

The potential ethical viability of the framework policy has at least five basic dimensions. First is the fairness of distributing the burden of LULUs among various groups or neighborhoods. Here the discussion of the ethics of environmental justice are germane. The second issue concerns the ethical rationale for establishing an alternative to our current system of allocating development rights to either the individual owner or to the state. In examining this second dimension, we need to answer the question: What is the ethical basis for creating neighborhood-level land use control? The third issue is the ethics of redistribution of existing property rights. Fourth is the fairness of the scheme for establishing the "price" or value of development rights, and finally, the ethical considerations related to the realignment of power that might occur upon establishment of neighborhood-level control of land use.

Ethics of Environmental Justice

Some general ethical objections to policies that are designed to further the goals of environmental justice were addressed at the beginning of Chapter 7. An ethical analysis that is more framework policy-specific, however, is in order. In this regard, the framework policy can be viewed as falling in the category of what Vicki Been has called proposals for "progressive siting" of LULU facilities. Part of the rationale for progressive siting, or the siting of new LULUs in neighborhoods that have less than a proportionate share of LULUs, is compensatory justice.[36] Compensatory justice is needed where past discrimination has harmed an individual or group. As noted earlier, however, the data on LULU site locations are not usually sufficient to prove intentional discrimination. Another justification for compensatory justice can be found in studies suggesting that LULUs in less advantaged neighborhoods will have a stronger or more negative impact than those sited in more advantaged neighborhoods. Reasons for such disparate impacts from what might be equal treatment (or equality of "opportunities" to live next to a LULU) are many. For example, if minority race residents in a particular neighborhood suffer from more health problems initially and have less ability to move out of the neighborhood than do majority race residents of another neighborhood, the siting of a noxious facility in the minority neighborhood could have a more negative impact on health than would be the case if the same facility were placed in the white, middle-class neighborhood. This is the case because in the latter neighborhood, the great majority of residents, being in good health, would be relatively unaffected by the siting, while the few who were affected would have the resources needed to move away from the source of the toxins. Hence, progressive siting, like progressive taxation, could induce a more equal sacrifice of comfort and happiness and in doing so impose the least loss of utility to society as a whole. Also, as argued above, progressive siting creates incentives for neighborhoods to reduce the number of LULUs needed.[37] Additionally, to the degree that neighborhoods use the framework policy to negotiate with LULU developers for adjustments in the design of the proposed LULU, progressive siting can also work to reduce the effects of each LULU.

Nevertheless, a number of arguments can be mustered against the compensatory justice rationale for progressive siting. First, as Vicki Been points out, our knowledge of individual and community utility functions (that is, how a particular LULU might affect different individuals or neighborhoods differently) is very tenuous. For example, the idea that disadvantaged neighborhoods would be more severely affected by the addition of another LULU is contradicted by studies suggesting that "the impact of an additional LULU is far less than the impact that the first LULU imposes on a neighborhood."[38] For ideological conservatives relying on a wealth-maximization criterion, this would be a persuasive argument. However, for most persons, this utilitarian argument is likely to ring hollow. Exposing a disadvantaged citizen to further, even though marginal, harm in order to save an advantaged citizen from the first quantum of LULU exposure is likely to be seen as unjust.

Second, if progressive siting were to make it more difficult to site future LULUs, existing LULUs in poor and minority communities would likely have to continue to operate or even expand, and additional LULUs such as social service facilities that would benefit disadvantaged minorities might never get built.[39] The dynamics of the framework policy, however, would work against this potential. That is, "hold-out" neighborhoods would experience increasing economic pressure (through the tax on unused development rights) to allow some LULU development.

A third argument has been made that the victims of regressive siting might be better served if the community were to focus more directly on quality-of-life measures (such as health, mobility, and so on) that make some neighborhoods more vulnerable to LULU effects in the first place. This argument has been implicitly addressed earlier in this text in the discussions of the need for governments to establish and protect a certain level of human dignity and equal protection. It is also addressed more directly below, where I argue that dignity and equal protection need to be part of long-term contractual relationships, just as they are part of how we order relationships involving social duties such as military service. Significantly, just as we do not let a draftee contract with another person to take his place in the service (even though this would be mutually agreeable) and we do not let a landlord provide substandard housing (even though it might come at a preferable price to some consumers), so too we would not want to see a developer of a toxic chemical plant be able to trade, say, her provision of a needed neighborhood health center in return for the neighborhood's acquiescence in the siting of the toxic facility.

No scheme for siting LULUs—framework policies included—can escape some of the practical problems of defining and operationalizing fairness. As such, framework policies need to be compared with and judged against other policy options, including the option of doing nothing. Such an undertaking, however, is beyond the scope of this book.

The Ethics of Initial Distributions of Control or "Spillover" Rights

The ethical case for framework policies that attempt to balance the values of equity, efficiency, environmental quality, and community viability is based on the idea that even where private property rights are assumed to be a basic and vital part of a democratic polity, there is need for some collective intervention to deal with conflict that will arise between the separate owners of private property. Alan David Freeman has described this process of collective regulation as most aptly being conceived as a property right that is separate from that of "basic ownership." Freeman calls this property "local environmental control," a concept that fits neatly with the LULU-development rights idea put forth in the sample framework policy. As suggested in various parts of this work, environmental control rights have not remained static or clearly allocated. Rather, these rights, which are realized through various legal mechanisms such as nuisance laws, land covenants, and zoning practices, have tended to fluctuate over the past century between the twin poles of expansionary and exclusionary interests in property.

Without some legitimate means for deciding between the two types of property interests, land users might establish their claims by force, but these types of claims tend to be unstable and therefore economically inefficient. Alternatively, such claims can be decided by prior designation of environmental control rights as part of property rights. Once the control rights are distributed and protected, the Coasean theorem would suggest that as long as bargaining is costless, efficient allocation of resources will result—no matter what the initial distributions. However, as the changes in nuisance law and zoning policies indicate, and as changes in the courts' understanding of takings suggest, the problem of the initial distribution of property rights is far from settled. Hence, the question that Professor Freeman poses and attempts to answer—what ethical criteria should be used to distribute environmental control rights initially?—is a crucial one. Freeman examines three potential criteria for an initial distribution of environmental control rights—economic efficiency, merit, and prior appropriation.

The economic efficiency criterion, he rightfully argues, is essentially irrelevant to the choice of an initial distribution scheme because an efficient allocation of resources can be achieved for any initial distribution of these rights as long as there is a sufficient distribution of wealth to allow for productive exchanges. The prior appropriation of environmental control rights, or what might be termed "first users' rights," is also an inappropriate guide to initial distribution, Freeman suggests, for three reasons. First, the term "first users' rights" implies an exiting initial distribution. Second, many existing claims for environmental control rights are tenuous and uncertain, as evidenced by the high level of land-use disputes in the last century and the continued extent of litigation in this area. The initial distribution of basic property rights through "first possession" has done little to quell disputes over spillover rights. Third, awarding first-user rights to environmental control might be very economically inefficient where a large number of highly productive, latecoming, but consistent land uses are opposed to a single, less productive first use. Freeman concedes that first users have a valid claim to the environmental control rights when they have been explicitly distributed to the property owner through a formal conferring. However, simply having a general expectation of environmental control in situations where the rule for the distribution of these rights is confusing or uncertain, or where it is clear that claims to environmental control (or "spillover claims") are revocable by public decision, would not be sufficient. Something else is needed to authorize property owners to develop their land in ways that could impose a negative spillover effect on their neighbors or the public in general. For Freeman, this "something else" is an ethical claim based on a system of initial distribution rights.

Freeman makes a cogent case for a system of initial distribution of environmental control rights that resembles the one suggested in the sample framework policy, namely, that these control rights should be allocated on the basis of a particular merit value. Generally, a merit value involves some feature of an activity or person, apart from what might be expressed through his ability to purchase particular goods or services, that provides external benefits for society. In Freeman's terms, the relevant merit value for an initial distribution of environmental control rights is "an agreed minimal level of residential environmental amenity."[40] In our argument, this merit value might be stated more broadly as an agreed upon minimal level of human dignity and public happiness, which in turn requires human and environmental habitats that can support these values. For both Freeman's and our own argument, a key merit value can be found in establishing a certain level of residential environmental control as part of the basic ownership rights of residential property. In particular, this control should be evident where there is a conflict between residents and business. The merit basis for an initial distribution of environmental control rights is less applicable to conflicts between firms or between residents because in these instances preferences as to environmental control rights can either be purchased (in the case of firm-versus-firm conflicts) or be easily regulated by nuisance standards that would apply across all residences.

Freeman argues that a minimal level of residential amenity should be considered a merit good (one that produces external benefits for society as a whole that would not be realized without collective provision) for several reasons. First, equality of opportunity cannot be realized if the disagreeable conditions of some people's living environment is so destructive to peace of mind that it negates any realistic chance of competing for life's rewards. Second, it is impossible to ensure a realistic basis for self-respect and human dignity for persons who are consigned to environments that do not meet minimal standards in this regard.[41] Additionally, Freeman's giving priority to residential property is supported by Margaret Jane Radin's recent analysis of the relationship between property and personhood. Radin analysis presents a "third strand of liberal property theory" between the libertarian/conservative ideas of property as sacred to personal autonomy and the communitarian and welfare-rights liberal ideas of property as reflecting the changing nature of the needs of persons within communities or of minimal individual needs. This third strand, Radin suggests, "focuses on personal embodiment or self-constitutions in terms of 'things.' "[42] For Radin, the property-personhood relationship potentially forms the basis for the state delineating property rights with higher or lower levels of protection. For example, she argues that residential property, which intuitively has a stronger association with a person's self-realization, should be given a higher level of protection. Radin's theory, in essence, avoids the obligation to defend all existing property relations and expectations with the same level of fervor. Freeman's designation of residential property as deserving of a major share of the initial distribution of environmental control rights is very much in line with Radin's property rights theory.

One potential criticism of Freeman's initial distribution of substantial control rights to residential owners is that this represents a redistribution of wealth to residential property owners. However, Freeman argues that the general arguments against the redistribution of wealth do not apply with regard to the distribution of local control rights, since basic spillover problems require some degree of public intervention to distribute these rights. In many cases, he suggests, there is no expropriation because there is no original vested right. Also, arguments for using income transfers to more effectively accomplish the goal of minimal residential amenity[43] are less persuasive, because such a scheme would not ensure that the merit good of residential amenity would be created. That is, it would substitute the efficiency value as the only criterion for initial distribution of environmental control rights. It should be made clear that Freeman does see a role for the efficiency criterion, but one that is limited to initial conflicts between firms or between residents and to resident-versus-firm conflicts once there has been an initial distribution of environmental control rights to residents.

The Ethics of Redistribution

The sample framework policy, in placing limits on LULU developments in neighborhoods that are in a vicious circle of deterioration, has the effect of directing further LULU development toward areas and neighborhoods that are currently the most exclusive. As such, it can be argued that the sample framework policy will tend to promote the economic integration of communities. Robert Nelson suggests that such integration efforts essentially constitute a redistribution of income to the poor. The poor, who would move into multifamily housing in more affluent neighborhoods, would receive a better environment and public services without substantial private expense. Nelson points out that because this redistribution is based on indirect "in-kind" assistance rather than direct income assistance, it is a less efficient means of assisting the poor. Assistance in the form of a better residential environment, Nelson argues, may not be appropriate or desired by the poor as much as other types of assistance. Also, he notes that "while some poor would have the good fortune to gain entry into desirable community environments, others would have to continue to live in much less desirable areas."[44] He concludes that transfer of income directly to the poor would be a more equitable solution. Nelson's criticism of the economic integration of communities is more extensive than is suggested by his critique of in-kind assistance. He believes that exclusionary zoning protections are needed for the establishment and maintenance of high-quality environments and public services. Without protection, he believes, such environments and public services would decline in quality and be replaced by private social institutions.

For Nelson, homogeneous community populations are desirable for a number of reasons. First, they provide for economic advantages. (For example, specialized shopping and public services can be designed to meet particular needs; private clubs will be able to orient their programs toward meeting common local needs.) Second, they result in a better fit between people's desire for public services and their willingness to pay. Where there is a mix of rich and poor, whichever group is in the majority will be able to force the other to accept a level of public service that is less than optimal. (For example, the poor might be forced to pay for municipal golf courses when they would prefer lower taxes and more income.) Third, decision-making or consensus-building costs are lower when people are more homogeneous. These advantages, for Nelson, suggest a particular policy innovation that reorders the public-private boundary in ways that give explicit public sanction to the creation of private neighborhood associations with full ownership of zoning or development tenures (including the right to sell these tenures).[45] In contrast to the sample framework policy, which gives spillover land-use control rights to a neighborhood collective but only within the limits of the framework restrictions on LULU siting, Nelson would place no constraints on the ability of neighborhoods to control their own destiny—even if it means that other neighborhoods are doomed to disintegrate under the impact of unwanted development. In essence, Nelson suggests giving up on the ideal of social integration because he believes that even if the inefficiencies could be overcome, forcing social integration through anti-exclusionary policies would simply result in the expansion of private provision of neighborhood amenities (such as the construction of more "walled and gated" residential developments).

Nelson has identified a major systems problem with policies designed to address the exclusionary nature of zoning—the flight of citizens in to private associations for the provision of services such as education, police, sanitation, and so forth. The question is whether his solution, which is to give into and give public approval the "inescapable reality" of homogeneous groupings, is a "syndrome friendly" innovation or, alternatively, one that involves moral hazards of the type identified by Gregory Alexander in his essay on group autonomy.[46] Alexander, in contrast to Nelson, sees a clear necessity for "groups to accept a civic obligation to maintain community within our society."[47] Because Nelson sees no escape from the disintegration of community into homogeneous groups (by either public or private means), he would place his hopes on maintaining public institutions—even if these institutions differed little from private ones and essentially place a public imprimatur on private associations that have as a prime purpose the exclusion of outsiders. While this blurring of the public and private sectors may have some economic and social benefits, without some mechanism for limiting the potential moral hazards involved, such policies seem to offer too little in short-term material benefits in return for too much long-term risk to democratic values. Matthew Crenson's finding that a little social conflict is healthy for citizen participation suggests that despite the seeming support for communitarian values found in Nelson's proposal for neighborhood governance of land-use control,[48] the effect of his proposal might be further reduction in the democratic spirit and civic activism. Additionally, while decreasing within-neighborhood divisiveness, Nelson's proposal would likely further divisiveness among neighborhood groups of citizens and thereby impede the achievement of a more integrated, democratic polity. When "factions" become confirmed in geographic realities and are provided public institutional status, there would seem to be much greater risk of the kind of destructive balkanization that is currently at work in the formerYugoslavia.

In response to Nelson's criticism of the economic integration of communities, several particular points can be made. First, the potential inequality of some of the poor getting the chance to live in affluent areas while others do not is mitigated by two factors: (1) Over time all neighborhoods will tend to have a similar level of residential amenities, at least with regard to the placement of unwanted land uses; and (2) the special advantages of the poor who choose to live in affluent neighborhoods may be offset by the higher tax rates and undesirable mix of public services that might accompany residence in these areas. Second, if we accept the proposition that property ownership involves social obligations to the community at large, providing public approval to community associations without also asking for some social responsibility in turn would undermine this principle. Bruce Ackerman, for example, argues that property owners have a particular moral obligation to "refrain from weaving the larger social injustice of the maldistribution of income into the fabric of [their lives], as [they] do when [they] embark upon . . . continuing relationship[s] [that embody this injustice]."[49] While Ackerman's proposition refers specifically to landlord-tenant relationships, the principle is relevant to larger social relationships within a local community and especially those relations that involve the placement of LULUs that benefit the entire community, but that of necessity also harm those who reside next to them. Most LULUs involve a continuing relationship with either those persons who are in need of care or with products and services generally consumed but whose waste streams are directed toward the more dependent neighborhoods. What makes LULU sitings different from straight forward inequality is the fact that such land uses become part of the built environment and therefore a fixture in the lives of both the poor who live in LULU-burdened neighborhoods and the affluent who benefit from the LULU but who do not take responsibility for it. Ackerman's suggestion to the slum landlord is also apt for the siting of LULUs: "Act so that in none of your ongoing relationships you permit another human being to exist under conditions which constitute a serious affront to his dignity as a person."[50]

Framework Policies, Efficiency and a Fair Price for Development Rights

The sample framework policy implicitly places environmental control rights at the neighborhood or residential level, but it goes one step further in that it allows local neighborhood collectives to manage these environmental control rights and set up a framework that reduces the barriers that potentially high transaction costs would pose to efficient exchanges if environmental control rights were simply distributed as an individual property. As such, framework policies, properly and flexibly implemented, can avoid the expected libertarian criticism that such policies would result in property remaining unused. The mechanism for taxing unused development rights also would work against the potential of negativism to triumph in non-libertarian systems of rights.

Also, because of the neighborhood-level management of these rights, there would seem to be greater opportunity to develop and protect a particular neighborhood character. This would be the case because neighborhoods would be able to shape their choices with respect to different LULU developments. That is, even though shopping centers might be rated, say, an eleven-point LULU development, for some neighborhoods that, for example, are particularly distant from shopping areas, a shopping center development would be less of a detriment than other types of LULUs. The neighborhood that chooses a shopping center as a preferred LULU could take steps to attract this type of development (by selling the development rights at a discount) rather than have another type of LULU developer make the choice for the neighborhood.

The framework policy also provides for the possibility of efficient exchanges (within the neighborhood jurisdiction) because the number of different types of units of exchange has been essentially reduced to one system of unitary and, therefore highly fungible, "LULU points."

The essential rule of the framework policy follows Freeman's suggestions in that beyond a minimal and free protection of residential amenity rights (that is, no neighborhood will be subject to a disproportionate share of LULU developments and no LULU will be placed adjacent to a residence without neighborhood consensus to sell the development right to an individual owner), neighborhoods will have to pay a premium for the privilege of acquiring greater levels of residential amenities than would be suggested by contemporary shared values. As Freeman writes,

> The agreed-upon content [of the initial distribution of residential amenities] should reflect contemporary shared values as the minimum quality of residential existence, excluding ostensibly residential uses that are actually inconsistent with residential use (such as the tuba player on the roof at night), and including ostensibly nonresidential uses that are regarded as consistent with residential amenity (for example, neighborhood shops, which might be permitted in residential districts if

> landowners are willing to purchase the rights). . . [T]hose who wish to acquire greater levels of residential amenity should . . . be required to pay a premium for the privilege.[51]

Advantages of Framework Policies over Freeman's Ethical Principles

What the sample framework policy offers over and above fulfillment of Freeman's ethical principles for the initial distribution of environmental control rights is a way of determining a fair price for the privilege of residential amenity rights that are more than the minimum—and a price that will eventually lead to the most privileged of neighborhoods bearing a fair share of the social responsibilities that LULU developments represent. The framework price for above-the-minimum residential amenities is fair because it is based on the idea that the concentration of LULUs above a certain level will be limited and that the remaining development (or control) rights will be distributed on a market-mimicking basis that will continually adjust the price of development rights, within the regulator frame, according to the law of supply and demand. In this process, the market value of the remaining development rights is continually reset, leading to an adjustment in the tax on the value of development rights and resulting in the proper level of economic incentives for social integration. Because the most privileged neighborhoods will tend to experience a rapid dwindling in their supply of development rights, the more they attempt to maintain a privileged level of amenities, the higher the premium will rise. Moreover, a framework policy makes the rise in the premium automatic, rather than dependent on periodic decisions by local government, which are likely to be subject to unwarranted influence by a more politically powerful and resource-rich class or interest group.

The framework policy also differs from Freeman's suggestions in that it would allow some trade-offs between residential and non-residential LULUs that Freeman would not allow. That is, in Freeman's scheme there is no level of density or other feature of residential use per se that would be considered a LULU, except for perhaps a neighbor's behavior that would cause a nuisance. Hence, developers would be free to continue to develop, without limit, high-rise apartments in otherwise LULU-dense neighborhoods, just as they would also be able to build such developments in more privileged neighborhoods. In essence, whereas Freeman's scheme provides a type of classic liberal, minimal protection, the framework policy is more encompassing in that it attempts to consider the larger issue of what the overall land-use picture would look like after the policy reform is in place.

Visualizing the potential outcomes of Freeman's approach in comparison with the sample framework policy points to a third difference between the two. Freeman's approach would go a long way toward making properties that are zoned residential more livable in terms of some of the environmental qualities that are of concern when people point to environmental racism. However, the approach would do little to protect these neighborhoods from a clustering of environmental LULUs just across the border from the residential zone. Also, because Freeman's scheme does not address how facilities such as community care homes, high-density housing, half-way houses for the mentally ill, juvenile delinquents and the like, could be truly integrated into neighborhood life, it would do little to address social justice concerns beyond simply opening up neighborhoods that are currently closed to these developments. Freeman's proposal does not consider that properties in these currently closed neighborhoods are more valuable than those in more vulnerable neighborhoods. This situation leads cost-conscious state agencies and non-profit organizations to choose the poorer areas for locating their social-type LULUs. Hence, although Freeman would deregulate the siting of these more institutional residences, he has not provided for any mechanism to broadly distribute the civic responsibility for community care. Low-income neighborhoods would still bear a disproportionate share of this responsibility.

In essence, instead of creating a minimal environmental control right in the tradition of classic liberalism—one that leaves both the social and environmental LULU policy issues only partially resolved—the sample framework policy is designed more along the lines of social-republican reforms, thereby promoting a generalized amelioration of both types of LULU-generated problems. To accomplish this feat, however, environmental control rights are partially collectivized at a neighborhood level.

The Ethics of Community Mobilization

A final ethical concern that the framework policy attempts to address is the tendency of more affluent communities to mobilize to affect specific zoning decisions. Because less affluent communities participate less effectively in zoning decision-making than affluent ones, the more affluent communities are typically more able to steer LULU developments away from their neighborhoods (such as by successfully protesting rezonings or maintaining a political hegemony that reduces the tendency for developers to even attempt to rezone these areas).[52] The aggregate effect of numerous such steering decisions will be the concentration of "necessary" LULUs in the less affluent neighborhoods. Framework policies address the inequality of participation by, first, providing a level of strict protection to neighborhoods that have been the historical victims of decisions that have steered LULU development away from more privileged neighborhoods, and, second, by reducing the size of the jurisdiction. Although reducing the size of jurisdictions does not eliminate the influence of elites,[53] most observers who have studied the effects of decentralization now believe that the political power of people in the lower socioeconomic classes is less likely to be diluted or undermined in local politics than in national politics. In local politics, leadership, political office, and political participation are more equally distributed among persons of different classes than is the case in larger political units. Additionally, in small jurisdictions, political representatives to governance bodies are more likely to resemble the full mix of constituent characteristics and their policy opinions than is the case in larger jurisdictions.[54] Furthermore, because of the high level of geographic segregation by socioeconomic class within individual towns and communities, it would seem plausible that creating neighborhood-sized jurisdictions would have a substantial impact on the inequality of participation.[55] That is, if political participation by the less privileged is increased by moving from national- to local-level politics, where socioeconomic inequality is still substantial, such participation should increase to an even greater extent if the jurisdiction is reduced to a neighborhood size where, because of homogeneous development, there is less likelihood that persons in the lower socioeconomic groups will have to wrestle with the more privileged for influence and positions of leadership.

Even though short-term prospects for effective participation by lower-class citizens in neighborhood-sized polities would be good due to the existing pattern of homogeneous development, the long-term tendency of framework policies to promote social heterogeneity within neighborhoods[56] could lead to a reduction in relative participation levels by poorer citizens. However, one might expect, as Benjamin Barber and other advocates of strong, participatory democracy do, that the practice of participation early on in homogeneous groups, especially by those in the lower socioeconomic strata, will lead to greater skill and self-confidence such that participation will continue in more heterogenous forums.[57] Moreover, as Crenson's research suggests, increased neighborhood heterogeneity should result in greater informal, but informed, direct action to create neighborhood public services on the part of rich and poor citizens alike.[58]

WHAT ABOUT DESEGREGATION?

The framework policy outlined above is designed to address directly the neglect of equity concerns in the governance of new locally unwanted land uses. The effect of this policy would be most immediately felt in the area of social justice concerns that is sometimes referred to as environmental racism. By directing the siting of community care facilities toward those neighborhoods that have not traditionally been the hosts of such facilities, the framework policy would more directly distribute the burden of social responsibility.

In addition, the sample framework policy should also have some indirect effects on racial segregation through the more direct effects on segregation by income. That is, the outlined framework policy would provide strong incentives for neighborhoods that have practiced or benefited from exclusionary zoning to begin to open their doors to the types of persons who have traditionally been excluded. Because the framework combines environmental and social LULUs, exclusive neighborhoods and communities will continually be faced with a choice between accepting higher density, multiple-family developments that can serve the needs of low-income citizens or accepting more noxious LULUs such as landfills or toxic waste disposal facilities. One can surely suspect that many communities, preferring social justice over environmental blight, will vie to be the host to new low-cost housing and community care facilities.

Providing for more low-cost housing in neighborhoods that are currently exclusive, does not guarantee racial integration. In fact, controlled studies of the relationship between income and racial segregation suggest that income differences between whites and African Americans can explain only 10 percent to 35 percent of the racial segregation typically observed in America.[59] Richard Sander's recent review of the various explanations for continued racial segregation in housing suggests that a number of factors are likely to be at work, including: blacks and whites choosing to live among members of their own race, lack of enforcement of fair housing laws, the slowing of economic progress among African Americans, and the continuation of informal discrimination in the form of real estate brokers' steering blacks toward all-black neighborhoods.[60] While Sander does not reject these theories entirely, he suggests that they do not tell the whole story or provide an explanation that is congruent with historical observation. He notes that these theories only explain why individual African Americans would end up in black neighborhoods; they do not explain the historical pattern of residential choice being dominated by group behavior rather than individual behavior. He points out that if integration could be achieved by the transfer of housing units from whites to blacks, then the fact that 50 percent of middle-income blacks between 1967 and 1971 moved into a unit previously occupied by whites should have resulted in increased integration.[61] In most of the cases where such integration was started by middle-income blacks, it did not last. Instead, once the barrier of segregation was broken in a particular neighborhood, the neighborhood would, often quite rapidly, become resegregated. Both initial integration and later resegregation, Sander points out, would often take place in neighborhoods that were adjacent to existing ghettos, leading to an expansion of the ghetto, rather than its elimination. The resegregation process occurs despite the evidence that a large percentage of both whites and black prefer to live in integrated neighborhoods.[62] The problem, Sander suggests, is related to the dynamics of housing markets in which the preferences for integrated housing differs between whites and blacks. That is, while whites will be comfortable in integrated neighborhoods, their sense of the optimal ratio of blacks to whites (that is, one to five) in an ideally integrated neighborhood is different from the view of most African Americans, who tend to see an ideally integrated neighborhood as being from 30 percent to 50 percent black.[63] In part because of these different preference curves, Sander argues, the demand among African Americans for integrated neighborhoods often exceeds the supply. This occurs because African American demand for housing in integrated neighborhoods will not drop off until blacks constitute about 50 percent of the neighborhood's population, yet after a neighborhood has become only 25 percent black, whites, "fearing that the neighborhood is losing its integrated character," will begin to drop their demand for residences in the neighborhood. Sander's argument suggests that resegregation will occur not just because of "white flight," but also because of slight differences in white and black demand for integrated communities. The latter process is likely to be much slower in working than the former, but it may be just an inexorable, Sander points out.[64] The group dynamic nature of the problem of segregation is furthered by the fact that the African Americans following the "pioneers" who initially integrated an all-white neighborhood will face fewer discrimination costs than the original pioneers as residents, realtors, and bankers come to view the neighborhood as integrated.[65] Integration pioneers face both higher search costs in terms of overcoming residual discrimination among residents, realtors, and bankers, and higher personal costs in terms of facing all alone the potential hostility of neighbors. As a consequence, "blacks leaving the ghetto are far more likely to move into areas where some blacks already reside, rather than areas that are all-white or nearly all-white."[66]

Because of the group dynamic nature of residential segregation, most efforts to enforce fair housing laws have been futile. The forces leading to resegregation cannot be substantially affected by simply eliminating discrimination. In essence, the market for housing is not framed in a way that would lead to the creation of stable integrated neighborhoods. Current policy efforts to promote residential integration, as Sander points out, generally use a form of "benign discrimination" to help create more integrated situations, such as when the state established quotas for blacks and whites in public housing that favor those persons whose presence in a particular situation will promote the goal of integration. The way such benign discrimination policies have typically been crafted, however, has opened them to constitutional challenge. That is, these policies have tended to burden blacks more than whites, have often not been narrowly tailored, have often been burdensome to innocent parties, have not followed the intent of fair housing legislation, and have often led to behavior indistinguishable from outright discrimination.[67] Most of the policies that have been developed to date that are likely to have substantial effects on segregation are open to such constitutional challenges, Sanders believes.

Sander offers an alternative solution to the segregation problem that is designed to address the group dynamics nature of residential segregation. This policy combines: (1) sliding-scale mobility grants to African Americans who act as pioneers in desegregating all-white or nearly all-white neighborhoods; (2) equity insurance designed to combat the fear of homeowners in all-white areas who fear that property values will fall upon integration of the neighborhood; (3) the substitution of rental vouchers for public housing and placement of caps on the percentage of any neighborhood's housing units that could be publicly assisted;[68] and (4) redevelopment of the ghetto through programs that "consciously preserve economic integration" (such as through "sweat equity" opportunities and other programs designed to limit the displacement caused by gentrification).[69]

Sander's policy alternative to traditional residential integration processes provides a combination of temporary market incentives (such as mobility grants) with more permanent framework policies (such as caps on LULU publicly assisted housing and programs to counter the displacement caused by gentrification). Sander's policy alternative is innovative and highly practical. He suggests, moreover, that once integration has become a widespread phenomenon rather than a concentrated and rapidly disappearing one, neighborhoods will tend to stabilize in terms of racial patterns: Whites will not have any all-white neighborhoods to fly to and blacks will have more substantial choices in neighborhoods because they will not have to pay the high costs of being a "pioneer."

As a market-based policy proposal, Sander's idea of the mobility grant represents an individual-choice policy option that changes the incentives for individual consumers of one race. In essence, it redirects the demand for integrated housing away from those neighborhoods that group-dynamic effects in combination with natural market forces determine to be the low-cost choices. Individual African-Americans, given the proper level of incentive, will now search for housing in areas that without the incentives would present higher market-set costs. Sander's mobility grants in this sense represent a demand- or consumer-side policy alternative for addressing the housing segregation problem.

A more framework-based policy—one that addresses the supply side of integrated housing and that fits neatly with the framework policy outlined for LULU development—can also be imagined. One framework policy alternative—the assignment of racial quotas that would limit the ability of property owners to sell property to persons of a race that would "tip" the neighborhood away from an integrated status—is clearly unconstitutional, having many of the constitutional problems that Sander identifies with "benign discrimination." A second alternative—assessing neighborhood property taxes based on the degree of integration achieved—is a more constitutionally feasible policy, but one that if applied evenly to both races would face a challenge on the basis that it burdened blacks living in ghettos as much or more than it burdened residents of all-white neighborhoods. However, a variation of this alternative—charging property tax surpluses only on properties in neighborhoods that are all- or nearly all-white—would represent the supply-side alternative to Sander's mobility grant.

As policy analysts have discovered in a number of policy areas, the most effective policies are often those that combine both demand- and supply-side features. In this respect, and given how difficult the problem of racial segregation has been to resolve, a combination of market demand-side incentives, and framework, supply-side incentives might provide the combination necessary to overcome the difficult group dynamic nature of this problem. Sander implicitly recognizes this notion in calling for the institution of a framework-type cap on publicly assisted housing.

SUMMARY AND CONCLUSION

The framing, through the creation of mediating institutions, of a limited market in LULU development rights would enable the community to shape opportunities for socially desirable development and an equitable sharing of the burdens of unwanted development. Socially responsible development occurs when: (1) investment and improvement of property are encouraged by limiting the level of LULUs in any one neighborhood; (2) the external or social costs associated with the creation of a new collective property right are shared equally among neighborhoods; (3) individuals can exercise political liberty by giving and taking "voice" and participating in democratic talk about the siting of unwanted developments; and (4) a mixture of political and economic mechanisms allows individuals to actively shape the nature of the decision, indicate the level of their desire, and be provided with benefits and pay costs in proportion to their contributions and appropriations. Such mechanism should be at work in an individual's decision to develop a LULU on his property and to avoid the siting of a LULU nearby.

Governing Our Collective Responsibilities: The Tragedy of the Commons in Reverse

The social framing of a market in LULUs is based on the idea that just as a "tragedy of the commons" will likely occur when a common access resource (such as a fishery or common grazing land) is left ungoverned, so too, a different type of tragedy of the commons occurs when communities do not govern their collective responsibilities. Elinor Ostrom's work on governing common pool resources suggests a lesson for governing collective responsibilities.[70] She has persuasively argued that neither market nor central government regulation has led to a satisfactory solution to the commons problem. As an alternative, Ostrom has suggested that enduring local collective-choice institutions can exist under some conditions (such as a well-defined boundary for the resource). Her research on common pool resource governance is clearly applicable to governing issues of common responsibility, and while the framing of a market for LULU development rights being suggested here does not go as far as fully establishing the kind of institution that she describes, it goes a long way in the direction of neighborhood control and collective choice nested within the larger obligations of community and state citizenship. In particular, by establishing clearly defined boundaries to a geographically small collective, the framework policy being proposed should tend to foster greater neighborhood activity and renewal around development and planning issues.

Moreover, as larger governments charge neighborhoods to become socially responsible while simultaneously authorizing and supporting the development of neighborhood institutions, neighborhoods are likely to invest in their overall self-improvement.[71] More important, they are also likely to invest the time, energy, thought, and resources needed to integrate the facilities and people originally seen as being unwanted.[72] The devolution of a large measure of authority over land-use control to neighborhood associations would seem to run counter to the forces of economic development and modernizations. Such forces, historically at least, have tended to favor both large-scale, private-sector institutions and facilities for production and distribution, and correspondingly large-scale public institutions to regulate the private sector ones. However, as a people, Americans have perhaps assumed too much that large economies of scale are inherent in the work that needs to be done and that any "bias toward bigness" is simply a necessary evil accompanying the benefits of modern life. In their highly influential book, *The Second Industrial Divide*, Michael Piore and Paul Sabel suggest that this bias may be more a matter of our making only semi-conscious choices for mass production technologies and scale. While these choices were reinforced by historical events such as the destruction (during the world wars) of competing models of production, the choice itself, for mass production on a large scale, was not driven by outright economic necessity. Piore and Sabel point out that alternative models of industrial organization that depend less on mass production techniques and scale and more on flexible specialization, individual craftsmanship, and collective support for advancing the state-of-the-art in skills development have survived and even thrived in certain areas of Europe. Moreover, they suggest that these alternative models have become increasingly successful in meeting the needs of emerging niche markets.[73] As basic needs are increasingly being met by high levels of industrial capacity and total social wealth expands, such niche markets for specialty, custom-made goods will likely increase even further. Consequently, if Piore and Sabel are correct, there may be opportunities to move away from the bias toward bigness that has dominated American industrial organization, and therefore land-use patterns as well, and move toward a more modern version of Jefferson's vision of a society of small-scale, groups of independent yeoman farmers and craftsmen—though with many more craftspersons and many fewer farmers.

Since the 1920s, when Louis Brandeis fought a heroic but seemingly futile battle against what he termed the "curse of bigness,"[74] there has been an unquestioned assumption that to reduce bigness would automatically result in less efficient production and distribution and therefore less aggregate material comfort. Brandeis did not question this assumption (as Piore and Sabel's research does), but instead argued that it was irresponsible to trade one's birthright of liberty and responsibility for the "mess of pottage" offered by large-scale, mass production and chain store distribution.[75] In 1911, Brandeis wrote: "I have considered and do consider that the proposition that mere bigness can not be an offense against society is false, because I believe that our society, which rests upon democracy, can not endure under such conditions."[76] The question that Brandeis struggled with and that we must continue to attempt to answer is whether there is a way to enjoy the benefits of industrialization without becoming slaves to a mass production machine driven by managers of capital and aggregated by a global-scale drive toward profit and growth. For Brandeis, the answer was to be found in small-scale institutions that would allow citizens to participate in the control of their lives and that would "maintain a link between liberty, democracy, and responsibility."[77]

A bias toward bigness, as Brandeis complained, has been built into laws that allow corporate entities to exercise as permanent rights what ought to be merely temporary privileges, since rights are prerogatives traditionally reserved for real people, rather than for the "legal fictions" that corporations represent. The framework policy presented in this book provides one means of land-use governance, perhaps an indirect one, of addressing the curse of bigness that Brandeis identified. However, the ability of such a governance structure to achieve its intended effect will be dependent on the ability of people to challenge assumptions that are traditionally made about the efficient scale of residential and industrial facilities. Some observations in this regard can be made. First, studies of the long-term economic viability of different types of housing and office facilities suggest that the large-scale, high-rise dwellings and office buildings may be less efficient, especially in terms of long-term costs, than was originally believed. Oscar Newman's study of the different development and maintenance costs of large-scale, high-rise dwellings with those of more modest-scale, three-story "walk-ups" is telling. In comparing developments of equal density, Newman discovered that the development costs, including the costs of environmental reviews, planning and architectural fees, capital and construction cost, were over 70 percent higher for the large-scale high-rises, and maintenance costs were nearly 50 percent more than was the case for the three-story, three-family homes.[78] Additionally, large-scale developments have been associated with more frequent, and therefore more costly, facility replacement, higher rents, and higher rates of crime. It is the size or scale of the building, not the density of the neighborhood, that is associated with higher crime rates. In fact, once one subtracts the effect of larger-scale buildings (both retail and residential), density appears to be associated with decreased criminal activity as small-scale retailers and residents act as informal "street managers" in ways first suggested by Jane Jacobs.[79]

In essence, the choice of large-scale development may have more to do with the aggregation and organization of capital within large-scale corporate structures than with any inherent advantage of scale in any particular instance of land use. As Alfred Chandler, the business historian, has suggested, the development of our business patterns may have more to do with the "visible hand" of business in collaboration with, or having influence over, government than with pure market forces.[80] This conclusion, moreover, may be becoming increasingly inescapable if one considers the alternatives paths of development that the information revolution could take us down.

Observers of this revolution suggest that we have a choice as to how we use and develop the potential of information technologies: We can make information cheap, ubiquitous and part of an interactive network in which all the nodes (that is, individual human beings) have equal power to submit and receive information, or alternatively, these same technological possibility could be used to channel information from centralized hubs that register a charge for the data, keep potentially embarrassing records of the information accessed, and use the technology to monitor and control individual behavior.[81] Benjamin Barber has outlined a number of ways in which these emerging information technologies can be harnessed to promote and re-energize citizen participation and a fuller democracy. He suggests, for example, establishing civic communication cooperatives, experimental electronic balloting, and a civic videotext service as a start.[82]

In addition to the choice between social and organizational hierarchy or heterarchy, these technologies can provide choices that affect the ultimate scale of production and service business facilities. As Michael Hammer has noted in his analysis of the potential for using information technologies to re-engineer business operations, these technologies allow one to "treat geographically dispersed resources as though they were centralized."[83] What this re-engineering principle suggests is that new information technologies may make it possible to provide the flexibility and higher level of consumer services associated with decentralization without sacrificing the organizational efficiency and economies of scale that have been the mark of centralization.[84] One likely result of establishing neighborhood controls over developments in their immediate environment would be to provide some impetus for businesses to develop alternatives to large-scale, neighborhood-unfriendly facilities. As an organized interest with possession of substantial development rights, neighborhoods can push businesses to use the emerging information technologies to reduce their scale of operations and to otherwise make them more acceptable to neighborhood residents. Without an organized, neighborhood-level force to resist the corporate bias toward bigness, the potential for information technologies to support new heterarchial relationships and more human-scale and rational land-use development might never be realized.

The potential of emerging information technologies is only one reason to question assumptions about the appropriate scale of industrial, office, and residential operations. Unfortunately, there is often great difficultly in distinguishing between real economies of scale and those that are assumed to exist because the only surviving operations are those of a particular scale. In some circumstances, it is market power and levels of capitalization that determine survivability rather than actual economies of scale.[85] As such, the assumption of the need for larger-scale operations is made where it may not be appropriate. Currently, for example, many local governments and private providers in the business of waste management have assumed that in order to meet new federal "Subtitle D" guidelines for making landfills safer, it will be necessary, for economy-of-scale purposes, to create mega-size landfills. Empirical studies by environmental groups have questioned this otherwise untested assumption—one that in some cases has already been built into solid waste management planning software. These studies suggest that smaller, more locally based landfills can be efficient and, just as important, can provide additional stimulus for treatment of waste to reduce toxicity and stabilize organics as well as for the reuse, recycling, or composting of waste that need not enter a landfill. Additionally, because no landfill operation is leakproof, small-scale operations provide for greater opportunity to catch a leak early and offer fewer opportunities for the kind of damage to groundwater and human health that only high concentrations of toxins can cause.[86]

Large-scale operations such as mega-sized landfills can create a level of "unwantedness" in a LULU equation that might be unnecessary; moreover, they force some localities or neighborhoods to bear a greater share of the social burden of handling the wastes that come from modern industrial production. As the links between liberty, democracy, and responsibility that Brandeis and others have seen as so important to our civic culture become more tenuous, it is more likely that citizens will reject even those unwanted facilities that truly are necessary or that truly could lead to greater social or environmental benefit. That is, without reforging the link between liberty, democracy, and responsibility, through framework governance of LULUs or otherwise, the negative side of the NIMBY politics might threaten even responsible and socially desirable development.

The more we unwittingly accept large scale as an inherent feature in land use, the more difficult it will be to reforge these links and create communities that are both democratic and socially responsible in the best sense of these ideals. The human rescaling of business and the deinstitutionalization of social care will demand a new framework in which to forge these links and realize these ideals. The sample framework policy presented in this book most likely has numerous conceptual holes. The framework, however, is not meant to be definitive; rather, it is offered as a potential stimulus to further thought on how best to approach land-use problems from environmental and social justice perspectives. That these problems are intricately tied to complex social and economic systems is enough to cause advocates of potential policy solutions to pause. However, without some attempt to address these problems, the current situation has many features suggesting the operation of vicious circles at work, leading to an ever worsening situation in terms of the key values of equity, efficiency, community viability, and environmental quality. Such a situation may call for creative policymaking, and although all policymaking tends to have an ideological basis, the sources of inspiration for creative policy making, as this book has attempted to suggest, may lie in the spaces between traditional ideological boundaries. From such spaces between traditional liberal and communitarian ideologies, framework and other innovative policies for land-use control might emerge.

Perhaps such policies in conjunction with others can reverse the social forces that are leading toward further segregation, political corruption, social inequity, and environmental irrationality. Establishing a framework for social responsibility is, I believe, the key. With such a framework, wealthy neighborhoods and citizens, instead of foisting on others the responsibility for community care of the homeless, the mildly mentally ill, or juvenile offender, or for the storage of noxious waste, will begin, once firmly faced with their responsibility, to lead the way toward more humane and socially integrated treatment of people needing help and toward more responsible and effective management of our waste.

NOTES

1. A number of authors suggest that in order to "get people to the table" it is necessary to provide the necessary motivation, skills, and other resources (such as a place to meet, coordination, ways of recording agreements, and so on). See Fisher, Roger, and Brown, Scott. (1988). *Getting Together*. Boston: Houghton Mifflin; and Laue, James. (1990). "Getting to the Table." *CCAR Newsletter*, Fairfax, Va.: George Mason University, Center for Conflict Analysis and Resolution. pp. 1, 7-9.

2. Kendig, Lane. (1980). *Performance Zoning*. Washington, D. C.: Planners Press, American Planning Association.

3. Nelson suggests a similar use of first refusal rights at the community level. Communities could purchase from neighborhoods development rights that would otherwise be sold to developers who might wish to use the land in ways that would be more costly to the community as a whole than whatever other individual or neighborhood benefits might be provided. See, Nelson, Robert. (1977). *Zoning and Property Rights*. Cambridge, Mass.: MIT Press.

4. For a description of a compensation scheme, see Ellickson, Robert. (1973). "Alternatives to Zoning: Covenants, Nuisance Rules, and Fines as Land Use Controls." *University of Chicago Law Review* (Summer): 40:4:681-719.

5. Margulies, Peter. (1992). "Building Communities of Virtue: Political Theory, Land Use Policy, and the 'Not in My Backyard Syndrome.' " *Syracuse Law Review* 43:945 96. Margulies argues that most fixed-distance provisions (requiring a certain distance between any two facilities) are inadequate because the distance required is so large (for example, more than half a mile) that the provision resembles a kind of quarantine of citizens in community care facilities. At first glance, the sample framework policy might seem to have a similar failing. However, because the framework policy combines environmental and social LULUs, the potential for synergistic patterns of LULU sitings (such as putting compatible social services in neighborhoods that serve such populations) are feasible as long as the final pattern of LULU sitings establishes a rough overall equity (for example, a neighborhood that is exempted from social service LULUs would likely bear a greater share of the burden of environmental LULUs).

6. Been, Vicki. (1993). "What's Fairness Got To Do With It? Environmental Justice and the Siting of Locally Undesirable Land Uses." *Cornell Law Review* 78:1001-85.

7. Ibid., p. 1024.

8. Barber, Benjamin. (1984). *Strong Democracy : Participatory Politics for a New Age* Berkeley, Calif.: University of California Press.

9. Crenson, Matthew A. (1983). *Neighborhood Politics*. Cambridge, Mass.: Harvard University Press.

10. Nisbet, Robert. (1974). "The Decline of Academic Nationalism." *Change* (Summer): 28.

11. Nelson, Robert. (1977). *Zoning and Property Rights*. Cambridge, Mass.: MIT Press.

12. For a survey of group home statutes, see: Jaffe, Martin, and Smith, Thomas P. (1986). "Siting Group Homes for Developmentally Disabled Persons." *American Planning Association Planning Advisory Service* 397:11-13.

13. Been, "What's Fairness Got," p. 1069.

14. H.R. 2105 103 Congress, 1st Session (1993).

15. Noah, Timothy. (February 14, 1994). "Order to Be Issued on Civil Rights, Pollution Link." *The Wall Street Journal*.

16. H.R. 495. 103rd Congress, 1st Session, 1993.

17. Been, "What's Fairness Got," p. 1071.

18. N. Y. City Charter, Section 203(a), 1989.

19. N.Y. City Charter.

20. Been, "What's Fairness Got," p. 1081.

21. Sterk, Steward E. (1988). "*Nollan*, Henry George, and Exactions." *Columbia Law Review* 88:1731-51.

22. Nelson, Zoning, pp. 91-96, 208-13.

23. Sterk, "*Nollan*" p. 1744.

24. Nelson, Robert. (1979). "A Private Property Right Theory of Zoning." *The Urban Lawyer* 11:4:713-732. Nelson describes this tendency as "doorslamming" and suggests that is occurs after the balance of political power has shifted away from the initial favoring of development (by the original owners of an undeveloped area) to attempts to restrict development (by those want to protect the character of the now established community).

25. Sterk, "*Nollan*," p. 1745.

26. Ibid., p. 1747.

27. Bernard, Michael M. (1979). *Constitutions, Taxation, and Land Policy*, Vols. 1 and 2. Lexington, Mass.: Lexington Books.

28. Ellickson, Robert. (1977). "Suburban Growth Controls: An Economic and Legal Analysis." *Yale Law Journal* 86:450-75.

29. Kmiec, Douglas W. (1981). "Deregulating Land Use: An Alternative Free Enterprise Development System." *University of Pennsylvania Law Review* 130:28-130. See specifically, p. 118.

30. *Metro 500 Inc. v. City of Brooklyn Park*, 297 Minn. 294, 211 N.W.2d 358 (1973).

31. *Stone v. City of Maitland*, 446 F.2d 83 (5th Cir. 1971). For discussion of classification of commercial properties, see: Blaesser, Brian, and Weinstein, Alan C. (1989). *Land Use and the Constitution: Principles for Planning Practice*. Chicago: American Planning Association.

32. *Cussack Co. v. Chicago*, 242 U.S. 526, 37 S.Ct. 190, 61 L.Ed. 472 (1917); and *State of Washington ex. rel. Seattle Title Trust Co. v. Roberge*, 278 U.S. 116, 49 S.Ct. 50, 73 L.Ed. 210 (1928).

33. Hagman, Donald, and Juergensmeyer, Julian Conrad. (1986). *Urban Planning and Land Development Control Law*, 2nd. edn. St. Paul, Minn.: West Publishing, p. 135.

34. Ibid., p. 135.

35. Blaesser, Brian W., and Weinstein, Alan C. (1989). *Land Use and the Constitution.* Chicago: American Planning Association, p. 171.

36. Taylor, Dorceta. (1992). "The Environmental Justice Movement." *EPA Journal* 18:23-24.

37. Been, "What's Fairness Got," p. 1048.

38. Ibid., p. 1050.

39. Ibid., pp. 1047-52.

40. Freeman, Alan David. (1976). "Give and Take: Distributing Local Environmental Control Through Land-Use Regulation." *Minnesota Law Review* 60:883-970.

41. Ibid., p. 896. See also, Michelman, Frank. (1973). "In Pursuit of Constitutional Welfare Rights: One View of Rawls' Theory of Justice." *University of Pennsylvania Law Review* 121:962-89.

42. Radin, Margaret Jane. (1982). "Property and Personhood." *Stanford Law Review* 34:957-78.

43. Ellickson, Robert. (1985). "Inclusionary Housing Programs: Yet Another Misguided Urban Policy," In *Inclusionary Zoning Moves Downtown*, edited by Dwight Merriam, David L. Brower, and Philip D. Tegeler. Washington, D.C.: American Planning Association, Planners Press, pp. 83-90.

44. Nelson, *Zoning*, p. 183.

45. Ibid., pp. 182-88.

46. Alexander, Gregory. (1989). "Dilemmas of Group Autonomy: Residential Associations and Community." *Cornell Law Review* 75:1-61.

47. Ibid., p. 60.

48. See generally, Crenson, *Neighborhood Politics*.

49. Ackerman, Bruce. (1971). "Regulating Slum Housing Markets on Behalf of the Poor: Of Housing Codes, Housing Subsidies and Income Redistribution Policy." *Yale Law Journal* 80: 1093-1172.

50. Ibid., p. 1171.

51. Freeman, "Give and Take," p. 913.

52. See Hutchinson, John, and Prather, James. (1988). "Community Mobilization and Participation in the Zoning Process." Urban Affairs Quarterly 23:3:346-68.

53. For an argument that decentralization can actually leave the less powerful members of society under greater control by elites, see McConnell, Grant. (1966). *Private Power in American Democracy*. New York: Knopf.

54. See generally, Mansbridge, Jane. (1983). *Beyond Adversary Democracy*. Chicago, Ill.: University of Chicago Press, p. 280. See specifically, Hare, Paul. (1976). *Handbook of Small Group Research*. New York: Free Press; Baird, L. L. (1969). "Big School, Small School: A Critical Examination of the Hypothesis." *Journal of Educational Psychology* 60:253-60; and Dahl, Robert, and Tuft, Edward. (1973). *Size and Democracy*. Stanford, Calif.: Stanford University Press.

55. Fowler, Edmund P. (1992). *Building Cities That Work*. Montreal, Canada: McGill-Queen's University Press.

56. This tendency for the framework policy to promote social-class heterogeneity might be frustrated at first by the existence of a tax on development rights. That is, as this tax applies to neighborhood residents, it would seem to present a barrier to less affluent persons wanting to enter the neighborhood. However, when the dynamic of the framework taxing policy finally lead even the most affluent neighborhood to relent and accept some LULUs, the neighborhood at that point would have to decide on how best it might attract the particular type of LULU that, all else being equal, would have the least negative impact. In this situation, it is highly likely that the neighborhood, in trying perhaps to avoid having to accept a high-impact LULU, will want to attract one or more type of residential facility that can be successfully integrated into the existing neighborhood. Their success at doing so, however, will be dependent on there being a market for such facilities. If the price is too high because of the development rights tax, the neighborhood might negotiate a subsidy to the builder or the consumers of the facilities in order to avoid a more undesirable LULU. However, as LULU sitings begin to approach equilibrium among communities, the tax differential will cease to be a barrier to more heterogeneous communities.

57. For a discussion of this process, see, Ventris, Curtis. (1985). "Emerging Perspectives on Citizen Participation." *Public Administration Review* (May/June):433-40; and Barber, Benjiman. (1984). *Strong Democracy: Participatory Politics for a New Age*. Berkeley, Calif.: University of California Press.

58. See generally, Crenson, *Neighborhood Politics*.

59. Taeuber, Karl, and Taeuber, Alma. (1965). *Negros in Cities: Residential Segregation and Neighborhood Change*. Chicago, Ill.: Aldine Pub. Co., p. 85; and Darden., Joe T. (1982). *Race, Housing, and Residential Segregation : A Selected Bibliography of Basic References*. Chicago, Ill.: CPL Bibliographies; and Schnare, Ann Burnet. (1977). *Residential Segregation by Race in U.S. Metropolitan Areas*. Washington, D.C. : Urban Institute.

60. Sander, Richard H. (1988). "Individual Rights and Demographic Realities: The Problem of Fair Housing." *Northwestern University Law Review* 82:3:874-939.

61. Ibid., pp. 887-902. As his source, Sander cites Long and Spain. (1978). *Racial Succession in Individual Housing Units*. Washington, D.C.: Bureau of the Census, Current Pollution Reports, Series P-23, No. 71, Table 4.

62. Ibid, pp. 887. As his source, Sander cites Taylor. (1979). "Housing, Neighborhoods, and Race Relations: Recent Survey Evidence." *Annals* 26:441.

63. Ibid. p. 888. As his source, Sander cites Farley. (1979). "Barriers to the Racial Integration of Neighborhoods." *Annals* 441:97-109.

64. Ibid., p. 897.

65. Ibid., p. 900.

66. Ibid., p. 901.

67. Ibid. pp. 926-27.

68. Sander reports that a pilot program of this type was created by agreement of the parties in *Hills v. Gautreaux*, 425 U.S. 284, and was evaluated by J. Rosenbaum, L. Rubinowitz, and M. Kulieke in *Low-Income Black Children in White Suburban Schools*, available from the Center for Urban Affairs, Northwestern University.

69. Sander, "Individual Rights," pp. 930-33.

70. Ostrom, Elinor. (1990). *Governing the Commons*. Cambridge, England: Cambridge University Press.

71. Lurcott, Robert, and Downing, Jane. (1987). "A Public-Private Support System for Community-Based Organizations in Pittsburgh." *APA Journal* 53:4:459-68.

72. Gambrill, Eileen, and Paquin, Gary. (1992). "Neighbors: A Neglected Resource." *Children and Youth Services Review* 14:253-72.

73. Piore Michael J., and Charles F. Sabel. (1984). *The Second Industrial Divide*. New York: Basic Books.

74. Brandeis, Louis. (1934). *The Curse of Bigness: Miscellaneous Papers of Louis D. Brandeis*, edited by O. Fraenkel. New York: Viking Press.

75. Brandeis, Louis. (1925). *Business—A Profession*. Boston: Small, Maynard.

76. McCraw, T. (1984). *Prophets of Regulation*. Cambridge: Harvard University Press; and McCraw, T. (1981). "Rethinking the Trust Question." In *Regulation in Perspective: Historical Essays*, edited by T. McCraw. Cambridge, Mass.: Harvard University Press.

77. Adelstein, Richard P. (1991). "Deciding for Bigness: Constitutional Choice and the Growth of Firms." *Constitutional Political Economy* 2:1: 7-30.

78. Newman, Oscar. (1980). *Community of Interest*. New York: Anchor Press.

79. See generally, Fowler, *Building Cities That Work*, pp. 82-106; Jacobs, Jane. (1961). *The Death and Life of Great American Cities*. New York: Random House. Or more specifically, Rhodes, William M., and Conly, Catherine. (1981). "Crime and Mobility: An Empirical Study." In *Environmental Criminology*, edited by Paul Brantingham. Beverly Hills, Calif.: Sage Publications; Roncek, Dennis. (1981). "Dangerous Places: Crime and Residential Environment." *Social Forces* 60:1: 74-96; and Roncek, Dennis "Density and Crime: A Methodological Critique." *American Behavioral Scientist* 18:6:843-60.

80. Chandler, Alfred D. (1977). *The Visible Hand*. Cambridge, Mass.: Harvard University Press.

81. For alternative views of the potential for these two paths of development, see, Shaiken, Harley. (1986). *Work Transformed: Automation and Labor in the Computer Age*. Lexington, Mass.: Lexington Books; and, Gilder, George. (1991). "Into the Telecosm." *Harvard Business Review* 69:2:150-64.

82. Barber, *Strong Democracy*, pp. 1-320.

83. Hammer, Michael. (1990). "Reengineering Work." *Harvard Business Review* 90:4:105-14.

84. For an example of how Hammer's principles might affect the delivery of educational services, see O'Looney, John. (1993). "Redesigning the Work of Education." *Phi Delta Kappan* 74:5:375-81.

85. Perrow, Charles. (1986). *Complex Organizations: A Critical Essay*. New York: Random House.

86. Pallats, Leonard. (January 12, 1994). "Are Big Regional Landfills Better for Rural Georgia?" *Athens Banner-Herald*, and personal conversations with Laurie Fowler, executive director of the Georgia Environmental Policy Institute, April 22, 1994.

Index

About the Author

JOHN O'LOONEY is human services research associate at the Carl Vinson Institute of Government, University of Georgia, where he provides consultation and technical assistance to local and state agencies, primarily in human resource management and organizational development. He holds two doctorates, one in political science, another in language education, and is a frequent contributor of articles to the scholarly and professional journals. His second Quorum book will be a study of ways to redesign the work of human services.

www.ingramcontent.com/pod-product-compliance
Ingram Content Group UK Ltd.
Pitfield, Milton Keynes, MK11 3LW, UK
UKHW020235290926
15470UKWH00002B/554

9 780899 309408